Time Out
Mumbai & Goa

timeout.com/mumbai

D1511019

Published by Time Out Guides Ltd, a wholly owned subsidiary of Time Out Group Ltd.
Time Out and the Time Out logo are trademarks of Time Out Group Ltd.

© **Time Out Group Ltd 2008**
Previous edition 2006.

10 9 8 7 6 5 4 3 2 1

This edition first published in Great Britain in 2008 by Ebury Publishing
A Random House Group Company
20 Vauxhall Bridge Road, London SW1V 2SA

Random House Australia Pty Limited 20 Alfred Street, Milsons Point, Sydney, New South Wales 2061, Australia
Random House New Zealand Limited 18 Poland Road, Glenfield, Auckland 10, New Zealand
Random House South Africa (Pty) Limited Isle of Houghton, Corner Boundary
Road & Carse O'Gowrie, Houghton 2198, South Africa

Random House UK Limited Reg. No. 954009

Distributed in US by Publishers Group West
Distributed in Canada by Publishers Group Canada

For further distribution details, see www.timeout.com

ISBN: 9781846700637

A CIP catalogue record for this book is available from the British Library

Printed and bound by Firmengruppe APPL, aprinta druck, Wemding, Germany

The Random House Group Limited supports The Forest Stewardship Council (FSC), the leading international forest
certification organisation. All our titles that are printed on Greenpeace approved FSC certified paper carry the FSC
logo. Our paper procurement policy can be found at www.rbooks.co.uk/environment

Time Out carbon-offsets all its flights with Trees for Cities (www.treesforcities.org).

FROM THE HIMALAYAS PRESENTING

THE WORLD'S FINEST RARE MONOFLORAL HONEY

MILLÉ FIORII™

For details please log on to **www.millefiorii.com** or call +91.98117 28123
Available at select luxury five star hotels

Contents

Edited and designed by
Time Out Mumbai
Paprika Media Pvt Ltd
Essar House
11 KK Marg
Mahalaxmi Mumbai 400 034
Tel +91 (0)22 6660 1111
Email letters@timeoutmumbai.net
www.timeoutmumbai.net

For
Time Out Guides Limited
Universal House
251 Tottenham Court Road
London W1T 7AB
Tel + 44 (0)20 7813 3000
Fax + 44 (0)20 7813 6001
Email guides@timeout.com
www.timeout.com

Editorial

Editor Leo Mirani
Proofreaders James Mathew, Mandy Martinez
Researchers Suhani Singh, Nikhil Subramaniam, Sanjeevani Thorat, Neha Sumitran
Indexer Navin Mohit

Managing Director Peter Fiennes
Financial Director Gareth Garner
Editorial Director Ruth Jarvis
Deputy Series Editor Dominic Earle
Editorial Manager Holly Pick
Assistant Management Accountant Ija Krasnikova

Design

Art Editor Arindam Duttgupta
Designer Navin Mohit
Picture Editor Ashima Narain
Digital Imaging Pravin Pereira, Amit Pradhan

Advertising

Commercial Director Mark Phillips
International Advertising Manager Kasimir Berger
International Sales Executive Charlie Sokol
Advertising Assistant Kate Staddon
Sales Managers (Mumbai) Vishal Pai, Nishit Kumar

Production

Group Production Director Mark Lamond
Production Manager Brendan McKeown
Production Controller Caroline Bradford
Production Coordinator Julie Pallot

Time Out Group

Chairman Tony Elliott
Financial Director Richard Waterlow
Group General Manager/Director Nichola Coulthard
Time Out Magazine Ltd MD Richard Waterlow
Time Out Communications Ltd MD David Pepper
Time Out International MD Cathy Runciman
Group IT Director Simon Chappell

Contributors

Introduction Leo Mirani. **History** Jerry Pinto (*Who is Shivaji, anyway?* Leo Mirani; *Mumbai or Bombay?* Iain Ball; *The Empire strikes out* Chetna Mahadik). **Mumbai Today** Leo Mirani (*Slumbai* Iain Ball; *Building blocks* Himanshu Burte). **Communities** Jerry Pinto. **Bollywood** Nandini Ramnath, Rachel Dwyer (*You too can be a star* Leo Mirani). **Where to Stay** Iain Ball, Leo Mirani (*Crowning glory* Iain Ball). **South Mumbai** Chetna Mahadik (*Port whine* Rachel Lopez; *Munificent Mumbaikars* Rachel Lopez; *A Beatle in Bombay* Iain Ball). **The Suburbs** Jerry Pinto, Iain Ball (*Local heroes* Iain Ball; *Village life* Rachel Lopez). **Day Trips** Naresh Fernandes, Jerry Pinto. **Restaurants & Cafés** Iain Ball, Divia Thani-Daswani, Vikram Doctor, Roshni Bajaj Sanghvi and contributors to *Time Out Mumbai* (*Café culture* Che Kurrien; *Vast food nation* Vikram Doctor; *Street eats* Iain Ball; *Bombay mix* Antoine Lewis; *Paan handling* Iain Ball). **Pubs & Bars** Leo Mirani and contributors to *Time Out Mumbai*. **Shops & Services** Divia Thani-Daswani (*Curio city* Roshni Bajaj Sanghvi; *The fab three* Roshni Bajaj Sanghvi; *Cotton on* Nandini Ramnath; *Reel Mumbai* Roshni Bajaj Sanghvi). **Festivals & Events** Nikhil Subramaniam. **Children** Meher Marfatia, Amrita Bose. **Film** Nandini Ramnath (*Metromorphosis* Chetna Mahadik). **Galleries** Srimoyee Mitra, Jerry Pinto, Deepanjana Pal. **Gay & Lesbian** Vikram Doctor. **Mind, Body & Soul** Tanvi Chheda, Divia Thani-Daswani, Vidya Balachander. **Music** Amit Gurbaxani. **Nightlife** Leo Mirani (*The Bombay sound* Amit Gurbaxani). **Sport & Fitness** Jamie Alter, Che Kurrien, Vidya Balachander. **Theatre & Dance** Pronoti Datta (theatre), Suhani Singh (dance). **Goa** Vivek Menezes, Iain Ball (nightlife). **Getting Around** Deepanjana Pal, Leo Mirani **Resources A-Z** Naresh Fernandes (media), Suhani Singh, Nikhil Subramanian, Neha Sumitran. **Further Reference** Naresh Fernandes, Nandini Ramnath.

Maps mapsofindia.com

Photography pages 7, 34, 47, 64, 71, 79 (left), 82, 96, 100, 103, 113, 126, 129, 135, 136, 157 Poulomi Basul; pages 3, 35, 43, 70, 73, 77 (bottom), 144, 155 Amit Chakravarty; pages 11, 21, 24, 32, 36, 60, 61, 65, 68 (left), 74, 75, 76, 77(top), 80, 84 (left), 89, 91, 101, 108, 127, 128, 134, 137, 161 Chirodeep Chaudhuri; pages 5, 63, 72, 79 (right), 87, 90, 102, 111, 115, 149, 159 Apoorva Guptay; pages 28, 45, 48, 68 (right), 78, 83, 85, 98, 99, 104, 107, 114 (bottom), 118, 138, 152, 153, 154 (left), 163 Vikas Munipalle; pages 15, 33, 109, 112, 114 (top), 120, 133, 140 Janak Shah; all Goa images Vivek Menezes.
Others page 26 Ambika Bhatt; page 84 (right) Dinodia Picture Agency; pages 14, 16, 22, 23 (Bombay The Cities Within) Eminence designs; pages 13, 19 Naresh Fernandes Collection; page 147 Sunil Gupta; pages 18, 20 Leo Mirani Collection; page 162 Bajirao Pawar 162; page 187 courtesy Goa Gil.

The Editor would like to thank: Ashima Narain, Deepanjana Pal, Iain Ball, Naresh Fernandes, Neelam Kapoor, Smiti Ruia and all at *Time Out Mumbai*.

Introduction

Visitors often dismiss Mumbai as not being representative enough of 'the real India', accusing the city of being too urban, too Western, too unlike what they want India to be. The fact is that Mumbai is India on steroids: 168 square miles bursting at the seams with the hopes and dreams, cultures and cuisines, languages and races, petty quarrels and disgruntled compromises of a billion people. Appropriately, Mumbai is the economic engine that drives India's growth; home to the country's central bank, two stock exchanges, the commodities markets and the headquarters of thousands of companies. More wealth is created and very conspicuously spent in Mumbai than anywhere on the subcontinent. It's not just commerce that keeps Mumbai on the move: the city is India's biggest manufacturer of popular culture – film, television, music, dance and fashion. It has dominated the popular Indian imagination through the hundreds of books, movies and songs it has inspired, its headline-grabbing gangsters and supercops and some of the country's greatest cricket heroes.

But if the 'real' India is supposed to be shockingly poor, with appalling living conditions and a gross neglect of basic human rights, then Mumbai is disastrously real – too real for the 55 per cent of its population that lives in slums. The city's infrastructure is crumbling, property prices are too high for the lower- and middle-class to afford proper housing, the roads are too narrow and battered to handle the exploding traffic, clean water is scarce and the electric supply is dwindling. After decades of civic mismanagement, misappropriation of funds and widespread corruption, the citizens of Mumbai are paying the price for the short-sightedness of their elected officials.

Yet, Mumbaikars rarely seem to do anything more than complain about the conditions in which they live. The city carries on with its day-to-day business as though the floods, religious riots, nativist demonstrations and occasional terrorist bombings are little more than traffic diversions. Disruptions are forgotten quickly and life goes on as normal. On 11 July 2006, when seven bombs went off on commuter trains across the city during the evening rush hour, services were up and running again the same night. People were back at work the next day.

As much the real India but thoroughly unreal in every way is Goa. Three hundred and seventy miles south of Mumbai, the former Portuguese colony was folded into India in 1961, 14 years after the rest of the country achieved independence from the British, and it retains a Latinate character to rival any Mediterranean or South Atlantic destination. Though it is no longer the untouched paradise discovered by the original flower children of the 1970s, packed as it is with the burgeoning Indian middle class, British charter tourists and nu-rave neo-hippies, Goa remains charmingly relaxed and thankfully unspoiled away from the main tourist areas.

Neither Mumbai nor Goa can claim to be all of India but they make up two ends of the spectrum – one a too-real adrenaline shot of urbs in extremis, the other an unreal promised land where the party never stops.

ABOUT TIME OUT CITY GUIDES

Time Out Mumbai & Goa is one of an expanding series of Time Out City Guides, produced by the people behind the successful listings magazines in London, New York and Chicago. Our guides are all written and updated

by resident experts who have striven to provide you with all the most up-to-date information you'll need to explore the city or read up on its background, whether you're a local or a first-time visitor. The guide contains detailed practical information, plus features that focus on unique aspects of the city.

THE LIE OF THE LAND

We've divided this book into two parts – a Mumbai city guide and a guide to Goa beginning on page 169. In Mumbai, we focus on the historic southern part of the city, the most interesting area for visitors, but we've also cast an eye on the vibrant suburbs to the north. Mumbai is a narrow strip of land where one neighbourhood follows the next, but finding your way through it all can be difficult; street names are infrequently used and locals usually navigate by reference to landmarks. Many street names have changed but locals continue to use the old names. To make life easier, we've put landmarks in our listings under 'Taxi' wherever possible and used street names with the most currency. We've also indicated whether the entry is on the east or west side of the local train station, for example, 'Bandra (W)'. Sights also have a grid reference and page number that points to street maps at the back of the book (starting on page 247).

ESSENTIAL INFORMATION

For all the practical information you might need for visiting the area – including emergency phone numbers and details of car hire and local transport, turn to the Directory chapter at the back of the guide. It starts on page 227.

THE LOWDOWN ON THE LISTINGS

We have tried to make this book as easy to use as possible. Addresses, phone numbers, local train stations, opening times, admission prices and credit card details are included in the listings. However, owners and managers can change their arrangements at any time – and they often do. Some restaurants and bars close to the public for private parties. Arts and cultural events are often finalised late and liable to change. We would advise you wherever possible to phone ahead and check opening times, ticket prices and other details. Pick up a copy of *Time Out Mumbai* magazine, published fortnightly, for up-to-the-minute listings. While every effort has been made to ensure accuracy, the publishers cannot accept responsibility for any errors it may contain.

PRICES AND PAYMENT

We have listed prices in rupees (Rs) throughout and noted where venues such as shops, hotels, restaurants and bars accept the following credit cards: American Express (AmEx), Diners Club

(DC), MasterCard (MC) and Visa (V). Few places except major hotels accept travellers' cheques.

The prices in this guide should be treated as guidelines, not gospel. It's not uncommon for taxi drivers and street vendors to double or triple prices for foreign visitors. Elsewhere, if they vary wildly from those we've quoted, ask if there's a good reason. If not, go elsewhere. We aim to give the best and most up-to-date advice, so we want to know when you've been badly treated or overcharged. Wherever possible, we have factored in taxes, which many restaurants and hotels leave out of the advertised rates.

TELEPHONE NUMBERS

The country code for India is 91. The area code for Mumbai is 022; numbers usually have eight digits. The area code for Goa is 0832, usually followed by a seven-digit number. If you're dialling from abroad, use the country code 91 for India, followed by 22 or 832 (thereby dropping the zero from the area code) and the number.

MAPS

The map section at the back of the guide includes an overview map of Mumbai and its suburban train network. There are also detailed street maps of south Mumbai and part of the suburb of Bandra. The Goa section contains an orientation map of the state and more detailed maps. The Mumbai map section begins on page 247, and pinpoints specific locations of hotels (❶), restaurants (❶) and pubs and bars (❶).

LET US KNOW WHAT YOU THINK

We hope you enjoy the *Time Out Mumbai & Goa* guide, and we'd like to know what you think of it. We welcome tips for places that you consider we should include in future editions and will take note of your criticism of our choices. You can email us at guides@timeout.com.

Advertisers

We would like to stress that no establishment has been included in this guide because it has advertised in any of our publications and no payment of any kind has influenced any review. Opinions given in this book are those of *Time Out* writers and entirely independent.

There is an online version of this book, along with guides to over 50 other international cities, at www.timeout.com.

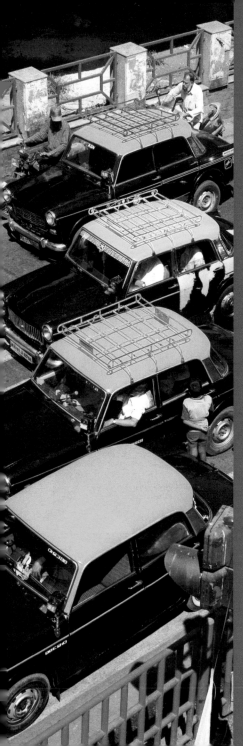

In Context

South Mumbai's **Maidan** at the turn of the 20th century.

History

From marshland to metropolis.

Somewhere underneath the vast, overcrowded urban explosion that is Mumbai lies a cluster of seven disjointed islands, populated only by Koli fisherfolk and mosquitoes. The city that exists today grew up around this unremarkable archipelago, engulfing it as it expanded, first by building causeways to connect the islands, then by filling in the sea until only the names of these blobs of land remained. It is from such mundane beginnings that the financial, media, glamour and film capital of India has arisen, and it's only 350 years old.

All that remains of Mumbai's early history are occasional scraps of activity in between centuries filled with what we can only suppose was the incessant hiss of the Arabian Sea, the cursing of Kolis, the city's original inhabitants, and the thump of falling coconuts. There are almost no records of those times, but the channels between the islands were so deep they must have been often impossible to cross, with monsoon storms leaving each island isolated from the others. Despite their ordinariness, Ptolemy marked the islands in his maps and the ancient Greeks knew them as Heptanesia (literally, 'Seven Islands'). But even when the legendary warrior king-turned-Buddhist, Ashoka – ruler of the Mauryan Empire – turned his attention to the region in the third century BC, he ignored the islands, instead colonising areas located beyond the northern limits of

modern Mumbai. In those days, Nalla Sopara (now a 15-second commuter stop for trains on their way north to the end of the line) was a bustling town, located at the crossroads of ancient trade routes, and became a patronage centre for magnificent Buddhist monasteries. You can still see the remnants of some of them in the Kanheri caves at Borivali.

What is known is that around the seventh century AD, a prince of the Chalukya Dynasty – a political dynasty that ruled large parts of the western and southern regions of the country – constructed the breathtaking cave-temples at Gharapuri, now called Elephanta Island, with an iconography that represents an early dialectic between Buddhism and Shaivism (the worship of Shiva). The Silhara kings of the Konkan region in the south moved north to take control of all seven islands in the ninth century; this was the first recorded instance of what was to be the first of many battles for control of the region, with the seven islands being batted between competing powers like a tennis ball over the next 1,000 years. Even with the Silharas in control, the islands and their Koli inhabitants remained undisturbed; the Silharas instead established their regional capital in Thane, on the northern limits of present-day Mumbai.

In 1127, the Walkeshwar Temple in what is now Malabar Hill, with its sacred Banganga

Bombay Harbour with Bombay Castle to the right and St Thomas' in the background.

tank, was constructed by Lakshman Prabhu, a minister in the court of the Silharas. It was an extraordinary achievement and a measure of the Silharas' devotion to Lord Rama, the Hindu god and hero of the epic *Ramayana*, who is supposed to have created the tank by shooting an arrow into the ground and bringing forth the waters of the Ganges. The terrain was difficult and required extensive infrastructure to transport masonry from one island to another. The Silharas managed to retain control of the islands until 1343, when the Sultan of neighbouring Gujarat took over and ruled it for the next two centuries.

Over the following five centuries, the islands that came to be known as Bombay underwent an extraordinary metamorphosis into the contiguous finger of land that now stretches south-west from the mainland. The story of that transformation begins with the Portuguese.

IMPERIAL AMBITIONS

Portuguese explorers had already arrived in Goa in the 16th century, on a mission to wrest control of the near-priceless spice trade from the Arabs and win souls for Christendom. One of the first recorded visits of the Portuguese to Bombay was in 1508, when a ship halted briefly at Mahim Island while travelling to an outpost at Diu in Gujarat. For the next two decades the Portuguese kept making short visits to the islands and in 1532 they finally seized Bassein (now Vasai, just north of Mumbai's municipal limits) from Sultan Bahadur Shah of Gujarat. From here the Portuguese took the entire region, including the seven islands. At that time, the Arabian coast was a bustling region of trading ships and seaside outposts. The Portuguese already possessed Goa, Daman

and Diu, and Vasai became an important part of their maritime trade network.

To protect their shipping routes, the Portuguese fortified the islanded region, establishing cannon-equipped outposts at Mahim, Sion, Bandra and of course in Bassein. It was around this time that the region got a new name – 'Ilha da Boa Vida', meaning 'the island of good life' in Portuguese. When the Portuguese first came to the place they called 'Bandora', now Bandra, they found an ideal spot: a strategically important point overlooking the sea, amply supplied with drinking water from nearby freshwater springs. In 1640, they stationed a permanent garrison of troops here and built a small fort, which they called the Castella de Aguada ('The Water Point'). Armed with a pair of cannons, the garrison kept watch over sea lanes crucial to Portuguese trading interests. Anxious about the spiritual wellbeing of their troops, they also built the Chapel of Nossa Senora de Monte ('Our Lady of the Mount') nearby and cut a road linking it to the fort.

> **'It was around the 1500s that the region got a new name – Ilha da Boa Vida – Portuguese for "the island of good life".'**

Over the next 100 years the region's social history was shaped by Portuguese religious, economic and political impulses and resembled other Portuguese outposts – including Goa and Daman in India and Malacca in Malaysia. Many village communities from Mahim to Vasai converted to Christianity and the landscape became punctuated with churches and chapels. The Portuguese destroyed the Walkeshwar Temple, which was eventually rebuilt in 1715 by a wealthy Hindu trader. Over 350 years later, the Nossa Senora de Monte church – now known as Mount Mary – is still a place of worship. At the fort, only ruins remain (now restored and home to a gorgeous amphitheatre). Thane, to the north east of the islands, became an attractive township of villages, temples and churches nestled between lakes and coconut groves.

For all the development, the Portuguese still didn't see much trade potential in the area and it remained a backwater. Instead it was their rivals, the British East India Company, who cast a covetous eye over the area from their headquarters in Gujarat. They considered it a perfect natural harbour for the Company's first Indian seaport. The main attraction of course

was the deep bay on the eastern waterfront overlooking the mainland. The Surat outpost began pressing its London headquarters to purchase the islands from the Portuguese. They finally got their hands on them in 1661, when they were given to King Charles II as part of the dowry for his marriage to Portuguese princess Catherine de Braganza. Apparently, Charles was not exactly sure where his wedding present was; he initially thought that the islands were somewhere in Brazil. In 1668, he leased the islands to the British East India Company for the sum of 10 pounds a year and the Company quickly established a colony in and around an existing Portuguese fort, which grew rapidly from 10,000 people in 1661 to 60,000 by 1675.

In 1687 the East India Company transferred its headquarters from Surat to what the British now called Bombay.

Who is Shivaji, anyway?

When you land in Mumbai and go from the airport to your South Mumbai hotel, you will no doubt experience a sense of déjà vu. Getting into a cab at Chhatrapati Shivaji International Airport, you pass Shivaji Park in the middle of the city before you arrive downtown, where you might drive by the magnificent Chhatrapati Shivaji Terminus and the Chhatrapati Shivaji Maharaj Vastu Sangrahalaya as you turn in on Chhatrapati Shivaji Marg towards Colaba. So who is Chhatrapati Shivaji?

The son of an officer in the court of Bijapur in western India, Shivaji Bhonsle laid the foundations for the modern state of Maharashtra, of which Mumbai is the capital. In the late 17th century, Shivaji established a rebel fiefdom within Bijapur and by the age of 30 successfully gained control of a significant chunk of land in and around the Pune region, commanding 40 forts, 7,000 horsemen and 10,000 foot soldiers. As his power grew, he took on the mighty Aurangzeb, king of the most powerful empire in India at the time, the Mughals. Shivaji's battles against the Mughals have been widely recorded and retold in folk tales, tbooks and Marathi performances and his legend continues to inspire Maharashtrians. But what makes his

exploits of great value to today's politicians is that he succeeded in establishing a Hindu kingdom in a land then run by Muslims.

Scholars continue to debate whether Shivaji set out to be what historian James Laine calls a 'Hindu King in Islamic India'. Cambridge University's *The Marathas* contends that Shivaji was never one to propagate a Maharashtrian or Hindu state, nor that he ever discriminated against Muslims, instead welcoming them into his state and his army.

None of this is of much concern to the local right-wing nativist political party, the Shiv Sena (Shivaji's Army), which rode to power on a wave of anti-Muslim rhetoric following religious riots and bomb blasts in the city in 1992-93. One of their first acts in power was to rename the city from the colonial Bombay to the Marathi 'Mumbai'. In the following years, they renamed several landmarks after the warrior king who evoked native pride and anti-Muslim sentiment. The Shiv Sena hasn't been in power at state level since 1999, but they won the last municipal elections in 2007 and currently control Mumbai's local government. Though the Shiv Sena has mellowed in recent years, a breakaway party, the Maharashtra Navnirman Sena, continue to harp on about 'outsiders'.

BIRTH OF A TRADE HUB

Bombay's early population mostly comprised Koli fisherfolk, East India Company officials and migrants from Gujarat who set up shop to service the outpost. Among the migrants were an émigré community of Iranian Zoroastrians known as Parsis (*see p30* **Communities**), who were to become a decisive commercial and political force in Bombay's development. That was foreshadowed earlier in the colony's history by the actions of a Parsi trader, Rustomji Dorabji: just two years after the Company moved to Bombay, the outpost was beset by a plague outbreak. At the same time, a nearby Africa-descended tribe called the Sidis launched an attack on the colony from their base down the coast in Janjira (near present-day Alibag). Despite the chaos caused by the plague, Dorabji managed to raise an impromptu army from the local Kolis and repelled the Sidis in a counterattack – saving the colony and killing the Sidi chief in the process.

> **'In 1689, Bombay was beset by a plague outbreak. At the same time, a nearby tribe launched an attack on the colony.'**

That the size and influence of the Parsi presence was strong very early in Bombay's history is proved by the fact that a Tower of Silence – a traditional Parsi funeral place, where bodies are left to be consumed by vultures – was built on Malabar Hill in 1672. In 1708 the first Parsi *agiary* (fire temple) was built – the Banaji Limji Agiary – with a second in 1733. Two years later, the Parsis set up a shipbuilding industry which later became one of the largest suppliers of ships to the British Royal Navy. A young Parsi shipbuilder

from Gujarat, Lowji Nusserwanji Wadia, was invited to Bombay by the East India Company to build them ships, an enterprise that led to the Wadia dynasty of shipbuilders.

The Parsis remained at the forefront of the city's development and in 1777, its first newspaper, the *Bombay Courier*, was published by Rustomji Keshaspathi. The city's main activity was as an import-export hub: diamonds, tea, paper, porcelain, raw silk, calicoes, pepper, herbs and drugs sailed out to Britain and lead, quicksilver, woollen garments, hardware and bullion sailed in. Bombay's status was further boosted by an increase in cotton trade with China after 1770, an exchange that continued over the next century.

During this period the city saw a continuous migration of traders from Surat, which further energised the economy. Some historians suggest that the rise of Bombay as a successful trading hub precipitated the decline of Surat, which soon lost its cherished status as a major port. In subsequent years, the islands began to attract many Gujarati traders (both Hindu and Muslim), including Parsi shipbuilders from the mainland. Most people lived in and around a fort at the heart of the colony, originally built by the Portuguese and further developed by the British. Known as Bombay Castle, it was essentially a walled township in the area of the city today known as Fort.

A fragment of the fort wall still exists next to St George's Hospital. By 1813, almost half of the 10,000 people who lived in the Fort area were Parsis. As it became more and more crowded and often prone to disease, its richer inhabitants began to move out to new townships beyond the walled city, building bungalows and mansions in the city's first suburbs: Byculla, Mazgaon and Malabar Hill.

SHAPING THE CITY

By the beginning of the 19th century, business in Bombay was booming, so much so that in

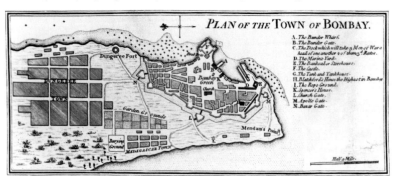

Mumbai or Bombay?

In 1995, the Shiv Sena, a far-right Maharashtrian political party, changed the city's official name from Bombay to Mumbai, the Marathi name for the city. It was the centrepiece of a drive to eradicate British Raj-era place names in the city, which included renaming the Victoria Terminus as Chhatrapati Shivaji Terminus. 'Mumbai' is derived from Mumba, a name for the Hindu goddess Mumbadevi, and *aai*, meaning 'mother' in Marathi, the language of Maharashtra.

Visitors often assume that it's politically incorrect to use the old name and are surprised to discover that almost every English-speaker in Mumbai – of whom there are millions – still calls the city Bombay. The fondness for the old name is mostly just a case of old habits dying hard, but for some it's also a rejection of the Shiv Sena and their violent, anti-outsider politics. But it's even more complicated, as each name also carries distinct class connotations – 'Bombay' implies the English-speaking elite, 'Mumbai' the middle and working classes. Either way, as a visitor you're unlikely to upset anyone whichever name you use.

1801 the British Government sent a reporter to document the extent of the city's trade. His reports convinced them to end the East India Company's monopoly on trade in 1813, encouraging even greater commercial expansion. A few years later, a massive civil engineering project to reclaim land from the sea was commissioned, its aim to fuse the disparate islands of Bombay into a single land mass. Over the next few decades, as the city took shape, a large middle-class population emerged that drove a huge demand for newspapers, schools and colleges.

> **'In the 1860s, the British began a construction programme designed to signal to the natives that they were here to stay.'**

In 1822, India's first Indian-language newspaper, the Gujarati daily *Mumbai Samachar*, was published in Bombay. Still running today, it's the country's oldest newspaper. The first copy of the *Bombay Times* (the forerunner of the *Times of India*) rolled off the presses in 1838. Grant Medical College was founded in 1845 and within another 15 years, Wilson College and Bombay University were established. Other colleges like Elphinstone College and St Xavier's went up within a decade. Both the new media and colleges were largely patronised by children of Gujarati merchants and traders, the indigenous Christian populations and Maharashtrians. Middle-class suburbs sprung up in the new neighbourhoods of Kalbadevi, Girgaum, Gowalia Tank, Mohammed Ali Road, Thakurdwar and Walkeshwar.

By the middle of the 19th century, the knitting together of Bombay's islands through land reclamation was nearly complete. Causeways linked Bombay, Sion, Salsette and Colaba; Mahalaxmi and Worli were joined; and in 1845, Mahim and Bandra were connected by the Mahim causeway thanks to a rich Parsi – Lady Avabai Jamsetjee Jeejeebhoy – who paid Rs 157,000 for it. Legend has it that she prayed at several religious sites for the survival of a sick child. When the child recovered after she prayed at Mount Mary Church, Lady Avabai built the causeway to allow more devotees access to the Virgin Mother without having to take a ferry.

As the physical landmass came together, Bombay's political and commercial links with the Empire were tightened. A regular steamship service between the city and London was established in 1843; fifteen years later, direct British Government control of the Indian colony was established after the First War of Indian Independence (the 'Sepoy Mutiny') in 1857, which led to all of the East India Company's formal political powers being handed to the Crown.

URBS PRIMA IN INDIS

By 1845, the basis of a modern city had been created with land covering 170 square miles – a complex landscape of fields, coconut groves and outsize colonial structures, of cosmopolitan enclaves and sleepy villages. Bombay was the starting point of India's first passenger railway line in 1853, connecting the city to Thane in Maharashtra.

In the 1860s the British began a construction programme, erecting architecture that was designed to signal to the natives that they were here to stay – a direct response to the Indian uprising of 1857. Victoria Terminus, the Prince of Wales Museum, Bombay University, the

The 'native town' of **Kalbadevi** in the early 1900s. *See p17.*

General Post Office, the Old Customs House, Elphinstone College, the Public Works Department Building – all were begun in the 1860s. With typical imperial hyperbole, they began to refer to Bombay as 'urbs prima in Indis' – the first city of India.

In 1864, The Bombay, Baroda and Central India Railway (later merged with other railways to form what is now the Western Railway) was extended to Bombay, boosting the flow of cotton from the hinterlands. Cotton now dominated trade through Bombay. Raw cotton from Gujarat was shipped to Lancashire in England, processed into cloth and then shipped back via Bombay to be resold in the Indian market. Although cotton trading was the city's main activity, businessmen began to recognise that bigger profits could be made by spinning the cotton themselves. In 1854 the first cotton mill, The Bombay Spinning Mill, was opened by a Parsi, Cowasji Nanabhai Davar.

It was met by vociferous opposition from Lancashire mill owners anxious to avoid the 'outsourcing' of the cotton spinning business, and was only pushed through thanks to the influence of the British manufacturers of the cotton looms. In 1870, around 13 mills were in operation in Bombay. The shipping of raw cotton was still the main engine of the city's economy, however, and it received a massive boost when the American Civil War broke out in 1861. The war forced global markets to look for alternative sources of cotton for the booming textile industries of Britain and other countries in Europe. Bombay consequently became the world's foremost cotton supplier, with money pouring into the city until the war ended in 1865.

Within a year of the war's end, however, most of the companies were liquidated and many speculators went bankrupt. In spite of this, the city continued to grow, using the wealth generated during the boom to make itself over by shifting more and more into cotton spinning. The city's strategic location as a trade hub was given a further boost with the opening of the Suez Canal in 1869. By 1895 there were 70 mills in the city, rising to 83 in 1915 before stagnating in the global recession of the 1920s. Despite continued British political control, most of Bombay's cotton mills were owned by Indian families. In 1925, only 15 mills were British-owned, and even then the management was mostly Indian.

With the growth of the mills, Bombay's population rapidly increased as thousands of Maharashtrians migrated to the city to work the looms. The workers, usually male, initially lived in hostels and dormitories but eventually the 'chawl' – a tenement still in use today in which each family has one room, with all sharing a common verandah and toilets – emerged as basic housing for workers and their families. The workers settled close to the mills, with new neighbourhoods springing up in Byculla, Lalbaug, Parel and Worli. These neighbourhoods were often referred to by one name – Girangaon – the 'Village of Mills'. It was a dynamic cultural space and spawned generations of writers, poets and dramatists in Marathi and Gujarati. As the city grew, more land was reclaimed and more roads, causeways and wharves were built. The population had already increased from 13,726 in 1780 to 644,405 in 1872. By 1906 it had become 977,822.

The British continued to develop the city's infrastructure, with innovations such as the drainage system that continues to serve the city today. It was in 1860 that piped water began to flow to the city from Tulsi and Vihar lakes, and in 1870, the Bombay Port Trust was officially formed. The Princess Dock was built in 1855, followed by Victoria and Mereweather Dry Docks in 1891 and Alexandra Dock in 1914.

TOLERATE THY NEIGHBOUR

From its early beginnings, Bombay had been a vibrantly diverse city of Europeans and Indians from across the subcontinent, and by the 19th century, the lines between communities had been drawn – but an uneasy tolerance prevailed. Europeans socialised amongst themselves in sports clubs, with cricket as the main recreation. The Bombay Gymkhana was set up in 1875, exclusively for Europeans, spurring other communities, including Muslim, Hindu and Parsi, to set up their own gymkhanas, all in a line by the sea along Marine Drive. A friendly rivalry developed between them, with a regular 'Pentangular' cricket tournament (the fifth team was called, and made up of, 'The Rest'), never failing to make headlines in city newspapers.

The British maintained their control in the city through a paradoxical combination of a reputation for fairness and a shameless policy of divide-and-rule. In the 1880s, the commander of the Bombay police was a British superintendent named Charles Forjett, who was greatly admired by Indian residents for his harsh treatment of corrupt policemen and for conducting regular operations against the Parsi mafia who controlled the illegal liquor business in the Falkland Road region. The British were concerned about the power of

religious festivals to encourage a desire for political independence, and tried to regulate them, albeit tentatively.

The nationalist and freedom fighter Lokmanya Tilak saw the same potential and transformed the Ganpati festival, once celebrated on a small, domestic scale across Maharashtra, into a large-scale, outdoor event. He brought his supporters to Bombay's beaches, ostensibly to immerse idols of the elephant-headed Ganesha in the sea as per tradition, and then gave fiery speeches about their political responsibilities and the dream of *swaraj* (self-government). The British were checked from interfering too much in religious issues by the lessons of 1857, in which a rumour about rifle cartridges being made with pig and cow fat (thereby offending both Muslims and Hindus) had sparked an army rebellion which nearly lost them the colony. The British left Tilak largely alone and mass immersions during the Ganpati festival continue to this day, with its freedom-movement origins largely forgotten.

> **'The British maintained control through a combination of fairness and a shameless policy of divide and rule.'**

Instead of direct action, the British responded to such challenges to their authority with the same divide-and-rule-policy they had used all over the country – by playing Hindus and Muslims off against each other. It was hardly difficult for the British in Bombay, a city where communities were already naturally

South Mumbai's **St Thomas' Cathedral** in the early 1800s.

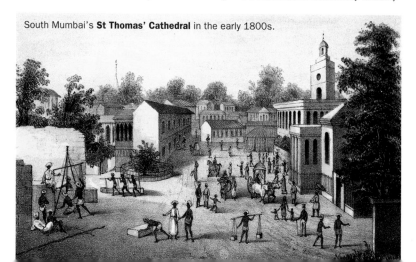

The **Eros** cinema in the 1940s.

Churchgate
New Reclamation,
Bombay

divided into different enclaves. With so little official thought put into planning residential neighbourhoods for the poorer or even middle-class populations, the only support network for those looking for homes or the means to build them came from within their own ethnic groups. As the city became increasingly politicised, communal riots began to plague Bombay for the first time.

A NEW CENTURY
Bombay was still a city among other Indian cities. But in 1875, the basis for its current status as India's economic capital was established with the Bombay Stock Exchange – then referred to as the Native Share and Stockbrokers Association. As the cream of India's professional talent flooded into the city, political movements began to flourish (*see p21* **The Empire strikes out**). Political ferment saw the establishment of the Indian National Congress – the first Indian political party – in 1885 at the Gokuldas Tejpal College in South Bombay.

> **'As the city became increasingly politicised, communal riots began to plague Bombay.'**

By this time a lack of adequate urban planning was causing large parts of the city to choke from over-congestion, a problem that became disastrous just a few years before the end of the 19th century, when bubonic plague broke out, possibly carried by rats on grain ships from Hong Kong. Thousands fled the city and Indian and foreign ports

quarantined all goods arriving from Bombay, with ruinous consequences for the city's economy. The tragedy was compounded by the failure of the monsoon in 1899, leading to one of India's worst-ever famines. The British authorities responded to the catastrophe by setting up a City Improvement Trust to encourage the development of the suburbs and relieve pressure on the southern part of the city.

By the beginning of the 20th century, the first outlines of the character of modern Bombay had begun to emerge. By 1906, the city's population had topped one million. It quickly became a hot-bed of the new politics that would lead to Indian Independence, fired up by Mahatma Gandhi's return from South Africa in 1915. Gandhi took a house called Mani Bhavan in Gamdevi, from where he began to rally citizens to the cause. Prominent Bombay businessmen, traders, workers and professionals became his votaries. Technological innovations that had slowly emerged in the West were implanted in Bombay in rapid order, with the first transmission lines of the Tata Power Company criss-crossing the city's skyline in 1915. In 1926 the first motorised bus service started between Afghan Church and Crawford Market. The first electric train started in 1927, an intercity service from Bombay to Pune and Igatpuri. A few years later the first electric commuter train (still known in Mumbai as 'EMUs' – Electric Multiple Units) rolled out. In 1932, the Parsi industrialist JRD Tata flew the first scheduled airmail flight from Karachi to Bombay via Ahmedabad, landing his single-engined de Haviland Puss Moth on a grass strip at Juhu Aerodrome.

The Lumière Brothers' Cinematographe showed four silent short films at the Watson's Hotel in Bombay in 1896, charging an entry fee

The Empire strikes out

The political force that would shape India's destiny was born in Bombay on a mild December day in 1885. A delegation of 70 Indian lawyers, professors and journalists congregated at the Gokuldas Tejpal College to establish the Indian National Congress, India's first national political party. There was no formal political forum in which it could speak or debate legislation – Indian independence was still 62 years away. However, the Congress led over 70 million Indians in the struggle against British rule and, after freedom finally came in 1947, dominated independent India's politics for the rest of the century. In Delhi, the Congress is still in power today.

Had he lived to see it, the Congress's founder would have been shocked. His name was Allan Octavian Hume, a retired civil servant from Kent. An ardent but puritanical social reformer, Hume served as the INC's General Secretary until 1908, during which time its official stance was not outright opposition to British rule, just a demand for greater say for Indians in government. It was only after repeated British refusals that their politics became radicalised.

Bombay remained at the centre of events throughout the Indian freedom struggle, despite being much younger and smaller than Calcutta or Delhi. Lacking the rigid social structures that prevailed in other cities, social reform was already underway in Bombay. The city admired ability and rewarded merit,

attracting India's best and brightest. It also had a cosmopolitan and enlightened middle class and an array of colleges and cultural institutions. This combination allowed Bombay to take the lead in making Indian political history, producing the first Indian to be elected to the British Parliament in 1893.

Mohandas Gandhi, commonly known as the Mahatma ('Great Soul'), chose Bombay as his base upon his return from South Africa, living in the now-famous Mani Bhavan in Gamdevi. It was from here that Gandhi planned and co-ordinated civil disobedience movements, and introduced his revolutionary concepts of non-violence, satyagraha ('truth force') and swadeshi (loosely, 'buying Indian goods'). He found enthusiastic support from the people of Bombay, financially and by way of manpower.

When the fatal blow to British rule finally came, it was struck from Bombay. Gandhi launched the Quit India movement on 8 August 1942 at Gowalia Tank (now August Kranti Maidan), with Congress support. He urged Indians to act as citizens of an independent nation and use non-violent civil disobedience to frustrate British control. Hundreds of thousands across India responded. Soon after, Gandhi and other members of the Congress Working Committee were arrested, but it was too late – Gandhi's call spread like jungle fire across the city and a large crowd gathered at Gowalia Tank the next day. Just five years later, the British empire fell in India.

Models of **Gandhi** at one of many trials for agitating British rule.

of one rupee. It was a phenomenon that the *Times of India* described at the time as 'the marvel of the century', and quickly fired the imaginations of a generation of Indians. The Indian film industry was born in Bombay a few years later. A man named HS Bhatavdekar filmed the city's first documentary in 1899, of a wrestling match, which he showed across the city to general acclaim. The first full-length feature film, *Raja Harishchandra*, was made in 1913 by Dadasaheb Phalke and shown at Bombay's Coronation Cinematograph. By 1920, the Indian film industry was fully formed, with Bombay at its heart. By 1931 about 207 films were being made every year (but it wasn't until the 1990s that the term 'Bollywood' was coined).

GROWING PAINS

After 'freedom at midnight' gave birth to independent India on 15 August 1947, Bombay continued to expand beyond the suburbs of Mahim and Bandra – erstwhile Portuguese areas – swallowing up everything as far north as Mankhurd, Mulund and Dahisar. The city became the capital of Bombay State, a political creation that included the whole of what are now the two separate states of Gujarat and Maharashtra. In the following years Bombay became a battlefield for political movements based on language groups, mainly its Gujarati- and Marathi-speaking populations. The Samyukta Maharashtra Andolan was a major political force of socialists, trade unions and artists that fought fiercely for the formation of an independent state for Marathi-speaking

Kala Ghoda ('Black Horse') statue, moved to Byculla in 1965.

people, with Bombay as its capital. They finally achieved their wish and Bombay State was split into two in 1960, but only after 105 of the movement's supporters had been shot dead by police during tumultuous political protests around Flora Fountain earlier the same year. A memorial at what is now called Hutatma Chowk commemorates the dead with an eternal flame.

'On 12 March 1993 came "Black Friday". Thirteen bombs exploded at locations across the city.'

Bombay's politics in the 1960s and 1970s remained dynamic and dominated by the Left, with the working class mill areas of central Bombay as a Communist heartland. But a splinter of the Samyukta Maharashtra Andolan morphed into a nativist movement – the Shiv Sena ('Army of Shivaji'), which won continued influence with its Right-wing anti-outsider politics in the face of growing slum encroachment by immigrants from outside the city. During the 1970s the city overtook Calcutta as the most populous city in India. A lack of political will, cushioned by a healthy economy benefiting from cheap labour, allowed slums to proliferate on a scale that had never been seen before (*see p26* **Slumbai**). In the process, the Shiv Sena fired the imagination of the working class, displacing the old dominance of the Left. Its founder, a former cartoonist named Bal Thackeray, came to dominate the city's political landscape using a combination of brutal mafia-like force and a string of local election victories. The decline of the textile industry contributed to this political shift and, after a catastrophic mill workers' strike in 1982-83, the century-old cotton-spinning industry effectively died in Bombay. With its passing, the mill workers lost their key position in the city's economy and politics.

The 1970s and early '80s were an exciting decade in the city's cinematic history, with the emergence of filmmakers determined to set themselves apart from the mainstream Hindi film industry. They began to make realist and neo-expressionist films with strong elements of social commentary. Shyam Benegal's *Ankur* (The Seedling, 1974), introduced the stunning actress (and later MP) Shabana Azmi and was the first film to articulate the new conflict between India's educated, urbane city dwellers and the feudal traditions of the countryside. Rabindra Dharmaraj's *Chakra* in 1981 was a searing look at the slums of Bombay, seen through the eyes of actress Smita Patil.

Bombay's western bay in the 1880s...

...and in the 1990s.

City authorities made few infrastructure improvements in the 1970s and '80s, despite the alarmingly rapid growth in the city's population. The largest was a plan to create New Bombay (now known as Navi Mumbai) – a parallel city across the harbour on the mainland, built to decongest the island city. It began slowly, faltered, and even today has yet to live up to its original aims.

The Shiv Sena continued to rise throughout the 1980s, thanks to the decline of the Left and increasingly visible corruption in the Congress. It was a political combination that proved to be lethal, culminating in the horrendous Bombay riots of 1992-93 – incidents that were in fact state-sanctioned and party-sponsored pogroms against Muslims. The violence erupted after the Babri Mosque was razed by Hindu militants in the city of Ayodhya, in the North Indian state of Uttar Pradesh. Hundreds of Muslims were killed by Hindu fundamentalists during the riots. On 12 March 1993 came 'Black Friday', when 13 bombs exploded in one day at locations across the city, including the Bombay Stock Exchange and the Air India Building.

Two hundred and fifty-seven people were killed in what were revenge attacks by a Muslim group for the slaughter two months previously. The riots and bombings were a shattering blow to Bombay's self-image as a cosmopolitan, secular city that for years had avoided the communal violence that afflicts other Indian cities. It paved the way for the Shiv Sena's rise to power at both city and state levels and, in 1995, they changed the official name of the city to Mumbai (*see p17* **Mumbai or Bombay?**). Since then, Mumbai has been the victim of sporadic terrorist attacks, most recently in July 2006, when bombs tore through the first class compartments of seven commuter trains on the Western Line, killing more than 200 people.

Since 1991, a series of economic reforms have liberalised India's economy, unleashing Mumbai's entrepreneurial energy. It aspires to become a new global city with a modern spirit close to that of its former identity as a trade hub. But while Mumbai may be the financial capital of a superpower-in-waiting, its citizens are still waiting for a transformation of its infrastructure, social housing and polluted air.

Mumbai Today

Many worlds, one city.

In November 2007, more than 300 urban planners, economists, geographers, anthropologists and architects from around the world assembled in Mumbai's posh Taj Mahal hotel for a conference called Urban Age. They hoped that studying the swirl of life outside the hotel's hushed confines would provide some clues about the potential problems the majority of the world's people will face in the 21st century – and how these pitfalls can be avoided. Already, more than half the world's population lives in cities and that number will rise to 75 per cent by 2050, according to experts at Urban Age. Mumbai and its sister megacities, said the organisers of the conference – the London School of Economics and Deutsche Bank – will 'provide the testing ground for our urban future'.

If this is the future, the world would have good reason to be a little alarmed. With the normal big city problems of overcrowding, strained water and sewage systems, almost no public housing, very few parks or open spaces, high levels of pollution and packed public transport, Mumbai is a perfect example of how not to do things.

All of this has turned Mumbai into a fertile field of study for academics from around the world. In fact, they've even coined a new word for this new endeavour: 'Bombayology'. Dozens of seminars have been organised in the last couple of years to contemplate the future of the city and it sometimes seems impossible to turn a corner in Dharavi, one of the city's most extensive slums, without bumping into Fulbright scholars, fellows from the American Institute for Indian Studies, PhD candidates, masters students and independent researchers collecting data on micro-finance schemes or women's organisations.

For students of urban planning, Mumbai is an endlessly fascinating challenge. A peninsula that extends south-west into the Arabian Sea, Mumbai is roughly one-third the size of Greater London. But with a population of 13 million within its city limits, it has nearly twice as many residents as Britain's capital. Another five million live in the suburbs and small towns in the hinterland, which puts the number of people in the Mumbai metropolitan region at just two million less than the population of Australia. Each day, six million of these people board

Mumbai's intensely overcrowded suburban commuter trains and head into the city for work. Most businesses and government offices are concentrated at the southern tip of the city, leading to chronic traffic jams, overlong train journeys and carriages so packed that the railways had to invent a word to describe the situation: they call it the 'superdensecrushload'. At peak hour, trains meant for 1,700 passengers routinely carry 4,700 people, with 17 bodies crammed into a single square metre of space. Every day, eight people die while commuting, often from falling off the train or hitting a signal pole while hanging out the coach.

> **'Roughly 55 per cent of Mumbai's population lives in slums – eight to ten people sharing a home smaller in area than an SUV – but they occupy only six per cent of the city's land.'**

In an attempt to ease commuting woes, the Mumbai Metropolitan Region Development Authority, the government organisation that has the weighty task of guiding the city's growth, proposed a sea-link – a bridge off the western waterfront that will connect the suburbs and South Mumbai. The first section of the bridge will reduce commuting time between the western suburb of Bandra and the mid-town district of Worli from 40 to 20 minutes. But this ambitious project, which will cost Rs 13.06 billion ($323 million) – three times the initial estimate – will benefit only the 1.6 per cent of Mumbaikars who travel to work by car. Twenty-nine out of every 1,000 Mumbaikars own a car, the lowest number of any Indian city, yet most transport projects in the city benefit this group of people.

CIVIC WOES

Yet, somehow the city keeps functioning. Mumbai's binary nature – conspicuous consumption juxtaposed with starvation, apparent anarchy with a low crime rate, a thriving economy amid obvious poverty – has over the last few years been the source of increasing global interest. Everybody, it seems, is trying to figure out how Mumbai continues ticking despite all odds.

Mumbai's average population density is 27,348 per square kilometre. Higher than even New York (9,551) or Mexico City (5,877), this number rises to 113,605 in the most crowded areas. Roughly 55 per cent of the city lives in slums – eight to ten people sharing a home smaller in area than an SUV – occupying six per cent of the city's land.

Thanks to the problems peculiar to the island's geography, there is only limited space in which to build and only one direction in which development can continue: north. But the tony addresses are in the south and western suburbs, which means developers are always seeking out old bungalows and small buildings to tear down so that they can be replaced with 15-floor apartment blocks and commercial complexes. Zoning restrictions seem to have almost been abandoned and the new buildings often lack sufficient parking space for all the residents, so many Mumbai streets are clogged with stationary cars. Water shortages are a chronic problem and in the summer of 2007, for the first time ever, the city faced the prospect of power cuts. Though it didn't come to pass, it's only a matter of time before the only city in India without electricity problems ceases to enjoy uninterrupted supply.

The rampant construction has hurt Mumbai's fragile ecosystem. The Mithi River, which runs from Borivali National Park in the north of the city to the Arabian Sea in the west, has been reduced to a sewage canal, and its once-wide

Gridlock is a daily feature of Mumbai life.

Slumbai

Roughly 55 per cent of Mumbai's citizens live in *zopadpattis* – slums of varying sophistication. Some are little more than bamboo-and-tarpaulin shacks; others are three-storey brick-built rooms stacked precariously on top of each other and supplied with electricity and water connections. Slum-dwellers perform vital roles in Mumbai's economy, working as labourers in the city's booming construction sector or as domestic servants in wealthier households. A staggering 40 per cent of Mumbai's police officers live in slums. Slums are everywhere in Mumbai, and it has the dubious distinction of being home to Dharavi, popularly referred to as Asia's largest slum. But it wasn't always like this. Slums first started appearing in Mumbai in the 1950s, as immigrants from other parts of Maharashtra state, and from poor rural states across India – particularly Uttar Pradesh and Bihar – began to arrive in search of work in a city seen as a land of opportunity. With no low-cost housing available, they began building shanties on patches of empty land.

It was the beginning of Mumbai's transformation into what locals ruefully call 'Slumbai', greased by gangsters, corrupt officials and conniving politicians. As immigration accelerated, the Mumbai mafia muscled in as slumlords, charging rents to slum-dwellers and threatening the private landowners whose land they had stolen. Police, bureaucrats and politicians were paid to look the other way as public land was grabbed. Politicians quickly realised they could benefit from these vast new additions to their electorates and used their clout to protect slums from demolition and provide them with some basic amenities. The slum-dwellers became 'vote banks' – blocks of support for any politician who would protect them from the law. By the 1970s, the slums had made a major impact on the character of the city, swallowing up many of its green spaces. The smallest patch of land is a potential slum, with shanties along roads, on bridges and even lining the city's railway lines. Every year, around 1,000 slum-dwellers are killed crossing train tracks just getting to and from their homes.

Numerous slum rehabilitation schemes have been launched over the years, with little impact. In 1995, the Shiv Sena government promised all slum-dwellers free 225sq ft flats. Their plan called for a million homes in five years, to be built by private developers in exchange for lucrative development rights. Ten years later, the scheme was widely seen as yet another scam, allowing builders to grab prime public land for a pittance, while building less than 40,000 homes. However, the scheme is still in operation. Ironically, free housing is not something slum-dwellers have ever asked for – after all, they all pay rent to slumlords. Housing experts say that slum-dwellers instead need access to mortgages.

The most ambitious scheme is the Dharavi Redevelopment Project, which aims to raze a 2.23 square kilometre slum, home to 350,000 residents, and erect a warren of skyscrapers in its place. The plans are to rehabilitate those residents who settled before 1995 (while leaving the rest to fend for themselves) in eight-storey blocks while using the rest of the area for large-scale commercial development. The government altered the rules to allow the proposal to pass without the requisite consent from 70 per cent of the area's residents. Despite concern over the sheer unworkability of the resulting population density and the effect the scheme will have on the area's thriving local economy and the city's commuting patterns, the Maharashtra government remains unmoved and is determined to see the project go through.

mouth has been narrowed by decades of reclamation – to build the swanky business district of Bandra-Kurla in the 1990s and, more recently, for the construction of the Bandra-Worli sea-link. Mangrove swamps along the city's coast, which protect the shore from the battering of the monsoon, have been illegally reclaimed, uprooted and destroyed.

On 26 July 2005, a freak cloudburst caused nearly a metre of rain to fall on Mumbai in 24 hours, flooding the entire city and killing 452 Mumbaikars. The deluge shut the city down – phones stopped working, power supply was cut, trains stopped – and cost Mumbai an estimated $3.5 billion in damage and lost business hours. The worst affected were the poor: in the northern suburb of Andheri, a landslide killed 72 slum-dwellers. In the days that followed the flood, they were the ones most susceptible to the waterborne diseases floating around the city.

CULTURAL RENAISSANCE

For all its chaos, though, Mumbai is a thriving and lively city, producing more wealth and culture than any other city in India. Perhaps thanks to the frantic energy of Mumbai, the rush to succeed in a traditionally business-oriented city or just a complete lack of introspection, Mumbaikars rarely do more than complain before getting on with life. There's no doubt that Mumbai in the 21st century is a tremendously exciting place to be; the city's stock index is soaring, business is booming and middle-class Mumbaikars now have access to goods and services they couldn't have imagined a few years ago. Faced with a looming economic crisis in 1991, India began the process of dismantling its protected economy, the results of which are apparent in the country's new-found reputation as an emerging giant.

> **'For the middle-class and upper-class Mumbaikar, there has never been a better time to live in the city, and for the visitor, Mumbai has never been more attractive.'**

Already the home of Indian popular culture, with the film, TV and advertising industries based in Mumbai, the city's culture and media are flourishing in sync with the economy. Perhaps that's why as many students of 'Bombayology' spend their time researching Bollywood orchestras or the art district of South Mumbai as they do slum economies and urban planning.

Over the last few years, a high-profile magazine has launched every couple of months, three new newspapers have been set up since 2005, dozens of new television channels have started operations and voluminous books about the city have invigorated international interest in Mumbai. A dozen new art galleries have opened over the last couple of years and well-established Indian artists are increasingly using Mumbai as an element in their works. The city's nightclubs bypass the global cool of house and trance to play a home-grown mishmash of remixed Bollywood meets electronica via hip hop. The country's first symphony orchestra was formed in Mumbai in 2006, and two years later the city hosted a full-fledged locally produced opera – Giacomo Puccini's *Madama Butterfly*. New clubs that fly down international acts are packed every night and major pop and rock stars have started including Mumbai on their world tour schedules.

For the middle-class and upper-class Mumbaikar, there has never been a better time to live in the city and for the visitor, Mumbai has never been more attractive. Free of the clinical sterility of other Asian megacities, but safer and friendlier than metropolises like Lagos or Sao Paolo, Mumbai offers the unique experience of being not one city but many worlds: equal parts exhilarating, disheartening, charming, revolting, addictive, unfathomable and uncontrollable, but never boring.

IN A BAD STATE

After all, the city's difficulties with overcrowding, poverty, infrastructure, open spaces, public transport or a shattered ecosystem aren't insurmountable. Instead, Mumbai's biggest problem is bad governance. Local politicians seem to spend more time debating issues of language and culture than how to fix the housing crisis. In 1995, the city's name was changed from Bombay to Mumbai by the Shiv Sena, a nativist political party on the far right (*see p17* **Mumbai or Bombay?**). In the decades before that, scores of streets shed their colonial names and took on the names of local figures. Since then, the names of the airport, the city's biggest railway terminus and the museum have all been homogenised with a single name (*see p15* **Who is Shivaji anyway?**). Yet, the problems that plague Mumbai are the same as those that afflicted Bombay.

Even when it had opportunities to attempt to solve Mumbai's problems, the government managed to let them slide. Mumbai's mills, once the engine of its economic prosperity, fell into disuse after disputes between management and trade unions in the 1980s. Located in the heart of the city, 54 mills occupy 600 acres of prime land worth roughly Rs 210 billion ($5.2 billion), of which the government owns 285 acres. According to a 1991 state law, the land was meant to be divided in three equal parts for public housing, open spaces and commercial development. But the state government altered the law in 2001 to allow large-scale private development, and when a high-court ruling reinstated the law, the state went to the Supreme Court of India to have it overturned. An opportunity to regenerate the city with open spaces and low-cost housing was squandered by greedy politicians and builders.

Like other emerging cities in Asia, there is a plan. In fact, there are numerous plans, including the Mumbai Urban Transport Project, the Mumbai Urban Infrastructure Project, the Mumbai Metropolitan Region Development Association plan 1996-2011 (with a sequel that stretches from 2011 to 2021 reportedly in the works) and the catchily titled Vision Mumbai drawn by the consulting firm McKinsey for Bombay First, a business lobby. There are also plans for a second airport outside city limits, for the Mumbai metro rail and smaller in size but as ambitious in scope, plans to rebuild all of the 2.23 square kilometre slum known as Dharavi (*see p26* **Slumbai**) and perhaps all of C Ward, a 1.78 square kilometre neighbourhood with a population of 202,216 people, located a couple of kilometres north of downtown. Yet, on its third

Building blocks

One expects great cities to have great architecture. But Mumbai clearly reveals how misplaced such expectations are. For long the focus of India's modernist aspirations, the city still has very little to show for itself by way of great modern architecture. If you are looking for bravura architecture, go to Chandigarh, where you get certifiably great architecture (but, from a Mumbaikar's perspective, no city) or to New Delhi (not Gurgaon), or even Bangalore (but not Whitefield). But if you're that truly liberated enthusiast who finds the accidental (and always in progress) collage of urban form deeply intriguing, then this is the city for you.

Mumbai has always been hot, rainy and ridiculously expensive (at least in terms of real estate). It has also always been in a hurry, and on the make. Like much else, its architecture has been shaped by these mental, meteorological and monetary drivers. Not unsurprisingly, Bollywood's prodigious output holds a steady mirror to Mumbai's culture of building. Both are driven by numbers and both make up in quantity what they slur over in quality. Both the world of real estate and that of film production also fancy themselves as 'industries' on the flimsiest of pretexts and routinely attract the interest of the underworld. What they have produced, actually, are exceptionally buzzing

birthday in 2007, the government of the state of Maharashtra, of which Mumbai is capital, boasted only of starting some projects, completing studies into plans and issuing a few calls for bids on infrastructure projects.

If Mumbai is to change, it will be because citizens' groups are becoming increasingly vociferous about the city's chaotic administration. For instance, in 2007, Mumbai's municipal corporation announced a plan that amounted to giving the city's parks away to private organisations – 'caretakers' would be allowed to maintain the city's parks and playfields in return for which they would be allowed to build a clubhouse. But heated public protests killed the plan. Some of the city's nicest open spaces – including Bandra's Carter Road and Bandstand promenades, and the fort and amphitheatre at Land's End – were created thanks to local citizen's groups, with the help of the local members of parliament.

Like Mumbai's problems, the solutions are age old. Bombayologists point out that Mumbai has been complaining about extreme congestion, flawed drainage systems and corrupt administrators for the last 350 years. But each crisis, these historians emphasise, has been overcome because citizen's groups and philanthropists have ensured that Mumbai continues to not just survive but thrive.

ambiences that, when you go close, pixelate intriguingly into blocks upon blocks (films or buildings), each tattier than the other.

Two pixels – the *chhajja* (weathershade) and the balcony – tell us much about the way rain, money, law and desire have given Mumbai its face. It's unlikely that any element has troubled the modern Indian architect more than the *chhajja*. If he could have his way, he would just turn off the rain. Modern architecture, as every novice knows, needs a clean slate of a wall (in any colour as long as it's white), outsized voids and surprising scatters of windows placed just right. But the driving rain compels *chhajjas* to be placed over all windows, and since most buildings in Mumbai are apartment or office blocks, their unrelenting profusion defeats any possibility of 'composition'. In the typical Mumbai building this either leads to monotonous clutter or severe continuous bands. Some architects give up the fight and simply don't put in any *chhajjas* at all. It is then left to the middle class desperados behind the windows to fashion their own weather protection using the detritus of the local industrial economy – steel angles, wonky aluminium sheet, tar and prayer. That's how the city gets its DIY appearance, the look of incessant enterprise.

The tight footprint teaches you to push the envelope overhead. One of Mumbai's great contributions to the modern Indian architectural argot must surely be the box grill. Fixed to the *chhajja* above and to the walls on three sides of the window, the box grill is a pouch that the room pushes out over the street (if not for a law that restricts *chhajjas* to a depth of around 2.5 feet, we would have entire room-cages projecting out of otherwise legit buildings). Its contents begin with potted plants, but run through bored students, broken tricycles and study tables. In many homes, this is the only alcove you can carve out of a city mean about space.

But one legitimate architectural element once used to make a poetic experience of dwelling possible in this crowded, sweaty, polluted and endearing city has disappeared. The projecting balcony – never more than three feet deep by law since the 1970s – once bridged the gulf between public and private space. It was often assimilated into the connected room, by closing the space above the parapet with sliding glass windows. The colours of film on the glass, and the aluminium used for framing, changed from window to window on the same building. Add to that the many patterns of window grills, flat or boxed, black or white, and you get a picture of Mumbai's architectural mish-mash.

Buildings, even by small developers, are much more completely controlled now. The architecture they favour is seemingly modelled on confectionery. The standardised allure (like that of Bollywood films) is quickly produced, quick to act and entirely disconnected from the core content of architecture – the life lived within. The wrapping (in masonry) is fixed two and a half feet away from the real skin of the building, and the balcony has finally been absorbed into the building to provide a smooth façade. But this has swallowed up the most heartening feature of Mumbai's streetscape – the men or women in vests and nighties peering out peacefully at the city.

The writer, Himanshu Burte, is an architect.

Communities

Author **Jerry Pinto** sorts out Mumbai's identity crisis.

First the ABC charts in primary school did their dirty work, introducing us to apples and zebras. Then the Good Habits chart told us that we should brush our teeth, not with neem twigs but with toothbrushes and toothpaste. Next we were shown a 'People of India' chart and we struggled to find ourselves reflected in it.

As a Roman Catholic, I remember being slightly surprised to find that my father's native dress was supposed to be a suit and my mother was supposed to have bobbed hair and wear a dress.

I went home from school that day and asked my father why he didn't wear a suit.

'In this heat?' he asked.

I showed him the chart.

He laughed. 'Well, they couldn't put us in loincloths, could they?'

A cold thrill ran down my snobbish little spine. Yes, my father had been a tiller of the soil in his native Goa. Yes, he had walked eight miles to school and back after he had watered the red bananas of which his village, Moira, was proud. I remember thanking my stars that we were once removed from the loincloth and that the chart of the communities of Mumbai had chosen to put us into double-breasted suits.

Today, of course, many years later, it is the height of chic to be the son of a farmer who actually carried his wares to the market and clawed his way out of poverty. The stereotyped representations on that chart no longer have the power to astonish/amuse/offend us. With our kitsch-tinted glasses, we can see ourselves as others see us and laugh in our new-found confidence as one of the largest consumer markets in the world, as the economic driver of the subcontinent, as the city where the stock market only has to cough for the national antibiotics to be trotted out. But like this city, built on rotting fish-heads and palm leaves, retrieved from a history of mosquitoes and amnesia, it is a shaky self-confidence.

THE MUMBAI MYTH

The urban myth of Mumbai's secular and classless self-image reads roughly like this: it was inherited from the older urban history of Surat, a port city in Gujarat situated on ancient trade routes that attracted settlers from across the Asian and African continents. As Surat declined, Mumbai emerged as a regional player and people migrated here in large numbers. Since they had already rubbed shoulders with the world, they brought with them their tolerance.

> **'Today, of course, it is the height of chic to be the son of a farmer who actually carried his wares to the market and clawed his way out of poverty.'**

The city had dismantled the barriers of caste simply by making it impossible to follow traditional proscriptions about purity and avoiding pollution. On the train and on the bus, in the mill and in the canteen, at the mess and on the cricket field, it was impossible to worry too much about who ate beef and who didn't, who was 'clean' and who was 'unclean'.

Cram millions of people on a patch of land and they must either learn to co-exist or kill each other. Mumbaikars did not learn the

Saraswati Chitra Kala's 'People of India' educational picture chart

CHRISTIAN   खिती   सीख

SIKH   वाऊवी
बोहरा

DAWOODI BOHRA

Amar Akbar Anthony (1977) – emblematic of Bollywood's cosmopolitanism.

virtue of tolerance on their own; they were forced into it by the congestion of the big city.

We were also in the habit of saying that there was only one God in Mumbai and his name was Mammon. No one was sure who actually had ever worshipped Mammon but we were proud of his classicism and, like the penguin-shaped dustbins that the municipality put on our streets because penguins are the only creatures with no religious associations, he was secular. We had not Kuber, the Hindu god of wealth, or even a Calvinist god of capitalism. He was just that ugly monster to whom we could all pretend allegiance so that we could laugh at the rest of the country when it went mad over symbolic acts of desecration – the slaughter of a cow near a temple, the mosque bedaubed with pig's blood. We were far too busy, far too intent on the good life, far too western-looking, to bother about that kind of thing. As Bombayites, we left that to the excitable natives of the subcontinent. Our little finger of land was, we believed, too busy making money.

In 1992, we found that we weren't quite so different after all. Far away, in Ayodhya, in Uttar Pradesh, the forces of the Hindu Right went on a rampage and destroyed a mosque that they claimed stood on the birthplace of Lord Ram, the ninth avatar of Vishnu, the Purushottam or perfect man, the hero of one of India's seminal epics, the *Ramayana*. No one ever believed that the mosque would be demolished. Even when the mosque came down, no one believed that the rage and the despair would come home to us. It did.

Mumbai's cosmopolitan façade went up in flames. Riots took over the city, hundreds were murdered, and we put to rest the idea of the national melting pot, the *bhelpuri* city, the idea that Mumbaikars had voluntarily exiled themselves from their roots to float free in the city. The next state election returned a coalition government between two right wing

Hindu parties. The city was renamed Mumbai, another symbolic act of reversal.

But Mumbai is endlessly volatile and we want to go back to that prelapsarian age when the question 'What's your caste?' was not about whether you were going to be burnt alive or not. In the old days, that question wasn't even about caste. It was about identity, an attempt to place you, geographically, psychologically, socially, sometimes even politically.

Declare that you are a Pinto, which puts you firmly into a supposedly casteless religion like Roman Catholicism, and your fellow Catholics will ask you your village. This will help them discover exactly what kind of Pinto you are: whether you are from upper-caste stock or a convert from the lower orders.

As a Pinto, I might be a Goan, one of a large wave of migrants washed in from Goa who settled around the port areas, especially Dhobi Talao (the long-since drained 'Lake of the Laundrymen'). I would speak Konkani at home and the rice cooked in my home would have salt in it.

Or I might be an 'East Indian' Pinto, even though Mumbai is on the west coast of India. The term applies to the many converts the Portuguese made when they arrived here and who chose that name for themselves over the term 'Bombay Portuguese' by which they had been known. 'East Indians', they thought, would endear them to the East India Company, which until 1857 was the representative of colonial British power. As an East Indian Pinto, I would speak Marathi at home.

I might even be a Pinto of Koli origin, fiercely proud of being one of the first inhabitants of the islands, perhaps a generation away from fishing, but still offering coconuts to the sea on Nariyal Poornima, to appease the waves after the storms of the monsoon.

For in Mumbai, as in India, no community is solid, no religious persuasion unites all its members. Thus the Mumbai Hindu is sub-divided according to caste (which still persists) but is also acutely aware of his or her family origins. Village life may be a distant memory for many Mumbai residents but it still, in many ways, determines identity.

In any case, even if the large majority of the city is Hindu, that's not much of an identity at all, except for outsiders. You have only to read the matrimonial columns of the local newspapers to see how many different ways the term can be sliced, with caste only one of them.

MUMBAI MASH-UP

The very term Hindu may be seen as a misnomer, an inclusive term created by the British as a bureaucratic convenience to make their censuses easier. Hinduism itself is difficult to define as a religion because it has no single defining text. There are hundreds of Hindu texts of different importance to different communities. The four Vedas (ancient religious texts dating back to around 1,800 BC, but this is a contested date) are often held to be central, but the epics, the *Ramayana* and the *Mahabharata*, constitute the core of most Hindus' connection with their religion.

Hinduism has been called a way of life but this is also misleading about a deeply complex and seemingly self-contradictory religion. Hinduism offers a dualistic path in which God and Man are separate entities and a non-dualistic one in which Man's only duty is to recognise the godhead within him. It sanctions great excess as a route to the divine but encourages great asceticism as well. It has 330 million gods, with their own distinct identities; and a single deity into which all of them can be collapsed. It is possible, as one observer remarked, to say two completely opposing things about Hinduism and find scriptural support for both.

No one ever answers 'Hindu' to the question of caste. One might say 'Saraswat' and straight away that answer would suggest that the speaker is from Goa, migrated to Mumbai and belongs to the Brahmin orders. Or one might say 'Pathare Prabhu' and evoke a group that came to Mumbai in the 13th century with the king Raja Bhimdev from Patan in Gujarat. Or one might say 'Tamilian Dalit' and order up another lineage of social revolution, of an underclass that is beginning to be mobilised by affirmative action, of the tanneries in what is often (mistakenly) called Asia's largest slum, Dharavi. Or one might say 'TamBram', meaning 'Tamilian Brahmin', and another set of images – of classical Carnatic music concerts and tight-lipped morality – would be set into play. All these are stereotypes and as soon as you bump into the real human being behind them, they begin to fade. But they are, nevertheless, a legacy of that school chart.

> **'Hinduism has 330 million gods, each with their own distinct indentities; and a single deity into which all of them can be collapsed.'**

Islam, you might think, would be easier. Muslims are supposed to be one people in their submission to Allah, their adherence to the Koran, right? But beyond the obvious Shi'a and Sunni divide there are regional differences as well. There are 'Dawoodi Bohras' from Gujarat, 'Memons' from Kutch and from Halai, 'Khoja Ismailis' (also called 'Aga Khanis'), 'Konkani Muslims' from the Konkan

The Bahu Daji Lad Museum presents the headgear of Mumbai communities. *See p73.*

Stuck in the caste

Caste is an uncomfortable phenomenon that most Mumbaikars just don't want to acknowledge. The word 'caste' is derived from the Portuguese word *casta*, meaning 'category'. The Portuguese and, subsequently, the British, saw caste as a way of organising communities on a hierarchy based on the *varna* system. The *varna* system is derived from classical Hindu texts that divide societies into four parts: **Brahmins**, the highest group, represented by priests and teachers; **Kshatriyas**, warriors and kings; **Vaishyas**, who are the merchants and traders; and **Shudras** (also known as Dalits), at the bottom of the hierarchy as labourers and peasants. Some texts hold the '**untouchables**' (later referred to by Gandhi as the Harijan – the 'children of God') as a fifth caste who did jobs considered polluting: handling corpses and collecting excrement from homes without a sewage system.

However, many sociologists believe that explanations of caste that rely on the *varna* system are flawed. They argue that castes are not discrete but themselves divided into numerous sub-categories. Even people of the same caste may be forbidden from marrying because of these divisions. Brahmins may be ritually superior, but in wealth and status they may actually be dependent on other castes below them on the *varna* scale.

According to some social historians, the caste system has served mainly to perpetuate the domination of elite priests, rulers and merchants. Those now regarded as the lower castes may have originally been forest tribes absorbed into larger kingdoms. The theory of *karma*, in which people are doomed to their status in life by their deeds in past lives, can be seen as an ideological tool that helped suppress desires for political change. But caste can also be seen in other ways, for example as a means of organising a division of labour that gave rise to highly productive economies in India's past.

In Mumbai, caste still connects the modern city to the ancient history of the subcontinent. The city still relies to a large extent on 'scavengers' – known as ragpickers – to deal with waste. Most of these scavengers belong to castes that have always been scavengers. Look harder and you'll find a city in which the majority of its teachers still come from the upper castes, and most businessmen belong to communities that have dominated business for centuries. Caste even shapes where people live: over 75 per cent of slum dwellers are from lower castes. That's a far cry from Mumbai's self-image as a meritocratic city of opportunity. No one talks of the slums of Dharavi as a Dalit colony but, effectively, they are.

In many ways, Mumbai does not encourage casteism. Many Dalits see the city as a place that frees them from the oppression of rural caste politics. Mumbai is a major centre of Dalit art and literature, and plays an important role in Dalit politics. In the 19th and 20th centuries, it was a centre of Indian social reform and helped weaken caste-based politics. But Mumbai continues to struggle with caste and with those who see advantage in dividing people on the lines of their birth.

coast, 'Irani Shi'as' who trace their lineage to Iran, 'Mapilahs' and 'Khoyas' from Kerala.

Walk down Mohammed Ali Road and you'll see an enormous variety of mosques and Muslim groups running businesses, groups who share very little except their submission to Allah. A Muslim from the Malabar coast will not speak the same language as a Muslim from the northern plains of India. They may eat together (each thinking very little of the other's food) but they will not intermarry.

THE ARCHIVE OF IDENTITIES

But if you're walking around South Mumbai, the imprint of another migrant tribe, the Parsis,

will be dominant. The Parsis are Zoroastrians, followers of the prophet Zoroaster, who were driven out of Iran by Muslim persecution. They arrived in Gujarat in the eighth or ninth century and sought asylum from the local king. He is said to have sent them a glass of milk full to the brim – his way of saying that his kingdom was full. The Parsi elders conferred, added some sugar to the milk and sent it back – to suggest that they would mix thoroughly and sweeten the life of the community. Thus the Parsis, true to their word, still speak Gujarati at home. And though, as good businessmen, they have been involved in a fair share of dirty dealing (the opium trade,

Every God has his day

Mumbaikars are a naturally tolerant lot. They'll happily worship Ganesha on a Tuesday, Mother Mary on a Wednesday and Allah on a Friday. If it wasn't for the religious right-wing, mutual respect would be the norm. Most places of worship will let you in regardless of faith, but make sure you're dressed in a way that won't offend – both men and women should cover their arms and legs. You should also cover your head before entering a Muslim or Sikh shrine – a knotted handkerchief will do. You can usually buy one outside or borrow one within. Be warned that visiting a temple on its most popular day may take a whole day.

Babulnath

Babulnath is Shiva, the god of destruction and also of generativity, who is often represented by the *lingam*, or phallus. Devotees see Monday as sacred to Shiva, and the temple is very crowded on that day. *Babulnath Temple, Babulnath Road. Grant Road station.* **Map** p254 A15.

Ganesha

Mumbai's most popular God, the elephant-headed Ganesha or Ganpati is the son of Shiva. He is the 'remover of obstacles' – no enterprise should be undertaken without his blessing. His idol is immersed in the sea every year at a city-wide event called Ganesh Chaturthi (*see p136*). His most famous temple is the Siddhivinayak Temple at Prabhadevi, where garland vendors gather outside (*pictured right*). Devotees arrive on Monday night, often walking miles barefoot, for *darshan* (a viewing that has been described as seeing and being seen by God) on Tuesdays, Ganesha's sacred day. *Siddhivinayak Temple, Prabhadevi. Dadar station.*

Haji Ali

Haji Ali was a Muslim holy man who died on pilgrimage to Mecca. Legend has it that his body then floated across the Arabian Sea and washed up back in Bombay. He is now interred in a spectacular *dargah* (tomb) on a rock off the mainland that can only be reached via a narrow causeway. If you press your forehead against his tomb and offer a covering (*chaddar*), your wishes will be granted, it is believed. *Haji Ali, Mahalaxmi. Mahalaxmi station.*

Mahalaxmi

The reigning deity of a commercial city is naturally the Goddess of Wealth, Mahalaxmi. She is the consort of Vishnu, the Preserver

for one) they have done their civic duty as well. Many of Mumbai's public institutions were built by the Parsi tradition of community service (*see p71* **Munificent Mumbaikars**).

Today the Parsi population has tragically declined, with no more than 50,000 left in the city, and a mere 120,000 worldwide. I would often suggest to a Parsi friend that I was going to start Project Parsi, much like Project Tiger.

'Yes, with radio collars to track us wherever we go,' he would retort, with the trademark good humour that gave us Parsi theatre, one of the grand-daddies of the Bollywood film.

'And report on mating habits,' I would add.

'If mating was a habit amongst us, would you need a project?' Few communities can take so much slander with such good humour.

The decline of the Parsis has found a sad parallel in the sudden decline of the white-backed vulture in South Asia and beyond.

The vulture plays a crucial role in traditional Parsi funerals, in which the body is left at the top of the 'Towers of Silence' where vultures pick it clean. This tradition is endangered because the vultures are dying out.

Mumbai's communities define and redefine themselves and each resident can be seen as a moving archive of identities. That taxi driver may be from the northern state of Uttar Pradesh but to most of his passengers, he is a 'bhaiyya', a word that used to mean 'brother' but now means a northerner. That nurse may see herself as an Orthodox Syrian Christian but to most of her patients she is a 'Mallu' (someone who speaks Malayalam, the language of Kerala) or just an 'Anda-Gundu' (a name intended to evoke hilarity at the supposedly muddled sounds of a Dravidian language).

For this is a city that has had many visitors. It has been home to groups like the Sidis (with

of the Universe. On the nine nights of Navratri, a harvest festival, the goddess' devotees arrive in thousands for *darshan*. *Mahalaxmi Temple, Mahalaxmi. Mahalaxmi station.*

Mauli Mary/Our Lady of Perpetual Succour

Mauli Mary is the local name for the Virgin Mary at the Basilica of Mount Mary (*pictured left*) in Bandra. During her feast in September she is offered a variety of odd-shaped wax objects including houses (from devotees with accommodation problems), airplanes (from those who want to emigrate) and body parts (from the sick). Mary's most popular avatar is Our Lady of Perpetual Succour, worshipped at St Michael's Church on Wednesdays. *Virgin Mary at the Basilica of Mount Mary, Mount Mary Road, Bandra (W). Bandra station.* **Map** p249 A6. *St Michael's Church, Mahim (W). Mahim station.*

Makdoom Shah Baba

Shah Baba Ali Mahimi (1372-1471) was a secular Sufi saint who embraced all religions. He is also the patron saint of the Mumbai police. His *dargah*, which is said to be about 350 years old, is accompanied by the tombs of his mother, his maid servant and his pet goat. Fridays bring the faithful to this spot. *Makdoom Shah Baba Dargah, Mahim (W). Mahim station.*

Mumbadevi

When the city was being plagued by a sadistic demon, Mumbaraka, locals offered prayers to Brahma, who pulled a six-armed goddess out of his body. The goddess defeated Mumbaraka, who then pleaded with her to take his name. She did so and became Mumbadevi, a manifestation of Shakti, the female embodiment of power. *Mumbadevi Temple, Zaveri Bazaar. Masjid Bunder or Marine Lines station.* **Map** p253 G14.

Sitladevi

The goddess of small pox, ritually appeased to protect children from infection. She is supposed to be an Ancient One, a goddess who predates the four Vedas that some call the defining texts of Hinduism. Many scholars believe she was first a tribal goddess and incorporated later into the Hindu pantheon. *Sitladevi Temple, Sitladevi Temple Road, Mahim (W). Mahim station.*

Zoroaster

There are barely 50,000 Parsis left in the city but their religious shrines, *agiaries* (fire temples), are everywhere. Non-Parsis are forbidden from entering, but you can admire a fine example from the outside at Cusrow Baug, a Parsi housing colony in Colaba. *Cusrow Baug, Colaba Causeway, Colaba. CST or Churchgate stations.*

roots in Africa), many of whom still live in Dongri; the Iranis, who created the glorious institution known as the Irani restaurant; the Chinese, who were a significant presence in Mazgaon before the 1962 Indo-China War; along with Anglo-Indians and Armenians.

And there were Jews from the Maharashtra coast – referred to as 'Bene Israelis' – believing they were among the lost tribes who arrived in India before the destruction of Jerusalem's Second Temple. They moved to Mumbai in the early 19th century, but today they number less than 5,000; many have moved to Israel since 1947. In the 19th century, Bombay played host to a wave of Jews from Baghdad. The most famous family among them were the Sassoons, who built some of the city's major landmarks.

But if there is one space where Mumbai's ethnic diversity is represented in its full glory, it is the Hindi film industry. It may be a little puzzling that Mumbai should be home to a cinema whose language it does not speak very well. Most northerners flinch at the sound of a Mumbaikar speaking Hindi, as well they might. We mangle the language, throw in words from every tongue (including English) and don't bother with honorific or subtlety. But then that's why this city created a cinema that was so easily portable. Largely cosmopolitan and secular, Bollywood is truly representative of the city's diversity, even if much of it is behind the camera. When communities are caricatured and stereotyped, it is usually done with an insider's sanction. It was this that ultimately made the Hindi film such a mobile force that spread a little of the spirit of Mumbai across India.

Jerry Pinto is a well-known Mumbai journalist and author, most recently of Helen: The Life and Times of an H-Bomb, *on racial and community stereotypes in Hindi cinema.*

Bollywood

A billion people can't be wrong.

No one knows for sure who coined the term 'Bollywood', which first gained currency in the early 1990s, though there are several candidates – mainly journalists and movie producers – vying for parentage. However, it's a neologism that's spread through the subcontinent like wildfire. The Bengali film industry, based in the Calcutta (now Kolkata) district of Tollygunge, is now commonly referred to as 'Tollywood', movies made in Madras (now Chennai) are said to come from 'Mollywood', while 'Lollywood' is used to describe the Pakistani film industry centred in Lahore. The term Bollywood is despised by many in the Hindi film industry, not least for defining Hindi films in relation to Hollywood, but it remains an unrivalled catch-all phrase for describing the farrago of emotion, action, song and humour that animate almost every Hindi film.

Ever since films by the Lumière brothers were first screened at the Watson's Hotel in Kala Ghoda in 1896, Mumbai has remained at the heart of the Hindi film industry. The first talkie in Hindi, *Alam Ara*, emerged in 1931 from the traditions of the city's theatre circuit. *Alam Ara* was directed by theatre director Ardeshir Irani, and established two

unshakeable pillars of Hindi cinema: it had over ten songs mimed and enacted by the movie's cast, and its plot was drawn from a play – an early indication of how Hindi cinema would evolve its form and language from Indian dramatic traditions, from classical Sanskrit theatre to folk forms.

Today, Bollywood continues to outperform Hollywood at the Indian box office, with a loyal and passionate fan following for its biggest stars. The melodramatic style that defines the Hindi film industry hasn't changed fundamentally over the past half-century: Sturm und Drang interspersed with song and dance. The 1970s and '80s saw action movies, multi-starrers and family weepies. With the 1990s came the rise of the so-called multiplex film, which refers to a movie that is produced with a relatively small budget, has an urban theme and actors who speak an urbanised Hindi that often weaves in English and slang. But the big-budget Hindi movie continues to thrive – Bollywood has borrowed extensively from Hollywood in attempting to make movies that are slick and punchily written. The song-and-dance routine now resembles MTV; some song sequences in new Hindi movies (intentionally) look like hip hop videos.

Spiced-up versions of Hollywood movies have always been a Bollywood staple, but there's now a marked tendency to borrow extensively from other movies right down to the last frame. The movie *Kaante* (2002) was a remake of Quentin Tarantino's *Reservoir Dogs* and was set in Los Angeles; the same director remade Chan-wook Park's *Oldboy* as *Zinda* (2005). A great deal of importance is now given to production design – sometimes at the cost of the plot, another tendency borrowed from Hollywood. Most movies are now shot on sets and in foreign locations. There's a veneer of modernity and urbanity in new Hindi movies. Actors now actually kiss, as they did before a puritanical streak hit the movies between the 1950s and late '90s, when the camera would cut away as their faces moved closer. But the basic values remain the same: the family is the core unit of stability and identity; marriage is the goal of romance; women look best when they're standing by their men; and wealth is sexy.

This new love for slickness means that Mumbai is increasingly losing its once-central role in Hindi films. For decades, the city was an evergreen star of Bollywood movies. The Marine Drive promenade in South Mumbai plays a role as the frontier of journey, hope, liberation and solace, as have the city's industrial zones, including its mills, factories and docks, the bustling streets and flyovers, the beaches, the brothels, bars and nightclubs. Mumbai's unique character types have influenced and shaped Hindi movies: the smuggler, the industrial worker, the bar dancer/prostitute, the industrialist, the dreamy-eyed migrant, the street-smart small-time criminal, the cop. It's difficult to judge who influenced whom: was the typical swagger associated with Mumbai characters picked off the streets, or do citizens learn their strut from the movies? It's hard to tell any more, but Mumbai's people are a bit like characters from their movies: loud, brash, romantic, anxious, hot-headed, money- and glamour-hungry, foolish at times, but always entertaining to watch.

INDIAN EMOTION

Hindi films are without equivalent in other cinema traditions. Unlike Hollywood, mainstream Hindi movies have always fused fancy with realism to the extent that descriptions of them as 'unrealistic' become almost meaningless. Instead, Hindi cinema employs melodramatic conventions that are close to those of opera. Just as in, say, *La Traviata*, a woman with an obviously fine

You too can be a star

It's surprisingly easy to get cast as an extra in a Bollywood movie. Most big-budget films are now set (and shot) in foreign countries to appeal to the Indian diaspora, who pay many pounds or dollars for the pleasure of watching their countrymen gambol in the middle of Times Square. Since bits of the film are still shot at Mumbai sets – nightclub scenes or dance numbers, for example – directors need a crowd of foreign faces in the background to make it look like New York or London or wherever is the flavour of the month. Take a walk down Colaba Causeway, the road that leads from the Taj Mahal Hotel to the Radio Club, or generally loiter around the bars and cafés in Colaba and, if you're clearly not Indian, a casting agent may well approach you with an offer. Though it may sound sleazy at first ('Excuse me, do you want to be in a Bollywood movie?'), nearly all of them are above board. Often, they might be casting for advertisements instead of movies, so you're as likely to find yourself co-starring with a sports hero as a film star. These are usually last-minute things, so if you answer in the affirmative, you will be expected to be free either immediately or the following day. For your efforts, which is mostly standing around and dancing a little, you get lunch, a few hundred rupees and if you're lucky, the chance to meet a famous star. As with any activity while travelling, use common sense: ask for a business card or some sort of credentials and don't go off alone with strange men. Away from the camera, it's often possible to spot stars and starlets shaking their stuff at select expensive nightspots, among them Olive and Poison in Bandra, and Aurus and Enigma in Juhu.

pair of lungs can sing about dying of consumption, the lack of Western-style realism in Bollywood is beside the point; what Hindi films seek to convey is emotional realism, taken to its purest form through the use of music. A good Hindi film may lack a logical or original narrative but it will make perfect sense to the emotionally literate. In *Kal Ho Naa Ho* (2003), Shah Rukh Khan is dying; his heart is failing, but he teaches others how to have a heart, to love their neighbours and put family and community at the centre of their worlds. He may run through New York, dance a mean bhangra and then linger on his deathbed, all in defiance of medical science, but millions of filmgoers have sobbed through these moments because they find them emotionally real and affirm that emotions lead to moral action as much as thoughts.

Hindi films are not just about romantic love but family love and friendship; the dramatic tension on screen often arises from conflict between romantic love and family duty. In the enormously successful *Dilwale Dulhania Le Jayenge* (1995), Simran (played by Kajol) is in love with Raj (Shah Rukh Khan) but is already engaged to the son of her father's friend. Simran respects her family so eloping is not an option. Instead Raj's goal is to make her father accept him. Often, such conflicts are pushed to melodramatic extremes, so the family will only accept the couple when death threatens, such as in *Bobby* (1973), when the couple seem headed for a *Romeo and Juliet*-style tragedy.

Hindi film stories also often revolve around the breaking and restoration of the moral order. A woman who has sex outside of marriage may do so in an irresistibly erotic moment, but she will have to pay for her sin. One of the many reasons for the enduring popularity of actor Amitabh Bachchan is his talent for conveying moral outrage; his characters are determined to restore the moral order, even if that means breaking the law or dying in the process.

Unlike Hollywood, Hindi cinema isn't ruled by genre, although many films have elements of multiple genres rolled into one – the *masala* (mix of spices) summed up by the word 'Bollywood'. The leading man in a Hindi movie must be more versatile than his Hollywood counterpart – he needs to know how to cry buckets as well as land a punch.

Hindi films are often dismissed as escapist entertainment, but there's nothing trivial about that. Turkish writer Orhan Pamuk wrote that the rest of the world will only understand the changes in India when 'we have seen their private lives reflected in novels'. But it's more likely to be in Bollywood that the fantasies and fears of modern India will find their clearest expression.

Star cast

A guide to the Bollywood A-list.

Aamir Khan

Aamir Khan hit gold with his second starring role in the teenage romance *Qayamat Se Qayamat Tak*. After a series of flops in the 1990s, Khan bounced back with scene-stealing performances in films like *Raja Hindustani*, *Rangeela* and the Oscar-nominated *Lagaan*. Adored by fans for his attention to performance over preening, Khan has often been described as a director's nightmare for the extraordinary interest he takes in the making of his movies. In 2007, he finally went ahead and directed his first feature, *Taare Zameen Par*, which opened to widespread acclaim.
Definitive films *Lagaan, Rangeela, Taare Zameen Par.*

Aishwarya Rai

A former Miss World, Aishwarya Rai has had an indifferent box-office track record but her near-perfect looks and recent wedding to Abhishek Bachchan, the son of Amitabh Bachchan, ensure lifelong membership to the A-list. Rai entered films after a successful modelling career, and acted in Tamil movie *Iruvar* before moving into Hindi films. Rai has since packaged herself as an Indian crossover actress, in the mould of *Memoirs of a Geisha* star Zhang Ziyi, but hasn't yet managed to work her charms on the North American box office.
Definitive films *Devdas, Hum Dil de Chuke Sanam, Josh.*

Amitabh Bachchan

Known as 'the Big B', Amitabh Bachchan became a superstar after the gangster flick *Deewaar* in 1975. Now in his sixties, Bachchan remains one of the most successful actors ever to emerge in Hindi cinema. His appeal lies in his brooding looks, versatile acting skills, and a deep voice that's as recognisable to Indians as the national anthem. Bachchan's films are now counted among the contemporary classics: *Sholay, Amar Akbar Anthony, Don* and *Namak Halal*. His popularity dipped in the 1980s, but he bounced back in the '90s by hosting an Indian version of the TV show *Who Wants to be a Millionaire?*.
Definitive films *Deewar, Don (1978), Sholay.*

Deepika Padukone

The latest dream girl made a dream debut with Shah Rukh Khan in *Om Shanti Om* in November 2007. Her classic Indian looks, used to great effect in *OSO* where she played a 1970s Bollywood star, and her acting talent mark her for bigger and brighter things.
Definitive film *Om Shanti Om.*

Hrithik Roshan

The son of director Rakesh Roshan, Hrithik Roshan is India's answer to Brad Pitt. His good looks, superb physique and ample acting talent place him squarely in the superstars' gallery. After a superb debut in *Kaho Naa... Pyaar Hai*, Roshan went through a lean patch before bouncing back with a bang with *Dhoom 2* and the superhero-themed *Krrish* in 2006.
Definitive films *Dhoom 2, Kaho Naa… Pyaar Hai, Mission Kashmir.*

Kareena Kapoor

The younger sister of actor Karisma Kapoor and a member of one of the oldest Bollywood families, Kareena Kapoor is the most camera-friendly of her generation. Blessed with strong movie genes, a confident face and tons of ambition, Kapoor's noteworthy roles include *Chameli, Kabhi Khushi Kabhie Gham, Asoka* and *Jab We Met.*
Definitive films *Chameli, Jab We Met, Refugee.*

Priyanka Chopra

This former Miss World has worked very hard on her looks and her career, and the results are there for all to see. The twentysomething Chopra has been in Hindi films for a little over four years, and has already snagged A-list projects such as *Krrish* and *Don*, where she bats her eyelashes at no less than Shah Rukh Khan. If there's any actor who can give Kareena Kapoor a run for her money, it's Chopra.
Definitive films *Aitraaz, Don (2006), Mujhse Shaadi Karogi.*

Rani Mukerji

The Rani Mukerji story started in 1997 with *Raja Ki Aayegi Baraat* – a turkey that couldn't sink her talent or quell her ambition. After a memorable turn in Karan Johar's *Kuch Kuch Hota Hai* the following year, Mukerji steadily worked on her acting and appearance. Mukerji's image is that of the girl next door who made it. Her warm good looks, passionate acting and hard work has pushed her into Bollywood's stratosphere.
Definitive films *Bunty aur Babli, Hum Tum, Saathiya.*

Saif Ali Khan

The son of actor Sharmila Tagore and cricketer Mansoor Ali Khan Pataudi, Saif Ali Khan's career took forever to kick-start. But once he got going with films like *Dil Chahta Hai* and *Ek Hasina Thi*, there's been no stopping him. A versatile actor who can switch effortlessly from buffoonery to baseness, Khan has reached the sweet spot desired by all actors in Bollywood: he can play almost any role.
Definitive films *Dil Chahta Hai, Ek Hasina Thi, Omkara.*

Salman Khan

The son of Salim Khan, the ace scriptwriter who co-wrote some of Bollywood's most iconic films in the 1970s and '80s, Salman Khan established his credentials as a romantic hero with *Maine Pyar Kiya* in 1989. His career has rollercoastered since then as he has gone from loverboy to macho action hero with some comedy thrown in for good measure. However, most of the drama has been off-screen: Khan is currently in court for killing two endangered blackbuck, and for drunkenly running down and killing a homeless man in Mumbai. On-screen, Khan is often portrayed as a toughie who's a fool for love.
Definitive films *Jaan-e-Mann, Karan Arjun, Maine Pyar Kiya.*

Shah Rukh Khan

Amitabh Bachchan is the only modern actor to command a guaranteed box office opening and worldwide fan following. Born in 1965 in Delhi, Khan studied theatre and acted in television serials before making the leap to Bollywood. Khan has experimented with several images through the past decade – anti-hero, common man, wealthy businessman – but will forever be remembered as the lover-boy extraordinaire, thanks to blockbusters like *Dilwale Dulhaniya Le Jayenge.*
Definitive films *Baazigar, Chak De India, Dilwale Dulhania Le Jayenge, Om Shanti Om, Swades.*

Where to Stay

Taj Mahal Palace & Tower. *See p43*.

Where to Stay

From flash five-stars to colonial-style charmers.

Ever since the Indian economy managed to get itself some excellent press and become a nation of a billion consumers rather than one of the world's most desperately poor nations, it seems like everybody wants a piece of the country. Whether it's business travellers or independent explorers, the crowds are pouring in and hotels in Mumbai have mushroomed to accommodate them. Over 1,200 rooms have been added since 2001 and as we go to press, the **Four Seasons** is putting the finishing touches to its spanking new midtown hotel, while at least two other major properties are in the offing.

But for tourists, the results of the hospitality boom have been mixed, as prices have shot up and some have nearly doubled over the last two years. South Mumbai, particularly around Colaba, Marine Drive and Churchgate, is the first choice of most foreign travellers, but you won't find yourselves spoiled for choice nor will you find rooms as cheap as you might expect. The explosion of hotels has been at the top end and the boutique hotel is almost unknown in Mumbai, with the refreshing exception of the **Gordon House Hotel**, which single-handedly fills the gaping hole in Mumbai's hotel offerings between high-end and moderate. The landscape is dominated by luxury five-stars, charging a minimum of around Rs 14,000-Rs 18,000 for a double room, with the top choice being the century-old **Taj Mahal Palace & Tower** (*see p43*), perched next to the Gateway of India and the harbour. The five-stars aren't just for tourists or foreign businessmen; these hotels have always played an important role in the city's social life, providing restaurants, bars, nightclubs, shopping and private party venues for Mumbai's wealthiest. Travellers looking for something cheaper can find themselves hitting characterless and unappetising mid-range business hotels built in the 1970s that are often not worth the rates they charge. A better option is to seek out cheaper hotels built in the 1930s and '40s, which have the virtue of period character and manage to convey some of the sleepy charm of an older Bombay. That's usually not by design but by default – the

managements simply haven't got around to changing anything in the last 60 years. Room rates at such places vary from budget (up to Rs 2,000) to moderate (Rs 6,000). We haven't listed anything that isn't scrupulously clean and decently maintained, but be prepared for hotels that are often a little rough around the edges.

INFORMATION AND BOOKING
We've included some Bandra and Khar hotels for those who want to step outside of the mainstream into the Bandra suburb, which has rapidly morphed into the city's hottest shopping and partying destination. If it's your first trip to the city, you may want to opt for the more tourist-friendly offerings of Churchgate, Marine Drive, Colaba and Fort in South Mumbai and check out Bandra by train or taxi. We've also listed some hotels close to the airport in Juhu and Andheri for those on brief stopovers. With high demand for rooms across the city, it's imperative to book ahead, especially if you're visiting in the peak winter season. The simplest way is to book via the web – even the cheapest hotels have their own websites. Many hotels in Colaba, Churchgate, Marine Drive and Juhu are close to the Arabian Sea, but not all provide sea views. You need to specify if you want a sea view when you book and you may be charged a higher rate.

The best Hotels

For shameless luxury
Taj Mahal Palace & Tower (*see p43*), the **Oberoi** (*see p51*) and **InterContinental Marine Drive** (*see p49*).

For a taste of old Bombay on a budget
Bentley's (*see p47*), **Sea Green Hotel** and **Sea Green South Hotel** (*see p51*) and **West End Hotel** (*see p48*).

For boutique style
The **Gordon House Hotel** (*see p43*).

For staying in the suburbs
Grand Hyatt (*see p52*), JW Marriott (*see p54*) and **Taj Lands End** (*see p51*).

---

❶ Green numbers given in this chapter correspond to the location of each hotel as marked on the street maps. *See pp249-255.*

Gordon House Hotel.

PRICES AND CLASSIFICATION

We don't list official star ratings, which tend to reflect facilities rather than quality; instead we've classified hotels within each area according to the price of a double room per night, beginning with the most expensive. All of the rates we've included are for rooms with air-conditioning and attached bathrooms. Some of the cheaper hotels also offer rooms without these facilities for cheaper rates. Breakfast is often included at the cheaper hotels, and many of the hotels in Juhu and Andheri offer a complimentary airport pick-up and drop-off.

Some hotels sneakily quote prices exclusive of the ten per cent sales tax. Always check. We've included the tax in the rates listed here, but room prices change frequently, so please make sure you verify before you book.

FACILITIES AND ACCESSIBILITY

In this chapter, we've listed the main services offered by the hotel. Concierges can often arrange far more than listed here, including restaurant reservations, dry cleaning and minor clothes repairs. We've also listed which hotels offer rooms adapted for disabled customers, but these vary and it's always best to ring ahead to confirm the precise facilities.

Colaba

Deluxe

Taj Mahal Palace & Tower

Apollo Bunder (6665-3366/www.tajhotels.com). CST or Churchgate stations. **Rates** Rs 18,000-Rs 21,000 double. **Credit** AmEx, DC, MC, V. **Map** p251 G5 ❶
Mumbai's most famous, oldest and most beautiful hotel, and an integral part of the city's social scene. (*see p44* **Crowning glory**).
Bars (2). Business centre. Concierge. Disabled-adapted rooms. Gym. Internet (wireless). No smoking rooms. Parking. Pool (outdoor). Restaurants (7). Room service. Spa. TV.

Expensive

Fariyas Hotel

25 Off Arthur Bunder Road, Colaba (2204-2911/ www.fariyas.com). CST or Churchgate stations. **Rates** Rs 8,500-Rs 11,000 double. **Credit** AmEx, DC, MC, V. **Map** p250 G4 ❷
There's not much to distinguish this standard 1970s-built, ten-floor five-star aimed at business travellers, although it does fill a useful mid-range gap in Colaba between the Taj Mahal and the cheap hotels that feed on its scraps. Rooms are neat, standard and serviceable, although rather on the small side – as are the pool and tiny gym. Despite space constraints, they've managed to pack in a perfectly decent sauna and steam room, accessed via a maze-like staircase. The position on a street off Apollo Bunder means that only the corner rooms get a slice of sea view, with north-side rooms getting a view of the Colaba skyline.
Bar. Business centre. Gym. Internet (wireless). Parking. Pool. Restaurant. Room service. TV.

Gordon House Hotel

5 Battery Street, Apollo Bunder, Colaba (2287-1122/www.ghhotel.com). CST or Churchgate stations. **Rates** Rs 10,500 double. **Credit** AmEx, MC, V. **Map** p251 G5 ❸
Mumbai needs more hotels like the Gordon House. It's the city's only real boutique hotel, offering a modern, stylish alternative to the standard five-stars at a competitive price. Smart, cool and beautifully designed, the courtyard atrium at its heart is a sanctuary of calming pine wood, wheatgrain tiles and soothing blues and whites under a high glass roof. Rooms on each of the three floors are themed: vibrant colours and smooth tiles on the 'Mediterranean' floor, cool blues and light woods on the 'Scandinavian' floor, and a homey, warm feel on the 'Country' floor. There's no gym on site, but a Bullworker is provided in each room, and internet access is free. This is a very popular hotel and there are just 29 rooms, so it's definitely worth booking well in advance.
Bar. Business centre. Concierge. Free parking. Internet (dial-up/wireless). Restaurants (2). Room service. TV.

Crowning glory

Taj is Hindi for 'crown', which makes the **Taj Mahal Palace & Tower** (*see p43*) – locally known as just 'the Taj' – the crown prince of Mumbai's hotels, situated right in front of the Gateway of India and the harbour. More than a hotel, it's a tourist attraction in its own right, admired for its broad, imposing presence, its grand dome, and an architecture that blends Florentine Renaissance and Moorish styles. The Taj has served innumerable illustrious guests over the years, including Queen Elizabeth II, President Gamal Abdel Nasser of Egypt and John Lennon.

The legend of the Taj is that its creator, the renowned Parsi industrialist Jamsetji Nusserwanji Tata, ordered its construction after being refused entry to the now-defunct European-only Pyrke's Apollo Hotel, with the aim of running a grand hotel without racist entry restrictions. (His nephew JRD Tata said that he built the hotel as a reaction to an offhand remark that Bombay has no good hotel.) When it was completed in 1903, it was by far the finest hotel in the city, with the latest imported conveniences such as electric lights, electric passenger lifts and its own soda-water factory. An urban myth persists that its architect, WA Stevens, was so appalled when he saw the completed hotel that he leapt to his death from its dome; it's said that builders had misread his plans and built the hotel the wrong way round, with the rear facing the sea. In boring old reality, the hotel is built the way it was originally designed and Stevens died of natural causes.

A second wing (the Tower wing) was added in 1972 but without doubt the Palace wing offers the original Taj experience – hence the difference in price, with base-category Palace wing rooms commanding prices far above the highest-category Tower wing rooms. The Palace wing entrance opens on to a vast stone staircase winding its way around the walls of the dome, which is supported by ornate stone arches reminiscent of a cathedral. At the dome's distant apex, stained glass admits a kaleidoscope of coloured light. The Palace rooms are steeped in period feel, with double doors leading from a marbled entranceway into elegant high-ceilinged rooms with antique furnishings and white marble bathrooms, and with widescreen plasma TVs as a concession to the 21st century. Rooms in the modern Tower wing offer elegant, contemporary design in soft cream and pastel shades, with fabulous views of the Gateway.

Moderate

Ascot Hotel

38 Garden Road, Colaba (6638-5566/
www.ascothotel.com). CST or Churchgate stations.
Rates Rs 5,500-6,000 double. **Credit** MC, V.
Map p250 G4 ❹
The Ascot is a little gem: not quite a boutique hotel,
but easily superior to most hotels in the same price
range, including all of the neighbouring hotels on
Garden Road. It resides in a charming 1930s building remodelled from top to bottom inside to create a
smart, contemporary hotel with ample use of light
wood floors, mirrors and glass, and a soft, cream
colour palette. Rooms are spacious and airy, with
checkerboards of orange-and-yellow fabric above
the beds, plants and glass tables. Most of the rooms
have flat-screen TVs and some have DVD players.
Add friendly and efficient staff and the Ascot is easily a top mid-range choice.
Bar. Internet (wireless). Restaurant.
Room service. TV.

Garden Hotel

42 Garden Road, Colaba (2284-1476/ 2283-1330).
CST or Churchgate stations. **Rates** Rs 4,000 double.
Credit AmEx, MC, V. **Map** p250 G4 ❺
The Garden Hotel looks almost identical to its
next-door neighbour, the Godwin; both are glass-
and-concrete towers built in the 1970s on a street
full of old Colaba buildings from the 1930s and
'40s. Inside is not much better, with a breathtak-
ingly ugly three-metre waterfall in the lobby made
of plastic climbing plants and artificial tree
stumps. Still, the rooms are clean and the staff
friendly; overall, a cheap and serviceable option
for bedding down for the night.
Internet (shared). Room service. TV.

Hotel Godwin

41 Garden Road, Colaba (2284-1226/2287-2050).
CST or Churchgate stations. **Rates** Rs 4,000 double.
Credit MC, V. **Map** p250 G4 ❻
A 1970s-built concrete tower similar in external
appearance to the Garden Hotel, but a superior
option, with smarter decor and a spacious ninth-
floor terrace offering sweeping views of Colaba,
complete with plant pots and plaster pillars
wrapped with rope lights. A front-facing room is
the best choice, with large windows displaying
views of the dome of the nearby Taj Mahal hotel.
The suites can sleep five people, six if you request
an extra mattress for the floor. The rooms are nothing to get excited about but are spacious, neat and
clean, and only slightly marred by the tatty red
sofas and dusty plastic chandeliers.
Room service. TV.

Sea Palace Hotel

26 PJ Ramchandani Marg, Apollo Bunder,
Colaba (2284-1828/2285-4404/www.sea
palacehotel.com). CST or Churchgate stations.
Rates Rs 3,800-Rs 6,600 double. **Credit** AmEx,
MC, V. **Map** p250 G4 ❼

Old-world charm at the **Regency Inn**.

The best feature of the Sea Palace is its location:
right on the peaceful waterfront road about ten minutes' walk from the Taj Mahal hotel, with perfect
views of the harbour. It's well worth shelling out for
the most expensive rooms, which have seafacing
views; open the window and you can lean out and
gaze at the Gateway of India. Rooms are plain and
simple, and you have to go for a 'deluxe' double (Rs
6,600 a night) for decent furnishings – smart beds,
lime-green walls and large, airy bathrooms. The garden at the front of the hotel is little more than a narrow strip with tables and umbrellas, but breakfast
here is a very pleasant way to start the day: clean
sea breezes, bobbing yachts in the harbour and the
clipping of the occasional horse-drawn trap.
Parking. Room service. TV.

Cheap

Regency Inn

18 Lansdowne House, MB Marg, Apollo Bunder,
Colaba (2202-0292/2282-3948). CST or Churchgate
stations. **Rates** Rs 3,000 double. **Credit** AmEx, MC,
V. **Map** p251 G5 ❽
The Regency is a small, 21-room hotel on the first
floor of a 19th-century colonial building of high ceilings and ancient wooden staircases. The reception
and lounge areas manage to mix some of that
old-world charm with modern touches – so we have
a 180-year-old Belgian chandelier alongside wood-
and-chrome Hunter fans, and modern chairs and
tables alongside antique chests and an ornate
old mirror. It works well and this could rank as a
budget boutique hotel if they paid similar attention

The best guides to enjoying London lif

(but don't just take our word for it)

'More than 700 places where you can eat out for less than £20 a head... a mass of useful information in a geuinely pocket–sized guide'

Mail on Sunday

'Armed with a tube map and this guide there is no excuse to find yourself in a duff bar again'

Evening Standard

'I'm always asked ho up to date with shopp and services in a city as London. This guide the answer'

Red Magazine

'Get the inside track on the capital's neighbourhoods'

ndependent on Sunday

'A treasure trove of treats that lists the best the capital has to offer'

The People

Rated 'Best Restaurant Gui

Sunday Times

Available at all good bookshops and imeout.com/shop from £6.99

100% Indepen

to the rooms, which are spacious but lacking in character, with old brown blankets on the beds. It's clean and neat, though, and one of the better budget options in the area. *Photo p45.*
Room service. TV.

Regent Hotel

8 BEST Road, Colaba (2287-1854/2204-1518/ www.regenthotelcolaba.com). CST or Churchgate stations. **Rates** Rs 3,850 double. **Credit** AmEx, MC, V. **Map** p251 G5 ⑨

The floors are marble, the walls are marble, the reception desk is marble. They like marble at the Regent – there's acres of the stuff. Add wingtip leather armchairs and prints of horses and Mughal emperors, and the decor practically hits you over the head with a (marble) hammer and screams, 'Classy, isn't it?' And it is, sort of. The paint is peeling in a few places but the rooms are spacious and the design has a genuine kitsch charm that elevates it above most city hotels in the same price range, with pastel tones, high ceilings, more of those wingtip armchairs and a faux-Edwardian feel. The location is central – just behind the Taj Mahal hotel – and the staff professional and friendly.
Internet (wireless/shared). No smoking rooms. Room service. TV.

Strand Hotel

PJ Ramchandani Marg, Apollo Bunder, Colaba (2288-2222/2288-0059/www.hotelstrand.com). CST or Churchgate stations. **Rates** Rs 2,500- Rs 3,000 double. **Credit** MC, V. **Map** p250 G4 ⑩

Right next door to the Sea Palace Hotel (*see p45*) is this peach harbour-front hotel, which manages to hang on to some of its art deco charm in the face of 'improvements' like the gratuitous marquee stuck on to its frontage. It doesn't offer much in the way of amenities but the location and value for money makes this one of the most popular cheap hotels in Colaba. Rooms are airy and clean, with high ceilings, a cream-and-brown colour scheme and simple furnishings. A few period touches have survived, like ornate designs on some of the windows and art deco balconies. Book ahead for one of the six 'deluxe' doubles (Rs 3,000 a night) for a wonderful view of the harbour and the Gateway of India.
Room service. TV.

Budget

Bentley's Hotel

17 Oliver Road, Colaba (2288-2890/www. bentleyshotel.com). CST or Churchgate stations. **Rates** Rs 2,000 double. **Credit** MC, V. **Map** p250 G4 ⑪

Nothing quite captures the faded elegance of Colaba like Bentley's, on a quiet, tree-lined street just off Colaba Causeway. Spread over three buildings built in the 1930s, the hotel is a strictly no-frills affair with plenty of period Bombay atmosphere, with antique furniture, wooden staircases and checkered black-and-white floors. A stay at Bentley's is a trip back

to an older, less frenetic Bombay, with servants cleaning mosaic-tiled floors with floorcloths under their bare feet, sleepy watchmen on the gate and the only noise the clatter of the cage lift door. Oliver Road looks like a suburban London street, lined with 1930s properties all in need of care and attention, but just five minutes' walk from the bustle of Colaba Causeway. The superior doubles offer views of a nearby park.
Room service. TV.

Hotel Moti

10 BEST Marg, opposite Electric House, Colaba (2202-5714/2202-1654). CST or Churchgate stations. **Rates** Rs 1,500- Rs 1,800 double. **No credit cards. Map** p251 G5 ⑫

Hotel Moti sits on the ground floor of an elderly building very close to the Taj Mahal hotel and a one-minute stroll from Colaba Causeway. An excellent-value budget option for the price, it's very basic but clean and secure, with 11 spacious rooms all equipped with fridges and attached bathrooms, and a few surviving period touches, including ornate stucco work on the ceilings.
TV.

YWCA International Guest House

18 Madame Cama Road, opposite National Gallery of Modern Art, Colaba (2202-5053/2202-9161/ www.ywcabombay.com). CST or Churchgate stations. **Rates** Rs 2,000 double. **No credit cards. Map** p251 G6 ⑬

Pay a Rs 50 temporary membership fee – it doesn't matter if you're male – and you can gain access to the YWCA's international guest house. Simply but comfortably furnished, with attached bathrooms and balconies, the YWCA rooms make a great budget option which includes buffet breakfast, lunch and dinner in the attached dining hall – and just a few minutes' walk from the Causeway. The price listed above is for air-conditioned rooms; cheaper rates are available for non-AC rooms.

Bentley's Hotel.

Lounging in the lobby of the **West End Hotel**.

Churchgate

Expensive

Ambassador Hotel

*Veer Nariman Road, Churchgate (2204-1131/
www.ambassadorindia.com). Churchgate station.*
Rates Rs 11,000 double. **Credit** AmEx, MC, V.
Map p251 & p252 E8 ⓲
This survivor of the 1970s doesn't do much for the
aesthetic sense – it's essentially a 14-storey tower of
dull concrete, but it's famed in Mumbai for being
home to the city's only revolving restaurant, the
Pearl of the Orient (*see p98*), on the 12th floor, which
offers some breathtaking views of the arc of Marine
Drive and the Arabian Sea. Inside, a '70s Indian
vision of opulence is still maintained, with acres of
marble and wood panelling, an ornate gold-painted
ceiling and golden elevator doors. The 'Society' bar
and restaurant on the lobby level once set the local
standard for 'luxury' kitsch against some tough
competition. Rooms are standard five-star fare, functional and comfortable, although none offer inspir-
ing views of the sea or the city.
*Bar. Business centre. Concierge. Gym. Internet
(shared). Restaurants (2). Room service.*

Moderate

Astoria Hotel

*4 Jamshedji Tata Road, Churchgate (6654-1234).
Churchgate station.* **Rates** Rs 5,000-Rs 6,600 double.
Credit AmEx, MC, V. **Map** p251 & p252 F7 ⓯
Just a minute's walk from Churchgate station, the
Astoria was once home to a popular jazz band
and part of the lively jazz strip that dominated

Churchgate in the 1950s and '60s. Recently renovated, the Astoria's lobby has been given a contemporary makeover, with soft, diffused lighting,
wooden floors and an elegant glass fountain. Sadly,
the rooms are not nearly so smart, with the obligatory wobbly fans and plain modern furniture, but
they're clean, neat and airy, with high ceilings.
Bathrooms are walk-in Indian style, with showers
and toilets sharing the same space.
Internet (shared). Restaurant. Room service. TV.

Ritz

*5 Jamshedji Tata Road, Churchgate (2285-0500/
2282-0141). Churchgate station.* **Rates** Rs 7,000-
Rs 8,000 double. **Credit** MC, V. **Map** p251/2 F7 ⓰
Mumbai's Ritz isn't at all ritzy, but this 50-year-old
hotel offers spacious, clean rooms with decent-sized
beds and large white-tiled bathrooms. The furnishings may be staid and the mini-bar in each room consists of just a single bottle of Kingfisher beer, but it's
neat and functional, the bathrooms are roomy, and
the location is good – just a few minutes' walk from
Churchgate station. Room 408A is a good choice: a
standard room but with impressive views of
Churchgate station and its own balcony. Be warned:
some of the rooms do not have wall-to-wall carpets,
balconies or bathtubs – you have to specify whether
you want these when you book.
Bar. Restaurant. Room service. TV.

West End Hotel

*45 New Marine Lines (2203-9121/www.westend
hotelmumbai.com). Churchgate or Marine Lines
stations.* **Taxi** opposite Bombay Hospital.
Rates Rs 4,300 double. **Credit** AmEx, DC, MC, V.
Map p252 F10 ⓱
Built in 1948, the popular West End has retained its
mid-20th century charm, with plenty of dark wood
and original features. Scrupulously well-maintained,
the spacious rooms are very simply but comfortably
furnished, with bright whitewashed walls, high ceilings and black marble bathrooms with generously
sized bathtubs. Rooms at the front of the hotel
have small balconies overlooking the crowded
New Marine Lines, always buzzing with traffic to
Bombay Hospital, and a nearby temple.
*Bar. Free parking. Internet (wireless). Restaurant. Room
service. TV.*

Cheap

Chateau Windsor

*86 Veer Nariman Road, Churchgate (2204-4455/
www.chateauwindsor.com).* **Rates** Rs 3,500-Rs 4,400
double. **Credit** AmEx, MC, V. **Map** p251/2 E8 ⓲
The family that has been running Chateau Windsor
for the last 60 years are not given to understatement,
as the Raj-era grandeur of the name will tell you. In
the brochure they inform us that Chateau Windsor
is a 'luxurious' and 'elegant' corporate hotel, which
is somewhat of an overstatement. It is, however, a
cheap and cheerful place with a fantastic location –
on a main street and just a few minutes' walk away

from both Marine Drive and Churchgate station. It's popular with families, tourists, budget business travellers and even the members of the Symphony Orchestra of India. The rooms, spread across three floors of narrow, sprawling corridors, are basic but clean, with garish bedcovers and curtains, and cheap-looking 1970s furniture. Staff are professional and friendly, and the hotel is equipped with a closed-circuit TV system. Your morning tea or coffee is complimentary, as is the shoe-shine service. *Internet (shared). Parking. Room service. TV.*

Marine Drive

Deluxe

Hilton Towers
Nariman Point (6632-4343/www.hilton.com). CST or Churchgate stations. **Rates** Rs 14,000-Rs 20,000 double. **Credit** AmEx, DC, MC, V. **Map** p251 D6 ⑲
The Hilton Towers is the sister of the landmark Oberoi Hotel next door, and it's possible to walk through from one lobby to the other along various brass-handled staircases and designer store-fringed corridors. The Hilton may be the poor sister – rates here start marginally lower than at the Oberoi – but it is impressive, with a vast lobby, some excellent restaurants and a bougainvillaea-fringed swimming pool with sea views. The superior rooms are comfortable, if a little staid, with city-facing views and the kind of inoffensive design, fixtures and furnishings to make granny feel at home. Deluxe ocean view rooms offer a much more civilised experience, with outstanding views of the Arabian Sea.
Bar. Business centre. Concierge. Disabled-adapted rooms. Gym. Internet (wireless). Non-smoking floors. Parking. Pool (outdoor). Restaurants (3). Room service. TV.

InterContinental Marine Drive
135 Marine Drive (6639-9999/www.mumbai. intercontinental.com). CST or Churchgate stations. **Rates** Rs 14,000-Rs 18,500 double. **Credit** AmEx, MC, V. **Map** p251 &p252 F8 ⑳

With a prime location right on the 'Queen's Necklace', it would be a shame not to fork out the extra cash for one of the InterContinental's sea-facing rooms: the views of the Arabian Sea are second to none. The view and the plush rooms put the InterCon firmly in the top rank of South Mumbai's five-stars. Rooms are spacious and smart, with wood floors, plasma TVs, Bose music systems and DVD players. You can even have the music or the TV piped through into the bathroom, which has Bvlgari toiletries and is walled off with a glass partition so you can keep watching the TV while you shower, should you desire. Or you could just go for a suite, like the massive apartment style lodgings on the top floor, where the bathrooms all have TVs anyway. The InterContinental is also home to South Mumbai's coolest rooftop bar, the sexy and sophisticated Dome (*see p113*), and a couple of the city's most impressive hotel restaurants.
Bars (2). Business centre. Concierge. Disabled adapted rooms. Gym. Internet (wireless). No smoking floor. Parking. Restaurants (2). Room service. TV.

Marine Plaza
29 Marine Drive (2285-1212/www.hotel marineplaza.com). CST or Churchgate stations. **Rates** Rs 16,500 double. **Credit** AmEx, MC, V. **Map** p251 & p252 E7 ㉑
The five-storey atrium of this seafront hotel just screams Indian nouveau riche: gold-topped glass elevators glide up and down walls of black and white marble edged with more gold. On the ground level sits a glass table supported by the tails of giant glass fish, with paintings of laughing and crying clowns on the walls. If that's a bit too much, just avert your gaze to the atrium ceiling and admire fellow guests' backstrokes in the glass-bottomed rooftop swimming pool. The rooms are not nearly as gaudy: they're modern and smart, with outstanding sea views from front-facing rooms. If the city starts to get to you, just march downstairs to the Marine Plaza's ersatz 'English' pub, Geoffrey's.
Bar. Business centre. Gym. Internet (wireless). Pool (outdoor). Restaurants (2). Room service.

InterContinental Marine Drive.

timeout.com

The hippest online guide to over 50
of the world's greatest cities

Oberoi

*Nariman Point (6632-5757/www.oberoimumbai.
com). CST or Churchgate stations.* **Rates**
Rs 15,000-Rs 21,000 double. **Credit** AmEx, DC,
MC, V. **Map** p251 D6

The Oberoi vies with the Taj to take the top slot in
the rankings of South Mumbai's luxury hotels. One
of the city's first modern five-stars, it has hosted Bill
Clinton, Bill Gates, Michael Jackson and numerous
visiting heads of state in its fabulously ornate
Kohinoor Suite (Rs 165,000 a night), a palatial 2,100-
sq ft apartment with dramatic sea views. The deluxe
ocean view rooms (Rs 21,000) offer a little taste of
that luxury, with broad picture windows and spacious, airy rooms decked out in warm wood tones
with half-bottles of Moët & Chandon in the mini-bar.
Each room comes equipped with a butler-on-call,
who can be summoned at any time with the press of
a large red button. The Oberoi also offers a selection
of top restaurants, including the superb Kandahar
(see p95) and Vetro (see p97).
*Bar. Business centre. Concierge. Disabled-adapted
rooms. Internet (wireless). Gym. Non-smoking floors.
Parking (free). Pool (indoor). Restaurants (3). Room
service. Spa.*

Green's the word at the **Taj Lands End**.

Cheap

Sea Green Hotel

*145 Marine Drive (6633-6525/2282-2294/
www.seagreenhotel.com). CST or Churchgate
stations.* **Rates** Rs 3,400 double. **Credit** AmEx,
MC, V. **Map** p251 & p252 E8

This green-and-white art deco hotel located on
Marine Drive was originally built in 1940 as quarters for British soldiers before being converted into
a hotel in the '50s. The threadbare red carpets look
as if they haven't changed since then but the Sea
Green is spotlessly clean and does manage to conjure up period charm, with high ceilings, some original features and the sleepy atmosphere of an older
Bombay. Each room has a balcony and is reasonably spacious, although the mattresses are a little
hard. Shell out a few hundred more rupees for a corner suite with an attached sitting room arrayed
with 1970s furniture, where the views of the
Arabian Sea are just as good as the lower floors of
the plush InterContinental a few minutes up the
road. If the Sea Green is full, go next door to its
sister, the Sea Green South Hotel.
Room service. TV.

Sea Green South Hotel

*145 A Marine Drive (6633-6535/2282-1613/
www.seagreensouth.com). CST or Churchgate
stations.* **Rates** Rs 3,400 double. **Credit** AmEx,
MC, V. **Map** p251 & p252 E8

The neighbour of the Sea Green Hotel shares the
same building and is identical in every respect, right
down to the room rates, but run under different management. The 1940s feel is even more pronounced
thanks to the gorgeous wood-panelled cage lift.
Room service. TV.

Bandra & Khar

Deluxe

Taj Lands End

*Bandstand, Bandra (W) (6668-1234/www.
tajhotels.com). Bandra station.* **Rates** Rs 22,500-
Rs 25,000 double. **Credit** AmEx, DC, MC, V.

Without doubt Bandra's most luxurious hotel,
the 18-storey Taj Lands End stands close to a 16th-
century fort where Portuguese cannons once kept
watch over maritime trade routes. It's not uncommon to spot Bollywood stars strolling in for dinner
(Shah Rukh Khan lives just down the road) and the
restaurants are equipped with private dining rooms
for just that purpose. The hotel is so large and self-
contained that it's virtually a miniature village, with
enough designer shops and restaurants to serve
Bandra's elite and keep guests – mostly business
travellers – distracted. The vast, plant-festooned
central atrium leads through to a large outdoor
swimming pool and sprawling landscaped lawns,
with fine views of the sea and the nearby fort. Rooms
are spacious and thanks to some cunning design, all
offer views of the sea through broad windows.
*Bar. Business centre. Concierge. Gym. Internet
(wireless). Parking. Pool (outdoor). Room service.
Restaurants (3). Spa.*

Moderate

Executive Enclave

*331 Dr Ambedkar Road, Pali Hill, Bandra (W)
(6696-9000/2649-0227/www.executiveenclave.com).
Khar station.* **Rates** Rs 5,000 double. **Credit** AmEx,
DC, MC, V. **Map** p249 C2

One of the few mid-range options in Bandra, Executive Enclave is a small, 54-room hotel a short walk from half a dozen pubs and bars to the south and a whole range of small restaurants and cafés and the seafront promenade to the west. The rooms are spacious and clean, and while the multicoloured plastic-panel aesthetic may not be to everybody's liking, the rooms are simply furnished and predominantly free of unattractive accoutrement.
Internet (wi-fi). Restaurant. Room service. TV.

Hotel Metro Palace
355 Hill Road, Bandra (W) (6774-4555/ www.uniquehotelsindia.com). Bandra station. **Taxi** opposite Globus shopping centre. **Rates** Rs 5,500-Rs 6,600 double. **Credit** AmEx, MC, V. **Map** p249 D5 ㉖
The Metro Palace offers a decent no-frills deal for a stay in the heart of lively Bandra. Rooms are clean and of reasonable size, but very plainly furnished, with a typical effort at a decorative touch being a large poster of some kittens in a basket. Some of the rooms are wood-panelled and most have balconies.
Bar. Room service. Restaurant. TV.

Ramee Guestline Hotel
757 SV Road, Khar (W) (2648-5421/2648-5422/ www.ramee-group.com). Khar station. **Rates** Rs 8,800-Rs 11,000 double. **Credit** MC, V. **Map** p249 D2 ㉗
The Ramee manages to pack quite a lot into a small space – as well as a hotel there's an 'Irish' pub, a Chinese restaurant, a hall-for-hire and a discotheque. There clearly wasn't a lot of room left over for the hotel lobby, or indeed the rooms, which are highly compact. Still, this is one of Bandra-Khar's better options for the price, and despite space constraints the Ramee has managed to squeeze in broad, comfortable beds and some smart, modern design, including attractive headboards of polished wood. The hotel has a good central location for access to Bandra and central Mumbai.
Bar. Internet (shared). Parking. Restaurant. Room service. TV.

Cheap

Hotel Jewel Palace
Fifth Road, Khar (W) (2604-5488/2604-8662). Khar Station. **Rates** Rs 2,750-Rs 3,300 double. **Credit** MC, V. **Map** p249 D2 ㉘
Nobody is going to go home from the Jewel Palace singing paeans about its wonderfulness but if you're staying in the 'burbs, it's hard to beat for both location and price. At seven stories, it towers over the bustling Khar market, where fruit and veg vendors haggle with local aunties. South Mumbai is easily accessible from Khar railway station, which is a two-minute walk and all of Bandra's nightlife and eating options are a short rickshaw ride away. The rooms are cramped – with a double bed taking up most of the floor space – but they're clean and the room service fellows are cheerful.
Bar. Restaurant. Room service. TV.

Vakola & Vile Parle

Deluxe

Grand Hyatt
Off Western Express Highway, Santacruz (E) (6676-1234/http://mumbai.grand.hyatt.com). Santa Cruz station. **Rates** Rs 15,000-21,000 double. **Credit** AmEx, MC, V.
The Grand Hyatt may have the internationally inoffensive and anonymous façade of glass and concrete, but its grey-blue walls are actually an apt reflection of the city in which it is located. It blends right in like yet another unfinished concrete shell. On the inside, it gives you everything you would expect from a business hotel set less than a mile away from Bandra-Kurla Complex, the city's shiny new glass-and-steel CBD: open-plan lobby with the restaurant and bar just barely set back from the public area; 547 clean, clinical rooms in cream and white; and an efficient staff who smile a lot. Set in an as yet undeveloped wasteland, the huge complex houses five restaurants, one of the city's most popular bars, China House (*see p115*), and a shopping arcade with a nice deli. Fortunately, the designers took their culturally barren location into account and the Hyatt features the city's best collection of art outside of a gallery. If you do actually venture out of this ten-acre township, Bandra is just 15 minutes away.
Bars (2). Business centre. Concierge. Disabled-adapted rooms. Gym. Internet (broadband, Rs 562/hour, Rs 1124/day). No smoking rooms. Parking (free). Pool (outdoor). Restaurants (5). Room service. Spa. TV/DVD on demand.

Orchid Hotel
Near the Domestic Airport, Nehru Road, Vile Parle (E) (2616-4040/www.orchidhotel.com). Vile Parle station. **Rates** Rs 12,500-Rs 18,000 double. **Credit** AmEx, MC, V.
This pleasant 245-room hotel is Mumbai's only ISO-certified eco-friendly hotel. It won't knock you out with sharp design, but the environmentally smart design is arguably more impressive, with furniture made with wood from sustainable forests, all-recycled paper products, smart water-saving bathrooms, and energy-saving air-conditioning, among other innovations. The seven-storey atrium has an attractive 70-foot 'waterfall' that is actually a circle of plastic wires carrying individual water droplets. An open-air rooftop restaurant and bar offer relaxed dining, and there's a medium-size, non-chlorinated rooftop swimming pool. The environmental concern isn't just a gimmick – Mumbai is under intense environmental pressure and five-star hotels are notorious producers of waste and consumers of energy. Fortunately, the Orchid's example is something of which neighbouring hotels have started to take notice.
Bar. Business centre. Concierge. Disabled-adapted rooms. Gym. Internet (wireless). Non-smoking floors. Parking. Pool (outdoor). Restaurants (3). Room service. TV.

ITC The Maratha. *See p55.*

Juhu

Deluxe

JW Marriott

*Juhu Tara Road, Juhu (6693-3000/www.marriott.com).
Vile Parle station.* **Rates** Rs 16,500-Rs 21,500 double.
Credit AmEx, DC, MC, V.

The JW Marriott is nothing less than a mini-city
of five-star luxury, set back from the mad scram-
ble that is Juhu Tara Road behind high walls (and
the city's toughest hotel security) with no less than
six restaurants, a bar, a club and one of the city's
best spas. Ninety per cent of the rooms have sea
views and are tastefully and sumptuously decorated, with attractive jute headboards, marble
bathrooms prettily stencilled with flower designs
and elegant shutters opening from the entranceway into the executive rooms. The Ocean Suite,
although not the largest nor the most expensive,
is arguably the most attractive of the suites, with
floor-to-ceiling windows offering fabulous views
of the palm tree-fringed beach that are not available in the more expensive Lotus Suite. You can
even admire the view from the bath and shower,
which is stocked with Bvlgari toiletries. Beach
access is closed because of security concerns but
the outside area offers no less than three swimming pools, including a children's pool with a
water slide and a large main pool with stone chairs
for aquatic lounging.

*Bars (2). Business centre. Concierge.
Disabled-adapted rooms. Gym. Internet (wireless).
Non-smoking rooms. Parking. Pools (outdoor).
Restaurants (6). Room service. Spa. TV.*

Expensive

Hotel Sea Princess

*Juhu Beach (2661-1111/www.seaprincess.com).
Santa Cruz station.* **Rates** Rs 17,500 double.
Credit AmEx, DC, MC, V.

This 20-year-old hotel is a traditional Juhu stand-
by. It recently acquired a new wing for conferences,
but the design and decor of the hotel don't seem to
have changed much since the mid-'80s, except for
the addition of wall-mounted flatscreen TVs to go
with loud-patterned bedspreads and carpets, staid
furniture and Pre-Raphaelite prints on the walls.
The rooms feel a little cluttered, but the excellent
sea views – Juhu Beach is just behind the hotel –
help take the edge off. The outside pool area is
calm, spacious and pleasant, and there's beach
access plus a scattering of tables and chairs to sit
by the water and sip beer or eat lunch. There's also
a separate children's pool.

*Bar. Concierge. Disabled-adapted rooms. Gym.
Internet (wireless). Non-smoking floor. Pool
(outdoor). Restaurant. Room service. TV.*

Sun 'n' Sand

*39 Juhu Beach, Juhu (6693-8888/2620-1811/
www.sunnsandhotel.com). Vile Parle station.*
Rates Rs 16,000 double. **Credit** AmEx, MC, V.

Muscle-bound Bollywood superhunk Hrithik
Roshan wanders through the lobby after a photo-
shoot on Juhu Beach and no one raises an eyebrow
– it's just another day at the Sun 'n' Sand, suburban
Mumbai's first five star-rated hotel (it was the first
to get a pool) and a favoured destination for ad
shoots thanks to its easy access to the beach and
high service standards. Now over 40 years old, the
Sun 'n' Sand retains an aura of 1960s Bombay with
pastel shades, an easy-listening lobby soundtrack,
and furniture and decor that must have been
cutting-edge modern when it was built in 1964
– although recent renovations in some parts do it no
justice. Still a favourite with foreign film crews and
old-school Bollywood producers, the rooms at Sun
'n' Sand are spick-and-span with sparkling marble
bathrooms and broad windows with excellent sea
views. Room rates include airport pick-up and drop-
off and complimentary cocktails.

*Bar. Business centre. Free parking. Gym. Internet
(wireless). Non-smoking rooms. Pool (outdoor).
Restaurants (2). Room service. Spa. TV.*

Le Royal Meridien.

Moderate

Hotel Four Seasons

5 Juhu Tara Road, Juhu (2663-1441). Vile Parle station. **Taxi** opposite Juhu Church. **Rates** Rs 5,000 double. **Credit** MC, V.

Okay, it isn't fancy (and no, it's not *that* Four Seasons). The fans are wobbly, the rooms are plain, cramped and have no views, and the plastic climbing plants in the lobby look like they need watering. But it is clean, the cheapest decent hotel in Juhu, and former patrons include the Nobel Peace Prize-winner Shirin Ebadi, who stayed here during the 2004 World Social Forum. If it's good enough for her, it might be good enough for you. Convenient for both airports.

Restaurant. Room service. TV.

King's International

5 Juhu Tara Road, Juhu Beach (6692-2222/ 2618-4381/www.kingsinternational.com). Vile Parle station. **Taxi** near Prithvi Theatre. **Rates** Rs 5,500-Rs 6,500 double. **Credit** MC, V.

The lift door sticks occasionally and needs a gentle kick to get it to shut, but don't worry, the shambling old commissionaire in a peaked cap will do that for you. This small, 30-year-old hotel won't win any awards but it is perfectly clean and decent, with surprisingly good-sized, comfortable rooms provided with fridges and TVs, and friendly service. Room service includes dishes from the excellent Temple Flower restaurant nearby. The rates include a complimentary airport drop-off. A popular coffee shop/bar/pizzeria, Alfredo's, functions out of the same building.

Free parking. Room service. TV.

Andheri

Deluxe

Hyatt Regency

Sahar Airport Road, Andheri (E) (6696-1234/ www.mumbai.regency.hyatt.com). Andheri station. **Rates** Rs 15,000 double. **Credit** AmEx, DC, MC, V.

Cocooned behind a sweeping wall of glass are the plush confines of the Hyatt Regency: acres of dark grey marble, dark wood and frosted glass. Even standard rooms are smart here: spacious and airy, with step-down showers and glass basins, and with a design laid out according to the principles of *vastu shashtra* – the Indian feng shui. That's why there's a tiny bamboo plant greeting you as soon as you step into your room, and why the mirror in the bedroom is positioned off to one side and not directly in front of the bed – that would be bad vastu. The outdoor gardens include a large swimming pool and – a rarity – tennis courts, where you can play against one of the hotel trainers.

Bar. Concierge. Gym. Internet (wireless). Parking. Pool (outdoor). Restaurants (2). Room service. Spa. TV.

ITC The Maratha

Sahar Airport Road, Andheri (E) (2830-3030/ www.itcwelcomegroup.in). Andheri station. **Rates** Rs 16,500-Rs 24,500 double. **Credit** AmEx, DC, MC, V.

From the white *jali*-style lattice screens that cover the walls of the hotel's tall atrium of Agra red stone, to the ayurvedic shampoos in the bathrooms, the Maratha stands out from other new five-stars with a design that works to remind you that you are actually in India. Airy rooms are adorned with modern and traditional Indian art, including fine examples of local Warli tribal painting made with rice paste and straw. The restaurants cover Indian cuisines from north to south, with a nod to the British era in a club-like bar littered with over-stuffed wingtip leather armchairs. The happy marriage of five-star luxury and Indian style is tastefully restrained until you get to the outside pool, where they've let rip with six stone lion fountains and a giant iron and stone gazebo.

Bar. Business centre. Concierge. Gym. Internet (wireless). Non-smoking rooms. Parking. Pool (outdoor). Restaurants (5). Spa. Room service. TV.

Leela Kempinski

Sahar Airport Road, Andheri (E) (6691-1234/ www.theleela.com). Andheri station. **Rates** Rs 17,000-Rs 22,000 double. **Credit** AmEx, DC, MC, V.

The Leela feels a little past its prime compared to its newer five-star neighbours on the airport road. Its multi-level lobby is a sprawling field of cream marble and brass fittings, with an elderly shopping arcade and a small gallery of works by contemporary Indian artists. The centrepiece is a sunken lobby with a step waterfall rushing down to a gold-domed gazebo. Rooms are smart, spacious and tastefully decorated, each with a plasma TV.

Bar. Concierge. Gym. Internet (broadband). Restaurants (4). Room service. Spa. TV.

Le Royal Meridien

Sahar Airport Road, Andheri (E) (2838-0000/ www.leroyalmeridien-mumbai.com). Andheri station. **Rates** Rs 16,000-18,000 double. **Credit** AmEx, MC, V.

Some nice design touches raise Le Royal Meridien above the five-star herd, most strikingly the Crystal Lounge: a long oval room in silver, white and beige with a series of glass doors opening off to other parts of the hotel under a gigantic chandelier. It's like walking into a Fabergé egg. In the Chinese restaurant next door, tables are set with specially-commissioned dinner plates scrawled with the verse of Indian poet Harivanshrai Bachchan – translated into Chinese. Rooms are smart and contemporary, with wooden floors and spacious bathrooms complete with rubber ducks. The only disappointment is that the view through the broad windows is of the neighbouring wasteland.

Bars (2). Business centre. Concierge. Disabled-adapted rooms. Free parking. Internet (wireless). Gym. No smoking floors. Pool (outdoor). Restaurants (3). Room service. Spa. TV.

Where to Stay

The most authentic Oriental cuisine in town

shiro

The taste of nightlife

Sightseeing

Features

Flora Fountain. *See p66.*

clean water. It's the most basic human necessity. Yet one third of all poverty related deaths are caused by drinking dirty water. Saying *I'm in* means you're part of a growing movement that's fighting the injustice of poverty. Your £8 a month can help bring safe water to some of the world's poorest people. We can do this. We *can* end poverty. Are you in?

shouldn't everyone get clean water? I don't think that's too much to ask for

Let's end poverty together.
Text 'WATER' and your name to 87099 to give £8 a month.

Standard text rates apply. Registered charity No.202918

oxfam.org.uk

Oxfam

i'm in

Introduction

Welcome to the carnival of life.

Mumbai isn't the sort of city that rewards tourists who come armed with checklists. Just over three centuries old, it doesn't bear the burden of history that the rest of India must shoulder, nor does it have the manufactured modernity that afflicts so many major cities in Asia. Like a tree that adds rings for each year of its growth, Mumbai has grown organically, adding layer upon layer of construction, culture and sheer humanity. It is a city that is fascinating not for its museums (of which there are just a handful anyway), nor for the conservation of its architectural heritage (although even the most dilapidated buildings in the south of the city manage to conjure up an optimistic grandeur).

No, Mumbai is the sort of city that is relentlessly fascinating simply for not having imploded; for continuing to function despite the state of anarchy in which it appears to exist. It is in the people of Mumbai, the hectic activity of its streets and railway stations, the chaos of its bazaars, the visible frenzy of commerce, the ridiculous contrasts of appalling poverty and overblown wealth – and the complete indifference with which Mumbaikars deal with them – that the appeal of the city lies.

LIE OF THE LAND

We've divided the city into South and North Mumbai – with the former known to locals as just 'Town' and the latter as 'the suburbs'. **South Mumbai** (*see p61*) is still where Mumbai's wealthy work and play, and die-hard South Mumbai snobs wouldn't dream of going anywhere near the 'burbs, even though Bandra is now the city's hottest nightlife hub. Nariman Point continues to be a major corporate centre packed with airline offices, banks and consulates, although these days business is shifting northward to cheaper, more convenient locations like Parel and the Bandra-Kurla Complex. Most of the city's sites of architectural and historical interest are located in the south, especially **Fort** (*see p65*), named for the long-since demolished fortress established by the British in the 17th century, that became the nucleus of the city. The British influence is everywhere – not surprising for a city that was built by colonialism – and its oldest and most impressive buildings are all British relics. The **University of Mumbai** looks like an Oxford college with palm trees (*see p63*), while **Chhatrapati Shivaji Terminus** (*see p70*) bears more than a passing

resemblance to St Pancras. Although there's been an effort to clean up some of the city's heritage buildings, many remain desperately neglected, some wrecked by ill-conceived modifications or obscured by vast advertising hoardings. The **Suburbs** (*see p78*), once villages, have swelled with new businesses, shops, restaurants and entertainment venues, but possess few places of interest for sight-seers, although we've picked out a few gems that are worth the trouble. Many sights close on public holidays so ring ahead to check.

GETTING AROUND

The intense traffic, crowds, noise, heat, shocking poverty and poor infrastructure can make Mumbai an exhausting and overwhelming city. Be gentle on yourself and don't try to do too much at once. Drink plenty of water. Some areas are best appreciated on foot (*see p67* **A walking tour of Fort**), but

The best Sights

For Mumbai's must-sees
The **Gateway of India** (*see p62*), **Chhatrapati Shivaji Terminus** (*see p70*), **Horniman Circle** (*see p66*) and the **Asiatic Society** (*see p66*) and **Chhatrapati Shivaji Maharaj Vastu Sangrahalaya** (*see p65*).

For peace in the city
Marine Drive (*see p76*), **Banganga Tank** (*see p75*), **Mumbai Port Trust Garden** (*see p61*) and **Byculla Zoo** (*see p73*).

For spiritual uplift
Haji Ali Dargah (*see p75*), **St Thomas' Cathedral** (*see p69*), **Kenneseth Eliyahoo Synagogue** (*see p64*) and **Babulnath Temple** (*see p76*).

For going independent
Mani Bhavan (*see p77*), **Azad Maidan** (*see p70*) and **August Kranti Maidan** (*see p76*).

For getting out of town
Elephanta Island (*see p83*), **Land's End, Bandra** (*see p79*) and **Sanjay Gandhi National Park** (*see p81*).

most of the time you'll find taxis much easier and a relatively cheap way to get around. Getting out to the suburbs is almost always faster by train but if you can't face those packed carriages, you'll find it isn't that expensive to go by cab. Many street and place names have been officially changed in the last 20 years but most locals still use the old names. New names are often not recognised, even by taxi drivers, so in our listings and maps we've given both where appropriate and a prominent nearby landmark to aid navigation.

TOUTS AND SCAMS

Mumbaikars are warm and welcoming to foreign visitors, but around tourist-heavy sites like Colaba Causeway and the Gateway of India you're likely to be zeroed in on by persistent hawkers, beggars and the odd hashish dealer, especially in winter – peak tourist season. Some visitors find being repeatedly offered drums and oversize balloons for a 'very good price' distressing and tiresome, but be philosophical and just accept it as the price of admission. Scammers and con artists do operate but muggings – of either tourists or locals – are very rare. You might be ripped off by a cute 12-year-old asking you to buy her some powdered milk at a hugely inflated price, or an aspiring shoe-shine boy who just needs a hundred rupees to buy some polish and brushes, but you're unlikely to be robbed at knifepoint. Colaba is by far the worst spot for foreigner-focused hawkers and hustlers. If it's all getting a bit much, get out of Colaba for instant relief. If you go to Bandra, however, do watch out for the fake nuns 'collecting for the orphans'.

City tours

By bus

Bombay Safari (2281-0139; Rs 130), runs a tour of every conceivable sight across the city from the Gateway to Juhu Beach, and you're welcome to hop off (but not back on) wherever you like. **Neelambari** (2202-6713; Rs 40-90) is an open-top, double-decker bus that offers one-hour evening rides through Fort's heritage district. The commentary is poor but this is still a great way to see the old city lit by floodlights.

By foot

Shriti Tyagi of **Beyond Bombay Tours** (98677-64409/beyondbombay@gmail.com; Rs 2,000 and up) organises tours of art galleries, landmarks featured in *Shantaram* and Dharavi slums. **Bombay Heritage Walks** (2683-5856/info@bombayheritagewalks.com; Rs 100 upwards) organises walking tours of heritage areas, usually with an emphasis on architectural details, around Fort, Banganga, Bandra and Khotachiwadi, normally on the first Sunday of the month. Deepa Krishnan of **Mumbai Magic** (98677-07414; Rs 1,250 upwards) holds two-hour walks through Fort every Saturday, with handouts, a tea break and a souvenir, for two to six people. Customised tours of Chor Bazaar, Bhuleshwar, the Kala Ghoda art district, Elephanta Island and Mumbai's largest slum, Dharavi, are also available. **Reality Tours** (2283-3872; Rs 300 upwards) organise slum tours of the city and claim that 80 per cent of their profits go to non-profit organisations.

By boat

Harbour cruises (Rs 50 onwards) from Apollo Bunder in Colaba take leisurely rounds of the sea and offer views of the skyline, the docks and little neighbouring islands. The **Taj Mahal Palace and Tower** hotel (6665-3255; Rs 15,000 an hour) also has a luxury yacht available for hire for up to ten people if you book two days in advance of your trip.

By cycle

Jayesh Morvankar of **Odati Adventures** (98200-79802; Rs 750) takes you on a pedal-powered tour of Fort, Ballard Estate, Town Hall, Chhatrapati Shivaji Terminus, Marine Drive, Nariman Point and Colaba, pausing to learn about the city's history and development. Tours are usually conducted on weekends between November and February and take about half a day.

South Mumbai

Treasure island.

Colaba

Map p250

Colaba Causeway – the city's prime tourist stretch – was once a strip of land that connected the islands of Bombay in the north with Colaba (named for the Koli fisherfolk who inhabited the seven islands before Portuguese colonists arrived) in the south. Home to some of the most expensive real estate in India, the causeway today has shopping arcades, hotels, restaurants and bars on either side, but the island of Colaba sits just south of the causeway and goes on to the very edge of Mumbai, at Navy Nagar.

A recreation area for the British throughout the 18th century and populated solely by large numbers of deer released by the East India Company, Colaba changed dramatically after the British constructed the causeway in 1838. The island was initially developed as a military cantonment, which is what it remains today. Green, well-maintained and quiet, it remains one of the most pleasant parts of the city, thanks to the army and navy installations (all of which are off-limits to civilians) and the sprawling campus of the Tata Institute of Fundamental Research – renowned for its research in maths and physics.

In 1847, work began on the Church of St John the Evangelist. Known locally today as **Afghan Church**, it was built to commemorate the hundreds of British and Indian soldiers from Bombay who died in the disastrous First Afghan War of 1838-42. Horse-drawn trams followed a few decades later, lending the island a romantic charm.

Cuffe Parade was once one of the city's most desirable addresses, with mansions and bungalows – many owned by Parsi families – overlooking a genteel seafront promenade. Some of the mansions remain but the promenade has gone, as has the sea, pushed back over a mile by land reclamation in the 1970s. It was quickly built over with apartment blocks, a shopping arcade, the twin towers of Mumbai's own World Trade Center and a large slum. A few minutes' walk north is **Gita Nagar** at Back Bay, where the brightly painted wooden boats of Koli fisherfolk, the descendants of the city's original inhabitants, line the beach just as they did for centuries before the Portuguese came.

Colaba also possesses one of the city's finest public parks, the **Mumbai Port Trust Garden** (6-11am, 4.30-8.30pm daily), where Colaba residents go jogging and take in a stunning sea view. A little further north and you hit **Colaba Causeway**. Once a bridge connecting two islands, it is now the city's equivalent of Oxford Street. It's crammed with clothes shops, restaurants, bars, cafés, trinket stalls, wandering salesmen and, of course, tourists. The sidestreets here abound with mid-range hotels, handicrafts and jewellery shops, and some of South Mumbai's classiest bars, like perennial favourite **Indigo** (*see p112*),

The **Gateway of India**. See p62.

If you only have 48 hours

Day One

Take a stroll down **Colaba Causeway**, then sidetrack down to the harbour to the **Gateway of India** (*see below*) and the nearby **Taj Mahal Palace and Tower Hotel** (*see p44*). From here, stroll back down to **Regal Cinema** (*see p141*) and take in the **National Gallery of Modern Art** (*see p146*), and the impressive domes and balconies of the Chhatrapati Shivaji Maharaj Vastu Sangrahalaya, formerly the **Prince of Wales Museum** (*see p65*), across the street. If you're feeling peckish, walk up to **Kala Ghoda** past a stretch of colonial-era buildings and the landmark **Jehangir Art Gallery** (*see p145*) and tuck into some first-class curries at **Khyber** (*see p100*) or try the outstanding South Indian seafood at nearby **Trishna** (*see p100*). Close by is the faded but beautiful **Kenneseth Eliyahoo Synagogue** (*see p64*) and the cool clothes store **FabIndia** (*see p121*). From here, it's a quick stroll to the **Bombay High Court**, the **University of Mumbai** and the cricket at **Oval Maidan** (*see p63*). Still got some energy? Then walk up to **Flora Fountain** (*see p66*) and wander the hawker-packed pavement arcades nearby. It's a short walk down Veer Nariman Road to **Horniman Circle** and the **Asiatic Society** (*see p66*).

Day Two

You can't leave Mumbai without a taxi ride down the two-mile **Marine Drive** (*see p76*) for a stroll on **Girgaum Chowpatty** (*see p76*). From here it's another short taxi ride to **Walkeshwar** for the ex-colonial enclave of **Malabar Hill** and the holy and serene **Banganga Tank** (*see p75*). On the way back south, drive up Balbunath Marg past the **Babulnath Temple** (*see p34*) to nearby **Soam** (*see p102*) for some fabulous vegetarian Gujarati food. Then it's off to the old **Crawford Market** (*see p129*) for a wander around the city's liveliest and oldest food market. From here, take a cab down to Nagar Chowk and the breathtaking **Chhatrapati Shivaji Terminus** (*see p70*), an Indo-British confection in stone. Pop into the Barista across the street for an iced coffee, then amble down Waudby Road to cross the lawns of Azad Maidan past the elite **Bombay Gymkhana** (*see p70*) to Mahatma Gandhi Road and the open-air **Fashion Street** clothes market (*see p129*). Before 6pm, go back to Marine Drive for fabulous cocktails and views from the **Dome** bar (*see p113*) on the roof of the InterContinental Marine Drive. Then it's a short hop to the seafront **Salt Water Grill** (*see p101*) for a relaxed dinner on the sand.

on Mandlik Road. At the southern end of the Causeway there's **Sassoon Dock**, a hectic wholesale fish market where the local Koli fisherfolk bring in the night's catch at around 5am. If you can get up, it's an experience (and smell) you won't forget in a hurry. Go north and the entrance to **Colaba Market** appears on the right – an open and lively produce market crowded with fruit and vegetable stalls and a line of jewellery shops. Also on the causeway stands the massive, arched entrance of **Cusrow Baug**, a housing colony built in 1934 and reserved for members of the city's dwindling Parsi community. A watchman guards the gate, but if you ask nicely he might let you take a peek at its spectacular art deco-style *agiary*, or fire temple (from the outside only; non-Parsis are not admitted). *Baugs* (literally, 'gardens') were built for community living, and with its neat, geometrical buildings and gardens, Cusrow Baug has since catapulted into a prime Mumbai address.

A right turn at Electric House on the Causeway leads you to the back of the **Taj Mahal Palace and Tower** hotel (*see p44*), which dominates the seafront. The city's most famous hotel, it was built by Parsi industrialist Jamsetji Nusserwanji Tata in 1903 (*see p71* **Munificent Mumbaikars**). Built in a blend of Moorish and Florentine Renaissance styles, it's worth visiting even if you're not planning on staying. The Taj is just yards from the waterfront **Gateway of India** (*photo p61*), a towering archway of yellow basalt built by the British to commemorate the visit of King George V and Queen Mary to India in 1911, the only visit of a reigning British monarch to the jewel in the Empire's crown. Designed by architect George Wittet, it provided a ceremonial entranceway to the subcontinent for George and his queen after stepping onto dry land, but that one was made out of papiermâché – the stone version wasn't completed until 1927. In 1948, the last British troops to leave Indian soil exited through the Gateway.

Overlooking the Gateway and its garden is the elegant **Royal Bombay Yacht Club** (Apollo Bunder, 6752-7200, www.royalbombay yachtclub.com), established in 1846 and still

Sightseeing

one of the city's most exclusive private members' clubs, steeped in colonial-era atmosphere – but you'll need permission from the club secretary to step inside. At the end of Colaba Causeway is **SP Mukherjee Chowk** – a traffic roundabout with an ornate stone fountain. Under British rule it was named Wellington Circle, after the Duke of Wellington, and the base of the fountain is inscribed with an inventory of the Iron Duke's battles. Locally, the roundabout is known as **Regal**, after the striking Art Deco cinema (*see p141*) built in 1934 that sits at the end of the Causeway.

Oval Maidan & Churchgate

Map p251 & p252

The Arabian Sea lapped at the edge of **Oval Maidan** (*maidan* means 'ground') until a land reclamation project in the 1920s extended the peninsula nearly half a mile westward to Marine Drive. As a result, there's a striking contrast between the Victorian Gothic buildings on the *maidan*'s eastern side and the art deco apartments to the west. This half-mile-long recreation ground between Maharshi Karve Marg (Queen's Road) and Karmaveer Bhaurao Marg (Mayo Road) was once a venue for dog-and-horse shows for the entertainment of British colonists in the 19th and early 20th centuries, before falling into disrepair. Now lovingly restored by residents of Queen's Road, it is the city's premier venue for impromptu cricket matches. On weekends there are dozens of games taking place simultaneously, overlapping to the point where it's almost impossible to tell where one ends and another begins. Visitors are very welcome to join the mêlée. On the Oval's eastern side is a row of some of the city's most impressive Victorian buildings. Next to the **Old Secretariat** and the **Sessions Court** at the southern end of Mayo Road are the curlicued stones and spiral staircases of the **University of Mumbai**, built in 1874 in the style of old English universities. Attached to the University Library and looming over the Oval is the **Rajabai Clock Tower**, constructed in 1878. To the left is the **Bombay High Court**, outside which down-on-their-luck itinerant lawyers in threadbare black suits tout for work. Visitors are allowed inside, which is highly recommended for courtroom scenes straight out of Dickens' *Bleak House*. Inside, look out for the satirical animal sculptures decorating the cornices and tops of pillars, like the monkey judge holding a hopelessly unbalanced scale, and foxes and wolves in lawyer's outfits. Across the street from the court is the **Bhika Behram Well**, built in 1725. It's a sacred well for the Parsi community

(*see p31* **Communities**), surrounded by green benches where elderly Parsis read their holy book. The canopy above the well features vivid stained-glasswork depicting the winged Ashofarohar, a Zoroastrian divine messenger. Only Parsis are allowed in. Westward along Veer Nariman Road sits the **Western Railway Headquarters**, built in 1899, with white domes rising above dark stone minarets. The staid concrete structure opposite is the **Churchgate Terminus** where the suburban Western Railway line ends. Every weekday, around three million commuters pass through here. Opposite Churchgate is the **Eros Cinema** (*see p141*), another art deco gem built in 1938, now run-down but as busy as ever.

Rajabai Clock Tower

Mumbai University, Karmaveer Bhaurao Marg, next to High Court, Oval Maidan, Churchgate (www.mu.ac.in). Churchgate station. **Open** 10.30am-6.30pm Mon-Sat. **Admission** free. **Map** p251 G7.

The chimes of the Rajabai clock tower, which rises 280 feet above the Mumbai University Library, have been sounding across the Oval Maidan every half-hour, with a few interruptions, since 1880. Modelled on London's Big Ben, the tower was built with a Rs 400,000 donation from Mumbai's first rogue trader, Premchand Roychand. In return, the clock tower was named after his mother, Rajabai. It was designed by Sir Gilbert Scott in Gothic Revivalist style and features stone heads of Shakespeare and Homer peering out from the crossed arches under the main spiral staircase. Look out for the pretty stained-glasswork around the staircase, and the flower-like teakwood library ceiling.

Western Railway Headquarters.

Sightseeing

Chhatrapati Shivaji Maharaj Vastu Sangrahalaya
– aka the Prince of Wales Museum.

Kala Ghoda

Map p251 & p252

South Mumbai's art district, **Kala Ghoda**
(which means 'Black Horse') sits off the
intersection of K Dubash Marg (Rampart Row)
and Mahatma Gandhi Road. It's one of the city's
most attractive areas, with some well-restored
heritage buildings. Kala Ghoda owes its name
to a 13-foot bronze equestrian statue of King
Edward VII (he reigned from 1901-10), which
was installed here in 1879 (*photo p22*) in what
is now a car park, to commemorate his visit
three years earlier. Edward sat there for the
next 86 years, surviving long after the last
British troops departed in 1948. The statue was
finally removed in 1965 in a drive to eradicate
British-era statues from public places. Edward,
unlabelled and stuck on a patch of grass, now
greets visitors to the Byculla Zoo (*see p73*).

Since Independence, the area has evolved
into Mumbai's premier art district, with eight
galleries nearby. The largest are the **National
Gallery of Modern Art** (*see p146*), which
stands off the Regal Circle, and the **Jehangir
Art Gallery** (*see p145*). Artists also display
their work on the pavement outside the
Jehangir, which stands on one corner of the
sprawling compound of the **Chhatrapati
Shivaji Maharaj Vastu Sangrahalaya**
(*see p65*), formerly known as the Prince of
Wales Museum, on Mahatma Gandhi Road.

Overlooking Kala Ghoda on the western
side of the street is the **David Sassoon
Mechanical Institute and Library**, built in
1870 and named after its founder, a renowned
Jewish businessman and philanthropist from
Baghdad whose family built many of the city's
civic and cultural institutions. Sassoon's face

peers out of the building's façade above its
arched entrance and there's a life-size statue
of him in traditional Jewish robes inside.
Upstairs, a peaceful balcony overlooking Kala
Ghoda is a popular spot for readers to while
away the afternoons. To the institute's left
stands **Elphinstone College**, Mumbai's
oldest college, instituted in 1835 and taking
up residence in this beautiful building in
1888. The college building had for decades
been a dark grey mess until renovation restored
the exquisite golden stonework a few years
ago. Similar magic was worked on the **Army
& Navy Building** to its right, named for
the Army & Navy Departmental Store it once
housed. The Army & Navy recently became a
department store once again, named Westside,
which has a small but decent café. Next door
is the decrepit **Esplanade Mansion**, once
the city's most luxurious hotel, Watson's.

Rampart Row, officially named K Dubash
Marg, runs along the site of one wall of the
17th-century British fort that became the
city's nucleus and was finally demolished
in the 1860s. On the other side of the popular
Rhythm House music store (*see p131*) the
narrow Dr VB Gandhi Road (Forbes Street)
leads to the sky-blue **Kenneseth Eliyahoo
Synagogue** (*photo p70*). Another Sassoon
family-funded institution, it was built in 1884
for the city's once-thriving Jewish community.
It's faded but still beautiful, especially in
the afternoons when its tall, stained-glass
windows cast a rainbow of light across the
prayer hall. Before Independence, the prayer
hall benches were packed elbow-to-elbow for
Saturday services; these days only a handful
come, as most of Mumbai's Jewish community
migrated to Israel and elsewhere after 1948.

From the Synagogue, the narrow Saibaba Lane leads back to Rampart Row, which is now lined with a stretch of smart restaurants, shops and art galleries. Keep an eye out for two mahogany trees in front of **Ador House** – legend has it that they were planted by the famous British explorer and missionary Dr David Livingstone on a visit to Mumbai in 1865. At the end of Rampart Row rises the tall spire of **St Andrew's and St Columba's Church**, built in 1819 and modelled on St Martin-in-the-Fields in London's Trafalgar Square. Mumbai's first Scottish Church, St Andrew's massive doors open onto a carefully preserved interior of Burmese teak and shining brass, surmounted by an antique pipe organ. St Andrew's only opens for Sunday services at 6.30pm. Opposite the church, along Rampart Row, stands the **Bombay Natural History Society**, hidden behind thick foliage at Hornbill House. The Society was formed by naturalists in 1884 to document the rich flora and fauna around Mumbai. Today, it conducts environmental projects and is at the forefront of efforts to save India's tigers. It's closed to non-members.

Every February, Rampart Row is closed to traffic for the two-week Kala Ghoda Arts Festival (*see p134*), when art installations, photographs, multi-media works and paintings spill out from the neighbouring galleries on to the pavements. Theatre, music and dance shows are performed on a makeshift stage on the road, which is lined with stalls selling street food, ethnic clothes and jewellery.

Chhatrapati Shivaji Maharaj Vastu Sangrahalaya

159 MG Road, Kala Ghoda, near Regal Circle (2284-4519/www.bombaymuseum.org). **Open** 10.15am-6pm Tue-Sun. **Admission** Rs 300; Rs 5 reductions; free under-fives. Rs 150 for audio tours in English, French and Japanese. **Map** p251 G6.
The city's largest museum, the Chhatrapati Shivaji Maharaj Vastu Sangrahalaya was built in 1914, and originally called the Prince of Wales Museum of Western India. The building is a fusion of British, Hindu and Mughal architecture – a style called Indo-Saracenic – pioneered by British architect George Wittet in the early 1900s. The domes are from Mughal architecture (its sculpted windows resemble those of traditional Rajasthani dwellings) while the balconies and façade are typically British. The museum has over 30,000 artefacts including bronze and stone sculptures, miniature paintings, arms and armour, as well as Far Eastern art. Don't miss the only Assyrian frieze in India, on display in the Pre- and Proto History Gallery. The explanatory labels are poor, but there is a 45-minute audio tour available.

Fort & Ballard Estate

Map p251 & p252

Under the Mumbai stink of petrol, dust and spices is that all-pervasive smell of fast money, and nowhere is it stronger than in Fort, the city's banking district, and Ballard Estate, the old shipping and finance district. The epicentre of Fort is the 28-storey **Bombay Stock Exchange**, which stands at the junction of Mumbai Samachar Marg and Dalal Street. The word *dalal* means broker, and Bombay's – and Asia's – first exchange was established here in 1875, then called the Native Share and Stock Brokers Association. The new building was built in the 1970s. On 12 March 1993, around 50 people were killed by a car bomb in the Exchange's basement during Mumbai's worst-ever terrorist attack, now known as 'Black Friday' (*see p23*). The narrow lanes around the exchange are lined with brokerages, banks, insurance and other financial institutions, and bulls and bears dominate the conversation at local *chai* stalls.

Mumbai Samachar Marg leads to **Horniman Circle**, a fenced circular garden surrounded by elegant heritage buildings, including the imposing neo-classical **Asiatic Society of Mumbai** (*see p66*). The circle was the heart of the city's cotton trade during its early boom years, and there's still an old trough near the western gate that was used to water the cattle carrying cotton bales to the market. After 1863,

The Hindu **Banganga temple**. See p75.

High hopes: **Bombay Stock Exchange**.

Sightseeing

the cotton market moved to Colaba, but profits from the boom paid for the Horniman Circle Garden and the buildings around it.

Ahead of the Asiatic Society, Shahid Bhagat Singh Road curves into Mint Road, site of the imposing **Reserve Bank of India**, the regulating bank. Hidden behind a wall next to the RBI is the **Bombay Mint**, built in 1827 to produce gold and silver coins and still pumping out the steel rupee coins used today. Close by is the **Monetary Museum**, on Sir Pherozeshah Mehta Road.

On Modi Street, parallel to Mint Road, stands the **Maneckji Nowroji Sett Agiary**, Mumbai's oldest Parsi fire temple, first built in 1733 and rebuilt in 1891. You'll have to admire it from outside, though, as only Parsis may enter. Inside burns an eternal flame, carried by Parsi refugees from Persia to India when they fled Muslim persecution around 800AD.

Ballard Road leads to the business district of **Ballard Estate**, a neat grid of elegant office buildings designed by George Wittet (the designer of the Gateway of India). The area was reclaimed from the sea around 1910 with material excavated for the building of the access-restricted **Indira Docks** that stand beyond. The buildings here housed shipping offices and hotels for arrivals at the docks. Most have closed down, replaced by some of India's biggest corporations, like **Reliance House**, the corporate office of Reliance Industries, a Fortune 500 company. Today, the office of the **Mumbai Port Trust**, which regulates all port activities and is the city's biggest landowner, and the **Customs House**, remain the Estate's most important administrative centres. A **War Memorial** for Mumbai Port Trust employees who died in World War I stands at the junction of Ballard Road, Sprot Road and Narottam Morarji Marg. The tiny **Ballard Bunder Gatehouse Navy Museum** on Ballard Road is a recent addition to the landscape.

Asiatic Society of Mumbai

Asiatic Society of Mumbai, Shahid Bhagat Singh Road, opposite Horniman Circle (2266-0956). CST or Churchgate stations. **Open** 10am-6pm Mon-Sat. **Admission** free. **Map** p251 H8.
This milk-white neo-classical building with sweeping steps and imposing pillars has starred in numerous Bollywood films, usually masquerading as the Bombay High Court. The Asiatic Society was formed in 1803 with the purpose of 'studying the Orient', although 'Orientals' themselves were excluded. It remained a Europeans-only club until Sir Cursetji Maneckji was admitted in 1840, after he pointed out the stupidity of banning Indians when they were free to join the Royal Asiatic Society of Great Britain, its sister organisation. Inside, the library's curving stone staircases and cosy alcoves are filled with life-size statues of British-era governors, officials and

philanthropists. The library is a repository of rare books, including an original manuscript of Dante's *Divine Comedy*, though sadly it's not on display.

Ballard Bunder Gatehouse Navy Museum

Ballard Road, Ballard Estate (no phone). CST Station. **Taxi** Ballard Pier. **Open** 9am-7pm Mon-Sun daily. **Admission** free. **Map** p252 J8.
This tiny museum was long overdue when it opened in 2005 – the first modern museum dedicated to Mumbai's illustrious maritime history. It's housed in a yellow stone gateway that was once lost behind a high wall after the Indian Navy took over the dockyards. The museum is filled with old black-and-white photographs, compasses, and intricate wooden models of ships and boats built by the Wadia family, once a famous Bombay shipbuilding dynasty.

Monetary Museum

Monetary Museum, Amar Building, Sir Pherozeshah Mehta Road (2261-4043/www.rbi.org.in/scripts/ic_museum.aspx). CST or Churchgate stations. **Taxi** RBI. **Open** 10.45am-5.15pm Mon-Sat. **Admission** Rs 10 adults; free for children. **Map** p251 H8.
Did you know that the world's smallest coins were panams from Kerala, with a diameter of less than 1/16th of an inch? If not, you need to educate yourself at the Reserve Bank of India's compact Monetary Museum, which offers a short, stimulating history of Indian money, from barter to credit cards. Crisp and informative text accompanies the displays, and colourful infographics deconstruct complex concepts for kids. It has an impressive collection of old Indian coins, and a thorough guide to spotting counterfeit notes.

Flora Fountain

Map p251 & p252

The hectic Flora Fountain intersection at the junction of Mahatma Gandhi Road, Dadabhai Naoroji Road and Veer Nariman Road is now officially known as Hutatma Chowk (Martyrs' Square), but locals still just call the area 'Fountain', referring to its central ornate fountain mounted with a statue of the Roman goddess Flora, carved from imported Portland stone and erected in 1864. Before that, this was the site of one of the three gates of the original Bombay Fort. There are several other public artworks nearby, including a statue of two martyrs with a flame built in memory of the 105 people shot dead here by police in 1960 during a protest for the creation of Maharashtra state (*see p22*). Commerce of all kinds keeps Fountain flowing; the streets are lined with the offices of the Hong Kong and Shanghai Banking Corporation, Standard Chartered Bank, the Central Bank of India and Bombay House, the corporate office of the Tatas, one of India's oldest and most respected business houses. Under Fountain's shaded pavement

A walking tour of Fort

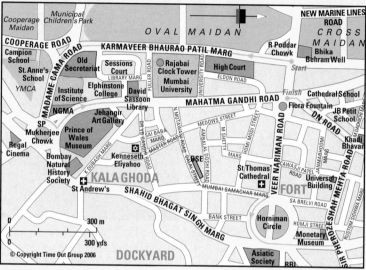

This tour of the area around the south-western part of the site of the old Bombay Fort takes about two hours. Start off at R Poddar Chowk, across from the **Bhika Behram Well** (*see p63*), situated between **Oval Maidan** (*see p63*) and **Cross Maidan** (so named for the cross put there by the Portuguese). Proceed down Karmaveer Bhaurao Patil Marg, lined with beautiful heritage buildings, including the **Bombay High Court**, the **University of Mumbai** (*see p63*) and the **Old Secretariat**, once the house of the British governor of Bombay.

Turn right on to **Madame Cama Road**, named for Bhikaiji Rustom Cama, a Parsi feminist and freedom fighter, made famous when she unfurled a prototype of the Indian flag at a socialist conference in Germany in 1907. At **SP Mukherjee Chowk** (*see p63*), better known as the Regal Circle, stands a fountain, built in 1865 and dedicated to Arthur Wellesley, the Duke of Wellington. On the southern side of the circle stands the art deco **Regal cinema** (*see p141*). Turn right on to Mahatma Gandhi Road, which runs along what was the western wall of the Bombay Fort. On the left are the exhibition halls of the **National Gallery of Modern Art** (*see p146*).

and on the right the impressive Chhatrapati Shivaji Maharaj Vastu Sangrahalaya, or **Prince of Wales Museum** (*see p65*).

Continue down past the **Elphinstone College** (*see p64*) and the **David Sassoon Library** (*see p64*) and take a right into **Kala Ghoda** (*see p64*). Keep the **Rhythm House** (*see p131*) music store on your right and head down into the narrow Dr VB Gandhi Road, once a covered gully called Ropewalk Lane, filled with cable makers for the city's docks. Just one rope shop remains. On the right is the charming **Kenneseth Eliyahoo Synagogue** (*see p64*). Cut left on to the narrow Master Road into the heart of the finance district on Dalal Street, near the **Bombay Stock Exchange** (*see p65*). Take a left on to Mumbai Samachar Marg past **St Thomas Cathedral** (*see p69*) to the grand **Horniman Circle** and **Asiatic Society** (*see p66*). Turn right on to Shahid Bhagat Singh Marg past the **Monetary Museum** (*see p66*) and left on to the hectic **Sir Pherozeshah Mehta Road**, lined with lively shops and stalls. From here dive left into the hawker-infested arcades along the pavements of **Dadabhai Naoroji Road** to **Flora Fountain** (*see p66*).

Sightseeing

A relief on the **New India Assurance Building**.

Haji Ali Dargah shrine. *See p75.*

arcades hawkers peddle everything from
second-hand books and T-shirts to bootleg
software, Bollywood posters and cheap
Chinese vibrators.

The façade of the **Pundole Art Gallery**
(*see p146*) is faced with a mural of black horses
by the renowned Mumbai artist MF Husain,
but even more impressive artwork graces
the frontage of the 1930s-built **New India
Assurance Company Building**, which
has a unique art deco-style depiction of rural
Indian workers. Along Veer Nariman Road,
just before Horniman Circle, stands **St
Thomas' Cathedral** (*see p69*), the first
Anglican Church of Mumbai, built in 1718.
On Medows Street, which also runs into the
Flora Fountain junction, stands the blue **St
Stephen's Armenian Church**, originally
built in 1876 for what was once the city's
flourishing Armenian community, of whom
just three members are left.

Further along Dadabhai Naoroji Road sits the
JN Petit Library, which features rare stained-
glasswork depicting Parsi philanthropists of
the late 1800s. Nearby is **Khadi Bhandar**
(*see p127* **Weave the people**), a handicraft
store dedicated to Gandhi, selling handmade
ornaments, furniture and traditional Indian
clothes made from homespun cotton.

A little off DN Road along Sir Pherozeshah
Mehta Road is the **Universal Building**,
where, in 1968, George Harrison spent five
days recording a soundtrack for the avant-

garde film *Wonderwall* with Indian classical
musicians (*see p72* **A Beatle in Bombay**).

There's a stark contrast between the crowded,
tangled bylanes to the east of Dadabhai Naoroji
Road and the smart, broad roads to the west.
Its eastern flank is known as **Bazaar Gate**,
a market area dating back to the early 18th
century, when the British Fort enclosed the
area. Its character hasn't changed much since
then, with teeming alleys filled with shops,
tailors, fruit stalls and the occasional massage
parlour. The area is dominated by Gujarati
Jains, and many of the buildings have Gujarati-
style wooden balconies and awnings, now hidden
under years of dirt. Clearer evidence of the
longstanding Jain influence can be found on
Maruti Lane at the 200-year-old **Shantinathji
Jain Derasar**, a multi-coloured Jain temple
with two stone guards manning its entrance.

The area of the city to the west of DN
Road was developed after the fort walls were
demolished in the 1860s to make room for
urban expansion. This area now has some of
Mumbai's most exclusive schools and colleges,
including **Cathedral and John Connon
School**, **JB Petit High School for Girls**,
and the **Alexandra Girls' High School**.
It's also home to **Siddhartha College**, set up
by Dr BR Ambedkar, the architect of India's
Constitution and a champion of the country's
lower castes, revered by the city's Dalit
community (*see p33* **Caste in stone**).

St Thomas' Cathedral

St Thomas' Cathedral, Veer Nariman Road, near Horniman Circle. **Open** 10am-5.30pm daily. **Admission** free. **Services** 7am & 8.45am Sun. **Map** p251 H8.

The Churchgate area is so named because of this church, built in 1718 near one of the gates of Bombay Fort, where Flora Fountain now stands. It was the first Anglican church in Mumbai and contains memorials to British colonists, many of whom seemed to have died from malaria before they reached the age of 30. The names include Katherine Kirkpatrick, mother of James Achilles Kirkpatrick, who scandalised colonial-era India by marrying Hyderabadi beauty Khair un-Nissa, and whose story is told in William Dalrymple's *White Mughals*. The church was recently restored, winning the UNESCO Asia-Pacific Heritage Award in 2004.

Nagar Chowk

Map p252

Dominating Nagar Chowk (meaning 'City Square' in Hindi) is the spectacular **Chhatrapati Shivaji Terminus** (*see p70*), Mumbai's main railway station and still known to many as 'VT' for its old name, Victoria Terminus. This area marks the northern boundary of the old British Fort; the last remnant of the fort wall still stands behind the terminus near **St George's Hospital**, unmarked and hidden behind a public toilet around the corner from the **General Post Office**. Across from the terminus on the corner between Mahapalika Marg and Dadabhai Naoroji Road stands the grand headquarters of the **Municipal Corporation of Greater Mumbai** – first set up in 1872 to take care of the city's upkeep, now a byword for inefficiency and corruption. In front of the building stands a statue of Sir Pherozeshah Mehta, the Corporation's creator. The Corporation is the favourite punch bag of most local newspapers, one of which is right next door at the **Times of India Building**, built in 1903 and home to the world's largest-selling daily English-language paper. Down Marzban Road, past the Barista café, sits the everpopular **Sterling Cinema** (*see p142*).

Next to Sterling Cinema stands **Tata Palace**, once the residence of India's foremost business family, now the offices of Deutsche Bank, mounted with circular galleries, stone lion heads and mock classical columns in form of Greek virgins. Nearby on Waudby

Port whine

For a port city, the docklands play a surprisingly minor role in Mumbai's daily life. The port, along with the mills, made Mumbai the economic powerhouse it is today. But unlike the mills, which are now part of the city's daily routine – albeit painted over, covered in glass and home to shopping malls or, worse, knocked down to make way for office towers – and were always something the city passed on its way to work every day, the docklands are largely off-limits to the public, despite making up one-eighth of the total area of the island city from its tip to Mahim.

The docklands have long been considered the last chance for urban renewal within the island city. They are owned and administered by the 134-year-old Mumbai Port Trust, which is the single largest holder of property in the Mumbai Metropolitan Region, with roughly 1,860 acres of land stretching from Sassoon Dock in the south to Wadala in the north. Yet, port activity and infrastructure take up less than 485 acres, and roughly 75 per cent of the Trust's land lies unused.

In 2007, the Port Trust mooted the idea of filling in two of the city's oldest docks, Victoria Dock and Prince's Dock, to construct

a container terminal and boost the port's cargo traffic. The Mumbai Docklands Regeneration Forum, a non-governmental body, said the idea had 'little merit', citing the increased vehicular traffic that would run through the city, and the availability of ports on the mainland across the harbour. Instead, the Forum has suggested a regeneration of Mumbai's docklands along the lines of cities like London or Melbourne, where once down-and-dirty industrial areas are now thriving entertainment, dining and recreational districts, attracting both locals and tourists.

Given the government's apathy towards public space – a similar battle saw 600 acres of defunct mill-lands in central Mumbai sold off to developers in the face of stiff public opposition – the Forum's suggestions seem idealistic at best. Still, the Port Trust seems occasionally willing to make concessions for the greater common good. There is news that it will allow the city to build an expressway over its land and isn't opposed to the idea of allowing the construction of ferry terminals for water transport along the eastern waterfront. If nothing else, at least Mumbaikars will finally get a chance to see an integral part of the city.

Kenneseth Eliyahoo Synagogue. *See p64.*

Road stands the 130-year-old **Bombay Gymkhana**, once a whites-only colonial enclave, now a private sports and social club for the city's elite, not open to visitors. On the other side of Azad Maidan, opposite the Gymkhana's front entrance on Mahatma Gandhi Road, is the vibrant **Fashion Street** (*see p129*), an open-air clothes market selling piles of fake Levis and reject export clothing to college students.

Chhatrapati Shivaji Terminus
Nagar Chowk. **Open** 4.30am-1am.
Map p252 H10.
If the central suburban railway line is Mumbai's main artery, then Chhatrapati Shivaji Terminus, built in 1808 and formerly known as Victoria Terminus, is its beating heart. Along with the western suburban railway line, which terminates at Churchgate (*see p63*), CST is the city's main transport hub and the busiest train station in Asia, with around three million people passing through on 1,350 suburban and intercity services every day. The building was designed by FW Stevens, who also designed the offices of the Municipal Corporation of Greater Mumbai facing the station. CST was declared a UNESCO World Heritage Site in 2004 for its blend of 'Victorian Italianate Gothic Revival architecture and Indian traditional buildings'. The ornate exterior is a jungle in stone, with a life-sized pair of lions guarding the doors to its administration offices, and peacocks, monkeys, owls, chameleons, rams, elephants and other beasts peering down on commuters from the façade. After the Taj Mahal in Agra, CST is the most photographed building in India.

Around Metro
Map p253
Mahapalika Marg is bordered by numerous Raj-era buildings and the sprawling **Azad Maidan**, or 'Freedom Ground', so named for being the site of many anti-colonial rallies during India's freedom struggle. It remains a popular site for political protests today. Past the Municipal Corporation headquarters is the **Presidency Magistrate's Court** (also known as Esplanade Court), which was completed in 1889, and the Gothic façade of the **Cama & Albless Hospital**, built in 1886. Ahead is **St Xavier's College**, established in 1891, now the city's best arts college. Around the corner of Lokmanya Tilak Marg is the **St Xavier's High School**, the courtyard of which displays a piece of a ship's propeller that landed here after an explosion in 1944.

The road ends at a square called **Dhobi Talao**, meaning 'Washerman's Pond' – once home to a community of workers who laundered the city's clothes in a lake that has long been filled in. The community now works at the Mahalaxmi **Dhobi Ghat** (*see p75*). On the southern side of Dhobi Talao is the **Metro Adlabs** cinema, a landmark art deco cinema built in the 1930s (*see p141* **Metromorphosis**). It's so famous in the city that many locals call the area around it 'Metro' instead of Dhobi Talao. The cinema has been turned into a multiplex but it retains its original splendour.

On the corner between Girgaon Road and Kalbadevi Road is the triangular **Jer Mahal**, an early 19th-century chawl – one of the first examples of the tenements that were built to house the thousands of immigrants who came to Mumbai to work in its cotton mills, with one room for each family. Millions of Mumbaikars continue to live in chawls. Although dilapidated, Jer Mahal is more attractive than most, with ornate wooden balconies and trellises. The lanes north of Dhobi Talao – Girgaon Road, Kalbadevi Road and Lokmanya Tilak Marg – are densely packed with shops, particularly sports goods and music stores. Lokmanya Tilak Road leads up to Crawford Market.

Crawford Market
Map p253 & p255
Sculptures of vegetable vendors adorn the arched entrance to the noisy and colourful **Crawford Market**, the city's first municipal market, built in 1869 to sell what it still sells today – fresh fruit, vegetables, spices, meat, imported foodstuffs and, in the back, live animals. It takes its name from its creator, Arthur Crawford, Mumbai's first municipal

Munificent Mumbaikars

Tourists, and indeed Mumbaikars, often think that all of South Mumbai's buildings of interest were made by the British. But while they may have been designed by architects from the Isles, neither the East India Company nor the Queen herself can claim credit for commissioning the historical heart of the city. A clutch of local businessmen, nearly all of them Parsis (*see p30* **Communities**), believed in the early years of Bombay's economic prosperity in giving something back to society and so funded the construction of hospitals, schools and infrastructure. Not altogether selfless, they also built wonderful mansions for themselves, some of which survive today.

The creamy-brown Fort House on DN Road, which, as trivia buffs will tell you, was the site of the first party in Mumbai at which iced drinks were served, was originally the home of **Sir Jamsetjee Jeejeebhoy**. Not one to let a good business opportunity pass him by, he made his fortune from the opium trade with China. He then used all his money for good, funding in part or full the JJ Hospital, the JJ School of Art, the JJ College of Architecture, and the establishment of the *Times of India*.

Mumbai University down the street may look like a classic example of architecture so beloved of English university towns, but much of it was built with Indian funds. **Cowasji Jehangir**, a businessman with strong political beliefs (he wanted votes to be weighted by levels of education, which meant that Parsis would have power far beyond their meagre numbers), contributed to the University's Convocation Hall, the Institute of Science, the Elphinstone College next door and the hall that is now the National Gallery of Modern Art.

The other great Mumbai University building and Fort's most iconic structure, the Rajabai Clock Tower (*see p63*), was financed by stockbroker and cotton merchant **Premchand Roychand**. He named it after his mother. Roychand made early money when he joined the Bombay Native Stockbrokers Association (later Bombay Stock Exchange) at the age of 18 as the first trader who could read and write English. In seven years, he created a near monopoly on shares, stocks and bullion. Roychand also made money on the back of the cotton booms, thanks in no small part to practices that weren't altogether legal.

The blindingly white neo-classical building, which houses Deutsche Bank, next to Sterling Cinema on Hazarimal Somani Marg, isn't British or even German. It's one of two mansions owned by industrialist **Jamsetji Nusserwanji Tata**, the founder of the vast Tata Group of Companies, which today make everything from cars to tea. An urban legend states that a tunnel runs between his two houses – the other is Esplanade House, the one with the statue of a dog at the entrance, opposite the Bombay Gym. Tata was a dazzling figure of staggering importance at the beginning of the 20th century who also built the Taj Mahal hotel (*see p44*) in Colaba and, in 1901, became the first Indian to own a car. The first Indian woman to drive a car was his sister-in-law Suzanne Tata, but she only got her hands on it in 1905, a year after he died.

Rajabai Clock Tower.

commissioner, who later resigned in a scandal over the market's financial mismanagement. It was the first building in Bombay to be lit by electricity but little else has changed, although recently the range of foods has increased as import tariffs have been slashed – California plums and Malta oranges now sit alongside Maharashtrian mangoes. There's an old sign asking visitors to only hire licensed porters but the wording is ambiguous and some porters like to suggest to foreigners that it's mandatory to hire them – it's not. Like so many of Mumbai's heritage buildings, Crawford Market is fraying at the edges, but Victorian touches survive intact, the most impressive being two elaborate fountains by J Lockwood Kipling, the father of Rudyard Kipling. Both have since been given a flamboyant multi-coloured paintjob. From 1865 to 1875, Lockwood Kipling was the dean of the **Jamsetjee Jeejeebhoy School of Art**, close to the market on Dadabhai Naoroji Road. Established in 1857, it was the city's first art school and remains one of India's premier art colleges. Rudyard Kipling was born in a bungalow on the college campus in 1865 and spent his early childhood there. Plans are afoot to convert it into a museum.

A short walk through the crowded lanes across the road from Crawford Market is the pristine white **Jama Masjid** on Sheikh Memon Street. It's an unusual mosque, built on a pond of tranquil, green water which has been incorporated into the design. Don't miss the intricate mosaic work on the exquisite marble staircase. North on Sheikh Memon Street, take a detour into the narrow passages of the **Moolji Jetha Cloth Market**, the oldest wholesale cotton market in Asia, built in 1881. Behind its high stone walls is a maze of 800 cotton shops, where shopkeepers and buyers lounge on white mattresses and pillows, negotiating the price of rolls of fabric over steaming glasses of *chai*.

Mohammed Ali Road

Map p253 & p255

A warren of narrow interconnecting lanes spread out on either side of Mohammed Ali Road, which bustles in the shadow of the JJ flyover for most of its length. The area is a commercial district dominated by the city's Muslim community, with numerous *dargahs* (tombs of saints), mosques and *burqa* shops along its length. A short distance up Mohammed Ali Road is the green-domed **Minara Masjid**, one of the city's oldest mosques, and closed to all but Muslim men. During Ramzan, or Ramadan, every year the lane next to the mosque turns into a hectic open-air barbecue in the evenings as thousands

A Beatle in Bombay

At 10am on 9 January 1968, a long-haired Englishman walked into the Universal Building on Pherozeshah Mehta Road in Fort (*see p68*) and bounded up the stairs to the third-floor HMV recording studio, then owned by Electric and Musical Industries Ltd. He was George Harrison, the Beatle, in Mumbai to record a soundtrack for an avant-garde movie called *Wonderwall*, starring Jacqueline Bisset. The recording sessions lasted five days, with contributions from some of India's most outstanding classical musicians, including *santoor* player Pandit Shiv Kumar Sharma.

Universal Building remains but the recording studio was long ago replaced by an insurance office. Derek Taylor, press agent for the Beatles for most of the 1960s, later wrote in his notes for a re-issue of the *Wonderwall* soundtrack what Harrison remembered of the Bombay recordings. 'I decided to do it as a mini-anthology of Indian music because I wanted to help turn the public on to Indian music,' Harrison told him. 'It was fantastic

really. The studio is on top of the offices but there's no sound-proofing. So if you listen closely to some of the Indian tracks on the LP you can hear taxis going by.

'Every time the office knocked off at 5.30pm we had to stop recording because you could just hear everybody stomping down the steps. They only had a big EMI mono machine. I mixed everything as we did it there, and that was nice enough because you get spoiled working on eight and 16 tracks.' *Wonderwall* premiered in London on 20 January 1969, but never got a general distribution deal. However, some of the music Harrison recorded in Mumbai made it on to the B-side of 'Lady Madonna' as 'The Inner Light'.

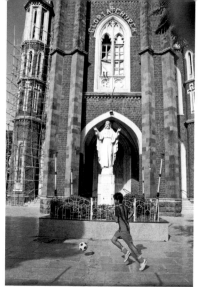

The tower and the glory: **Gloria Church**.

gather to break their fast. A narrow lane to the left of the **Jamsetjee Jeejeebhoy Hospital** and **Grant Medical College** up ahead leads to **Irani Masjid**, a beautiful mosque covered in a mosaic of blue tiles. Again, only Muslims are allowed to enter.

In the days of the Raj, Mohammed Ali Road was known, along with the Hindu-dominated Kalbadevi area nearby, as the 'Native Town'. The stark divide between the Hindu and Muslim communities is most evident at **Null Bazaar**, marked by a Hindu temple named **Gol Mandir**: to its west extends the Hindu colony, and to the east the Muslim precinct, extending to Mohammed Ali Road. Near the temple is the famous **Chor Bazaar**, which means 'Thieves' Market' (*see p129*), once a place for fencing stolen goods. Now it's a perfectly respectable place selling everything from recycled car parts to old Bollywood posters and gramophones. Wander down **Mutton Street** and you'll come across old coins and postcards, dog-eared film posters and magazines, antique porcelain and furniture, and much more. Be ready for some intense haggling.

Byculla

Byculla, at the end of Mohammed Ali Road, was uninhabitable until 1793, after the Great Breach at Mahalaxmi was sealed and a new road constructed. It became the city's first real suburb, settled by the British after venturing out from the overcrowded walled city of Fort. They built new streets, lined with spacious bungalows, and the first European social club, the Byculla Club, in 1833. The rural character of

the suburb changed dramatically with the opening of the city's cotton mills in the late 19th century. Byculla became part of Girangaon, the so-called 'village of mills', and home to a large migrant population of mill workers. As the area became increasingly congested, the British moved out to Malabar Hill (*see p75*). Nowadays, more than a few residents complain that it has returned to its old uninhabitable state: the mills are closed but Byculla is horrifically crowded and choked with traffic. Reminders of quieter times linger on in the form of the imposing **Gloria Church**, near Byculla Station, and **Magen David Synagogue**, near the police colony. Now fallen into disrepair and with a small tree growing out of its clock tower, the synagogue was built in 1861 by the Sassoon family – a philanthropic business family from Baghdad – for the large Jewish community that once lived here. A little ahead in a large compound, hidden behind a tall stone wall, is the **Christ Church**, the city's second Anglican church (after St Thomas' Cathedral at Churchgate), built in 1833.

Past Shepherd Road, the Sir Jamshetji Jeejeebhoy Road splits at a Y-shaped flyover. Stuck below the forking roads is the **Khada Parsi**, or the 'Standing Parsi', a bronze statue of the Parsi businessman and philanthropist, Sir Cursetji Maneckji (1863-1943), mounted on a 15-foot plinth. The right-hand road leads to the **Bhau Daji Lad Museum** (*see below*), which stands in the ground of the **Veermata Jijabai Bhonsle Udyan** (*see below*), a park and zoo.

Bhau Daji Lad Museum

Bhau Daji Lad Museum, Veermata Jijabai Bhonsale Udyan (city zoo), 91 Dr Ambedkar Road, Byculla (E) (6556-0394). Byculla station. **Taxi** *Rani Bagh.* **Open** *10am-5pm Mon, Tue, Thur-Sun.* **Admission** *Rs 100; Rs 50 under-12s; free under-5s.*
The Bhau Daji Lad Museum was built in 1872 and originally named the Victoria and Albert Museum. As its more famous counterpart did for the Empire, the museum was built to showcase Mumbai's industrial skills and craftsmanship. The building was recently restored to its original Renaissance Revival splendour with intricate iron pillars, ornate chandeliers, exquisite gold railings, and a dramatic painted ceiling. It won a UNESCO heritage award in 2005. Displays include models and maps of the city as it was in the late 19th and early 20th centuries, and 1,200 original glass negatives that include rare images of the gates of the old Fort.

Veermata Jijabai Bhonsle Udyan (Byculla Zoo)

91 Dr Ambedkar Road, Byculla (E) (2374-2162). Byculla station. **Open** *9am-5pm Thur-Tue.* **Admission** *Rs 10 adults, Rs 5 children.*
The Veermata Jijabai Bhonsle Udyan, or Byculla Zoo, has for years been a prime example of how

Sightseeing

The 'urban village' of **Gaiwadi**.

not to run a zoo: unhappy animals caged in tiny enclosures, with little or no information provided for visitors. It's locally known as Rani Bagh, meaning 'Queen's Garden', after its original name, Victoria Gardens. Formerly a 48-acre 'pleasure garden', it became a zoo in 1873. The types of animal on display has not changed much since then: lions, leopards, elephants, deer, crocodiles, tigers and hippos – although llamas and kangaroos are no longer in residence. The animal enclosures are often more depressing than educational; instead, the zoo's best features are its gardens and winding pathways, which are littered with Raj-era artefacts, like an ancient basalt elephant that the British recovered in pieces from Elephanta Island (*see p83*) and placed here. The first animal you encounter on entering is King Edward VII's horse. The statue was made in 1877 by JE Boehm, Queen Victoria's favourite sculptor, and once stood at Kala Ghoda (*see p64*).

Bhuleshwar & Kalbadevi

Map p253 & p255

It's said that the Hindu pantheon has about 330 million gods. At first glance, it seems that each one has a temple somewhere in the crowded lanes of **Bhuleshwar** and **Kalbadevi**. In fact, some locals believe that Bhuleshwar is so named because even the gods lose their way in the area's labyrinthine alleys: *bhula* means 'to forget' in Hindi, and *ishwar* means 'god'. But

actually the name just comes from the **Bhuleshwar Temple**, which was built by a wealthy fisherman by the name of Bhula. If you are ready to brave heaving crowds, get lost in the weaving lanes, evade wandering cows and leap over puddles of mud, then the area offers a wealth of colourful Hindu temples. The biggest is the **Mumbadevi Temple** (*see below*), named after the same goddess that Mumbai is named for. There's also the fuchsia-pink **Dwarkadheesh Temple**, nicknamed Monkey Temple by the British for the row of monkey statues across its façade; the **Ram Temple**, a one-stop shop for major gods, shared between Lord Ram, Ganesha, Maruti, Durga, Garuda, Vishnu, Laxmi and Hanuman; and the **Nar Narayan Temple**, where women peel peas on the temple porch under delicate carvings depicting stories from Lord Krishna's boyhood (dancing on a serpent's head, flirting with milkmaids and stealing butter). All three temples stand close together on Kalbadevi Road. Apart from the temples, Kalbadevi is also home to numerous *wadis* (urban villages) with names like Gaiwadi (cow village) and Phanaswadi (jackfruit village).

The arched green doorway to the **Bombay Panjrapole** stands at the end of the Bhuleshwar Road behind a tight maze of stalls selling flowers, incense, coconuts, puffed rice, milk and other bric-a-brac used in temple rituals. Inside the Panjrapole are dozens of cows – sacred animals for Hindus – who graciously deign to eat the grass given to them by Hindu devotees. Bombay Panjrapole is run by a 170-year-old trust which operates five similar cow sanctuaries across the city.

Mumbadevi Temple

Mumbadevi Temple, Mumbadevi Road, near Zaveri Bazaar. CST station. **Taxi** Mumbadevi Temple. **Open** 5am-noon, 4-8pm daily. **Admission** free. **Map** p255 G14.

If you should get lost searching for Mumbadevi Temple, look for long lines of flower-holding devotees snaking their way through the lanes and simply join them. Mumbadevi is the patron goddess of the Koli fisherfolk, the city's original inhabitants. The original temple stood at Azad Maidan near Nagar Chowk, but was demolished by the British along with a Roman Catholic church to make way for the city's expansion. The new temple was built in the 1830s and is one of the city's most popular. Generous devotees have provided the building with pure silver doors, while the walls teem with sculptures of vibrantly coloured gods and animals. Many temples have wishing wells, but Mumbadevi has wishing woodwork: devotees believe that the goddess will grant wishes if they embed a coin in the temple railings. The priests have recently banned the practice (it was wrecking the woodwork), but old coins still shine out from the beams.

Malabar Hill

When you have the Governor of the state of Maharashtra as your neighbour, you know you're on the top rungs of Mumbai's lengthy social ladder. The upper-crust residents of **Malabar Hill** – sitting atop a green hillock at the end of Marine Drive – literally look down on the rest of the city. Until the early 1870s, the area was a dense jungle where British officers went fox hunting. But the coming of textile mills to once-posh Byculla (*see p73*) sent the British community scrambling for a new, unsullied suburb. The stretch between Malabar Hill and Worli is still speckled with British-era bungalows, though most have been demolished and replaced with high-rise apartment blocks.

The precinct of **Walkeshwar** at Malabar Hill is lined with temples and Gujarati-style homes that were rebuilt in the 18th century after being destroyed by the Portuguese the previous century. The largest temple is **Walkeshwar Temple**, dedicated to Lord Shiva, which was rebuilt in 1715. The *shivalingam* inside is made from sand, hence the name of the temple, which means 'sand god'. The district around the temple still has the feel of an older and slower Bombay, with doors to homes left open and women in colourful saris exchanging local gossip in the streets. Nearby is the holy lake, or 'tank' of **Banganga** (*photo p65*), built sometime between the ninth and 13th centuries, and the oldest sacred Hindu site in the city. *Ban* means 'arrow' in Hindi and, according to legend, the water comes straight from the holy River Ganges some 1,000 miles away, brought forth by an arrow shot from the bow of Lord Rama. It's a place of rare serenity, with ducks gliding on the still, green waters and visitors relaxing on the worn basalt steps that lead down to them. Banganga usually becomes crowded in August, during the festival of Shravan, when Hindus come to pay their respects to deceased relatives by shaving their heads and purifying themselves in the tank.

There is also an unusual **Hindu graveyard** near the tank, notable because Hindus usually cremate their dead. But the Goswami community that lives here follows their own unique, centuries-old tradition of burying their dead in a sitting position. Men's graves are marked with a *shivalingam*, while the graves of women are marked with a footprint.

While most of Malabar Hill's greenery has been supplanted by concrete jungle, it still boasts one of the city's largest parks: **Kamala Nehru Park**, which provides a panoramic view of Marine Drive. Opposite the park are the **Hanging Gardens** (*see p139*), another spectacular viewpoint.

Mahalaxmi

Mahalaxmi, between Malabar Hill and Worli, takes its name from the **Mahalaxmi Temple** that stands here. It's an attractive temple, with bright exterior murals and carved wooden lintels. According to local folklore, Laxmi, the Hindu goddess of wealth, appeared in a dream to an engineer working on an ambitious land reclamation project to join the islands of Bombay and Worli in 1784. Laxmi revealed to him that an idol of her lay at the bottom of Worli Creek, which he recovered and later installed in a temple built on the reclaimed land. Close by is the spectacular **Haji Ali Dargah** (*see p34, photo p68*), a beautiful shrine of white, windswept domes and minarets built on a tiny island off Worli Seaface, to a Muslim saint named Haji Ali. The causeway that connects the island to the mainland is lined with beggars and vendors selling toys and religious images.

Mahalaxmi is often referred to as the city's lungs, thanks to the greenery provided by the 64-acre **Mahalaxmi Racecourse** (*see p163*), and the elite **Willingdon Sports Club**, which boasts Mumbai's oldest golf course. Both stand on either side of KK Marg, otherwise known as Racecourse Road. Entry to the uppity club, established in 1917, is restricted to members only, but the racecourse opens its 2,600-yard track to the public from November to May and is a popular walking spot. We recommend a quick visit to the **Mahalaxmi Dhobi Ghat**, on the left from the Mahalaxmi railway station exit, where over 200 *dhobis*, or laundrymen, wash clothes collected from local households in a maze of concrete wash pens. The *dhobis* then thrash the clothes on flogging stones, toss them into huge vats of boiling starch and hang them out to dry on long, criss-crossing clotheslines. It's become a popular tourist attraction for foreign visitors, with a few vendors now selling trinkets and postcards on the bridge by the station. Locals are, however, mystified as to why foreigners should take so much interest in what they consider an open-air laundromat.

Charming **Khotachiwadi**. See p77.

Marine Drive & Chowpatty

Map p251-p255

Ask the average Mumbaikar where Netaji
Subhash Chandra Bose Road is and he'll
probably give you directions to Thane.
Despite the change of name, Mumbai's most famous
boulevard is still known as **Marine Drive**
– a two-mile, palm-fringed arc sweeping along
the western bay from the business district
of Nariman Point to the wealthy enclave of
Malabar Hill. For most Indians, Marine Drive
is an iconic shorthand for the city of Mumbai,
made famous by appearances in numerous
Bollywood films. The other unofficial name is
the 'Queen's Necklace', coined by the British to
describe the illuminated curve of the bayfront
road at night. The seafront has a broad
promenade that's a favourite walking and
jogging spot, popular with young couples
looking for romance, anonymity and beautiful
sunsets. Marine Drive is lined with art deco
buildings built in the 1920s and '30s, most of
which are now in need of renovation. Still, this
is Mumbai's most exclusive address, and home
to some of the city's wealthiest residents. At
the southern end stands the luxury **Oberoi**
hotel (*see p51*). Fabulous views of the bay and
Marine Drive can be enjoyed over cocktails
at the elegant **Dome** bar on the roof of the
InterContinental Marine Drive hotel (*see
p113*). The road extends past the lacklustre
Taraporevala Aquarium and a line of
gymkhanas that host opulent weddings
during the winter season.

At the northern end of the promenade is
the popular **Girgaum Chowpatty** (*chowpatty*
means 'beach' in Marathi), a broad, curved
beach where spectacular idols of the elephant-
headed god Ganesha are immersed in the sea
during the festival of Ganesh Chaturthi (*see
p136*). Sunbathing and bikinis are out of place
here, and don't bother going for a swim – the
water is horribly polluted. Families and couples
come to Girgaum Chowpatty for a stroll on
the sands, for a stiff working-over by itinerant
head masseurs (*see p151*), and for the spicy
snacks sold at the lines of stalls.

From Chowpatty, P Ramabai Marg runs
north past Wilson College to **Mani Bhavan**
(*see p77*), once the Bombay home of Mahatma
Gandhi, now a museum dedicated to his life.
Nearby, at the western end of Laburnum Road
is **August Kranti Maidan** (also known as
Gowalia Tank) where Gandhi launched the
Quit India movement on 8 August, 1942, a mass
movement that spread across India and brought
British rule to an end five years later (*see p17*).

A little further ahead, past Chowpatty,
Babulnath Marg leads to **Babulnath Temple**
(*see p34*), dedicated to Lord Shiva and one of
the city's holiest Hindu sites. The steps leading
up to it are lined with traditional Gujarati
houses for priests and temple employees.
A short distance away on Hughes Road is
the attractive **Khareghat Colony**, a Parsi
housing complex. Behind the colony, higher up
the hill, are the **Towers of Silence** – sprawling
gardens that house a Parsi funeral site, where
bodies are left to be devoured by vultures as per

Chowpatty.

tradition. Rudyard Kipling, who spent his early childhood in Mumbai, once described finding severed human fingers near his house at the JJ School of Art (*see p71*); his mother believed they had been dropped by careless vultures returning from the Towers of Silence. Recently, the numbers of vultures has dramatically declined, and the traditional practice is under threat, but conservative members of the Parsi community refuse to consider any other means of disposing of their dead. The Towers are off-limits to non-Parsis, although visitors are allowed into the attractive gardens around it.

Mani Bhavan

19 Laburnum Road, off Ramabai Marg, Gamdevi (2380-5864/www.gandhi-manibhavan.org). **Open** 9.30am-5.30pm daily. **Admission** free.
Mani Bhavan was the home of the Mahatma (meaning 'Great Soul'), Mohandas Karamchand Gandhi, from 1917 to 1934, and the base for his civil disobedience movement that helped topple the British Empire in India. The museum contains many of his photographs, personal belongings and over 50,000 books and documents, including copies of his letters to figures such as Franklin D Roosevelt, Winston Churchill and Adolf Hitler. It also has a series of charming tableaux telling the story of Gandhi's life through clay models.

Opera House

Map p254

At the junction of Raja Ram Mohan Roy Road and Girgaum Road, the tranquil enclave of **Khotachiwadi** (*photo p75*) provides a snapshot of what much of Mumbai looked like before the coming of concrete. Once inhabited mainly by the East Indian community (*see p30*), it's a network of narrow, meandering lanes lined with pretty Portuguese-style bungalows with wooden porches, staircases, and balconies. The inhabitants have held out against intense pressure from local builders to sell up, instead restoring much of this neighbourhood's original charm.

The area around the junction of Girgaon Road and Sardar Vallabhbhai Patel Road is known as Opera House, after the once-magnificent **Royal Opera House** that stands on the crossroads. Built in 1925, the impressive frontage features neo-classical columns and elaborate sculpture-work of dancing figures playing musical instruments. The Opera House's timing was terrible though – film was taking off and cinema became the city's great passion. It closed down to reopen as a cinema hall in the late 1930s, and ran for the next 60 years before shutting down in the 1990s. Now closed to the public, it has become dilapidated, with plants growing out of its crumbling stonework.

The dilapidated **Royal Opera House**.

Mani Bhavan – Gandhi's former home.

Sightseeing

The Suburbs

Head north to see how Mumbaikers really live.

Sightseeing

The Mumbai suburbs, which officially start in Bandra (although we have included the mid-town neighbourhood of Dadar in this section) were once farmland and forests, punctuated every now and then by villages or clusters of bungalows. No more. Today, the western understanding of the word suburb has no place in Mumbai. There are no lawns and backyards, nor little semi-detached houses set in cul de sacs. In Mumbai, the suburbs are merely an extension of the city – just further away, and much uglier, because the buildings went up in an architectural era less interested in form than function. Yet, this is where most of Mumbai lives, and parts of it offer a hipper, younger, more chilled-out vibe than the south. Most notable among these is Bandra, home to Bollywood stars, loads of bars and restaurants, hidden villages (*see p82* **Village life**) and young professionals with money to burn. Also worth the trek are Goregaon and Borivali for their acres of greenery.

Dadar

Dadar station is a 25-minute train ride north from both Churchgate Terminus and Chhatrapati Shivaji Terminus. It was once an area for rice farming and became one of the first suburbs to be developed under the City Improvement Trust set up by the British after the city's bubonic plague outbreak and subsequent famine of the late 19th century. It's now a crowded and hectic heartland for the city's Maharashtrian community and site of the headquarters of the Shiv Sena, a right wing nativist political party. If you go by train, you'll find a thriving and chaotic produce market as soon as you step out of the station on the west. But Dadar's greatest charm, a short taxi ride from the station, is **Shivaji Park**, a seven-acre expanse of lawns that has been the training ground for some of India's greatest cricketers, including Sachin Tendulkar. It was created in 1925 by the British who, unusually for them, named it after the 17th-century Maratha warrior-king Chhatrapati Shivaji, a hero to the Maharashtrian people (*see p15* **Who is Shivaji, anyway?**). The park became an important venue for political rallies in the Indian freedom struggle and, after 1947, a focal point for the Samyukta Maharashtra movement, which sought and finally won the creation of Maharashtra state. The park still plays host to scores of overlapping cricket games as well as giant rallies for the Shiv Sena and other political parties. Across from the park, off Swatantrya Veer Savarkar Marg, is the **Mayor's Bungalow**, an attractive colonial home closed to visitors. The mayor holds a

Dadar Market.

Bandra Fort at Land's End.

Kanheri Caves, Borivali. *See p82.*

merely decorative post in Mumbai and several mayors have complained about the poor state of the bungalow's interior; so much so that one even threatened to move into the zoo at Byculla.

Bandra

Once a sleepy collection of mostly Roman Catholic hamlets (*see p82* **Village life**) dismissed as parochial by the sophisticates who lived in the city to its south, Bandra has recently morphed into Mumbai's hottest area. Flat prices have skyrocketed from around Rs 5,000 per square foot ten years ago to current highs of around Rs 18,000, and rural charm has been displaced by urban cool. A large part of Bandra's success is down to its location: it occupies a sweet spot between the south of the city and the new business districts in the north, with the sprawling business hub of the Bandra-Kurla complex on its doorstep. There's something here for everyone: a tradition of communal tolerance that draws the Muslim community; the gravitational pull of movie-star glamour for hipsters, models and wannabe actors; and a diversity of restaurants, smart bars and nightclubs for young well-paid professionals. In a choking city, what once made it parochial is now part of its charm: tree-lined roads and public spaces like Jogger's Park, Land's End and the Carter Road Promenade.

But Bandra has been so successful that its appeal is beginning to eat itself; the new landscape of glass and aluminium-clad towers has little to do with the balconies and verandas of the old Bandra. Traffic and pollution levels are spiralling, with Bandra now claiming some of the worst air quality in the city. However, Bandrawallahs take some comfort from their tradition of civic pride – a rarity in Mumbai. Determined citizens greatly enhanced the suburb's charms with the restoration of Land's End, a small peninsula leading to the **Bandra Fort**. Named Castella de Aguada by the Portuguese, who built the fort in 1640, it was equipped with cannons to protect shipping routes and supplied fresh water from a nearby spring to trading vessels on their way to Goa or Vasai. Today, despite the two gigantic hotels nearby, the Taj Land's End (*see p51*) and now-defunct SeaRock, the fort is a beautiful spot to take in the sunset. The area behind it has been landscaped with palm trees and an attractive stone amphitheatre. Not far away, **Carter Road** was similarly restored with a promenade along the seafront. Local kids tend to race up and down the stretch and the other side of the street is a popular spot for teenagers to hang around, smoke pot and generally watch the world go by. At the end of Carter Road is Road No. 5, better known as just 'Off Carter Road' – a lively strip of shops and restaurants with tables out on the street.

Local heroes

Whether it's floods, riots or bombs, Mumbaikars have a single litmus test for the state of their city: 'Are the trains working?' On 11 July 2006, when bombs exploded in the first-class compartments of seven trains along the Western Line during the evening rush hour, Mumbai ground to a halt – but only for a few hours. Services were up and running again the same night.

Mumbaikars spend large chunks of their lives on commuter trains, referred to as 'locals'. They talk of 'train friends', regular co-commuters with whom they sing songs, exchange life stories and who, most importantly, will 'catch place' for them – reserve them a seat, hopefully in the sweet spots. In the morning, the best seats are on the west side, facing south for the breeze; in the evening, it's the other way round.

Local trains have two classes: the first class has padded seats; the second class has wooden benches. They are almost equally crowded, but those who can afford it will shell out up to ten times the price of a second-class ticket for the unwritten rules: three to a bench in first, four to a bench in second; four at the door in first, six or seven in second.

The well-used ladies-only compartment is filled with women cleaning vegetables and rehashing old arguments about the rival merits of tailors. The 'general compartment' is mainly used by men, and where *bhajans* (religious songs) are sung, *prasad* ('blessed' food) is doled out and card games are played.

The compartments are scoured by vendors hawking everything from peanuts to fake moustaches to fish-shaped torches. Urchins run through with brushes, sweeping the dirt on to the tracks before asking for tips.

The crush of train compartments during rush hours, between 9 and 11am and again between 6 and 9pm, defies description. Sardines have it easy. Around ten per cent of passengers during these hours aren't even in the train – you'll see them hanging out of the sides, courting death by trackside pole. Some young men even climb on to the roof, partly because it's too crowded, partly out of sheer bravado. Inside, passengers have to start pushing their way to the door one stop before their station – any later and they'll never make it out in time. The rest of the day, though, there isn't a quicker, more efficient way of getting around Mumbai. But travel during peak hours and you'll have bragging rights for life.

Bandra has numerous churches, the most important of which is the **Basilica of Mount Mary** (*see p35*), on the hill along Mount Mary Road. A popular church, it brings thousands of devotees from across the city during the Mount Mary Fair in September. The original chapel was built in 1640 and destroyed in a Maratha raid in 1738. The life-sized statue of the Virgin Mary was rescued from the sea by fishermen and housed in the attractive Portuguese-style **St Andrew's Church** on Hill Road while a new church was being built. It was returned in 1761. Until around 30 years ago, this was Bandra's highest point, visible from Mahim beach. Also on Hill Road, **St Peter's Church** has some interesting frescoes and stained glass.

Many of the crosses that dot Bandra's streets are 'plague crosses', built around the turn of the 20th century as bubonic plague swept across the city, killing hundreds of thousands. Bandra residents built crosses near their homes, both to seek protection from the pestilence and later in gratitude for their survival. Crosses were also built to ward off evil spirits and simply to mark property boundaries. Among Bandra's oldest streetside crosses is the wooden one that stands at the junction of Bazaar Road, Chapel Road and Waroda Road, which dates back to 1698. Chapel Road eventually leads to **Bandra Reclamation**, which has a charming promenade that runs along the Mahim Creek and has a view of the city skyline.

Goregaon

Goregaon was a pretty tree-lined village until as late as the 1970s, before being turned into yet another noxious concrete mess. Respite remains, though, in the sprawling greenery of the **Aarey Milk Colony**, a dairy farming area with jungle-crested hills. It takes around 15 minutes to get here by autorickshaw from Goregaon Station, which is about an hour's ride on the train from Churchgate. The Aarey Garden Restaurant (2684-8119; open 11am-11.30pm), next to the central dairy, is popular with locals for alfresco dining amid the greenery and for its BYOB policy. The milk colony is also home to Goregaon **Film City**, on the Film City Road; a major studio built in 1978 on what was rural scrubland. Officially no visitors are allowed in, but the gate watchmen may be persuaded with a big smile and a little largesse. You could also get inside by being cast as an extra in a Bollywood movie (*see p37* **You too can be a star**). Much like its Hollywood equivalents, Film City tends to be a little surreal, with leftovers from sets scattered about, like the staircase that leads nowhere, along with a Hindu temple and helipad.

Borivali

There's only one reason to come this far north: the **Sanjay Gandhi National Park** (Borivali, 2886-0389, open 7.30am-6.30pm Tue-Sun, admission Rs 20), one of Asia's busiest national parks, with around two million visitors a year. Mumbaikars come here to escape the city, get lost in the greenery with lovers, play cricket, eat vast picnics and just cool off – the temperature here is about four degrees cooler than the city's average. And at 40 square miles, it won't be crowded. The nearest station is Borivali, about an hour and 15 minutes on the train from Churchgate. From there, it's around Rs 15 in an autorickshaw to the main entrance. To the west lie the neighbourhoods of Goregaon, Malad, Kandivali, Borivali and Dahisar; and Bhand up and Mulund to the east. In recent years, the park has been encroached by numerous slum dwellings, which is not only bad for the park but also for the slum dwellers – leopards have been known to mistake children for prey.

The park's two lakes – Vihar and Tulsi – supply Mumbai with water. The park's forest is a mix of deciduous and semi-evergreen and contains a great diversity of wildlife, including tigers, leopards, lions, pythons, cobras, spotted deer, black-naped hares, barking deer, porcupines and around 5,000 different kinds of insects. There are also crocodiles in Tulsi Lake. Swimming is not encouraged. The park is also home to 150 species of butterfly and the world's largest moth, the Atlas, which was discovered here. There is a Tiger and Lion safari bus tour (*see p82*) which departs regularly from the orientation centre around half a mile from the main entrance.

Village life

Two generations ago, Bandra was made up of villages, expansive bungalows, farmland and the occasional two-storey apartment 'tower'. As late as 1960, large parts of it were wooded, and even in the '70s school-children could knock on the front doors of unknown houses and come out with cake and biscuits. Today it's a concrete jungle, but there are still pockets where the village feel has survived.

Start at one of Bandra's oldest neighbourhoods, the area surrounding **Mount Mary Church** (*see p35*). Walk through the compound, to the Mount Mary steps at the back and down to the foot of the hill. From there, go down Chapel Road to **Ranwar Village**, where local-style Christian family cottages and new high-rises stand around the village square. The areas around Waroda Road and Veronica Road are filled with little lanes that are a joy to explore, with old homes teetering on either side.

Further north, past the cluster of restaurants, gyms and boutiques, is **Pali Village**, which takes its name from the Portuguese port of Pallem. Here, the labyrinth of villas is punctuated by modest apartment buildings, often housing different generations of the same family. It's reached via the lane behind Toto's Garage Pub (*see p115*).

Running parallel to the Carter Road seafront is Sherly Rajan Road, which gets its name from the adjacent villages of **Sherli** and **Rajan**. While educational complexes and swanky buildings now dominate the area, local communities continue to survive. The street still retains its quiet suburban charm thanks to its out-of-the-way location and the fact that it's an inconvenient thoroughfare.

At the northern end of Carter Road is **Chuim**, near the Koli settlements at Khar Danda (and technically out of Bandra's postcode). Perhaps the quietest of the villages, Chuim is no more than a one-lane village, with alleyways branching out in labyrinthine patterns from the main street.

Ranwar Village.

Also in the park are the **Kanheri Caves**, (*photo p79*), a total of 109 caves in which remarkable halls have been carved out of the rock and ornate statues and images of Buddha and the Boddhisattvas sculpted from the walls. The caves are located about 450 yards above sea level and command a panoramic view of the forest surroundings and the Arabian Sea in the distance. They date back to the Mauryan and Kushan Empires of the first century BC, although the carving continued well into the ninth century AD. Outside Cave No.3 are two 60-foot statues of Buddha that date back to the sixth century AD. The history of the caves is incomplete, but as there were also two ports nearby at Kalyan and Sopara, the area around must have been an important Buddhist settlement. Inscriptions found in the caves refer to the area as Krishnagiri, Krishnasila, Kanhasila or Kanhagiri. Their current name appears to have been derived from the Sanskrit word *krishnagiri*, which means 'black mountain'. Archaeologists believe that the caves began to be permanent residences for Buddhist monks in the first century AD.

Tiger & Lion Safari
Orientation centre (2886-0362). **Tickets** Rs 30 for a 10 min tour. **Tours** Every 20 mins during park hours.

A rickety green forest department bus takes visitors into two fenced compounds of tigers and lions. The lions tend to look a little bored (or might be asleep), but they do occasionally leap into action, with mornings being the best time to see some activity. Some years ago, before grated windows were put on the buses, one visitor opened a window and cheekily waved the edge of her sari at them; one of the lions duly jumped on to the roof and ripped off her scalp.

Day Trips

Far from the madding crowd.

Elephanta Island

Around the seventh century AD, a prince of
the Chalukya dynasty – a political dynasty that
ruled large parts of the western and southern
regions of India – is said to have constructed
the breathtaking cave temples at Gharapuri,
a small island about seven miles north-east
of the Gateway of India now called Elephanta
(admission Rs 250 foreigners; Rs 10 Indians,
closed Mon). A trip there and back takes at least
four hours, but it's more than worth it. There's
even a bar near the caves if you get thirsty.

Indian temples had always been built by
erecting base pillars and then laying plinths on
top to support the roof, but in Maharashtra the
brittle volcanic stone plinths kept breaking. At
Gharapuri, the ancients decided that the only
way to get round the problem was to find a
large chunk of stone and chisel away anything
that didn't look like a temple.

When the island was rediscovered (and
renamed) in the 16th century by the Portuguese,
they saw an elephant waiting for them as they
approached the island. It turned out to be made
of basalt, the first clue that the island was home
to something remarkable. Intrigued, they
decided to take it home with them, but ended
up dropping it into the sea. Many years later the
British recovered it and carried it back to the
mainland, where it now sits at the Byculla Zoo,
or Veermata Jijabai Bhonsle Udyan; *see p73*.

The triple-bayed entrance to the cave
doesn't look that impressive but, once inside,
everyone from Andre Malraux to Auguste
Rodin has been struck dumb by the sheer
spectacle of Sadashiva ('Eternal Shiva'), a
full-relief bust about 20 feet high, showing
three faces of Lord Shiva.

The central image is one of serene
contemplation; the left half-face is the face
of Aghora Bhairava, the vengeful, angry
Shiva; the right one is Uma, or Vamadeva,
the feminine side of this complex god. Some
have suggested that a fourth face remains
buried in the rock.

The temple sprawls across about 60,000sq
ft, with ornate pillars and exquisitely carved
sculptures, many of which have been badly
damaged. Demonstrating the kind of barbarism
that they repeated in Goa, the Portuguese used
the caves as a firing range. They must have
been not only blind to beauty but hard of hearing
too; the echoes would have been deafening. It's
possible to wander up to the top of the natural
rock mass to see one of the old cannons. There
are also a couple of villages on the island but
nothing of much interest to visitors. A word
of warning: don't be tempted to eat anywhere
near the monkeys who populate the island;
they're a rapacious bunch and have been known
to pounce aggressively on visitors with food.
Some locals will encourage you to take
photographs of them; they will expect a tip.

Elephanta Caves.

Vasai Fort.

Matheran.

Getting there

Boats to Elephanta depart every half-hour from the Gateway of India from 9am until 2.30pm and cost Rs 80-Rs 120. The journey takes about an hour. The last ferry leaves Elephanta for the Gateway around 5pm. There's nowhere to stay overnight on the island, so don't miss it.

Matheran

Matheran is a hill station 68 miles from Mumbai – a small township established in the Sahyadri Hills by British colonists to escape the city's humid summers. It's still a favourite day and weekend getaway for Mumbaikars for precisely the same reason. Once a quiet, wooded place filled with bungalows, these days it's a haven for commercial tourism, filled with restaurants, snack shops and ice-cream parlours. But much of its charm has been preserved, due partly to its traditional community of cobblers, who still produce leather shoes, but largely thanks to a wise decision to ban motor vehicles from its broad streets; horses are a common way of getting around here, and you'll see them tied up Wild West-style outside restaurants. The British also built a narrow-gauge train from Neral – the so-called toy train – that curved its way up and down the hill until it was wiped out by terrible flooding in July 2005.

The track has since been repaired (*see below*). The main thing to do in Matheran is to go walking into the woods along its red laterite paths and take in the spectacular views of forested hills and valleys from viewpoints like Panorama Point, Echo Point and Monkey Point – all of which live up to their names. There's a Rs 25 fee to enter the hill station.

Getting there

The nearest station is Neral, 55 miles from Chhatrapati Shivaji Terminus and 13 miles from Matheran. Return tickets cost Rs 26 for second class and Rs 300 for first class. The old narrow-gauge train up is a fun way to go and costs Rs 25. You can also hike it or take a taxi. If you opt for the latter, negotiate the price – around Rs 50 per head is reasonable.

Vasai Fort

At its peak in the 17th century, Vasai was known as Bassein, a jewel in the Portuguese crown. It boasted impressive public buildings, private mansions, soaring churches and an imposing seafacing fort. In 1557 it was the birthplace of India's only Catholic saint, Gonsalo Garcia, who sailed to Japan as a missionary. He was later accused of plotting to overthrow the Emperor Taiko-sama and crucified on a hill in Nagasaki. The Vatican declared him a saint in 1862. Today, the walls of Bassein Fort still stand, sprawled across 110 acres, although none of the buildings are completely intact. It's a calm, romantic spot of collapsing arches and decrepit belfries, half-overrun with forest. Still standing is the seaward entrance, the Porto da Mar, an iron-clad gateway that resolutely thwarted attackers over the years. Today it's scrawled with boasts of other conquests, like 'Sunil love Sunita'. Nearby, there's a shop with snacks and drinks.

Getting there

Trains to Vasai leave from Churchgate with Virar as their final destination. The first train leaves at 4.15am and takes an hour and a half to reach Vasai Road, the fifth stop after Borivali. The return fare is Rs 26 for second class, or Rs 300 for first class. The fort is 30 minutes from the station by rickshaw and costs around Rs 30-Rs 35. The last train from Vasai Road leaves for Churchgate at 12.05am. By road, it's 47 miles from South Mumbai along the Mumbai-Ahmedabad highway via Borivali, taking two to three hours depending on traffic.

Wine tasting in Nashik

Sula Wine Tasting Centre
Gate No. 35/2, Govardhan, Gangapur-Savargaon Road, Nashik (0253-223-1663). **Open** 11am-9pm Mon-Thur; 11am-10pm Fri-Sun.
Located about 110 miles from Mumbai, Nashik has become Maharashtra's own Napa Valley: it's home to the vineyards of Sula Wines, one

of India's leading brands. The vineyard was set up in 1997 on 30 acres and released its first wines three years later – sauvignons and chenin blancs. Eight years later, it's expanded to 400 acres, growing shiraz, zinfandel and merlot varieties. Sula has opened a wine tasting centre and offers tours of the vineyard, taking visitors through the wine-making process. You can taste the wines (they charge Rs 100 for five tasting samples) and then drink much more of them in their impressive tasting room – an elegant 2,000sq ft wine bar, with a beautiful balcony overlooking the vineyards. They also conduct tours of the winery every hour on the hour from 11.30am to 5.30pm. It's a long way back to Mumbai – about four hours by train – but after a few glasses it'll go in a flash.

Getting there

The first train for Nashik leaves at 6.10am from Chhatrapati Shivaji Terminus – you'll have to catch this one to make it there and back in one day. Return fares for seats in the relatively comfortable AC chair car cost Rs 475. Get off at Nashik Road station and take a cab to Gangapur Road for around Rs 200-Rs 250. The last train back to CST leaves Nashik Road at 6pm. By road, Nashik is 110 miles and takes about three hours. Check the Sula website (www.sulawines. com) for detailed directions and a road map. Organised tours of the winery are available from Tulleeho (93229-16506/www.tulleeho. com) and cost Rs 1,750 including travel.

Sula's tasting room in **Nashik**.

GRAND DINING EXPERIENCE AT GRAND HYATT MUMBAI

Authentic Sichuan and signature Chinese delicacies at China House.
Grill, Martini bar & wine library at M. Truly Italian home-style cooking at Celini.
Traditional Indian food at Soma. Indian & international cuisine at Grand Café.
Eclectic range of cocktails & spirits at The Bar & China House Lounge.
A dining experience grand in style, service and attention.

FEEL THE HYATT TOUCH®

For reservations contact 6676 1234

Off Western Express Highway, Santacruz (East), Mumbai – 400 055, India
TELEPHONE +91 22 6676 1234 FACSIMILE +91 22 6676 1235 mumbai.grand.hyatt.com

Eat, Drink, Shop

Soam. *See p102*.

Restaurants & Cafés

India on a plate.

Eat, Drink, Shop

Mumbaikars tend to eat out a lot. Busy lifestyles that leave little time for cooking, matchbox-size houses that wouldn't fit in very many guests anyway, and a profusion of restaurants that serve everything from kebabs from the North West Frontier Province to *dosas* from the southern tip of the country (and now, from sushi to Californian cuisine) mean that eating out has always been an integral part of the city's culture.

Indian cuisine is as diverse as the country itself and includes some entirely separate sub-cuisines like Bengali cooking. Luckily for us, nearly all of them are available in Mumbai, thanks to the millions of economic migrants who have come to the city from across the country over the last 200 years. The newly arrived émigrés stuck together, initially sharing familiar food in community kitchens or *khanevals*, which in time opened their doors to outsiders and became the city's first real restaurants. For a description of some of the different dishes available and where to find them, *see p99* **Vast food nation**.

For decades, the finest restaurants in Mumbai were confined to the insides of five-star hotels that were out of the reach of all but the city's wealthiest diners. Today, the five-star culture persists but in recent years it has been increasingly challenged by a new breed of high-quality, stand-alone restaurants eager to grab a share of the Mumbaikar's skyrocketing disposable income. Many of these have sprung up in and around Colaba, but the biggest explosion has been in the suburb of Bandra, a 30-minute train ride north. Standards vary, but the best of the five-stars and the new stand-alones offer food that compares well with top quality restaurants the world over – sometimes at international rates.

Chinese food is now virtually an Indian cuisine, and even the simplest restaurant offers Indianised hybrids like chicken Manchurian or chop suey dosas (*see p105* **Bombay mix**). In recent years, the increasingly well-travelled Mumbaikar has begun to demand much more

> ❶ Purple numbers given in this chapter correspond to the location of each restaurant and café as marked on the street maps. See pp249-255.

variety and sophistication in foreign cooking, with more and more new restaurants serving authentic Mediterranean and East Asian food, often prepared by foreign chefs. There's a lot of experimentation going on too, with pan-Asian restaurants throwing together dishes from across the continent, often with Indian twists.

It remains to be seen how many of the glut of new restaurants (around one high-profile opening a month in 2006 and 2007) will survive, but there's no doubt that there has never been a better time to eat in this city.

DOS AND DON'TS

Mumbaikars rarely make reservations, often happy to mill around outside a restaurant until a table becomes available, but to guarantee seating and avoid wasting time, it's always best to book in advance where possible. Mumbaikars usually like to eat late; around 9pm or 10pm is the busiest period. It's easy to spot a decent restaurant – it will be packed. Food poisoning is relatively rare and hygiene is generally not

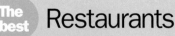

The best Restaurants

For killer kebabs
Bade Miya's (*see p89*), Kebab Korner (*see p101*) and Shalimar (*see p103*).

For fab fish
Konkan Café (*see p90*), Mahesh Lunch Home (*see p100*) and New Martin Lunch Home (*see p90*).

For curries
Delhi Darbar (*see p89*), Peshawri (*see p109*) and Kebabs and Kurries (*see p104*).

For vegetarian cuisine
Friends Union Joshi Club (*see p104*), Govinda's (*see p102*) and Swati Snacks (*see p104*).

For lazy weekend brunches
Indigo (*see p93*), Olive (*see p107*) and Samovar (*see p91*).

For regional delicacies
Jimmy Boy (*see p100*), Oh! Calcutta (*see p104*) and Rice Boat (*see p107*).

Wasabi. *See p95*.

Eat, Drink, Shop

something to worry about unless you're eating from street stalls (*see p102* **Street eats**). Most restaurants don't bother with non-smoking sections (although most expensive and five-star establishments do have them) and smoking is generally permitted throughout.

The pricier eateries are liable for taxes that are usually not included in menu prices, so be aware that your final bill may include a value-added tax of 12.5 per cent on food and 20 per cent on alcoholic drinks. This should be stated clearly on the menu, but you can't rely on that so it's better to ask. Most places serve alcohol, except in the cheaper restaurants, and we've listed where they do not.

Tipping is a standard practice, although at relatively low rates – generally between five and ten per cent. Service charges are sometimes included in the bill, so make sure you're not tipping twice. It's better to tip in cash; some establishments can't be relied upon to divide tips made by credit card to staff.

We've listed a range of meal prices for each place. However, restaurants often change their menus so these prices are only guidelines. For more on the latest restaurant openings in the city, pick up a copy of *Time Out Mumbai*.

Colaba

Indian

Bade Miya's

Tulloch Street, off Colaba Causeway, Colaba (2284-8038, 2285-1649). CST or Churchgate stations. **Open** 7pm-3am daily. **Main courses** Rs 30-Rs 70. **No credit cards**. **No alcohol**. **Map** p251 G5 ❶

Not a restaurant, but a hugely popular streetside stall just off Colaba Causeway serving up fabulous kebabs and rolls to Colaba's post-party crowd. Bade Miya's started as a single stall a decade ago, but grew with its fame; it now consists of a couple of hard-working skewer-laden grills and rows of plastic chairs and tables. Bade's has even colonised a derelict building across the road. It's not fancy, but it is delicious. Everything's good here but the top choices are the *baida rotis* (spicy mutton, chicken or beef with egg in a grilled wrap), the spicy chicken livers, the bhuna mutton and bhuna chicken. The vegetarian seekh kebab is also excellent. On Friday and Saturday nights expect lots of traffic, alcohol-fuelled patrons and a wait for tables (though you can take your kebab rolls to go).

Baghdadi

11 Tulloch Road, off Colaba Causeway, Colaba (2202-8027). CST or Churchgate stations. **Open** 7am-1am daily. **Main courses** Rs 50-Rs 80. **No credit cards**. **No alcohol**. **Map** p251 G5 ❷

Not so much a restaurant as a huge room with rows of six-seater benches and tables, Baghdadi is known locally as the 'poor man's Taj', after the Taj Mahal Hotel nearby. The portions are large, the food decent and the kitchen surprisingly clean. Even so, it's an experience best enjoyed if you leave your aesthetic sensibilities at home. The seating is a great leveller, with executives sharing tables with couriers, taxi drivers, African students and labourers. If there's space at your table you may be asked to slide a place down. Baghdadi is famous for its chicken biryani, topped with a special Baghdadi masala and buried under rice and browned onions, and the chicken masala fry, served in a sweetish red gravy. To mop it up, go for a plump, soft naan or one of their enormous rotis. Baghdadi is also one of the very few places in Mumbai where you can get a beef biryani.

Delhi Darbar

Holland House, Colaba Causeway, Colaba (2202-0235/5656). CST or Churchgate stations. **Open** 11.30am-12.30am daily. **Main courses** Rs 100-Rs 150. **Credit** AmEx, MC, V. **No alcohol**. **Map** p251 G5 ❸

An old-timer (it first opened in 1973) with a huge following, Delhi Darbar is nothing much to look at: it dispenses with atmosphere in favour of cooking fumes. Doesn't matter, though, it's the food that has been bringing diners back all these years. Darbar specialises in Punjabi and Mughlai cuisine with some truly excellent kebabs, curries and biryanis.

Healthy Bite

Tulloch Road, next to Gokul, opposite Bade Miya's, Apollo Bunder (99203-29501). CST or Churchgate stations. **Open** 4pm-1.30am daily. **Main courses** Rs 60-Rs 90. **No credit cards. No alcohol. Map** p251 G5 ④

Owner Smita Verma promises that the cuts of meat she uses are lean, and they're grilled over charcoal, so there isn't a drop of oil on them. The sauces are made with olive oil and the rumali roti wraps are made of wholewheat. In direct competition with kebab institution Bade Miya's (it's across the street), Healthy Bite's kebabs, the eclectic teriyaki chicken wrap and *pahadi aloo* along with the standards like chicken tikka and seekh kebab are tasty and won't weigh down your stomach.

Kailash Parbat Hindu Hotel

Sheela Mahal, 1st Pasta Lane, Colaba (2287-4823). CST or Churchgate stations. **Open** 11am-11pm daily. **Main courses** Rs 40-Rs 65. **No credit cards. No alcohol. Map** p250 F4 ⑤

If you're looking for mouthwatering Indian snacks like *bhel puri* and *ragda pattice* (a deep-fried potato patty in a spicy chickpea gravy), few places do a better job than Kailash Parbat, a 60-year-old Colaba institution. The split-level restaurant is always packed

Henry Tham. *See p93.*

and almost everything on the menu is worth a try. Be sure not to miss their *falooda* (a thick, creamy sweet drink), *gulab jamun* (milk powder balls in a sweet syrup) and other specialities from the Sindh province.

Konkan Café

Taj President, 90 Cuffe Parade (6665-0808). CST or Churchgate stations. **Open** 12.30-2.45pm, 7-11.45pm daily. **Main courses** Rs 800-Rs 1,000. **Credit** AmEx, DC, MC, V. **Map** p250 E3 ⑥

This is a beautifully planned and striking restaurant with a decor that mirrors that of village homes along India's Konkan coast, a region that begins in Maharashtra and extends through Goa into Karnataka. Chef Ananda Solomon is a proponent of 'slow food' – so he sticks to authentic seasonings and methods of preparation, including hand-grinding. Although the focus is definitely on seafood (including Mangalorean-style *gassi*, steamed fish in turmeric paste and Malwani shrimp curry – all fabulous), they also serve some exquisite lamb chops in East Indian masala, mustard seeds and curry leaves.

Koyla

Gulf Hotel, Arthur Bunder Road, Colaba (6636-4727). CST or Churchgate stations. **Open** 7.30-12.30pm Tue-Sun. **Main courses** Rs 200-Rs 400. **Credit** MC, V. **No alcohol. Map** p250 G4 ⑦

When the state government's slum demolition drive in 2005 ran into political flak, Koyla was torn down to defuse accusations that only illegal structures belonging to the city's poorest were being targeted. Like many of the slums, it was back in business shortly after. By far Koyla's best feature is its location – on the roof of a hotel overlooking the harbour and the rooftops of Colaba, with its tables laid out under white *shamianas* (canopies). A big hit with college kids, Koyla serves up some decent North-West Frontier dishes cooked over charcoal. There's no alcohol; flavoured tobacco is the substance of choice here, smoked in ornate hookahs.

Masala Kraft

Taj Mahal Palace & Tower, Apollo Bunder, Colaba (6665-3366). CST or Churchgate stations. **Open** 12.30-2.45pm, 7-11.45pm daily. **Main courses** Rs 450-Rs 1,350. **Credit** AmEx, DC, MC, V. **Map** p251 G5 ⑧

Contemporary Indian cuisine delivered with a Western twist, like cooking in olive oil – unheard of in traditional Indian cooking. It works fabulously: try the tandoori pink salmon dipped in sugarcane vinegar, or the paneer in a white sauce (another Western import) with black peppers. The combination is reflected in the decor – imposing dark wooden pillars conjure up a regal Indian vibe, contrasted with light pine furniture.

New Martin Lunch Home

Glamour House, Strand Cinema Road, Colaba, (2202-9606). CST or Churchgate stations. **Taxi** Strand Cinema. **Open** 11.30am-3pm, 6.30-10pm Mon-Sat. **Main courses** Rs 35-Rs 60. **No credit cards. No alcohol. Map** p250 F4 ⑨

Café culture

In Mumbai's unpretentious Irani cafés, time has stood still. Original 1940s furniture and weighing scales stand in the same positions they did 60 years ago, along with some of the same customers – wizened old Parsi gentlemen sipping on cups of tea and nibbling mawa cakes and buttered buns under slow-spinning fans. Mumbai's first Irani cafés were established in the late 19th and early 20th centuries by Zoroastrian Iranian émigrés, catering to industrial workers who didn't have kitchens in their chawls. The mood was tranquil and the food cheap and wholesome, if nothing close to Iranian cuisine (except **Britannia**, *pictured*, which still does a berry *pulao*). After the Shah returned to power in 1953 and the Iranian economy boomed, many sold up and went home; other cafés have since morphed into bars or fast-food outlets like the McDonald's opposite Chhatrapati Shivaji Terminus. But a few survive.

The area surrounding Metro cinema near Marine Lines station has a few famous Irani restaurants like Sassanian Boulangerie and **Kyani & Co**, famous not for any Iranian food but for their marble-topped tables, *mava* cakes, watermelon juice and 1940s charm. Kyani's upper level 'family section' is a favourite with young couples from nearby St Xavier's College. Lovers can switch on the wrought-iron table fans, huddle together and sip endless cups of tea.

Britannia
Sprott Road, opposite New Custom House, Ballard Estate (2261-5264). CST station. **Open** 11.30am-4pm Mon-Sat. **No credit cards. No alcohol.** Map p252 H8 ㉛
For review, *see p100*.

Café Brabourne
Jagannath Shankar Seth Road, Dhobi Talao (2205-6988). CST or Marine Lines stations. **Open** 6.30am-10.30pm daily. **No credit cards.** Map p253 F11 ㊲

Café Military
Ali Chambers, Meadows Street, Fort (2265-4181). Churchgate station. **Open** 8am-9pm daily. **No credit cards.** Map p251/p252 G7 ㊳

Kyani & Co
Jer Mahal Estate, near Metro Adlabs Cinema, Dhobi Talao (2201-1492). CST or Marine Lines stations. **Open** 6.20am-9pm daily. **No credit cards. No alcohol.** Map p253 F11 ㊴

Delicious Goan food, served simply – don't expect more from Martin's than five tables with benches and tube-lighting. But it's clean and the food is fresh and tasty. Most of the dishes are subtly different shades of red, yet the masalas are quite different. The top order here is the Goan sausage: sour, spicy and swimming in tasty fat which you can mop up with *pao* (bread). There's also great vindaloo, prawn curry, and the classic fried fish curry and rice.

Samovar
Jehangir Art Gallery, MG Road, Kala Ghoda (2284-8000). CST or Churchgate stations. **Open** 11am-7pm daily. **Main courses** Rs 50-Rs 150. **No credit cards.** Map p251 G6 ㉑
A sweet little restaurant within Jehangir Art Gallery, Samovar is popular with artists, students and long-time loyalists. It's a pleasant place to while away the afternoon drinking beer, eating prawn curry and rice, and staring at the museum garden.

International

All Stir Fry
Gordon House Hotel, 5 Battery Street, Apollo Bunder, Colaba (2287-1122). CST or Churchgate stations. **Open** noon-3pm, 7pm-midnight daily. **Main courses** Rs 400. **Credit** AmEx, MC, V. Map p251 G5 ㉒
The selling point of this trendy restaurant has always been its all-you-can-eat wok that allows patrons to custom-make stir fries to their tastes. Head to the noodle bar and fill your bowl with raw materials: noodles, vegetables and seafood/meats. Then proceed to the chefs, who will do the rest with your preference of sauces and condiments. *Photo p97.*

Basilico
Sentinel House, Arthur Bunder Road, Colaba (6634-5670). CST or Churchgate stations. **Open** 7.30am-1am daily. **Main courses** Rs 350-Rs 500. **Credit** MC, V. **No alcohol.** Map p250 G4 ㉓

Eat, Drink, Shop

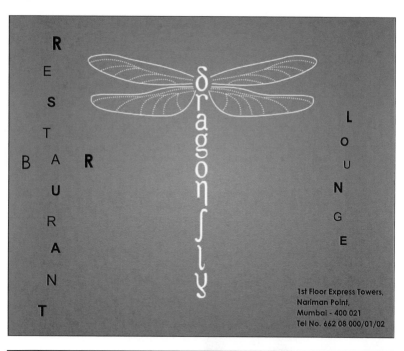

dragonfly

RESTAURANT BAR R

LOUNGE

1st Floor Express Towers,
Nariman Point,
Mumbai - 400 021
Tel No. 662 08 000/01/02

carpaccio

pekingduck

pomelosalad

Dimsum

vongwong

1st Floor, Express Towers, Nariman Point, Mumbai-400 021. Contact No. 022 2875633/34/35

This stylish wood-and-glass eaterie just off Colaba Causeway specialises in European cuisine with a Mediterranean slant, with some excellent sandwiches and mains, and some truly delightful coolers. There's also a deli section with fresh bread, pastries, and imported cheeses.

Busaba

4 Mandlik Road, off Colaba Causeway (2204-3769). CST or Churchgate stations. **Open** noon-3pm, 7pm-1am daily. **Credit** AmEx, MC, V. **Main courses** Rs 500. **Map** p251 G5

Busaba serves memorable pan-Asian cuisine while retaining a hip vibe. If it's dinner you're here for, skip upstairs to the peaceful dining room or the romantic enclosed terrace. Burmese *khao suey*, Korean *bipimbap* and *bulgogi*, Tibetan *momos* and Thai lime-chilly fish are favourites. The melting chocolate fondant with *crème anglais* is exceptionally smooth and succeeds in its attempt to impress.

Café Churchill

103B East West Court Building, opposite Cusrow Baug, Colaba Causeway (2284-4689). **Open** 10.30am-12.30am. **Main courses** Rs 300. **No credit cards. No alcohol. Map** p250 G4

An old favourite on Colaba Causeway, Churchill's is a small, friendly eaterie usually heaving with diners at both lunch and dinner, with a queue waiting outside. It specialises in 'Continental' cooking with a menu heavy on pasta dishes, decently done, and great burgers. The desserts cabinet is a must-visit, filled with terrific cheesecakes, gateaux and mousses. Tables are packed in tight and elbow room is at a premium, but food and atmosphere are abundant.

Golden Dragon

Taj Mahal Palace & Tower, Apollo Bunder, Colaba (6665-3366). Churchgate station. **Open** 12.30-2.45pm, 7-11.45pm daily. **Main courses** Rs 600-Rs 800. **Credit** AmEx, DC, MC, V. **Map** p251 G5

The provenance of Golden Dragon's food roams widely, even ocean-hopping to Singapore, but the majority of the dishes originate in China's Sichuan province. Here the Indianisation effect is the reverse of the usual – Sichuan is too spicy even for Indians, so the chillies have been taken out. Their master chef is Shi Xi Lin, a native of Beijing who was awarded the title of 'best Sichuan chef in China' in 1994. The hot and sour soup is a treat.

Henry Tham

Dhanraj Mahal, Apollo Bunder, near Regal Cinema (2284-8214). CST or Churchgate stations. **Open** 12.30-3.30pm, 7pm-midnight daily. **Main courses** Rs 450-Rs 1,000. **Credit** AmEx, MC, V. **Map** p251 G5

This Colaba restaurant with a downstairs lounge bar is contemporary in grand fashion, with minimalist decor, subtle lighting and nine-foot chairs. But the real beauty is in the food presentation, like the lightly fried tofu soy sauce served in an olive green, almond-shaped dish that resembles the pupil of an eye. It's good value too: the signature vegetarian and non-vegetarian set meals (Rs 550 and 825) offer five generous courses. This is contemporary

Peshawri. *See p109.*

Chinese cooking at its best. The showstopper is the fresh fruit platter, called 'One Tree Hill': slivers of melon and grapes, plus a twig and dry ice, arranged as a miniature enchanted forest. *Photo p90.*

Indigo

4 Mandlik Road, Colaba (6636-8999/8980). CST or Churchgate stations. **Taxi** behind Taj Mahal Hotel. **Open** 12.30-2.45pm, 7.30-11.45pm Mon-Sat; noon-4pm, 7.30-11.45pm Sun. **Main courses** Rs 500-Rs 800. **Credit** AmEx, MC, V. **Map** p251 G5

Indigo was revolutionary when it first opened in 1999, breaking new ground with a sophisticated European menu of the kind previously confined to five-star hotels. It's still one of the city's finest standalone restaurants, serving dishes like carpaccio, lobster bisque and goat's cheese on grilled apples, all well executed. They also do an addictive all-you-can-eat Sunday champagne brunch (Rs 2,025). The open terrace upstairs is without a doubt the nicest spot to dine here in the evenings, but book in advance as Indigo is always busy.

Indigo Deli

Chhatrapati Shivaji Maharaj Street, Colaba (6655-1010). CST or Churchgate stations. **Open** 9am-11pm daily. **Main courses** Rs 225-Rs 325. **Credit** AmEx, MC, V. **Map** p251 G5

Indigo's younger sister is not far away, a few minutes' walk from Regal Cinema and opposite Henry Tham's restaurant. There's a deli counter with a wide range of fresh breads, imported cheeses, meats, olives and more, plus a wall full of Indian and imported wines. The main attraction, though, is the sit-down dining area, smartly decked out in dark woods. Service is painfully slow, but the results are worth it, with some superb soups, salads and sandwiches. A great spot for breakfast or a snack, Indigo Deli also serves excellent coffees and smoothies.

Ling's Pavilion

19/21 KC College Hostel Building, Lansdowne Road, off Colaba Causeway, Colaba (2285-0023). CST or Churchgate stations. **Open** noon-11pm Tue-Sun; noon-3pm, 6-11pm Mon. **Main courses** Rs 200-Rs 350. **Credit** AmEx, MC, V. **Map** p251 G5

Eat, Drink, Shop

Ling's isn't a restaurant, it's an institution. This old-timer just off Colaba Causeway has been feeding South Mumbaikars their favourite Chinese dishes for the last 17 years and shows no sign of slowing down. A large part of its appeal is the decor: a miniature Chinese bridge crossing a fake stream, cute ceiling clouds, and an upper gallery roofed with Chinese tiles. But it's mostly about the food: delectable honey-glazed spare ribs (Rs 180), crab steamed with soy sauce (around Rs 1000) and whole steamed pomfret garnished with chicken and mushroom (Rs 700). Most of the regular dishes are available for around Rs 200-350, making it one of the city's best value-restaurants, with consistently high quality.

Paradise

Sindh Chambers, Colaba Causeway (6635-2714). *CST or Churchgate stations.* **Open** 11am-11pm Tue-Sun. **Main courses** Rs 150. **No credit cards.** **No alcohol.** **Map** p250 F4 ⑳
This small, unassuming eatery has been serving snacks and Parsi food for the last 53 years. The best days to go are Wednesdays and Sundays, when owner Mehroo Kadkhodai cooks her famous mutton *dhansak* (lentil and vegetable curry).

Thai Pavilion

Taj President, Lobby Level, Cuffe Parade, Colaba (6665-0808). CST or Churchgate stations. **Open** 12.30-2.45pm, 7-11.45pm daily. **Main courses** Rs 800-Rs 1,200. **Credit** AmEx, DC, MC, V. **Map** p250 E3 ㉑
The same Japanese design firm that designed Wink at the same hotel and China House at the Grand Hyatt has redone the finest Thai restaurant in the city (and possibly in India). Venture beyond *phad thai* and green curry to try the experiments that chef Ananda Solomon has introduced. If you're lucky, he might be cooking in the open kitchen himself, amidst all that glass shelving and wooden fretwork.

Wasabi

Taj Mahal Palace and Tower, Apollo Bunder, Colaba (6665-3202). CST or Churchgate stations. **Open** 12.30-3pm, 7-11.45pm daily. **Main courses** Rs 2,000. **Credit** AmEx, MC, V. **Map** p251 G5 ㉒
For Mumbai's fans of Japanese cuisine, Wasabi is sacred: its head chef is Masaharu Morimoto of Nobu fame; his locally recruited chefs maintain his sky-high standards matched by similar prices. Entered only via a narrow spiral staircase from a bar on the Taj's ground floor, Wasabi reeks of exclusivity and elegance. The food is fabulous, but there's only one saké on offer, its appeal extended by using it as a base ingredient in an array of cocktails. You'll have to reserve a table several days in advance; request one with a sea view. *Photo p89.*

Cafés

Barista

Cecil Court, Colaba Causeway, Colaba (6633-6835). CST or Churchgate stations. **Taxi** Regal Cinema. **Open** 8.30am-1.30am daily. **Credit** MC, V. **No alcohol.** **Map** p251 G5 ㉓

A highly successful Indian café chain, modelled on Starbucks, which has now spread across India, Sri Lanka and the Middle East. The snacks and cakes are passable, but the hot and cold coffees are quite good and the decor soothing. This one's usually packed with college kids, shoppers and tourists. **Other locations** *34 Chowpatty Seaface (2369-0104); Maker Towers, Cuffe Parade (2215-0562); Murzban Road, next to Sterling Cinema, near Chhatrapati Shivaji Terminus; Bandstand Building, Bandstand, Bandra (W) (2643-4287).*

Moshe's Café

7 Minoo Manor, Cuffe Parade, Colaba (2216-1226). CST or Churchgate stations. **Open** 9am-12.30am daily. **Main courses** Rs 250-Rs 550. **Credit** AmEx, MC, V. **Map** p250 E3 ㉔
Hidden behind a hedge on Cuffe Parade is this smart, high-ceilinged café with a small garden dining area. Better as a lunchtime stopover than a dinner place, Moshe's offers grilled sandwiches, salads and mains with Mediterranean flavours. There's also a wide range of coffees, desserts and coolers, like a killer limeade made with ginger, fennel and cloves, plus excellent smoothies – the papaya, yoghurt and vanilla are particularly good. *Photo p103.*

Olympia Café

Rahim Mansion, Colaba Causeway, Colaba (2202-1043). CST or Churchgate stations. **Open** 7am-midnight daily. **Main courses** Rs 30-Rs 60. **No credit cards. No alcohol.** **Map** p251 G5 ㉕
Olympia scores high on the 1940s period charm, with old chairs and tables, and lazy fans. It's cheap and popular with backpackers, office workers and taxi drivers crowded in together. A great spot for cheap biryanis and curries, and more exotic dishes like the brain fry. Finish with a caramel custard.

Theobroma

Cusrow Baug, Shop No 24, Colaba Causeway (6529-2929). CST or Churchgate stations. **Open** 8.30am-12.30am daily. **Credit** MC, V. **No alcohol.** **Map** p250 F4 ㉖
The name means 'food of the gods', and they aren't exaggerating. The decor is strictly terrestrial, but the food is divine; top quality sourdough loaves, fluffy focaccia, chocolate brownies, Danish pastries and freshly made, five-star hotel quality sandwiches. An excellent lunch and snack spot.

Nariman Point

Indian

Kandahar

The Oberoi, Nariman Point (6632-6210). Churchgate station. **Open** 12.30-2.45pm, 7.30-11.30pm daily. **Main courses** Rs 550-Rs 700. **Credit** AmEx, DC, MC, V. **Map** p251 D6 ㉗
Why go all the way to Afghanistan when you can sample outstanding North-West Frontier province cuisine in the outrageously plush surroundings of the Oberoi? High ceilings and broad windows with

Bespoke stir-fries are the order of the day at **All Stir Fry**. *See p91.*

gorgeous views of Marine Drive complement rich, skilfully prepared food including curries, biryanis, and juicy kebabs. The *raan* (leg of lamb) – a royal feast all on its own – is perhaps the city's finest. In the evenings, diners are treated to a traditional performance of *jal tarang*: music played on water-filled porcelain cups with wooden sticks.

Moti Mahal Delux

102 CR2 Shopping Mall, First Floor, Nariman Point (6654-6454). Churchgate station. **Taxi** INOX Cinema. **Open** noon-4pm; 7pm-midnight daily. **Main courses** Rs 250-Rs 400. **Credit** MC, V. **Map** p251 E6 ㉘

Moti Mahal (meaning 'Pearl Palace') is part of a chain of restaurants that originated in Peshawar in the 1920s. The Mumbai version is neat and contemporary: wooden floors and modern seating, sheer white drapes and a glass-wrapped live kitchen. Listen out for the twang of Delhi accents – this is where expat North Indians come for home-style food. Go for the tender *lasooni* kebabs (Rs 309) and the soft naans (Rs 59). The butter chicken (Rs 309) alone makes a trip here worthwhile. Finish off with a sweet, thick *lassi*.

International

India Jones

Hilton Towers, Nariman Point (6632-5757). Churchgate station. **Open** 12.30-2.45pm, 7.30-11.45pm daily. **Main courses** Rs 500-Rs 1,200. **Credit** AmEx, DC, MC, V. **Map** p251 D6 ㉙

China meets Japan via Thailand and Indonesia at India Jones, where the menu includes a mishmash of popular dishes from across South-east Asia, plus some fusion experiments. The *chao tum* (cooked prawn mousse on sugarcane skewers) is delightful. The appetisers are superb – you could skip the main courses and go straight for the appetiser platter.

Japengo Café

Ground Floor, CR2, Nariman Point (6633-4040). Churchgate station. **Open** 11am-11pm daily.

Main courses Rs 300-Rs 700. **Credit** AmEx, MC, V. **No alcohol. Map** p251 E6 ㉚

At the Mumbai branch of the Dubai-based chain of Japengo Café cafés the choices span everything from pasta and fish and chips to yakitori, houmous and dim sum. While the menu is rather alarmingly diverse – covering Italy, Lebanon, Japan, China and South-east Asia – it's hard to find fault with the cooking. The decor infuses a casual spirit into the place: bamboo twigs fall down the sides of ceiling lights, seating is a mix of minimal backless stools, high-backed chairs and a sit-down lounge area, and you get to watch the chefs at work. *Photo p100.*

Tiffin

The Oberoi, Nariman Point (6632-6205). Churchgate station. **Open** 6.30am-11.30pm daily. **Main courses** Rs 700-Rs 1,400. **Credit** AmEx, MC, V. **Map** p251 D6 ㉛

Another Oberoi restaurant, this one decked out in an understated white-and-grey that exudes off-hand elegance. The menu is short and changes every couple of months, with the emphasis on European cuisine, with some token Indian standards like *rogan josh*. They also serve some decent sushi and sashimi (Rs 300-Rs 650). The standard of dishes is uniformly high, although the servings can be a little small.

Vetro

The Oberoi, Lobby Level, Nariman Point (6632-5757). Churchgate station. **Open** 12.30-3pm, 7-11.30pm daily. **Main courses** Rs 750-Rs 1,800. **Credit** AmEx, MC, V. **Map** p251 D6 ㉜

One of South Mumbai's high-end Italian restaurants, with a beautiful interior design. Row upon row of coloured windows line the walls, reflecting the afternoon sunlight so that it forms criss-crossing rainbows. As soon as you enter you'll be invited for a wine-tasting session before you eat. There's a walk-in antipasti bar, including juicy stuffed olives and very good carpaccio, Parma ham and salads. The starters and salads are outstanding – so good in fact that they leave the mains a little in the shade.

Govinda's. *See p102.*

VongWong

First Floor, Express Towers, Nariman Point (2287-5633/2287-5634). **Open** 12.30-3pm, 7.30-11.45pm daily. **Main courses** Rs 600-Rs 1000. **Credit** AmEx, MC, V. **Map** p251 E6 ③

Occupying the space formerly used by the printing press of the *Indian Express* newspaper, VongWong is a gorgeous Chinese and Thai restaurant named for its chefs, the very talented Vong and Wong. Split into three sections, including a private dining room, VongWong is expansive in both size and menu: diners have over 300 dishes to choose from and the dim sum are particularly impressive.

Churchgate & Marine Lines

Indian

Panchvati Gaurav

Vithaldas Thackersey Marg, Marine Lines (2208-4877). Marine Lines station. **Taxi** Bombay Hospital. **Open** 11am-3pm, 7-10.30pm daily. **Thali** Rs 180. **Credit** MC, V. **No alcohol**. **Map** p252 F10 ③

One of the city's favourite *thali* places, Panchvati Gaurav specialises in Gujarati *thalis*. Still a regular destination for the office lunch crowd, it's unbeatable value for money and boasts excellent service. The sweet, milky Gujarati curry is light and tasty, the *farsan* (snacks) delicious with *papads* and pickles, and dessert included.

Samrat

Prem Court, Jamshedji Tata Road, Churchgate (2282-0942). Churchgate station. **Open** noon-11pm daily. **Thali** Lunch Rs 163, dinner Rs 197. **Credit** AmEx, MC, V. **Map** p251 & p252 F7 ③

Samrat is almost legendary in the city for its Gujarati *thalis*, attracting big crowds at lunchtimes from the offices around Churchgate and Nariman Point. The *thalis* are 'unlimited', with a smartly uniformed waiter on hand to make sure your *katoris* are constantly filled to the brim with four types of vegetables, two *farsan*, two sweet dishes, and mountains of *puris*, *papads* and rice. It's consistently fabulous – just don't plan on doing anything more strenuous than digesting for a few hours afterwards.

Shiv Sagar

Nagin Mahal, 82 Veer Nariman Road, Churchgate (2282-4862). Churchgate station. **Open** 9am-12.30am daily. **Main courses** Rs 70-Rs 170. **Credit** AmEx, MC, V. **Map** p251 & p252 F8 ③

A neat, clean but hectic Udipi joint serving lunch to the office crowd in the busy Churchgate district. Skip most of the menu and head straight for the South Indian fare – crisp *dosas* and soft *idlis* – and the tasty *pao bhajis*. They also do a good selection of street-style snacks, hygienically prepared.

International

Oriental Blossom

Marine Plaza Hotel, 29 Marine Drive, Churchgate (2285-1212). Churchgate station. **Open** 12.30-2.45pm, 7.30-11.30pm daily. **Main courses** Rs 400-Rs 1,200. **Credit** AmEx, MC, V. **Map** p251 & p252 E7 ③

House restaurant of the splendid Marine Plaza Hotel, the Blossom makes a very decent fist of Cantonese cooking. Some of the dishes are a little heavy on the sauces but the freshness of the ingredients wins out. Book in advance.

Pearl of the Orient

Ambassador Hotel, Veer Nariman Road, Churchgate (2204-1131). Churchgate station. **Open** 12.30-2.45pm, 7.30-11.45pm daily. **Main courses** Rs 350-Rs 1,200. **Credit** AmEx, MC, V. **Map** p251/2 E8 ③

Mumbai's only revolving restaurant, on the 12th floor of a 1970s-built concrete tower housing the Ambassador Hotel. It's an East Asian eatery with an emphasis on Hunan, Sichuan and Cantonese dishes, plus some sushi and Thai food – all competently prepared by a chef with a penchant for carving roses out of beetroots. It has spectacular views of the sea, the sweep of Marine Drive and the cityscape through its floor-to-ceiling windows, and the restaurant completing a circuit every 90 minutes.

Cafés

Mocha

Nagin Mahal, Veer Nariman Road, Churchgate (6633-6070). Churchgate station. **Open** 9am-1.30am daily. **Credit** AmEx, MC, V. **Map** p251 & p252 F8 ③

A trendy hangout for well-heeled college kids, with a Middle Eastern vibe complete with fez-adorned waiters. The thing to do here is lounge on a bolster passing around a flavoured hookah with your mates, whilst slurping on a pricey coffee. They also

Vast food nation

Sample the flavours of Mumbai.

Maharashtrian

The austere and healthy cuisine of the state of Maharashtra, of which Mumbai is the capital, Maharashtrian food is liberal in its use of whole grains and restrained with ghee and oil. It's also fairly mild, avoiding strong spices in favour of the more delicate flavours of sesame, turmeric and coriander.
Try these: *poha* (a light snack of beaten rice flakes, spices and peanuts); *sabudana vada* (chewy tapioca fritters); *kothimbir vada* (deep-fried squares of coriander and chickpea paste); *vada pav* (deep-fried potato with spices, served in bread).
Get it at: Jumbo King (*see p102*); Panshikar Aahar (*see p102*); Swati Snacks (*see p104*).

Coastal

A broad term covering the cuisines of India's west coast, from southern Maharashtra right down to Kerala, all sharing a holy trinity of coconut, rice and fish. Malvani cooking from southern Maharashtra uses coconut milk and the sour-fruity kokum fruit in simple, delicious curries. Goans add Portuguese colonial influences of vinegar, pork and *pav* (bread). Further down, Mangaloreans grind a thick base of spices and grated coconut for their seafood and chicken curries. And deep in the south, Kerala cooking makes use of banana flowers and stems.
Try these: Goan pork sausages; Mangalorean prawn *gassi* (a kind of curry); *neer dosa* (steamed rice bread); classic Goan fish curry-rice.
Get it at: Konkan Café (*see p90*); New Martin Lunch Home (*see p90*); Rice Boat (*see p107*); Sindhudurg (*see p106*); Sushegad Gomantak (*see p106*); Trishna (*see p100*).

Parsi

Parsi food is very rich (recipes routinely start with 'Take a dozen eggs'), heavy on the meat and slightly sweet, thanks to a Zoroastrian Persian tradition of cooking with dried fruits. It's a wonderful mélange of Middle Eastern cooking styles and Indian ingredients.
Try these: *dhansak* (a thick curry of meat, lentils and vegetables); *patra ni machchi* (fish cooked in banana leaves); *akuri* (spicy scrambled eggs).
Get it at: Britannia (*see p100*); Jimmy Boy (*see p100*).

Udipi

South Indian vegetarian cuisine, renowned for highly popular snacks made from fermented ground rice like *idlis* (steamed rice cakes), lentil batter dishes like *dosas* and more substantial *thalis*. Udipis are ubiquitous across Mumbai and a regular lunchtime destination for healthy, tasty and cheap food.
Try these: *appams* (thick round pancakes); *dosa* (thin, crispy, savoury pancakes); Udipi *thalis* served on banana leaves.
Get it at: Shiv Sagar (*see p98*).

Mughlai

Think kebabs and biryanis. Mughlai is an ultra-rich non-vegetarian Muslim cuisine but there are also simpler versions created in casual Chillia Muslim-run eateries. The best time to experience Mumbai's Muslim food is unquestionably the month of Ramzan (*see p134* **Festivals & Events**), when Muslim neighbourhoods like Mohammed Ali Road become vast outdoor dining extravaganzas after sunset.
Try these: *khichda* (thick stew of meat, wheat and lentils); *raan* (a tender leg of lamb, split so you get at the marrow); *khiri* (grilled udders).
Get it at: Shalimar (*see p103*), the streets around Minara Masjid.

Bengali

Pungent, with liberal use of mustard in both seed and oil form. Combine that with poppy seeds, freshwater fish and an inventive range of sweets made from cottage cheese and you have a strikingly different cuisine.
Try these: *maccher jhol* (Bengali fish curry); *chingdi malai-kari* (prawns cooked in coconut cream); smoked hilsa (a Bengali freshwater fish); *mocchar ghanto* (stir-fried banana flower); *bhaja mungher dhal* (roast mung beans); *mishti doi* (a fabulous yoghurt dessert).
Get it at: Howrah (*see p103*); Oh! Calcutta (*see p104*).

South Indian *idlis*.

serve wine and Bacardi Breezers – no beer – and a range of workmanlike Euro-dishes. The service is sluggish, so be prepared to spend a few hours here. **Other locations** *near Holy Family Hospital, Hill Road, Bandra (W) (2643-3098); Juhu Beach, Juhu Tara Road (2617-5495).*

Tea Centre
Resham Bhavan, 78 Veer Nariman Road (2281-9142). Churchgate station. **Open** 8am-10.30pm daily. **Main courses** Rs 300-Rs 400. **Credit** AmEx, MC, V. **Map** p251 & p252 F8 ⓸
A venture run jointly with the Tea Board of India, the Tea Centre is an eminently civilised showcase of India's finest teas, served by turbaned waiters in stiff uniforms. It's small, decked out in green and white and on offer are varieties of Assam, Darjeeling and Nilgiris, both hot and iced, plus street tea, train tea and a selection of tea 'mocktails', such as mint tea with ice-cream. They also offer snacks, sandwiches and decent set lunches.

Fort & Kala Ghoda

Indian

Britannia
Ram Gulam Road, Ballard Estate, near Fort (2261-5264). CST station. **Taxi** opposite New Custom House. **Open** 11.30am-4pm Mon-Sat. **Main courses** Rs 60-Rs 200. **No credit cards**. **No alcohol**. **Map** p252 J8 ⓸
Despite the dilapidated wooden interior, complete with wobbly chairs, peeling walls and dusty chandeliers, Britannia, a classic Irani restaurant of a type now slowly dying out (*see p91* **Café culture**), manages to exude a homely 1940s charm. Open only for lunch, it's famous for its fabulous berry *pulao*, a traditional Iranian dish of boneless mutton (Rs 240) or chicken (Rs 200) in a sweet, spicy masala and garnished with tart Iranian berries. If you still have room, follow it with a creamy caramel custard.

Jimmy Boy Café
11 Bank Street, Vikas Building, Fort (2270-0880). CST station. **Taxi** Horniman Circle. **Open** 11am-11pm daily. **Main courses** Rs 200-Rs 250. **Credit** MC, V. **No alcohol**. **Map** p251 & p252 H7 ⓸
Jimmy Boy is best known for its Parsi specialities, particularly *lagan nu bhonu* – Parsi wedding food. Try the delightful *murghi na farcha* (crumb-fried spiced chicken), *patra ni machchi* (chutney-stuffed pomfret wrapped in banana leaves), *jardaloo sali boti* (boneless mutton cooked with dried apricots and an onion and tomato gravy) and the signature Parsi dish, mutton *dhansak* (a lentil and vegetable curry). It's very popular with Parsis and non-Parsis alike, so make a reservation.

Khyber
145 MG Road, Kala Ghoda (2267-3227). CST or Churchgate stations. **Open** 12.30-3.30pm, 7.30-11.30pm daily. **Main courses** Rs 250-Rs 350. **Credit** AmEx, DC, MC, V. **Map** p251 G7 ⓸

Japengo Café: mimimal yet diverse. *See p97.*

A sprawling, two-level restaurant grandly furnished in wood and stone, Khyber is an old favourite of fans of North Indian cuisine, with consistently high standards. Top choices here include their tender *raan* – a slow-cooked leg of lamb – the biryani and their paneer korma.

Mahesh Lunch Home
8B Cawasji Patel Street, Fort (2287-0938). CST station. **Open** 11.30am-4pm, 6-11.30pm daily. **Main courses** Rs 150-Rs 250. **Credit** AmEx, DC, MC, V. **Map** p251 & p252 H8 ⓸
Less fancy in its decor than its Mangalorean seafood sister Trishna, Mahesh nevertheless keeps up with the competition with their food – excellent Konkan coastal and Magalorean cuisine, in particular some killer *gassi* and excellent curry-rice.

Mocambo Café & Beer Bar
23A, PM Road, Fort (2287-0458). CST station. **Open** 9am-11.30pm daily. **Main courses** Rs 200-Rs 300. **Credit** AmEx, MC, V. **Map** p251 & p252 H8 ⓸
A spruced-up old-timer, Mocambo does Parsi food, Goan curries and some of the best pork chops in town. An ancient gent on the mezzanine plonks away on a mini-piano as you eat and a CCTV allows diners to the enjoy the performance too.

Trishna
7 Sai Baba Marg, Kala Ghoda (2270-1623). CST station. **Taxi** behind Rhythm House. **Open** noon-3.30pm, 6pm-midnight daily. **Main courses** Rs 250-Rs 700. **Credit** AmEx, DC, MC, V. **Map** p251 G7 ⓸
A popular seafood restaurant famed for its South Indian Mangalorean dishes. The decor is ornate and the food good enough to keep the South Mumbai elite and the odd celebrity coming back. Favourites include the prawn *gassi*, the butter-pepper-garlic crab and stuffed pomfret.

International

Joss
K Dubash Marg, Kala Ghoda (6633-4233).
Churchgate station. **Taxi** *Rhythym House* **Open**
12.30-3.30pm, 7.30-11.30pm daily. **Main courses** Rs
320-Rs 975. **Credit** AmEx, MC, V. **Map** p251 G6 ❹
This smart, subtly lit place used to be a Thai
restaurant (hence the gold-and-glass Thai temple-
style wall decor); it's now become one of the city's
most impressive pan-Asian restaurants, with a
range of Singaporean, Indonesian, Thai, Chinese,
Japanese and Korean dishes, and fusion experiments like *aki miso*-marinated tenderloin thrown
in. All of the dishes are good, and there's an
impressive sushi menu.

Royal China
SP Corporation Building, behind Sterling Cinema,
Hazarimal Somani Marg, Fort (6636-5531). CST
station. **Open** noon-2.30pm, 7-11.30pm daily. **Main**
courses Rs 475-Rs 900. **Credit** AmEx, DC, MC, V.
Map p252 G10 ❽
Royal China is arguably the city's finest Cantonese
Chinese restaurant, one of the few places where
Mumbaikars can eat authentic Chinese food. Big
favourites with the local crowd are dishes in sauces
and with strong flavours, like the crispy aromatic
duck served with paper-thin pancakes and plum
sauce. Royal China is also the local pioneer of dim
sum – nowhere else comes close in terms of choice
or quality – with a dedicated chef who prepares up
to 50 different kinds daily.
Other location *192 Turner Road, Bandra (W)*
(6704-9553).

Howrah trumpets Bengali cuisine. *See p103.*

Indian

Kebab Korner
InterContinental Marine Drive, 135 Marine
Drive (6639-9999). Churchgate station. **Open**
12.30-2.45pm, 7.30-11.45pm daily. **Main courses**
Rs 450-Rs 1,100. **Credit** AmEx, MC, V. **Map**
p251 & p252 E8 ❾
Kebab Korner was an institution that shut down
years ago, before being recreated in 2005 with its
original chefs and traditional cooking style – the
kebabs here are made on a *sigri* (a kind of coal-fired
grill) instead of a tandoor oven. The results are stunning – tender and subtly flavoured seekh kebabs,
spicy butter chicken (Rs 680) and outrageously tasty
kali dal (Rs 600). The biryani is also to die for, as is
the house special 'Busybee' stuffed chicken kebab
(Rs 725) served with burnt onions and yoghurt chutney. Add a sea view and the sumptuous wood and
marble decor, and you have a Mumbai classic.

International

Pizzeria
Soona Mahal, 143 Marine Drive (6730-5626).
Churchgate station. **Open** noon-12.30am daily.
Main courses Rs 260-Rs 350. **Credit** AmEx, MC,
V. **Map** p251 & p252 E8 ❺
On the corner of Marine Drive and Veer Nariman
Road, Pizzeria offers a fine view of the bay, pass-
ing traffic and hurrying commuters. The pizzas are
thoroughly enjoyable Indian versions of old
favourites, but try the local inventions like the
Bombay Masala: plain cheese with spices. Perfect
to while away an afternoon drinking beer and
watching the world go by.

Salt Water Grill
Girgaum Chowpatty, Marine Drive (98925-78494).
Churney Road station. **Taxi** *Chowpatty.* **Open**
7.30pm-1am daily. **Main courses** Rs 350-Rs 750.
Credit AmEx, MC, V. **Map** p254 C14 ❺
The location is unbeatable – right on the Marine Drive
beach; lit-up palm trees sway above white cotton
canopies while Buena Vista Social Club plays over
the insistent whisper of the Arabian Sea; hammocks
loll, lounge chairs beckon, sand shifts underfoot. No
wonder this is the playground of Mumbai's celebrity
set. The food is sophisticated Euro-cuisine with an
emphasis on seafood. The cocktails are fab too.

Cafés

Bachelor's Juice House
Marine Drive, opposite Chowpatty beach (2368-2211).
Churney Road station. **Open** 10.30am-2.30am daily.
No credit cards. No alcohol. Map p254 C14 ❺
Easy to spot from the rows of fruit and parked cars,
Bachelor's isn't a 'house' at all. It's a street stall,
although a superior stall on a superior street – the
bayfront Marine Drive. Bachelor's has ice-cream,

Eat, Drink, Shop

milkshakes and fresh juices, all made with fresh fruit. Everything is superb, but the highlights are the watermelon, custard apple, mango, roast almond and green chilli ice-creams (Rs 55 for a large cup).

Girgaum

Indian

Govinda's

Sri Sri Radha Gopinath Mandir, 7 KM Munshi Marg, near Bharatiya Vidya Bhavan, Chowpatty (2366-5566/2366-5567). Churney Road station.
Open 11am-10pm daily. **Main courses** Rs 95-Rs 225. **Credit** MC, V. **No alcohol.** **Map** p254 A15 🚷

Run by the International Society for Krishna Consciousness, Govinda's serves vegetarian food but doesn't limit itself only to north Indian fare. They do stir-fries, south Indian *dosas*, and some excellent pizzas. Best of all, everything that comes out of their kitchen is first offered to, and blessed by, the gods themselves, which, say the temple staff, tastes different 'because it has been tasted by the lord so it is almost like it has his saliva on it'. *Photo p98.*

Panshikar Aahar

Govardhandas Building, Jagganath Sankarseth Road, Girgaum (2386-1211). Grant Road station.
Taxi Girgaum Church. **Open** 8am-10pm daily.
Main courses Rs 15-Rs 30. **No credit cards.**
No alcohol. **Map** p254 C15 🚷

Maharashtrian vegetarian food, Panshikar's speciality is the interesting category of *upvas* (fast) dishes, food meant to be eaten on traditional Hindu fast days that prohibit the consumption of 'sown' foods, meaning anything grown in a ploughed field. This includes fruits, roots and tubers. Panshikar makes most standard Mumbai snacks in *upvas* form.

Soam

Sadguru Sadan, Babulnath Road, Ground floor, Chowpatty (2369-8080). Grant Road station.
Taxi Babulnath Temple. **Open** noon-midnight daily. **Main courses** Rs 120-Rs 170. **Credit** MC, V. **No alcohol.** **Map** p254 A15 🚷

The true test of a Gujarati snacks joint is its *panki chutney* (pancakes steamed in banana leaves), and Soam passes with flying colours. The intense heat makes it almost difficult to touch, but hold up the banana leaf and the pancake falls off in one piece – perfect. Furnished in dark wood, ochre-coloured walls, bamboo blinds and comfy seating, Soam is

Street eats

Mumbai's street food is a cuisine in itself, built on Maharashtrian-Gujarati roots, with the added influence of every émigré community. Food stalls are everywhere, serving kids on their way to school, office workers on lunch breaks, commuters grabbing a bite before the train home. The signature street snack is the *vada pav*, a fried potato fritter in a soft roll with dry chilli-garlic chutney. Another is *bhel puri*, a dry snack of puffed rice, peanuts, chickpea noodles, onions and chutney. Then there's *pav bhaji*, spicy puréed vegetables eaten with buttered bread, and *pani puri* – crispy shells filled with chickpea dumplings, *mung* sprouts and spiced water. Pop it in, crunch, and it all explodes thrillingly in your mouth. *Bhutta* is roast corn-on-the-cob dusted with chilli powder and lime. It's all cheap – Rs 5-Rs 30.

You'll find street stalls everywhere, but these aren't always the cleanest places to eat; foreign visitors who aren't used to them risk getting sick.

Exercise common sense: stick to the most popular stalls, like those around Churchgate station and CST or at Chowpatty Beach. Ensure the cook observes basic hygiene and that the food is piping hot. Alternatively, you can find excellent versions of street cuisine at Swati Snacks (*see p104*), and *vada-paos* are now sold in fast-food chain Jumbo King. Here are some recommended stalls:

Jai Santoshi Ma Bhel Puri Bhandar

20 Bharati Bhavan, corner of Princess Street and Kalbadevi Road. Marine Lines station.
Map p253 F12 🚷

Jumbo King

308 Devji Kanji Street, Princess Street, Marine Lines (2206-6903). Marine Lines station.
Open 9am-10pm.
Map p253 E12 🚷

Vithal Bhelwallah

5 AK Naik Marg, near Sterling Cinema, Fort (6631-7211). CST station.
Open 11am-11pm.
Map p252 H10 🚷

Jumbo King's *vada pav.*

Get your Mediterranean fix at **Moshe's Café**. See p95.

Eat, Drink, Shop

the favourite alternative to South Mumbai's other hugely popular (and always crowded) Gujarati snack joint, Swati Snacks (see p104).

Crawford Market

Indian

Howrah
Sitaram Building, B Block, Crawford Market (2344-2690). CST station. **Open** 11am-4pm, 7-11.30pm daily. **Main courses** Rs 150-Rs 200. **Credit** AmEx, DC, MC, V. **No alcohol. Map** p253 H12
Howrah is a restaurant specialising in Bengali cuisine. Despite being right next to one of the city's most hectic markets, Howrah's one-flight-up terrace offers a relaxed dining experience, with old-fashioned ceiling fans and smiling, unhurried *dhoti*-clad waiters. Just think of a lazy afternoon in Kolkata, with a 1980s Bengali pop soundtrack to make expat Kolkatans (who account for most of the customers) feel at home. Howrah is best known for its fish dishes, especially freshwater fish like the delish *ilish*, a regional delicacy flown in from Bengal. Styles of preparation vary from a creamy cardamom gravy of *malai* curry to the complex *daab* style in which the fish is baked in a coconut shell. *Photo p101.*

Rajdhani
361 Sitaram Memon Street, near Crawford Market (2342-6919). CST station. **Taxi** Crawford Market. **Open** noon-4pm, 7-10.30pm daily. **Thali** Rs 190 Mon-Sat, Rs 225 Sun. **Credit** AmEx, MC, V. **No alcohol. Map** p253 & p255 G13
Rajdhani is an oasis of calm in a narrow, frantic side-street a few metres from the bustle of the historic Crawford Market. Getting here requires some

Frogger-style negotiation of the local traffic of hand-pulled carts, but if you make it, you'll be treated to a superior Gujarati *thali* with endless refills of *palak paneer* (spinach and cottage cheese), sweet *kadi* (a gram flour-based curry), *aloo subzi* (masala potato), kidney bean curry and more. Take a glass of *chaas* (buttermilk) and finish off with some *gulab jamun*.

Shalimar
Vazir Building, Bhendi Bazaar, Mohammed Ali Road (2345-6632/2346-5286). CST station. **Taxi** Bhendi Bazaar Fire Station. **Open** 8am-1.30am daily. **Main courses** Rs 35-Rs 250. **Credit** DC, MC, V. **No alcohol. Map** p255 G15
Meat, meat, and more meat... this is Mumbai Muslim food at its most carnivorous. Shalimar makes no concessions to health fads, serving up extremely rich and spicy kebabs and other delights. The traditional dishes are great – try the *raan*, a leg of lamb from the restaurant's own livestock, split so you can get at the marrow – but avoid the ill-conceived 'Mexican' and 'Chinese' fusion dishes. It's a little claustrophobic and usually packed, so expect a short wait for a table.

Mahalaxmi

Indian

Gallops
Mahalaxmi Racecourse, Keshavrao Khadye Marg, Mahalaxmi (2307-1448). Mahalaxmi station. **Taxi** Racecourse. **Open** noon-midnight daily. **Main courses** Rs 275-Rs 600. **Credit** AmEx, MC, V.
The greatest thing about Gallops is the location – next to a tree- and bougainvillea-fringed garden on the edge of the Royal Western India Turf Club,

with a view of the racecourse and the skyline beyond. The restaurant, decked out in acres of stone, wood and brass, offers Indian and 'Continental' cuisine – both competently executed. The ideal spot for lunch before an afternoon at the races.

International

CG'83
201 Om Chambers, 123 AK Marg, Kemp's Corner (2363-0841/42). **Open** 12.30-3pm, 7-11.30pm daily. **Credit** AmEx, MC, V. **Main courses** Rs 275-Rs 350.
Together with his sons, Eddie and Henry, Nelson Wang has tapped into the city's obsession with Oriental cuisine and created Chinese dishes influenced by the food of Vietnam, Singapore, Japan and the Philippines. Experiment, because everything is superb, from the baked radish *soong* (crisp buns stuffed with bland, soft strips of cabbage and radish) to spring rolls stuffed with vegetables, but with a delightful surprise of plum sauce and honey.

Tardeo

Indian

Oh! Calcutta
Rosewood Hotel, Tulsiwadi Lane, Tardeo (2496-3145). Mumbai Central station. **Open** noon-3pm, 7pm-midnight daily. **Main courses** Rs 300-Rs 450. **Credit** AmEx, MC, V.
Oh to be in Cal. Oh! Calcutta provides a culinary home-from-home for misty-eyed Bengali customers. The must-try dish here is the *ilish maacher apturi* – lightly spiced boneless hilsa fish from the Ganges marinated in mustard paste and green chillies, then baked. And there should be a law forbidding diners from leaving without trying the *mishti doi* – a creamy yoghurt dessert.

Swati Snacks
248 Karai Estate, Tardeo (6580-8406/2352-4994). Grant Road station. **Taxi** opposite Bhatia Hospital.

Open 11am-11pm daily. **Main courses** Rs 50-Rs 100. **Credit** MC, V. **No alcohol. Map** p254 B18
Back in the 1960s, Swati Snacks was little more than a shack on the street serving Gujarati food. Now, it's a swanky, shiny spacecraft of glass and stainless steel. The menu is packed with gorgeous Gujarati staples and some Mumbai street fare like *dahi batata puri* and *idlis*. Everything on the menu is outstanding, in particular the delectable *panki chatni* (rice pancakes steamed in banana leaves) and the *dal dhokli* – a thick lentil curry with a cinnamon flavouring, filled with soft squares of *chapati*. There's also a good selection of fresh juices. Be warned, lunchtimes here are packed; they don't accept reservations and 40-minute waits are not uncommon. Try their delicious sugarcane and ginger juice mix while you wait.

Kalbadevi

Indian

Friends Union Joshi Club
381A Kalbadevi Road, Narottamwadi (2205-8089). Marine Lines station. **Open** 11am-3pm, 7-10pm Mon-Sat; 11am-3pm Sun. **Thali** Rs 70. **No credit cards. No alcohol. Map** p253 & p255 F13
It's been around since before India became independent in 1947, but the FUJC remains tricky to find. Look for a large, bright red neon sign, go through the gateway underneath and take the staircase up to the first floor. It's worth discovering, as the Gujarati shop-keepers who eat there almost daily will tell you. It offers one of the tastiest all-you-can-eat Gujarati *thalis* in the city.

Parel & Lower Parel

Indian

Kebabs & Kurries
ITC Grand Central, Babasaheb Ambedkar Road, Parel (2410-1010). Lower Parel station. **Open** 12.30-2.45pm, 7.30-11.45pm daily. **Main courses** Rs 450-Rs 1,500. **Credit** AmEx, MC, V.
A sprawling five-star hotel restaurant of light stone and dark wood, serving a range of Indian cuisines, all cooked perfectly. Choose from Punjabi, Mughlai, Hyderabadi, Malayali and more, with extensive vegetarian options. Try the rich and tender *murgh aloo qaliya* – chicken and potato in a spicy sauce – and skip the rice for the soft, napkin-sized *roomali rotis*.

International

Lemon Grass
High Street Phoenix, 462 Senapati Bapat Road, Lower Parel (2495-4444). **Open** noon-3.30pm, 7-11.30pm daily. **Main courses** Rs 200-Rs 500. **Credit** MC, V.

Bombay mix

Indian-Chinese cuisine may have been born in Kolkata's China Town, but it was a Mumbaikar who invented chicken Manchurian. Heavily doused with soy sauce and flavoured with the potent triumvirate of ginger, garlic and chillies this hugely popular dish was rapidly adopted by restaurants across the country.

Indian-Chinese takes on many forms in Mumbai. Moderately spicy Sichuan cuisine, which was introduced to the country in Mumbai, quickly metamorphosed into the fiercely sour-pungent, heart-thumping, nose-watering version. Thrice as potent is the layered triple Szechwan, consisting of fried rice topped with meat in Szechwan sauce and garnished with crispy fried noodles and a double fried egg. If you hunt hard enough you might even find a culinary rapprochement between Indian, American and Chinese cuisines in the form of the Szechwan chop suey.

Finding a parallel between the crisp noodles of a chopsuey and *sev*, the crisp broken chickpea flour noodles used in *bhel puri*, creative restaurateurs mixed the sauce with the noodles and created Chinese *bhel* (*pictured*). Of course, you won't find any of these ingenious dishes on a fancy restaurant menu but they're freely available at any of the multi-cuisine restaurants that dot the city.

The city's most ubiquitous and popular fast food – South Indian cuisine – couldn't escape the Sino influence either. Szechwan *dosas* and *idli* Manchurian proliferate in quick-service Udipi restaurants. The *dosas* are prepared from a regular batter, with the normal dry potato filling and usual accompaniments; the only difference is that the inner surface of the *dosa* is smeared with a Szechwan chutney. The *idli* Manchurian however is slightly different: soft, fluffy *idlis* are deep fried till hard, cut into halves or quarters and served in a corn flour-thickened Manchurian sauce. Though it doesn't sound terribly tasty, it is popular enough to have made it to mid-level hotel buffets.

Inspiration has come from the west too and one of Mumbai's iconic snacks, the Frankie, is an adaptation of Middle Eastern *shawarma*. The pitta bread has been substituted with a soft Indian roti and the mutton, chicken and potato filling was made spicier, sourer and juicier. And yes, there is a Szechwan Frankie too.

Japanese food may have only arrived in Mumbai recently but the sizzler, a Mumbai invention based on the teppanyaki concept, has been around for a few decades. Sautéed red meat, chicken, fish or vegetable steak is accompanied with boiled vegetables, chips and noodles or rice and served on a hot cast iron plate placed in a thick wooden tray. Steaming and noisy, the sizzler is a loud culinary spectacle to behold – and tasty too. With Japanese cuisine catching on, it's only a matter of time before the city starts biting into a sushi *dosa* and tempura-style *pakodas*.

New Yorker
25 Fulchand Niwas, Chowpatty (6528-3338/2367-7500). Churney Road station. **Open** *11.30am-11.30pm daily.* **Map** p254 B15

Tibb's Frankies
Kiosk at Aga Brothers Restaurant, 16A Cusrow Baug, Colaba Causeway (2283-0692/www.tibbsfrankies. com). Also Churchgate station. **Open** *noon-9.30pm daily.* **Map** p250 F4*

Yoko Sizzlers
Junction of Cowasji Patel Street and Rustom Sidhwa Marg, Behind Citibank, Fort (6636-4606). CST or Churchgate stations. **Open** *noon-11.30pm daily.* **Map** p251 H8*

Eat, Drink, Shop

Lemon Grass started life as a cosy café in Bandra, but that upped and moved to the more spacious (and air-conditioned) premises at Phoenix Mills, complete with bar. The food is pan-Asian and decent Thai for those not too hung up on originality.

Monza

High Street Phoenix, opposite Quorum, 462 Senapati Bapat Marg, Lower Parel (2495-4852). Lower Parel station. **Open** 12.30-3.30pm, 6.30pm-midnight daily. **Main courses** Rs 250-Rs 400. **Credit** MC, V.

An innovative restaurant, unpretentious but chic, with a decor of black and white with copper accents. Try the excellent crêpes stuffed with wasabi-flavoured cottage cheese topped with tomato coulis (Rs 150) or the equally delicious chicken bruschetta with olives, mushrooms and cheese (Rs 150), which arrives on warm, crispy bread.

Dadar & Mahim

Indian

Pritam da Dhaba

Hotel Midtown Pritam, Station Road, Dadar (E) (2414-5555). Dadar station. **Taxi** Pritam Dadar. **Open** 11am-midnight daily. **Main courses** Rs 140-Rs 160. **Credit** AmEx, MC, V.

Your *dal makhani* is served in a copper bowl by a waiter clad in a pathani suit. You recline on a charpoy under open skies as you dine to the thump of bhangra. And isn't that a tiger lurking over there, lured by the aroma of your chicken tikka? Don't worry, it's just painted on the walls, along with a pastoral Punjab. Pritam da Dhaba's misty-eyed vision of the Punjabi heartland may be rose-tinted, but it's fun and the food is gorgeous. Skip the air-con section and make sure to go for dinner, because tables in the open-air courtyard are only operational after 7.30pm.

Sindhudurg

Sita, RK Vaidya Road, Dadar (W) (2430-1610). Dadar station. **Taxi** behind Shiv Sena Bhavan. **Open** 11.30am-3.30pm, 7-11.30pm daily. **Main courses** Rs 200-Rs 250. **Credit** MC, V. **No alcohol**.

This multi-storey, wood-panelled restaurant is an excellent place to sample dishes from the simple but delicious Malvani-style cuisine, in relative comfort. The basics to order are the prawn, fish and shellfish curries, but the fish biryani, prawn *pulao* and chicken curry are also good. Ask for seasonal specialities like fried fish roe (*gaboli*) and ask them to make their special flatbreads: *jowari* or *nachni bakhri*. Hearty and healthy.

Sushegad Gomantak

Shop No A11, Shiv Sagar Society, opposite Paradise Cinema, Mahim (2444-5555). Mahim station. **Taxi** Paradise Cinema **Open** 11am-4pm, 7pm-midnight daily. **Main courses** Rs 50. **No credit cards**. **No alcohol**.

Sushegad serves 'Gomantak' or Hindu Goan cooking as opposed to Catholic Goan cuisine. It's just as preoccupied with fish and rice but with unique masalas. Sushegad breaks out of the pomfret-rawas-surmai trinity of fishes that most restaurants offer, serving less famous but no less tasty fish like *mori* (shark), *bhingi* (a kind of herring), *tarlya* (sardines), *dhodiyare* (mullet) and *verlya* (similar to whitebait).

International

Tamnak Thai

274 Veer Savarkar Marg, Shivaji Park, Dadar (W) (2447-4646). Dadar station. **Open** noon-3.30pm, 7pm-12.30am daily. **Main courses** Rs 200-Rs 450. **Credit** MC, V.

Tamnak Thai seems to be one of the city's best-kept secrets, despite thousands of motorists passing it every day on their way to and from South Mumbai. That makes Tamnak Thai perfect for a quiet dinner, with sweet waiters and a great wine list.

Bandra & Khar

Indian

Papa Pancho da Dhaba

Gasper Enclave, St John Street, Pali Naka, Bandra (W) (2651-8732). Bandra station. **Taxi** Pali Naka. **Open** noon-12.30am daily. **Main courses** Rs 200-Rs 300. **Credit** MC, V. **No alcohol**. **Map** p249 B4 ⑥①

The decor is resolutely rustic: the holes in the plasterwork are fake, the sky is painted on the ceiling, and the parrots are plastic. It's a city dweller's idea of rural charm, turned into kitsch. Modelled on Punjabi roadside inns called *dhabas*, Papa Pancho serves classic, tasty Punjabi nosh like butter chicken, *dal makhani* and the inevitable chicken tikka. By the way, the restaurant's name is a bit naughty – pancho sounds to Indian ears a little like *behenchod*, which is a grievous insult relating to a gentleman's not altogether appropriate affection for his sister.

International

Mia Cucina

Gasper Enclave, St John Street, Pali Naka, Bandra (W) (6710-4000). Bandra station. **Taxi** Pali Naka. **Open** noon-midnight daily. **Main courses** Rs 225-Rs 400. **Credit** MC, V. **No alcohol**. **Map** p249 B4 ⑥②

Everything about Mia Cucina is impressive, not least the chef, Sanjay Kotian, who makes a point of going from table to table to recommend dishes and enquire about the quality of food. Dispense with the menu and ask him for suggestions. If you aren't the adventurous type, the old favourites are reliable – their Caesar salad (Rs 125) is as perfect as it gets and the quattro formaggio (Rs 300) is appropriately stinky. The spinach and goat's cheese (Rs 275) risotto is good too.

Olive Bar & Kitchen

4 Union Park, Pali Hill Tourist Hotel, Khar (W)
(2605-8228). Khar station. **Taxi** near Café Coffee
Day. **Open** 8pm-1.30am Mon-Sat; 12.30-3.30pm,
8pm-1.30am Sun. **Main courses** Rs 300-Rs 700.
Credit AmEx, DC, MC, V. **Map** p249 A1 ⑬

A super restaurant-cum-bar serving Italian cuisine
for an endless stream of Bandra models and hipsters. The salads, pastas and risottos can be a case
of hit and miss, so too with the funky cocktails – but
nobody is really there for the food anyway. Nights
are lively, Sunday brunches are lazy – especially in
the coolly-lit outside dining area. Calling ahead for
directions and a booking is recommended.

Pot Pourri

*4 Carlton Court, Turner Road-Pali Road Junction,
Bandra (W) (2642-9193). Bandra station.* **Open**
11am-12.15am daily. **Main courses** Rs 190-Rs 250.
Credit MC, V. **Map** p249 B4 ⑭

Buy an ancient *New Yorker* from the eclectic news-
stand outside and stroll on to Pot Pourri's open-air
veranda for a cappuccino and cake, or some well-
prepared, well-presented food, from burgers to
pastas to their signature chicken stroganoff. The
desserts are great. This highly popular lunch and
evening eaterie was one of the first to capture the
mood of modern Bandra – hip, young and with
new money to burn. The noisy, autorickshaw-
choked junction by the veranda is part of the
package, unfortunately.

Seijo & the Soul Dish

*Second Floor, Krystal, Waterfield Road, Bandra
(2640-5555). Bandra station.* **Taxi** ICICI Bandra.
Open 7pm-1am Mon-Sat; noon-4pm, 7pm-1am Sun.
Main courses Rs 400-Rs 600. **Credit** AmEx, DC,
MC, V. **Map** p249 D4 ⑮

Seijo is one of Bandra's more atmospheric pan-Asian
restaurants. Its tall glass walls are offset by winding wrought iron tubes, dark wooden walkways and
egg-shaped lavatories, all beneath a high, retractable
ceiling for open-air dining. It looks stunning, with
sprawling idols, candles, even a mini-waterfall. The
menu doesn't stray too far from the pan-Asian staples: a bit of sushi, some Thai curries and plenty of
noodles – but they're competently done, especially
the steamed mussels in Thai coconut sauce.

Cafés

Café Coffee Day

*1 Bandstand Apts, 212/A BJ Road, Bandstand,
Bandra (W) (3290-6436). Bandra station.* **Open**
9am-1.30am daily. **No credit cards. No alcohol.**

The coffee is bearable at best, the snacks are best
avoided but the view is to die for. Located along
the Bandra Bandstand promenade, a narrow street
and a walking track are all that separate the café
from the Arabian Sea and fabulous sunsets. The
street itself has a carnival-like atmosphere in the
evening, when families, joggers and couples come
out for some fresh air and streetfood. You could
also move to the slightly pricier but better Barista
next door (*see p95*).

Candies

*St John Road, near Pali Hill, Bandra (W) (2642-
4124/2642-2324).* **Open** 8.30am-10.30pm Tue-Sun.
Main courses Rs 70-Rs 150. **No credit cards.**
No alcohol. Map p249 B4 ⑯

Candies is a snack shop serving sandwiches, salads, samosas, rolls and even sushi, but more than
the food it's the atmosphere that makes it one of
Bandra's favourite cafés. Spread over five levels,
it's a sprawling space that seems to go on and
on, with mosaic tiles, metal-framed furniture
and a decidedly Mediterranean feel. Popular with
pretty Bandra girls and their equally pretty
boys, Candies is one of the nicest cafés in the suburbs. For something more substantial, pick up one
of their meal combos.

Juhu & Versova

Indian

Rice Boat

*Aram Nagar 2, JP Road, Versova, Andheri (W)
(2633-6688/2632-6688). Andheri station.* **Open**
noon-3.30pm, 7pm-midnight daily. **Main courses**
Rs 150-Rs 250. **Credit** AmEx, MC, V.

Duck under the shiny temple bell on a chain by the
entrance and pretend you're in Kerala. Rice Boat
offers a tour of Keralan cuisine, with dishes unique

China House. *See p109.*

to the state's Syrian-Christian community, like *kozhi varuthathu* (tender chunks of chicken roasted on bamboo skewers) as well as more familiar Keralite dishes like Travancore *konju vechathu* – a prawn curry with coconut and garam masala. A must-try is the *aatirachi peralan* – tender mutton and raw banana. Book a table in the upstairs room with a coconut thatch ceiling – Kerala houseboat-style.

International

Aurus
Nichani Kutir, Juhu Tara Road, near Nike showroom, Juhu (6710-6666). Santa Cruz station. **Open** 7.30pm-12.30am daily. **Main courses** Rs 500-Rs 800. **Credit** Amex, MC, V.
Aurus's outdoor deck is among the most pleasant places in the city to listen to the waves and watch the moon chart its course across the inky sky. Pretty Moroccan lamps sit on tables set with nouvelle American cuisine. The short menu is fairly exciting, featuring lemon-grass-rubbed prawns with wasabi foam and creole baby potatoes with blue-cheese dip, Moroccan lamb slices with mozzarella, jalapeno chicken with Camembert dip. The vegetarian mains draw heavily from the Mediterranean, with several pasta offerings. Reservations are recommended if you want to sit outside.

Penne
14 Silver Beach, opposite Spinach Supermarket, AB Nair Road, Juhu (2625-5706) Vile Parle station. **Open** noon-12.30am daily. **Main courses** Rs 350-Rs 500. **Credit** MC, V.

Located on a quiet backlane, Penne is a good place for a date, with its open courtyard seating, tables for two and understated elegance. The food is innovative and, for the most part, quite exciting.

Temple Flower
Kings International Hotel, 5 Juhu Tara Road, Juhu (6692-2222). Vile Parle station. **Taxi** Prithvi Theatre. **Open** 11.30am-3.30pm, 7.30pm-12.30am daily. **Main courses** Rs 150-Rs 250. **Credit** AmEx, MC, V.
The menu roams freely across borders but Temple Flower's heart lies in Thailand and Indonesia. The basics are done simply but supremely well – try the richly flavoured Thai yellow curry with prawns. Although modestly sized, it's a good-looking place, with slate floors and lots of dark, chocolatey wood.

Cafés

Bombay Baking Company
JW Marriott, Juhu Tara Road, Juhu (6693-3399). Vile Parle station. **Taxi** Marriott. **Open** 7am-10pm. **Credit** AmEx, DC, MC, V. **No alcohol**.
BBC, as it is known by locals, is a favourite with Bollywood stars meeting producers, scriptwriters and each other. A cute café just off from the Marriott's cavernous lobby, it has a little bookstore and does good sandwiches, salads and coffees.

Brio
Shopper's Stop, next to Chandan Cinema, JVPD Scheme, Vile Parle (W) (2625-6281). Vile Parle station. **Open** 11am-11pm daily. **Main courses** Rs 150. **No credit cards. No alcohol**.

Paan handling

There's nothing like a sweet *paan* to finish off a meal. *Paan masalas* are highly popular concoctions made from betel leaves and nuts and numerous other ingredients, sold by tiny *paanwallah* stalls on streets across the city. The key ingredient is shavings of betel nut, or *supari*, a mild stimulant that leaves a characteristic red stain on the teeth. It's chewed slowly and the juice spat out – hence the red stains on streets and walls across Mumbai. Different *paanwallahs* offer different versions, some bitter and some sweet, some from Benares, some from Calcutta.

Common ingredients include lime paste, cloves and cardamom. Others add coconut and sugar, or jellied fruits, dates and honey, all wrapped neatly in a betel leaf and sometimes covered in silver leaf. People often favour *paan* as a post-dinner digestive, but others take it for its alleged aphrodisiac properties, with the big daddy of *paan* Viagra

being the *palang-tod* ('bed-breaker'). You can find *paan* on any street corner usually for between Rs 5 and Rs 50, depending on the extravagance of the *paan*. Muchhad, named for the moustaches sported by the brothers who own the stall, is among the best-known in the city.

Muchhad Paanwala
Opposite Barista, Bhulabhai Desai Road (2369-0782/www.paan.com). **Open** 7am-1am daily.

Feast with the thesps at **Prithvi Theatre Café**.

Large windows along one wall afford diners a view of the tables ranged outside and a dark wood counter occupies the other wall, its glass shelves packed with pastries, tarts, pies, croissants, cookies and breads. The menu is partial to quick snacks and coffee with a selection of salads, pastas, crêpes and pizzas.

Prithvi Theatre Café
Prithvi Theatre, Janki Kutir, Juhu Church Road, Juhu (2617-4118). Vile Parle station. Open 11am-midnight daily. **No credit cards. No alcohol.**
This cosy alfresco café in Prithvi Theatre is the happy refuge of many a fledgling actor and director. Recently re-opened under new management, Prithvi Café hasn't lost an ounce of its character. While their famous, and extremely popular (non-alcoholic) Irish Coffee has been retained, the café has introduced famous dishes from restaurants and eateries across the city on its menu, making a great place to do a little culinary tour of the city in one place. Try the kebabs, the fresh fruit ice-cream, and the baked snacks.

Around the airports

Indian

Peshawri
ITC The Maratha, Sahar Airport Road, Andheri (E) (2830-3030). Andheri station. Open 7.30-11.45pm daily. **Main Courses** Rs 400-Rs 600. **Credit** AmEx, MC, V.
The single best import into Mumbai from the North-West Frontier Province, Peshawri at the ITC Maratha makes the sort of food that connoisseurs across the world fawn over. Food here is prepared authentically (and visibly in a glass-encased kitchen) in *tandoors* and gigantic bubbling vats. Kebabs are tender and juicy, *rotis* soft and crisp and the world-famous *dal* Bukhara (now also sold in a ready-to-eat format in branded cans) is cooked just as it should

be: overnight, with lots of cream and the subtlest of seasoning. Book in advance. *Photo p93.*

International

Celini
Grand Hyatt, Kalina, Santa Cruz (E) (6676-1234). Santa Cruz station. Open 12.30-3pm, 7.30pm-midnight daily. **Main courses** Rs 650-Rs 1,000. **Credit** AmEx, DC, MC, V.
This is where you go for the perfect pizza: thin and crisp, with toppings of Italian cheese, fresh vegetables and quality meats. Celini's open kitchen and wood-and-glass interiors make it contemporary and casual, with a kitchen philosophy that's focused on home-style cooking. Don't miss the gorgeous pannacotta.

China House
Grand Hyatt, Kalina, Santa Cruz (E) (6676-1234). Santa Cruz station. Open 12.30-3pm, 7.30pm-12.30am daily. **Main courses** Rs 300-Rs 650. **Credit** AmEx, DC, MC, V.
China House looks like a cross between an old Beijing tea house and a hypermodern Shanghai office tower. The decor is a mix of dark wood and shiny glass. Diners sit around five open kitchens (preparing appetisers, noodles and dumplings, Peking Duck, wok dishes and desserts) or in one of four private rooms. Though the menu at China House has a predisposition to Sichuan specialities, none of the dishes have the tongue-numbing spiciness most Indians chuck in. Instead, the food has strong, clear flavours, using spice to accentuate the taste of the ingredients rather than overwhelm them. *Photo p107.*

Pan-Asian
ITC The Maratha, Sahar Airport Road, Andheri (E) (2830-3030). Andheri station. Open 12.30-2.45pm, 7.30-11.45pm daily. **Main courses** Rs 500-Rs 1,400. **Credit** AmEx, MC, V.
A sprawling, gorgeous restaurant and possibly the big daddy of Mumbai's many pan-Asian restaurants, Pan-Asian has no less than five separate kitchens dedicated to different cuisines: Mongolian, Chinese, Japanese, Thai and Korean. It's also unique in offering tables with built-in grills for authentic Korean barbecues. The Cantonese roasted chicken here is particularly good.

Stax
Hyatt Regency, Sahar Airport Road, Andheri (E) (6696-1234). Andheri station. Open 7-11.30pm daily. **Main courses** Rs 700-Rs 1,000. **Credit** AmEx, MC, V.
Stax deftly combines modern steel-and-glass design and touches straight out of an Italian trattoria, with a live kitchen and a soundtrack of 1960s and '70s Italian hits. The food is top quality, with a stunning signature dish of seabass and leek fondue in Sicilian sauce and a gorgeous rack of lamb encrusted with pistachios in a bitter chocolate sauce.

Pubs & Bars

Dodgy dives, languid lounges and trendy taverns.

British Bombay was founded in an orgy of drunkenness and debauchery, with officials of the East India Company often dying young thanks to their intemperate habits. According to MD David's *History of Bombay 1661-1708*, Englishmen in Mumbai 'led a life which was shameful and loose with drinks, duels, frauds, luxury, immodesty and prostitution'. In the 18th century, the Company tried to restrain the number of punch houses by reducing the number of licences, much like today's Mumbai, where bars are a soft target for conservative outrage.

But the tradition of debauchery continues into the 21st century, with boozers of all descriptions catering to every sort of Mumbaikar: cheap and cheerless 'country liquor' bars; working class 'permit rooms' (*see p116* **Licence to swill**); lively white-collar and college-kid hangouts like Ghetto and Toto's; and fancy cocktail bars like Busaba and Zenzi for when you want to splash out. Spirits are the drink of choice in dives while beer (sold in 330ml bottles called pints or in 650ml bottles) continues to reign supreme in the posher bars. The most famous may be the ubiquitous Kingfisher, but there's a lot more choice (and arguably tastier beers) like Haywards 2000, Golden Eagle, and Royal Challenge. There's even a homegrown stout called Haywards Black. As major international brands eye India's loaded middle class, foreign brews and spirits have come pouring in and the choice of drinks is wider than ever before. Cocktails have become hugely popular in recent years, especially fruity twists on traditional mixes, and the venerable whisky-soda is in grave danger of being overtaken in popularity by the vodka-Sprite.

But a class distinction persists in the city's drinking culture: at most of the bars listed in this guide, you're unlikely to find yourself sharing a table with a postman or a grocer. The boundaries of Mumbai's social circles may not be spelt out in words but they are clearly circumscribed in action and rarely do different demographic groups meet. Not only does this make it difficult for locals to meet people they aren't already connected to in some obvious or arcane way, but it also restricts the citizenry's perception of their fellow Mumbaikars as well, for to hang out in Mumbai bars is to play a massive game of six degrees of separation. Then there's the gender thing: working-class

bars are exclusively male. Women from the upper-middle and elite classes frequent more expensive bars where it is considered acceptable, but for the mainstream, women who drink alcohol – especially without male company – are almost automatically considered to be made of low moral fibre. Many 'permit rooms' don't even have a loo for the ladies and some deny them entry altogether (citing women's safety as the reason). However, nobody seems to care very much.

DOS AND DON'TS

In country liquor bars or working-class haunts, female drinkers – especially foreigners – are likely to be the target of uncomfortable stares or unwelcome attention, so with a few clearly stated exceptions we've avoided listing them. We've divided bars and clubs on one criterion, whether there is a dance floor or not – *see p157* **Nightlife** for club listings.

> ❶ Pink numbers given in this chapter correspond to the location of each pub and bar as marked on the street maps. *See pp249-255.*

The best Bars

For stunning views
Aurus (*see p115*), **Dome** (*see p113*) and **Sea View** (*see p116*).

For fine cocktails
Busaba (*see p111*), **Henry Tham** (*see p111*) and **Wink** (*see p112*).

For mixing it with Mumbaikars
China House (*see p115*), the **Ghetto** (*see p113*) and **Shiro** (*see p114*).

For live music
Blue Frog (*see p113*), **Not Just Jazz by the Bay** (*see p113*) and **Soul Fry Casa** (*see p113*).

For inexpensive drinks
Indus (*see p112*); **Ivy** (*see p114*) and **Café Universal** (*see p112*).

By law, bars are required to close by 1.30am, unless they have special permission or, more frequently, have paid bribes to the local police. Bars inside five-star hotels are allowed to stay open until 3am. Expect to pay the equivalent of western prices at five-star hotel bars and most cocktail bars. All liquor is subject to 20 per cent tax. Most bars have table service; it's rare to have to fetch drinks from the bar. Tipping is at your discretion, usually around ten per cent.

Colaba

Busaba
4 Mandlik Road, off Colaba Causeway, Colaba (2204-3779/3769). CST or Churchgate stations. **Taxi** behind Taj Mahal Hotel. **Open** noon-3pm, 6.30pm-1am daily. **Credit** AmEx, MC, V. **Map** p251 G5 ❶
Neighbouring Indigo may be where South Mumbai's la-di-dah types go when they want to spend the GDP of a small African nation for an evening out but Busaba does the better (and slightly cheaper) cocktails and attracts a hipper crowd.

Café Mondegar
Colaba Causeway, near Regal Cinema, Colaba (2202-0591). CST or Churchgate stations. **Open** 8am-midnight daily. **Credit** MC, V. **Map** p251 G5 ❷
It's always ten degrees hotter inside Mondy's than out. It must be all the bodies they cram in: four to each table and as many tables wedged in as possible. The ear-splitting chatter from college students, foreign travellers and office workers competes with a chunky jukebox at the back, where Pink Floyd and the Doors seem to be on permanent rotation. Mondy's is as popular with Mumbaikars as it is with tourists, and the tile wall murals in the style of Goan caricaturist Mario Miranda make it a local landmark. Don't be offended by the service: they're as surly with locals.

Gokul
Nawaz Building, 10 Tulloch Road, off Colaba Causeway (2284-8504). CST or Churchgate stations. **Open** 11am-12.30am daily. **No credit cards**. **Map** p251 G5 ❸
Once a haven for the city's gay community, these days the crowd at Gokul is far less easy to bracket – an easy-going mix of foreign travellers, students, office-goers, habitual drunks and, sometimes, even families. It's a dim back-room haunt with four sections, some cavernous, some pokey; the liquor is marginally cheaper in the non air-con parts. Spirits come by the peg (30/60ml) or by the quarter bottle (180ml), the beer is always cold, and the food is down and dirty local Indian and Indian-Chinese.

Henry Tham
Dhanraj Mahal, Apollo Bunder, Colaba (2202-3186/2284-8214). CST or Churchgate stations. **Taxi** Gateway of India. **Open** 12.30-3.30pm, 7.30pm-1.30am daily. **Credit** AmEx, MC, V. **Map** p251 G5 ❹
Tham's is one of the few places in the city that actually gets the concept of a lounge, and strikes just the

Dome. *See p113.*

right balance between the understated and the ostentatious. There's a simple sophistication in the functional if familiar interior: wood flooring, plush, comfy sofas, South-east Asian artefacts, and an L-shaped design that accommodates plenty of standing room along the bar. The cocktails are expensive, the starters excellent and the crowd a mix of pinstripe shirts and pretty young things, while the music is a mix of sporadic gigs, thumping electronica and piped world music.

Dry days

Wine shops and bars are forbidden from selling alcohol on certain days of the year, known as dry days, usually out of respect for the occasion. These days range from the nation's Independence Day to Mahatma Gandhi's birth anniversary and even the 48 hours before an election. Even days when votes are being counted are dry, making India's tortuously long general elections a nightmare for those of us who like a tipple. By law, foreigners are exempt from the ban, but many bars just close for the day. The restriction doesn't apply to drinking at home and the dry day isn't midnight to midnight, but for the duration of a single working day. Most five-star hotel bars will serve alcohol to foreigners on production of a passport (though a non-Indian complexion will usually do).

26 January Republic Day
30 January Martyrs' Day
1 May Maharashtra Day
15 August Independence Day
August-September Ananta Chaturdashi & Gauri Visarjan (Ganesh celebrations)
2 October Gandhi Jayanti (anniversary of Gandhi's birth)
8 October End of Gandhi Week

Eat, Drink, Shop

Indus Cocktail Bar & Tandoor

Ground Floor, Hotel Diplomat, Apollo Bunder,
Colaba (2202-1661). CST or Churchgate stations.
Taxi behind Taj Mahal Hotel. **Open** noon-3.30pm,
6pm-1am daily. **Credit** MC, V. **Map** p251 G5 ⑤
Indus is a cute little cocktail bar that does happy
hours between 6pm and 8pm and serves some delicious kebabs (with *kali dal* gratis). The clientele is
a mix of tourists, couples, suits and yuppies, the
drinks are competent and the bartenders friendly.
It isn't particularly large but seats tend to free up
on a fairly regular basis.

Indigo

4 Mandlik Road, off Colaba Causeway, Colaba (6636-
8999). CST or Churchgate stations. **Taxi** behind Taj
Mahal Hotel. **Open** noon-3pm, 6.30pm-1.30am daily.
Credit AmEx, DC, MC, V. **Map** p251 G5 ⑥
South Mumbai's premier watering hole for the well-
heeled, Indigo is pretty much an institution. On
weekends it's packed wall-to-wall with strutting
women in strapless, backless dresses and their
pumped-up boys in print shirts. Nobody gets too
comfortable as seats are few; the ambience is chic
hotel lobby. After 11pm, the crush can get rib-crack-
ing, so head for the upstairs lounge, or even better,
the beautiful, candlelit terrace.

Leopold Café

Colaba Causeway, Colaba (2202-0131). CST or
Churchgate stations. **Open** 7.30am-midnight daily.
Credit AmEx, MC, V. **Map** p251 G5 ⑦
The default drinking destination for foreign travellers, Leo's has all the atmosphere of a railway station waiting room and staff are about as friendly as
the gent behind the station's enquiry counter when
you ask about a much-delayed train. Yet sheer size,
cheap drinks and its prominence in Gregory David
Roberts' *Shantaram* make Leo's a favourite.

Sports Bar Express

Regal Cinema Building, Colaba Causeway, Colaba
(6639-6682). CST or Churchgate stations. **Open** noon-
1am daily. **Credit** AmEx, MC, V. **Map** p251 G5 ⑧
Sports Bar Express doesn't offer much in the
way of character but it's conveniently located and

inexpensive. All American diner-ish in look and
decidedly Indian in choice of sport on the plasma
screen (cricket, cricket, cricket), it's a fair option for
a few drinks on a hot day. Avoid the snacks.

Wink

Taj President, Cuffe Parade (6665-0808).
Churchgate station. **Taxi** Taj President. **Open**
6pm-1.30am daily. **Credit** AmEx, MC, V. **Map**
p250 E3 ⑨
Hotel bars in Mumbai tend to be staid, unexciting
and, frankly, a waste of time. But Wink, at the
President, changed all that when it opened in 2006.
Intricate metal grills, angled brick walls and an
island bar designed by Japanese firm SuperPotato
fade into the background when you try their cocktails, mixed by some of the best bartenders in
town. Electronica forms an essential part of the
aural vibe but conversation thrives and the free
wasabi-flavoured peas are yummy.

Woodside Inn

Indian Mercantile Mansion, Wodehouse Road,
opposite Regal, Colaba (2202-5525/2287-5752).
CST or Churchgate stations. **Open** noon-1am
daily. **Credit** AmEx, MC, V. **Map** p251 G6 ⑩
One-time hole-in-the-wall dive, Woodside Inn was
recently refurbished and is now a cosy little tavern
with framed pictures of Mumbai, smiling staff and
cheap drinks. The music varies wildly from the
Beatles to the Red Hot Chilli Peppers but the lack of
pretension and the homely atmosphere make it a
nice escape from the madness of the Causeway.

Fort

Café Universal

299 Shahid Bhagat Singh Road, Fort (2261-3985).
CST or Churchgate stations. **Taxi** Ballard Estate.
Open 9am-midnight daily. **Credit** AmEx, MC, V.
Map p252 J9 ⑪
The 85-year-old Café Universal is an excellent exam-
ple of how to renovate an old bar without losing any
of its character or giving in to crass market forces.
It's big and bright, with lots of natural light stream-
ing in and the design is very art nouveau. Universal

Café Universal.

Shiro. *See p114.*

only does beer and wine but an extensive food menu includes Chinese and Zoroastrian food, as well as steaks, sandwiches and soups.

Soul Fry Casa
Currimjee Building, opposite Mumbai University, MG Road, Fort (2267-1421). CST or Churchgate stations. **Taxi** Kala Ghoda. **Open** 7pm-midnight daily. **Credit** AmEx, MC, V. **Map** p251 G7 ⑫
Kitschy adverts line the walls, an irony-laden colonial-era fog hangs heavy in the air and Konkani music fills the spaces in between. Munch on calamares and fried prawns and if it's a night with live music, you can watch bands play jazz standards and vintage pop or, if you're really lucky, drunken uncles singing 'Careless Whisper'. The bar is small but they don't really mind if you continue drinking in the dining area.

Churchgate

Café Oval
Eros Cinema, Churchgate (6634-5721). Churchgate station. **Open** 9am-11pm daily. **No credit cards.** **Map** p251 & p252 G8 ⑬
This tiny, Irani-run bar opposite the Oval Maidan is bare and spare but has its own 1940s-style Bombay charm, walls lined with crates of beer and the waiters sliding on to the old wooden benches to chat with regulars. The posters of Sachin Tendulkar have long since been replaced by Joss Stone, but little else changes here. This is a mostly male hangout but women need not feel unwelcome. After all, there's a wooden board on the wall declaring that 'Shop is open to all caste.'

Dome
InterContinental Marine Drive, 135 Marine Drive, (6639-9999/www.intercontinental.com). Churchgate

station. **Open** 6pm-1.30am daily. **Credit** AmEx, DC, MC, V. **Map** p251 & p252 E8 ⑭
Undoubtedly South Mumbai's finest hotel bar. Dome is a lounge/grill occupying the InterCon's eighth-floor rooftop terrace, overlooking the fabulous arc of the seafront promenade. The walls are white, the tiled floor is white and the abundant sofas and armchairs are all wrapped in white cotton. A raised platform holds the aqua-blue swimming pool, while a corner rotunda houses a sleek aluminium-and-glass bar counter with matching stools. Be sure to drop in before 6.30pm for the glorious pink-orange sunset. *Photo p111.*

Not Just Jazz by the Bay
Soona Mahal, 143 Marine Drive (2285-1876). Churchgate station. **Open** 12.15pm-3.15pm, 6pm-1.30am daily. **Credit** AmEx, DC, MC, V. **Map** p251 & p252 E8 ⑮
Locally known simply as 'Jazz', this sole survivor of Bombay's '50s jazz era is among the handful of live music options in the city. Wednesdays through Saturdays draw the older crowd for bands usually dishing out jazz, country and rock. Sundays through Tuesdays are reserved for the wildly popular karaoke nights for students and young professionals seeking therapy on stage. An entry fee of Rs 200 applies.

Mahalaxmi

Ghetto
30B Bhulabhai Desai Road, near Mahalaxmi Temple, Breach Candy (2353-8418). Mahalaxmi station. **Taxi** Mahalaxmi Temple. **Open** 7pm-1.30am daily. **Credit** MC, V.
This smoky rockers' hangout has been boozing for a decade and a half, and a fanatical band of regulars are permanently fixed to its barstools. The college pub-like atmosphere is deceptive – most patrons are thirtysomething media professionals who have been coming here since their first year of university. The walls are thick with graffiti (ask for a felt pen if you want to leave your mark) and Jim Morrison murals are illuminated by UV tubelights. Expect the obligatory 1980s rock soundtrack.

Lower Parel & Worli

Blue Frog
Todi & Co, Mathuradas Mill Compound, Senapati Bapat Marg, Lower Parel (4033-2300/ www.bluefrog.co.in). **Open** 7pm-1.15am daily. **Credit** AmEx, DC, MC,V.
Blue Frog is quite simply the best-looking nightspot in Mumbai. When you walk into the 6,000sq ft space, you can't help but be struck by its magnificence. Using circular seating 'pods', innovative lighting and an amphitheatre-like design, the architects have attempted to create an opera house-meets-warehouse hybrid. The post-industrial vibe is complemented by the funky visuals projected on the screens and the bump patterns on the walls (they're

there to help the acoustics). They host local bands on weekdays and fly in international acts on the weekends and the atmosphere is always electric. A Rs 300 entry charge applies.

Hard Rock Café
Bombay Dyeing Mills Compound, Pandurang Budhkar Marg, Worli (2438-2888). Lower Parel station. **Taxi** Kamala Mills. **Open** noon-1.30am daily. **Credit** AmEx, MC, V.
Anywhere else in the world, it's a tourist trap. In Mumbai, it's the playground for the city's young and tasteless. Still, the Hard Rock Café is worth a visit for its sheer size and to see where all those New India rupees are going and who's spending them. Its also hosts gigs on Tuesdays and Thursday, but if you're expecting hard rock, you're likely to be disappointed.

Ivy.

Hawaiian Shack.

Ivy
Indage House, Annie Besant Road, Worli (6654-7939). Mahalaxmi station. **Taxi** Worli Naka. **Open** 11am-1am daily. **Credit** AmEx, MC, V.
Ivy is everything you wouldn't expect a wine bar to be. It has none of that trying-to-be-posh hokum with dim lighting, wood panelling and leather sofas, and it doesn't expect its patrons to wear suits, smoke cigars and talk about how badly the Dow is faring while they sip their white Zinfandels. Instead, with bright lights, blazing pink walls and an all-embracing attitude, it's a cheerful, genial wine bar that attracts a crowd as mixed as any beer bar.

Shiro
Bombay Dyeing Mills Compound, Pandurang Budhkar Marg, Worli. (2438-3008). Lower Parel station. **Taxi** Kamala Mills. **Open** 7pm-1.30am daily. **Credit** AmEx, MC, V.
Located in a former mill and filled to the rafters with the city's swish set, Shiro is an East Asian-themed bar on acid. It's like drinking in Alice's wonderland. Curtains of red-glass teardrops greet you as you enter, as does a serenely oversized statue of a Buddhist monkette eternally pouring water from a pot in her palm. The walls are stone, occasionally recessed to accommodate Buddha busts and thick candles dripping wax all the way down to the floor; the beams are wood, and the drinks are stellar. It's important to remember though, that when logic and proportion have fallen by the wayside, the shrinking feeling you experienced extends to your wallet as well. *Photo p113.*

Bandra

Hawaiian Shack
16th Road, Bandra (W) (99873-97663). Bandra station. **Taxi** near Mini Punjab. **Open** 6pm-1.30am daily. **Credit** MC, V. **Map** p249 C3 ⑯
What makes Hawaiian Shack Bandra's most popular pub? Is it the outstanding service? The resemblance to the inside of an old wooden ship? Or could it be that a large number of Mumbaikars still think the 1980s had the best pop music? In any other country, a bar that played so much Madonna and Boney M would surely be a gay joint, but this is India, where the two men holding hands or dancing together next to your table are probably just good friends.

Janata
Ambedkar Road, Pali Naka, Bandra (W) (2600-4049). Bandra station. **Taxi** Pali Naka. **Open** 11am-1.30am daily. **Credit** MC, V. **Map** p249 B3 ⑰
Rub shoulders with retired technocrats, broke college students, yuppies tanking up before hitting the clubs, Bandra boys, immigrants, policemen and everyone in between. In part, its popularity is explained by the superlative food, but what really works for Janata is the great location, friendly service and all-embracing attitude. As a now gentrified 'permit room', a group of girls *sans* male escort need not feel uncomfortable.

Sea View tells it as it is. *See p116.*

Olive Bar & Kitchen

4 Union Park, Pali Hill Tourist Hotel, Khar (W)
(2605-8228). Khar station. **Taxi** near Café Coffee
Day, Carter Road. **Open** 8pm-1.30am daily. **Credit**
AmEx, DC, MC, V. **Map** p249 A1 ⑱
The suburbs' swishest spot for those who want
to see and be seen, packed to the gills with models, actors and Bandra's rich and shameless. The
Pulitzer Prize-nominated author of *Maximum City*,
Suketu Mehta, maintains that on Thursday nights
the most beautiful women in Mumbai come to
Olive. Pretty faces and pilates-toned bodies certainly abound, but one regular patron calls Olive
a gay bar and 'one of the best places in the city to
pick up men'. Then again, his female friends
seem to agree. This place can be tricky to find, so
call ahead for directions.

Seijo & the Soul Dish

Krystal, Second Floor, Waterfield Road, Bandra (W)
(2640-5555). Bandra station. **Taxi** Waterfield Road.
Open 7.30pm-1.30am daily. **Credit** AmEx, MC, V.
Map p249 D4 ⑲
Aimed at professional thirtysomethings, Seijo is
drenched in red and black hues, with Japanese pop
art splashed on the walls. They do good cocktails
and occasionally have live acts.

Toto's Garage

30 Lourdes Heaven, Pali Junction, Bandra (W)
(2600-5494). Bandra station. **Taxi** Pali Naka.
Open 6pm-1.20am daily. **Credit** AmEx, MC, V.
Map p249 C3 ⑳
Engine parts, hubcaps and number plates emblazon
the walls of Toto's Garage. One of the city's most
popular watering holes with office workers and students, with an air as casual as the waiters' denim
overalls. The playlist segues from the Doors to
Duran Duran to Rammstein without an eyebrow
being raised. It's cheap too.

Zenzi

183 Waterfield Road, Bandra (W) (6643-0670).
Bandra station. **Taxi** Waterfield Road. **Open** 7pm-
1.30am daily. **Credit** MC, V. **Map** p249 D3 ㉑

This gorgeous bar-restaurant is without a doubt a
perennial upmarket Bandra favourite. Zenzi
extends deeply off the street into a long bar/dining
area that's split by glass, decked out in natural
woods and lit by candlelight. Populated largely
by models, musicians, media types and other
assorted folk with what they like to call 'boho' job
descriptions, Zenzi treads a fine line between pre-
tentious and truly liberated.

Santa Cruz

China House

Grand Hyatt, off the Western Express Highway,
Santa Cruz (E) (6676-1234). Santa Cruz station.
Taxi Vakola Hyatt. **Open** 6pm-3am daily. **Credit**
AmEx, MC, V.
Designed by the same firm that did the President's
Wink, China House is located way out in the middle
of nowhere but that hasn't stopped it from becoming wildly popular. Perennially afflicted by the
Bollywood crowd, it's also full of pretty girls, their
goofy boyfriends and pretty much anybody who
still wants a drink in the suburbs after the 1.30am
deadline. Great cocktails, sexy design, energetic vibe
but rubbish music most of the time.

Juhu

Aurus

Nichani Kutir, Juhu Tara Road, between Nike & Reid
and Taylor showrooms, Juhu (6710-6666/67). Santa
Cruz station. **Taxi** Juhu Tara Road. **Open** 8.30pm-
1.30am daily. **Credit** AmEx, MC, V.
There is absolutely no finer place to sip a
cocktail than leaning against the railings high above
the sand watching the lights of airliners as they
slither across the silvery waves. The crowd at Aurus
is primarily the young and aspiring-to-be-famous
children of Bollywood movie stars and their hang-
ers on, but don't let that dissuade you. The entrance
is so discreet, you'll miss it if you don't know it, so
call ahead for directions.

Eat, Drink, Shop

Sea View

Behind the police station, Juhu Beach (2660-5942). Vile Parle Station. **Taxi** Juhu Beach. **Open** 9am-11pm daily. **No credit cards.**

In early 2008, cries of panic went up with the news that the 70-year-old Sea View had been sold. As old-timers mourned the death of an institution, the new management surprised everyone by not demolishing it to make way for a high-rise, instead only changing the furniture and raising the prices a little. The antithesis of froufrou, Sea View is a series of tables and chairs lined up against a low wall, but it's what's behind the wall that counts. With spectacular views of Juhu Beach, good-value beer (and only beer) and a very liberal policy on smoking, it's the closest you get to Goa without actually getting to Goa. *Photo p115.*

Vie Lounge & Deck

102 Juhu Tara Road, Juhu (2660-3003). Santa Cruz station. **Taxi** opposite Little Italy restaurant. **Open** 8pm-1.30am daily. **Credit** AmEx, DC, MC, V.

Vie's killer location on Juhu Beach is a good starting point, and the design makes the most of it. Sloping glass planes intersect with palms and the luminescent back-lit panels of the open-air deck glow under starlit skies. It's set back a little from the road and can be tricky to find, so call ahead for directions.

Licence to swill

In the hierarchy of Mumbai's drinking establishments, permit rooms fall somewhere between the pubs that cater to middle-management and the country liquor bars that attract the city's working class. According to an archaic law, the state of Maharashtra is still technically a land of prohibition, with any tippler required by law to carry a permit stating that he 'continues to require foreign liquor and country liquor for preservation and maintenance of my health'. Although this rule is largely ignored, the permit rooms that sprung up as prohibition began to wane continue to bear the name and are a safe haven for men who care little for ambience or atmosphere, concentrating instead on drinking large quantities.

Unconvinced of the need for ostentatious decor or music, permit rooms are generally little more than Formica tables and benches slapped together with maybe a television in one corner. Tables are often shared and the clientele is almost always male. Liquor is served in small (30ml), large (60ml), half nip (90ml) and nip (or quarter) (180ml) measures.

Mumbai's permit rooms have their own uniform aesthetics. The bars in the south are older and more beaten up. They have wooden chairs and spacious halls rather than narrow corridors and English-sounding names like Lord Irwin and Felicity. Many were Irani restaurants that found greater profits in liquor. In the suburbs, wooden chairs give way to beige and red plastic but the overall design remains the same.

Frequented largely by college students, low-level white-collar workers and small traders at the end of the day's work, permit rooms open early in the morning and close by midnight. Most patrons chose one over the other simply by virtue of location and convenience, but over the last few years some have been gentrified and now see large numbers of tourists, kids tanking up before hitting the clubs, spillover from nearby bars and even – gasp! – women. For a taste of the cheap, Mumbai way to drink, visit Café Oval in Churchgate (*see p113*) or Janata in Bandra (*see p114*). For a permit room with real character, check out Kit Kat, which is retro by virtue of never having been refurbished.

Kit Kat

Opposite Metro Adlabs, Dhobi Talao (2209-4112). Marine Lines station. **Taxi** Metro Cinema. **Open** 11am-midnight daily. **No credit cards. Map** p252 F11 ㉒

Shops & Services

A juxtaposition of markets and malls.

Until the last decade of the 20th century, Mumbaikars, like all Indians, wrote out long lists of requests for aunts, brothers-in-law or cousins twice removed who were planning trips abroad. Few imported consumer products were available in Indian stores, so even munching on a bar of Kit-Kat was a status symbol. All that has now changed, with economic liberalisation and lower import duties. Mumbaikars have adapted to shopping sprees with remarkable ease, without forgetting the speciality markets and old favourites that held them in good stead for decades past.

Colaba is king for kitsch and trinkets, as well as a good offering of mid-range and expensive shops, but other retail hotspots have sprung up that are great to shop around, and also make for an interesting portrait of the city's changing socio-economics and geography. Mumbai's glamour industry lives primarily in Bandra, where boutique stores abound with an eclectic mix of imported jeans and T-shirts, as well as homegrown designerwear. Lower Parel has become a hub of activity since its dilapidated mills were sold to private developers and converted into prime retail and residential spaces. The outsourcing boom has also made once-sleepy Malad a hot shopping destination, with the city's best-looking mall, InOrbit. With Mumbai's heat, dust and crowds, you should take the phrase 'shop till you drop' a little less literally than you would at home – give yourself plenty of time and carry lots of water.

THE BASICS

Most stores open by 11am and close around 8pm. Visa and MasterCard are accepted almost everywhere, except at markets and street stalls, where cash is king. Some marketwallahs and street vendors might double, triple or quadruple their prices for foreigners. Friendly haggling is required and a few Hindi phrases may come in

Haggle in Hindi

Ye kitne ka hai? How much is this?
Aap pagal ho kya? Are you insane?
Bahut zyaada hai That's very expensive.
Theek bhao bolo Quote the right price.
Bhao thoda kam karna Drop the price a bit.
Dhanyavaad! Thank you!

The best | Shops

For fine Indian fashion
Amara (*see p118*), **Aza** (*see p119*), the **Courtyard** (*see p120*) and **FabIndia** (*see p121*).

For manic Mumbai markets
Chor Bazaar (*see p129*), **Crawford Market** (*see p129*) and **Mangaldas Market** (*see p129*).

For jewellery
Amrapali (*see p125*), **Curio Cottage** (*see p125*) and **TBZ** (*see p125*).

For glittering Indian sweets
Brijwasi (*see p125*) and **Camy Wafer** (*see p125*).

For the latest Indian sounds
BX Furtado & Sons (*see p131*) and **Rhythm House** (*see p131*).

handy (*see below* **Haggle in Hindi**) but bargaining in shops is considered bad form.

Books

Crossword
Mohammed Bhai Mansion, Hughes Road, Kemp's Corner (2384-2001). Grant Road station. **Open** 11am-8.30pm daily. **Credit** AmEx, DC, MC, V.
The flagship store of Mumbai's best-known bookstore chain also sells music and movies, toys and games, and has a great café with pastries, sandwiches and coffee. They also host author readings, forums and children's events.
Other location Noor Mahal, Ground Floor, Turner Road, Bandra (W) (3956-5547).

Landmark
Second Floor, Infiniti Mall, New Link Road, Andheri (W) (2639-6010). Andheri station. **Open** 10.30am-8pm daily. **Credit** AmEx, DC, MC, V.
Mumbai's biggest bookstore, with the best collection. Landmark moves beyond bestsellers to stock titles that you won't find anywhere else in the city, including a great collection of graphic novels, film books and literary fiction. It's also one of the few bookshops in town where the staff actually seem to read the books they stock. Worth the trek to Andheri.

Nalanda
Taj Mahal Palace & Tower, Lobby Level, Apollo Bunder, Colaba (2202-2514). CST or Churchgate stations. **Open** 8am-midnight daily. **Credit** AmEx, DC, MC, V.
This is where to go for glossy coffee table books on Rajasthani palaces, Benarasi textiles and the *Kama Sutra*. Nalanda is small but has a strong India focus, and a strong collection of Indian non-fiction. It also stocks international magazines and newspapers.

New & Secondhand Bookstore
Kalbadevi Road, Near Metro Cinema, Dhobi Talao (2201-3314). CST or Marine Lines stations. **Open** 10am-7.30pm Mon-Sat. **No credit cards.**
Now in its second century, New & Secondhand Bookstore is a treasure trove of collectibles, odds and ends, and out-of-prints. Titles include travel guides to the Soviet Union, a history of Elephanta Island and political manifestos. It's as close to an antiquarian bookshop as it gets in Mumbai, and they have a 30 per cent discount on the marked price.

Strand Book Stall
Cawasji Patel Street, off Sir PM Road, Fort (2266-1994/www.strandbookstall.com). CST or Churchgate stations. **Open** 10am-8pm Mon-Sat; 10am-7pm Sun. **Credit** AmEx, DC, MC, V.
The favourite of journalists and novelists, this city institution is tiny and stuffed with piles and piles of assorted books. While the space is not very conducive to browsing, it does have a range of lesser-known writers and the staff let you linger as long as you like. Most importantly, they offer an average discount of 20 per cent on every purchase.

Strand Book Stall is all it's stacked up to be.

Department stores

Asiatic
Veer Nariman Road, Churchgate (2283-4541/28). Churchgate Station. **Open** 10am-8.30pm Mon-Sat. **Credit** MC, V.

Lifestyle
High Street Phoenix, 462 Senapati Bapat Marg, Lower Parel (6666-9200). Lower Parel or Mahalaxmi stations. **Open** 10.30am-9.30pm daily. **Credit** AmEx, DC, MC, V.

Westside
Army & Navy Building, Kala Ghoda (6636-0499/0500). CST or Churchgate stations. **Open** 10.30am-9pm daily. **Credit** AmEx, DC, MC, V.

Electronics

Croma
JM Marg, Vasundhara Chambers, opposite Utpal Sanghvi School, Juhu (6710-3333). **Taxi** near Chandan Cinema. **Open** 11am-8.30pm. **Credit** AmEx, MC, V.
You could spend days wondering around the aisles of Croma; the shop stocks everything you could ever want in electronics.

Vijay Sales
29 New Queens Road, next to Charni Road Station, Opera House (2363-9210). **Open** 10.30am-8.30pm daily. **Credit** DC, MC, V.
Vijay Sales is a one-stop shop for gadgets, with stock ranging from refrigerators and television sets to iPods and mobile phones.
Other locations 225 Pandurang Bhuvan, Lady Jamsetjee Road, Shivaji Park (2430-9660); 108 Lady Jamsetjee Road, Mahim (2445-7959); 3 Bhatia Building, Zarina Society, SV Road, Bandra (W) (2642-2119).

Fashion

Indo-western designers

Amara
Hughes Road, Kemp's Corner (2387-9687/2387-2530). Grant Road station. **Open** 10.30am-8pm daily. **Credit** AmEx, MC, V.
A large, ambitious project located on prime South Mumbai property, selling wares by a range of exclusive designers. It doesn't stop at retail therapy though, you can also get a deep-tissue massage and some inspired fusion food at the attached Rudra spa-cum-salon and Ambiir restaurant.

Ananya
Burani Mahal, 59 Nepean Sea Road, behind Kotak Mahindra Bank (6571-4888). **Taxi** opposite Priyadarshani Park. **Open** 11am-8pm Mon-Sat. **Credit** MC, V.
A fashionista favourite, Ananya was originally started up in London by sisters Ansuya and Nandita

Curio city

Cushions

Why take postcards or snapshots when you can curl yourself around old prints of Mumbai's heritage? Even though it's all grand architecture, the Asiatic Library, Chhatrapati Shivaji Maharaj Vastu Sangrahalaya and Crawford Market never looked cuddlier than on Contemporary Arts & Crafts' cushions.
Contemporary Arts & Crafts *19 NG House, Nepean Sea Road, Kemp's Corner (2363-1979).* **Open** *10am-8pm Mon-Sat; 10am-7pm Sun.* **Credit** AmEx, MC, V. From Rs 930.

Elephants

Yes there are elephants on the streets of Mumbai and animal rights activists are doing their best to get them off. But if you walk along Colaba Causeway you will see a completely different type of pachyderm: little ones stacked vertically in threes and carved in delicate filigree, from a single piece of wood. You can also get them in ersatz miniature paintings, on tracing paper and on dried leaves.
Street vendors along Colaba Causeway. From Rs 250.

Home accessories

Fashion designer Krsna Mehta has superimposed cheeky pop culture references on old city images to make kitschy cushion covers, tiffins, watches, lampshades and coasters with a quirky take on the city.
Bombay Project by Krsna Mehta and Sangita Jindal *Good Earth, Raghuvanshi Mills, Senapati Bapat Marg, Lower Parel (2495-1954).* **Open** *11am-8pm daily.* **Credit** MC, V. From Rs 800.

Maps & prints

Phillips Antiques stocks old Mumbai photographs, lithographs, postcards, maps and some delightful prints of old advertising posters from Mumbai, like the one that features a heavily decorated elephant carrying a giant bobbin on its back with a biplane hovering in the background.
Phillips Antiques *Indian Mercantile Mansion, Madame Cama Road, opposite Regal Cinema, Colaba (2202-0564/www. phillipsantiques.com).* **Open** *10am-7pm Mon-Sat.* **Credit** MC, V. From Rs 2,000.

Mugs

Whether you like your froth caffeinated or hoppy, Café Mondegar tumblers are big enough for both. Take some of Mumbai's love-struck couples and beery revellers back home with you on its variety of mugs. The designs are picked off Mondy's walls and screen-printed on espresso cups, large ceramic beer mugs, ashtrays and soup bowls.
Café Mondegar *5A Metro House, Apollo Bunder, near Regal Cinema, Colaba (2202-0591).* **Open** *8am-1am daily.* From Rs 125.

Mahtani. Showcasing a range of high-profile Indian designers as well as its in-house label, it has some of the country's most colourful and quirky looks. **Other location** Shop 3, Pluto Building, Turner Road, Bandra (W) (6593-0262).

Aza

21 Siffy Apartments, Altamount Road, off Pedder Road (2351-7616). Grant Road station. **Open** *10am-8pm daily.* **Credit** AmEx, MC, V.
Leafy green Altamount Road is better known for its profusion of consulates and wealthy residents (think old, old money) than its fashion quotient, but that's changed with the arrival of Aza. This big store stocks a large range of up-and-coming designers from across the country. The staff are courteous, the fitting rooms roomy and alterations are done while you wait.

Aza for Men

Cornelian, Shop No 4, 104 August Kranti Marg, Kemp's Corner (2352-0212). **Open** *10am-8pm daily.* **Credit** AmEx, MC, V.
Twenty designers, a mix of established and young, showcase everything from *sherwanis* to shirts and accessories to go with them. You may have to get your trousers somewhere else, though, as Aza for Men stocks just a handful.

Barefoot

Anand Villa, Pali Mala Road, Bandra (W) (3296-5067). Bandra station. **Taxi** Carter Road Police Station. **Open** *11.30am-8pm Mon-Sat.* **Credit** MC, V.
Undoubtedly one of Bandra's best stores, Barefoot isn't just about shoes (although the leather slippers are fabulous). It's about funky clothing, with plenty of cool accessories and striking jewellery as well.

Eat, Drink, Shop

Bombay Electric

Reay House, BEST Marg, Colaba (2287-6276).
CST or Churchgate stations. **Open** 11am-9pm daily.
Credit AmEx, DC, MC, V.
Taking its name from the street it shares with south Mumbai's electricity board, Bombay Electric has an eclectic collection of Indian and international clothes for men, women and children.

Courtyard

Minoo Desai Marg, behind Radio Club, Apollo
Bunder, Colaba. CST or Churchgate stations.
Open 11am-8pm daily. **Credit** AmEx, MC, V.
This chic enclave houses a mix of designer and boutique stores that sell everything from bridalwear and gold jewellery to Aigner handbags and bar accessories. Some top designers also have stand-alone stores here, including Suneet Verma and Narendra Kumar Ahmed.

Cypress

Windward Apartments, 21st Road, Khar (W)
(2646-1747). Khar station. **Open** 11.30am-8.30pm
Mon-Sat. **Credit** MC, V.
At 1,400sq ft, Cypress houses collections from a mix of top Mumbai and Delhi designers, including Sabina Singh.

Ensemble

Great Western Building, 130/132 Colaba Causeway,
Colaba (2284-3227/5167). Churchgate/CST
stations. **Open** 10am-7pm Mon-Sat. **Credit** AmEx,
DC, MC, V.
The pioneer of Indian clothes retailing, Ensemble was the first store to stock high-profile Indian designers in a luxurious space – at mostly unattainable prices – and its Lion's Gate location still symbolises exclusivity and quality for many Mumbaikars. Currently, Ensemble carries big label names such as Monisha Jaisingh, Manish Malhotra and Tarun Tahiliani, who is also an owner.
Other location West Wing, Whitehall Building, 143 August Kranti Marg, near Shalimar Hotel, Kemp's Corner (2367-2416).

Kimaya

3 Delstar Building, below Kemp's Corner flyover,
Kemp's Corner (2386-2432/99675-97778). **Open**
10.30am-8.30pm daily. **Credit** AmEx, MC, V.

Juhu's film crowd loves Kimaya because it saves them a trip to South Mumbai to buy all their favourite Indian designers. South Mumbai has now cottoned on too and has its own branch.
Other location 2 Asha Colony, Juhu Tara Road (98920-10003).

Melange

33 Raj Mahal, Altamount Road (2385-0288).
Grant Road station. **Open** 10am-7pm Mon-Sat.
Credit AmEx, DC, MC, V.
This pretty store is tucked away on Altamount Road, but has a dedicated crowd of buyers who prefer the more sober and grown-up, but no less stylish, offerings compared to what you'll find at most other boutique stores.

Mogra

High Street Phoenix, 462 Senapati Bapat Marg,
Lower Parel (2496-0808). Lower Parel station.
Open 10am-8pm daily. **Credit** AmEx, MC, V.
Glitz and glam is the rule at Mogra, which houses almost 100 young designers of both clothes and accessories in a brand new, massive space.

Oak Tree

18 Cusrow Baug, Colaba Causeway, Colaba (2281-
9031). CST or Churchgate stations. **Open** 11am-
8pm Mon-Sat. **Credit** AmEx, MC, V.
A small Colaba boutique packed with funky shoes, belts, bags, jewellery and Indo-western clothes.

OMO

204 Sagar Fortune, Second Floor, Waterfield Road,
Bandra (W) (6698-1804). Bandra station. **Open**
11am-8pm daily. **Credit** AmEx, DC, MC, V.
Way before folk became funky, OMO, or On My Own, was doing it, and it's still doing it better than most. OMO's also got the most die-hard loyalists we've seen of any store in Bandra.

You

2 Cornelian, Kemp's Corner, 104 August Kranti
Marg (2382-6972/73). Grant Road station. **Open**
10.30am-7pm Mon-Sat. **Credit** AmEx, MC, V.
Kitsch is cool at You, which stocks summer dresses, T-shirts and a changing assortment of accessories, including sequinned clutches, pretty beads and paisley *chappals*.

Courtyard.

Indian designers

Abu Jani-Sandeep Khosla
Om Chambers, No. 2, Kemp's Corner (2367-3401/3505). Grant Road station. **Taxi** Kemp's Corner. **Open** 10.30am-6.30pm Mon-Sat. **Credit** AmEx, MC, V.
India's most exclusive designer duo, Abu Jani and Sandeep Khosla, have dressed innumerable stars and celebrities, and created an Oscar ceremony dress for Dame Judi Dench.

Azeem Khan
Shop No. 1, Usha Sadan Building, Colaba (2215-1028/0372). CST or Churchgate stations. **Taxi** Colaba Post Office. **Open** 10.30am-7pm Mon-Sat. **Credit** AmEx.
When they want to add glitter to their look, Hillary Clinton and Naomi Campbell have used Azeem Khan's styles to bring on the bling. His penchant for shimmer is not surprising: he is the third generation of the SU Zariwala family, Mumbai's celebrated embroiderers.

Manish Arora
The Courtyard, Minoo Desai Marg, Apollo Bunder, Colaba (6638-5464). CST or Churchgate stations. **Open** 11am-7.30pm daily. **Credit** AmEx, MC, V.
Designer Manish Arora bears a signature style: gaudy colours that magically work, Indian pop culture references, over-the-top embellishments and a distinctly Mumbai feel.

Ritu Kumar
Block 9, Phoenix Mills Annexe, 462 Senapati Bapat Marg, Lower Parel (6666-9901). Lower Parel station. **Open** 10am-8pm daily. **Credit** AmEx, DC, MC, V.
The empress of traditional craft and colour, Kumar's creations are the kind you'll see in countless Bollywood wedding sequences.

Rohit Bal
The Courtyard, Minoo Desai Marg, Apollo Bunder, Colaba (6638-5478/5479). CST or Churchgate stations. **Open** 11am-7pm daily. **Credit** AmEx, MC, V.
Best known for dressing India's most high-profile grooms, Bal's prêt line includes excellent shirts and Nehru-style tunics. His work in linen is classy too.

Satya Paul
Delstar Building, below Kemp's Corner Flyover, Kemp's Corner (3251-0612). Grant Road station. **Open** 11am-8pm daily. **Credit** MC, V.
Satya Paul is always doing something new with his trademark printed saris and hip ties. Both make great gifts.

Tarun Tahiliani
Villar Ville, Ground floor, 16 Ramchandani Marg, Apollo Bunder, Colaba (2287-0895/2285-4603). CST or Churchgate stations. **Open** 11am-7pm Mon-Sat. **Credit** AmEx, MC, V.
India's reigning king of design, Tarun Tahiliani has been around for years and has mastered the art of sexily draping women in yards of fabric – and getting them to pay a large sum for it.

Casualwear

Chemistry
CR2 shopping mall, Nariman Point (6654-7966). CST or Churchgate stations. **Open** 11am-8pm daily. **Credit** AmEx, DC, MC, V.
Chemistry's got the formula right with good basics. Perfect for nice office shirts, fun tees and the occasional denim.
Other location 210 Govindham, Waterfield Road, Bandra (W) (2640-6601).

Cotton World Corporation
201 Ram Nimi Building, Mandlik Road, Colaba (2285-0060). CST or Churchgate stations. **Taxi** behind Taj Mahal Hotel. **Open** noon-8pm daily. **Credit** AmEx, DC, MC, V.
Mumbai's answer to the Gap, CWC has a host of basics like T-shirts, trousers, capris, shorts and shirts that are perfect for the warm, humid climate. Shame there aren't more stores like this.
Other locations Phoenix Mills, Lower Parel (2491-8801); Vipul Apartments, Tagore Road, Santa Cruz (W) (2605-1602).

FabIndia
137 MG Road, Kala Ghoda (2262-6539). CST or Churchgate stations. **Open** 10am-7.45pm daily. **Credit** AmEx, DC, MC, V.
One of Mumbai's most popular stores, selling stylish, high-quality Indian casualwear – from *kurtas* to *salwar kameez* – with a wide range in cotton and silk; and it's all made by rural artisans. There's also a home furnishing section.
Other location Navroze, Pali Hill, Bandra (W) (2646-5286).

Peppertree
Shop No. 3, Vaidya Mansion, near Noorani, Tardeo (2494-1905). Bombay Central station. **Open** 11am-8pm Mon-Sat. **Credit** AmEx, DC, MC, V.
Think Goa: bright colours, tie-dye, flowing skirts, large pants and affordable prices.

Men's chain stores

Color Plus
Cusrow Baug, Colaba Causeway, Colaba (2284-1821). CST or Churchgate stations. **Open** 10.30am-9pm daily. **Credit** AmEx, MC, V.
Excellent quality trousers and khakis; this is a chain of stores that says 'export quality', which probably explains the dropped 'u' in colour.
Other locations Phoenix Mills, Lower Parel (2496-4464). Shops 1 & 2, Satyam, Linking Road, Khar (W) (2648-2731).

Millionaire
132 Damodar Mahal, August Kranti Marg (2382-5555/2388-6018). Grant Road station. **Taxi** opposite Shalimar Hotel. **Open** 11am-9pm Mon-Sat. **Credit** MC, V.

Eat, Drink, Shop

MOON)RIVER

Looking for an Indian *sherwani* suit that won't break the bank? Millionaire should be a first stop, with an excellent variety of ready-to-wear versions of this classic Indian formalwear.

Provogue

Shop No. 9, Ground Floor, Cusrow Baug, Colaba (2284-0048). CST or Churchgate stations. **Taxi** Cusrow Baug. **Open** 10am-9:30pm daily. **Credit** MC, V.

Provogue started out as a party and loungewear brand for men, but the shop now has clothes and accessories for every occasion. These manage to look good even on regular people, not just the Bollywood stars who plug their products.

Raymond

RNA House, Veer Nariman Road, Churchgate (2204-5912). Churchgate station. **Open** 11am-8pm daily. **Credit** AmEx, DC, MC, V.

Raymond is one of India's best-known tailors for good reason: staff are able to tailor-make a suit in just a few days, and for a fraction of the price you'd expect to pay in Europe or the United States – and the quality of the work is outstanding. **Other location** 59A Bhulabhai Desai Road, Breach Candy (2351-1644).

Tuscan Verve

1 Lotia Palace, Linking Road, Khar (2648-0385). Khar station. **Taxi** Khar Citibank. **Open** 10.30am-9pm daily. **Credit** AmEx, MC, V.

Tuscan Verve shirts are as colourful, loud and funky as it gets; don't bother unless you have the chutzpah to carry them off.

Zodiac

Taj Mahal Hotel, Apollo Bunder, Colaba (6591-7138). CST or Churchgate stations. **Open** 10am-midnight Mon-Sat; 10am-7pm Sun. **Credit** AmEx, DC, MC, V.

Crisp shirts, great patterns and prints, cool ties, and prices that will make you want to buy them all. **Other locations** Linking Road, opposite Shopper's Stop, Bandra (6591-7121). Grand Hyatt Mumbai, Santa Cruz (E) (6591-7130).

Local designers we love

Narendra Kumar Ahmed

Ahmed understands how to design for men, keeping both structure and colour in mind. His 2007 Fashion Week collection was themed on wedding wear, but it was still refreshingly lean and spare, with brocade, chino, corduroy, velvet and shimmering linen. Colours are grey, blue and beige with some brocade and with muted embellishments as accents rather than the centrepiece of the outfit. Obsession with detail is visible in every perfectly lined-up stitch and strip. **Available at**: the **Courtyard** (*see p120*). From Rs 3,800.

Sabina Singh for Horn OK Please

An eye for the quirky – and a good dose of humour – gives Sabina Singh our vote for the designer who gets the most out of Mumbai. Her funky designs celebrate quirky localisms and transform them into hip Mumbai icons. Singh identifies and develops unique elements of Mumbai, like the sequinned double-decker bus T-shirts and tutu skirts. 'It's usually something visual that I pick off the street that inspires me – a slogan on a truck, for example,' she says. 'They're just catchy, everyday experiences that I try to translate and capture and take to another level. I'm a complete Bombay girl.' **Available at**: **You** (*see p120*). From Rs 1,800.

Taxxi & Vitamin K

Before they were store owners or even designers, Aarti Nichlani and Prachi Rashmi Bhatt of Taxxi were inveterate but dissatisfied shopaholics. This is why their clothes hit the high notes in both design and practicality. When their bright, fun collections started selling out from their counters at other stores they decided to team up with accessory designer Karishma Shanbagh of Vitamin K and get a place of their own. This is the spot to hit if you're looking for a little jump in your wardrobe. It's mostly cotton, more than just casual and will certainly get you noticed. *Shop 3 & 4, Kusum Kunj, Linking Road, opposite Citibank, Khar (W) (6525-9382).* **Open** 11am-8.30pm Mon-Sat. From Rs 350.

A **Taxxi** number.

Jewellery

Amrapali
Shop Nos. 39 & 62, Oberoi Shopping Arcade, Nariman Point (2281-0978/0981). CST or Churchgate stations. **Taxi** Oberoi hotel. **Open** 10.45am-7pm daily. **Credit** AmEx, DC, MC, V.
This Jaipur institution creates fine gold and silver jewellery, combining Indian tradition and craftsmanship with contemporary design and aesthetics. Naomi Campbell, Jennifer Lopez and the Prince of Morocco seem to like it.

Curio Cottage
19 Mahakavi Bhushan Marg, Colaba (2202-2607). CST or Churchgate stations. **Taxi** Regal Cinema. **Open** 10.30am-8pm daily. **Credit** AmEx, MC, V.
A favourite with both locals and visitors, Curio Cottage sells semi-precious jewellery that fills the pages of fashion magazines as well as tiny trinkets your friends back home will love.

Orra
58/60 Zariwala Mansion, Hughes Road (2368-0606). Grant Road station. **Open** 11am-7.30pm daily. **Credit** AmEx, MC, V.
This chain of stores is a reliable place to buy gold, diamond and platinum jewellery, as well as Indian mythology-inspired pendants.
Other location 2 AN Chambers, Turner Road, Bandra (2643-3423/3291-6064).

Sia
37 Maskati Corner, 110/112 Altamount Road (2381-2628). Grant Road station. **Open** 10am-8pm Mon-Sat; 10am-6pm Sun. **Credit** MC, V.
Sia sells stunning replicas of the kind of ornate, heavy Indian jewellery that you see on display at lavish weddings.

TBZ – The Original
Zaveri Bazaar, Bhuleshwar (2343-5001). Charni Road station. **Open** 10.30am-7.30pm Mon-Sat. **Credit** AmEx, DC, MC, V.
One of the city's oldest goldsmiths, Tribhovandas Bhimji Zaveri is known for its solid gold jewellery and for not having copyrighted its name. Dozens of inferior imitators have the same name, but this is the real deal.

Food & drink

Bakeries

Kyani & Co
Jer Mahal, Dhobi Talao (2201-1492). Marine Lines or CST stations. **Taxi** Metro Cinema. **Open** 6.20am-9pm daily. **No credit cards.**
The baked delights on offer at Kyani & Co have a sort of period charm to them – custard puffs, sweet buttered buns and other treats of the sort dreamed of by Billy Bunter. Don't miss the chicken patties and the cardamom-flavoured *mava* cakes, which are beloved of Parsis.

Paris Bakery
278 Cowasji Hormusji Street, Marine Lines (2208-6619). Marine Lines station. **Taxi** near Our Lady of Dolours church. **Open** 8am-9pm Mon-Sat; 8am-2pm Sun. **No credit cards.**
On a tiny street-side stall along a narrow potholed lane up from Our Lady of Dolours sits Paris, a well-loved institution with delicious cashew macaroons and garlic-butter breadsticks among many other treats.

Theobroma
Cusrow Baug, Shop 24, Colaba Causeway, Colaba (6509-0909). CST or Churchgate stations. **Taxi** Cusrow Baug. **Open** 8am-11pm. **Credit** MC, V.
The name means 'food of the gods', and it's not too much of an exaggeration; top-quality sourdough loaves, fluffy focaccia, chocolate brownies, Danish pastries, fresh sandwiches and possibly the only chip butty in Mumbai.

Beverages

Philips Tea & Coffee
Shop No. 8, Usha Sadan, Colaba Causeway, Colaba (2207-4793). CST or Churchgate stations. **Taxi** near Colaba Post Office. **Open** 9am-8pm daily. **No credit cards.**
Cheap, super quality, fresh Indian teas and coffee beans are available at this sleepy store.

Shah Wines
Sitaram Building, Ground Floor, Fort (2342-7997/www.shahwines.com). CST or Churchgate stations. **Taxi** Crawford Market. **Open** 10am-8.30pm Mon-Sat. **Credit** MC, V.
One of the city's biggest wine shops, Shah Wines sells a good range of Indian and imported wines, spirits and beers.

Indian sweets

Brijwasi
Narayan Building, near 1st Pasta Lane, Colaba Causeway, Colaba (2282-0963/www.brijwasi.in). CST or Churchgate stations. **Open** 10am-8pm daily. **No credit cards.**
A top choice for a glittering array of silver-wrapped *mithai* (sweets) in all their glory – try the *kaju anjeer* (cashew and fig) rolls and ghee-soaked *ladoos* (sweet balls). They also have a range of delicious fresh milk sweets and Bengali treats like *sandesh* – dry on the outside, sweet and juicy on the inside.
Other location Raj Mahal, near Ambassador Hotel, Veer Nariman Road, Churchgate (2282-2368).

Camy Wafer
5-6 Oxford House, near Colaba Market, Colaba Causeway, Colaba (2282-8430/www.camywafer.com). CST or Churchgate stations. **Open** 9am-9pm daily. **No credit cards.**
More *mithai* than you can shake a candy cane at, all superb quality. Camy also has an outstanding selection of savoury snacks, including *chivda* – dry snacks of puffed rice, raisins, nuts and spices.

Ravissant.

Other locations Second Taj Building, August Kranti Marg, Gowalia Tank (2389-2288); Shop 1 & 2, Crystal Building, Junction of 16th Road, Khar Danda Road (2604-1178).

Mishty Bela
Krishnaraj Building, Walkeshwar Road, Malabar Hill (2361-6690). Grant Road station. **Taxi** near White House. **Open** 9am-8pm daily. **No credit cards.**
A wide range of traditional Indian *mithai*, including sugar-free, all-natural fruit *mithai* made from almonds, raisins, walnuts, figs and more. Don't miss the tiny *rasmalai* – sweet, milky and juicy.

Gifts

Bombay Store
Western India House, Sir Pherozeshah Mehta Road (2288-5048/2288-5049). CST station. **Taxi** PM Road. **Open** 10.30am-7.30pm Mon-Sat; 10.30am-6.30pm Sun. **Credit** AmEx, DC, MC, V.
Perfect if you want to get a taste of everything, with plenty of potential for interesting presents and souvenirs – like the modernistic stone Ganesha statues small enough to sit on the palm of your hand. The Bombay Store brings together artefacts, home accessories, clothes, jewellery, stationery and various trinkets that proudly bear a 'Made in India' stamp.

Cheemo
High Street Phoenix, 462 Senapati Bapat Marg, Lower Parel (2493-0495). Lower Parel station. **Taxi** Phoenix. **Open** 11am-8.30pm Mon-Sat. **Credit** AmEx, MC, V.
Handbags galore – from bejewelled, embroidered and studded clutches that will turn heads back home to 'Prada-inspired' purses.
Other location Mangal Darshan, Waterfield Road, Bandra (W) (2643-2493).

Hidesign
CR2 shopping mall, Nariman Point (6654-1615). CST or Churchgate stations. **Taxi** INOX. **Open** 10.30am-8.15pm daily. **Credit** AmEx, DC, MC, V.
All manner of leather goods – from cool satchels to belts and jackets – made in Pondicherry and exported to fine stores across the world.

Other location High Street Phoenix, 462 Senapati Bapat Marg, Lower Parel (2496-4309).

Ravissant
New India Building, Madame Cama Road, Colaba (2287-3405/3406). CST or Churchgate stations. **Open** 9.30am-8pm Mon-Sat. **Credit** AmEx, DC, MC, V.
One of India's oldest fine brands, Ravissant is best known for its silver items handcrafted in Holland, Germany and Switzerland. If you're looking for a one-of-a-kind three-foot-high Ganesh statue or an actual swing set for your bedroom (both in silver), this is the place to visit.
Other location 131 August Kranti Marg, Kemp's Corner (2363-7003/2368-4934).

Shawlart
3 Jai Tirath Mansion, Barrack Road, behind Metro Adlabs Cinema (2203-1128). CST or Marine Lines stations. **Open** 10am-6pm Mon-Sat. **Credit** AmEx, MC, V.
This speciality store for shawls, scarves and stoles is happy to send a trunk full of wares based on your requirements and tastes, so you can shop from your hotel room. Or pop in for a look. There's lots of variety in embellishments, weaves and embroideries.

Hairdressers

b:blunt
Block No. 1, Ground Floor, 29 Hughes Road (6598-0301). Grant Road station. **Open** 11am-7pm Tue-Sun. **Credit** MC, V.
Adhuna Bhabani, the woman behind b:blunt, also sets the biggest hair trends in Bollywood. This salon houses a Kerastase centre.

Hakim's Aalim
Union Park, Khar (W) (2646-0044). Khar station. **Taxi** Olive restaurant. **Open** 11am-9pm daily. **Credit** MC, V.
This shiny salon looks more like a sports bar: it's spread over 2,500sq ft, with plasma screens and a resident DJ. But don't let the fluff distract you – it's quality.

Nalini of Nalini & Yasmin
Sagar Fortune, Second Floor, Waterfield Road, Bandra (W) (6698-2614). Bandra station. **Open** 10am-8pm daily. **Credit** MC, V.
Nalini and Yasmin are pioneers in every sense of the word and have been around long before hairstyling was considered a 'cool' thing to do in Mumbai. They have now split (amicably) but Nalini remains at their old venue.

Raih: Hair Reinvented
Arunodaya Building, 20 Nepean Sea Road (2363-5599). Grant Road station. **Taxi** opposite Contemporary Arts and Crafts. **Open** 11.15am-6.45pm daily. **Credit** MC, V.
One of the city's swankiest hair salons. Raih boasts a client book stuffed full of Mumbai's rich and pretty, including industrialist wives, celebrity regulars, sportspeople and fashion editors.

Home

Anokhi

*Rasik Niwas, Metro Motors Lane, off Hughes Road
(2368-5308/5761). Grant Road station.* **Open**
10.30am-7.30pm Mon-Sat. **Credit** AmEx, MC, V.
Rajasthani prints abound here on bed and table
linens, easy-to-wash curtains and seat covers.
Other location Govinda Building, Waterfield Road,
Bandra (W) (2640-8263).

Contemporary Arts & Crafts

*19 NG House, Nepean Sea Road (2363-1979).
Grant Road station.* **Taxi** St Stephen's Church.
Open 10am-8pm daily. **Credit** AmEx, MC, V.

CAC makes knick-knacks and essentials for the
home, ranging from brocade cushions to Christmas
lights, candlestands and lampshades. Cool designs
with Indian influences.

Dhoop

*First Floor, 101 Khar Sheetal Apartments, Dr
Ambedkar Road, Union Park, Khar (2649-8646).
Khar station.* **Taxi** near Carter Road. **Open** 11am-
8.30pm Mon-Sat. **Credit** DC, MC, V.
Dhoop's focus is on handicrafts made from
natural materials, but this isn't your average jute
bag shop – instead think coconut shells, bamboo,
banana, sugarcane, water hyacinth and many
more intriguing materials.

Cotton on

Khadi Bhandar is where you can find yards
and yards of the fabric that Mahatma Gandhi
called the 'sun of the whole industrial solar
system'. *Khadi* – coarse, handspun cotton
– played a significant part in India's freedom
movement, replacing imported cotton with
locally produced material, which made it
an important symbol of self-reliance.

Khadi Bhandar was set up in 1954 to
promote the Gandhian philosophy in general
and the fabric in particular, and has always
been distinctly uninterested in making money.
Remarkably unmoved by the post-1990s
'liberalisation' spirit, the store is run by a
12-member trust that strongly opposes plans
to upgrade. But then, the designers of the
original store knew how to charm shoppers.
Walking through Khadi Bhandar is like
entering Aladdin's cave, and even the poor
window and shelf displays and bored staff
can't tarnish the experience. The store is
spacious and well ventilated, creating a
relaxed shopping vibe, even during sales.

The ground floor stocks *khadi* garments.
This is one section where the selection for
men scores over the offerings to women.
The ready-made *kurtas* and shirts for men
are better tailored than the shapeless *kurtas*
for women. The smarter option is to hop into
the next section, a treasure trove for shoppers
with tailors. Bales of plain and coloured khadi
and gorgeous silks are stacked on shelves,
as are towels, napkins and handkerchiefs.
One counter stocks honey, soaps, lotions,
incense, health drinks, and tonics such as
Nari Yog, for 'unmarried, newly married and
mature women', and Special Shaktiprash for
'the body and mind'. In a corner is 'ahinsak
leather' footwear, made out of carcasses
rather than by killing animals.

The floor above houses sandalwood, papier
mâché dolls, leather bags and stone jewellery;
animals carved out of stone, marvellously
carved rosewood elephant figures and
teakwood furniture are also sold.

Anti-slick salespersons, quite the opposite
of the type you find in lifestyle stores, slouch
over counters. It's always been fashionable
to bash Khadi Bhandar, especially because of
its close association with a past that appears
more irrelevant every day, but there's certainly
some pleasure to be had from visiting a store
that doesn't care too much for profit or PR. In
a city that's being led by its nose by builders,
a 14,242sq ft space where you can shop
without bumping your handbag into another
shopper is a thing of joy.

Khadi Bhandar

DN Road, Fort (2207-3280). **Open** 10.30am-
6.30pm Mon-Sat. **Credit** MC, V. From Rs 50.

Eat, Drink, Shop

High Street Phoenix – from mill to mall.

FabIndia
137 MG Road, Kala Ghoda (2262-6539). CST or Churchgate stations. **Open** 10am-8pm daily. **Credit** AmEx, DC, MC, V.
Indian textiles and artistry at their best in a range of cool home furnishings and accessories, all at very affordable prices. They have great Burma teak furniture too.

Good Earth
Raghuvanshi Mills, Lower Parel (6572-0345/0342). Lower Parel or Mahalaxmi stations. **Open** 11am-8pm daily. **Credit** AmEx, DC, MC, V.
This large, pretty store sells everything from dining tables to chandeliers, spa products to coffee cups. None of it is overtly ethnic, but it is lovely.

India Weaves
Near Cymroza Art Gallery, Bhulabhai Desai Road (2368-6366). Grant Road station. **Open** 10am-8pm Mon-Sat. **Credit** MC, V.
For that majestic look and feel that comes from luxurious Indian silks and rich tissues, head to India Weaves where they can help you create just that.

Yamini
Wodehouse Road, Colaba (2218-4143/4145). CST or Churchgate stations. **Open** 10.30am-7.30pm daily. **Credit** AmEx, DC, MC, V.
Yamini is the best place to go for affordable, Indian-inspired linens, textiles, bags, home accessories and delightful lamps.
Other location 380 Shanti Nivas, 14th Road, Khar (W) (2646-3645/3647).

Salim Asgarally
99 Abde Villa, SV Road, Khar (W) (6529-5265/66). Khar station. **Open** 11am-8.30pm daily. **Credit** MC, V.

Furnishings that are wildly decadent and jewel-toned home accessories. Turn your home into an Indian-style palace.

Bungalow 8
E-F Block, Wankhede Stadium North Stand, D Road, Churchgate (2281-9880). Churchgate station. **Credit** MC, V.
Maithili Ahluwalia's store is situated under the stands of Wankhede cricket stadium. Her choice of dinnerware, home accessories, clothes and jewellery is as eclectic as her choice of location.

Malls

Atria
Annie Besant Road, opposite Poonam Chambers, Worli (2481-3333). Mahalaxmi station. **Taxi** opposite Poonam Chambers. **Open** *Shops* 9.30am-9pm. *Restaurants* 9.30am-1am daily.
The all-glass structure near the Planetarium has enough shopping, entertainment and leisure on its five levels to keep you entertained for a whole day, including a sushi counter, 4D cinema and India's only Rolls-Royce showroom. There's a good mix for both big spenders and mall-rats, and a food court on the top level.

CR2
Opposite Bajaj Bhavan, Nariman Point (6524-6470). Churchgate station. **Taxi** INOX. **Open** *shops* 10am-8pm; *restaurants* 10am-midnight daily.
Fashion brands including Versace JC, restaurants like the tatty American chain Ruby Tuesday on the ground floor and South Mumbai's most popular multiplex on the top floor make this mall a popular evening and weekend hangout. The delicious kebabs at Moti Mahal have earned the place a cult following, but don't drive down the spiral car park exit right after a meal.

High Street Phoenix
462 Senapati Bapat Marg, Lower Parel (2496-4307). **Open** *shops* 9.30am-10pm; *bowling* 10am-12.30am; *restaurants* until 1.30am daily.
The zenith or nadir of Mumbai consumerism, depending on your political leanings, this massive mall was formerly a mill. There's very little you don't get here but it's best known for South Mumbai's best bowling lanes, accessible local designerwear, nightclubs and home grown restaurant chains. An international hotel and a seven screen multiplex are works-in-progress on the site.

Orchid City Centre
Opposite BEST Bus Depot, Mumbai Central (6610-4300). Mumbai Central station. **Open** 11am-10pm daily.
Going just by noise levels alone, this mall in the heart of Central Mumbai is mighty popular. You can buy vegetables, clothes, accessories, books, music, electronics, furniture, luggage and then some. The multi-cuisine food-court swings from burgers to thalis.

Markets

Nowhere is Mumbai's mercantile instinct more evident than in its wide range of specialised markets that sell everything from pickles to zebra-striped fabric. Credit cards are very definitely not accepted, and don't expect a money-back guarantee. Here's a selection of the city's most colourful and quirky trading zones.

Antiques at Chor Bazaar

Mutton Street, opposite Null Bazaar. CST or Marine Lines stations. **Open** 10.30am-7pm Sat-Thur.

From ancient 78 RPM records by Gauhar Jaan to elaborately carved cupboards, from ships' wheels to 1950s Bollywood posters and old cameras, Chor Bazaar ('Thieves' Market') has it all. Thought to have its origins as a market where stolen goods were fenced, today it's a warren of respectable stores peddling antiques and assorted bric-a-brac. Though the shops are shut on Fridays, an informal flea market thrives in the afternoons, after 3pm.

Clothes at Fashion Street

Mahatma Gandhi Road, along Azad Maidan. CST station. **Open** 10.30am-7pm daily.

Wondering why shopping in Mumbai isn't as inexpensive as you expected? Head to Fashion Street, the unofficial name for a stretch of Mahatma Gandhi Road along Azad Maidan, where stalls sell all kinds of clothing for cheap. Some export surplus makes its way here. Don't forget to bargain.

Antiques aplenty at **Chor Bazaar**.

Everything at Crawford Market

Opposite Police Headquarters, Fort. CST station. **Open** 11am-7pm Mon-Sat.

Crawford Market, which opened its iron gates to the public in 1865, is a Mumbai institution not to be missed. As well as the four broad lanes packed with stalls selling fruit, vegetables, kitchenware, spices, dry fruits and foreign foodstuffs, you'll find bloody warehouses for poultry and mutton and even live pet stores. Watch out for the wigs at the Hair House for the Bald and Beautiful, just one of the oddities.

Fabric at Mangaldas Market

Sheikh Memon Street, near Chhatrapati Shivaji Terminus. CST station. **Open** 10am-7pm Mon-Sat.

A glorious array of colours and textures and a somewhat chaotic atmosphere make this the city's most vibrant and frantic fabric market.

Fireworks at Mohammed Ali Road

Near the junction of Paltan Road and Mohammed Ali Road. CST station. **Open** 10am-8pm Mon-Sat.

Diwalis past have seen natural disaster-inspired fireworks Tsunami, Katrina and Rita hitting this market, but recently it's been back to Bollywood bombshells. During Diwali, temporary stalls stretch down the pavement for kilometres. The rest of the year, weddings and other festivals keep the five firework shops here in business.

Jewellery at Zaveri Bazaar

Bhuleshwar. **Open** 11am-7pm Mon-Sat.

India is said to consume about one-third of all the gold produced in the world – roughly 800 tons every year – and one visit here is all you need to believe it. Zaveri Bazaar offers customers highly competitive rates for an astonishing variety of gold and silver jewellery. Larger stores sell diamond jewellery as well, making this a one-stop shop for brides-to-be.

Leather at Dharavi

Sant Rolida Marg, Sion-Bandra Link Road, Sion (W). Sion station. **Open** 11am-8pm Mon-Sun.

Die-hard leather fans swear by Dharavi, where world-class leather products are produced in innumerable dingy workshops. Dharavi, which has the dubious distinction of being the largest slum in India, houses over 125 shops that retail and export leather goods to Europe and West Asia. This is where Indian fashion designers source accessories like handbags, jackets and shoes for catwalk shows. Those hot pink knee-high leather boots would find little use elsewhere.

Saris at Dadar

NC Kelkar Road, near Dadar Station, Dadar (W). Dadar station. **Open** 9am-9pm daily.

During the winter wedding season, the Dadar sari market – 25 shops on a half-mile stretch – is packed with women taking saris out on to the street to ensure that it is the exact shade of yellow or green. Prices start at Rs 150 for synthetics and go up to Rs 40,000 for hand-woven Paithani saris.

Eat, Drink, Shop

Shoes at Linking Road

Linking Road, Bandra (W). Bandra station.
Open 11am-9pm daily.
Hundreds of slippers, stilettos and sandals for men, women and children. A steady river of people flows along its periphery, selling everything from fruit trays to silk pouches and fluorescent yo-yos.

Snacks & pickles at Lalbaug

Chivda Galli & Achar Galli, off Dr B Ambedkar Road, Lalbaug. Chinchpokli or Lower Parel stations.
Open 10am-7pm daily.
Ten fragrant outlets line Chivda Galli, a lively lane near Lalbaug market. The *chivdas* (savoury snacks) sold here are made out of *dagadi poha* (thick rice flakes), with chillies and raisins deep-fried and tossed together with a spice mix in a round-bottomed *kadhai*. They sell for around Rs 65-Rs 90 per kilo. Next door is Achar Galli, which sells the traditional Maharashtrian *loncha* (made with lime) as well as pickles of raw mango, chillies and berries.

Wedding cards at Girgaum

Khandilkar Road, opposite Gaiwadi, Girgaum, Churney Road (E). Churney Road station.
Open 10am-8pm Mon-Sat.

Before you walk down the aisle, take a stroll down Khandilkar Road for a look at its dizzying array of thousands of ready-to-print wedding invitations. There are around 200 stores, each with hundreds of clever samples on display. Most are adorned with the elephant-headed Ganesha, who symbolises new beginnings and good luck. But stores also feature at least one wall of 'Muslim, Catholic and non-religious wedding cards'. Fun to browse.

Music

CDs

Planet M

Times of India Building, Dadabhai Naoroji Road, Fort (6635-3875). CST station. **Open** 11am-9pm Mon-Sat; noon-8pm Sun. **Credit** MC, V.
The country's largest music store chain has outlets across Mumbai but their flagship, in the *Times of India* building, is the most impressive. Modelled on successful international chains such as HMV and Virgin Megastore, this 10,000sq ft flagship store has an impressive range – you'll find music from all genres. A good place to pick up the latest releases.

Reel Mumbai

Didn't get to play a Bollywood extra? Get yourself a consolation prize.

Bollywood in a bottle

Pop culture creations by Bharati Pitre that appeal to both aesthetics and funny bones. It's Andy Warhol meets Bollywood, with caricatures of Bollywood stars on bottles and cushions in all shapes and colours. She lives in Pune, but give her a call and she'll have her work delivered to Mumbai. *Bharati Pitre (98200-24791).* **No credit cards.** From Rs 2,000.

Poster boys

Before there was digital printing, Bollywood heroes' faces turned fern green and bubblegum pink in shadows and highlights. For ample evidence, visit Shahid and Zahid Mansoori's store in Chor Bazaar. From a tin plate advertisement of Atlas Cycles showing Amitabh Bachchan in the movie *Coolie* to Raj Babbar with fuchsia lips in mid-grimace or Poonam Dhillon playing a busty village belle, Mini

Market keeps posters, original photographs, lobby cards, prints and synopses of movies released between the 1940s and '80s. *Mini Market, 31/33 Mutton Street, Chor Bazaar (2347-2427).* **Open** 11am-7pm Sat-Thur. **Credit** MC, V. From Rs 250.

Stars at your feet

Have tea every morning with old flames Amitabh Bachchan and Rekha. As a special for a street shopping festival, Chetan Sharma and Gayatri Rao of Raw Works decided to spice up some plain stools, lamps, mirrors and coasters by fixing iconic Bollywood posters on them and finishing with a glossy varnish. When they sold out, the Apun Ka Mumbai collection became a regularly ordered item from their Santa Cruz studio. Good enough to make a song and dance about. *To place orders with Raw Works call Romel Dias on 93246-36073.* **No credit cards.** From Rs 850.

Rhythm House

40 K Dubash Marg, Fort (2284-2835). CST or Churchgate stations. **Open** 10am-8.30pm Mon-Sat; 11am-8.30pm Sun. **Credit** MC, V.

One of Mumbai's oldest music stores, this city institution is the best place to find old Hindi film soundtracks. In addition to current chart hits, it also stocks a wide range of Hindustani classical and fusion/lounge music and sells tickets for gigs. Best of all, most of the red jacket-clad shop assistants actually know their music.

Musical instruments

Bhargava's Musik

4/5 Imperial Plaza, 30th Road, Bandra (W) (2641-1842). Bandra station. **Open** 10am-1pm, 2-7.30pm Mon-Sat. **Credit** MC, V.

A one-stop shop for all Hindustani and Carnatic musical instruments, including *sitars, tablas, sarods* and more. This 54-year-old shop counts renowned *santoor* player Shivkumar Sharma and flautist Hariprasad Chaurasia among its clientele.

BX Furtado & Sons

Jer Mahal, Dhobi Talao (2201-3105). CST or Marine Lines stations. **Taxi** Metro Cinema. **Open** 10am-7.30pm Mon-Sat. **Credit** MC, V.

Around since 1865, Furtado's focus is on Western musical instruments but they also sell Indian classical instruments, a large collection of music books, music software, speakers and amplifiers, and pedals and processors in two stores, BX Furtado and LM Furtado, that are around the corner from each other. BX is the only place in the city that stocks albums by local rock bands.

Shoes

Catwalk

Bhulabhai Desai Road, near Gangar opticians, Kemp's Corner (2367-8488). Grant Road station. **Open** 10am-9pm Mon-Sat; 11am-9pm Sun. **Credit** AmEx, DC, MC, V.

Diamanté-studded stilettos, strappy wedges and other shoes for a night on the town.
Other location Infiniti Mall, New Link Road, next to Fame Adlabs, Andheri (W) (3241-5335).

Inc 5

Bhulabhai Desai Road, opposite Breach Candy Hospital (2361-8616). **Open** 10am-9.30pm Mon-Sat. **Credit** MC, V.

Inc 5 carries a mix of party shoes, labels like Guess and Tommy Hilfiger, and a small but practical range of boots, which, despite the climate, Mumbai can never get enough of.
Other location High Street Phoenix , 462 Senapati Bapat Marg, Lower Parel (2495-1352).

Metro Shoes

Metro House, Colaba Causeway (6656-0444). **Open** 10am-10pm daily. **Credit** AmEx, MC, V.
Swarovski crystals on your toes? Look no further.

Rinaldi

67/68 Sea View Terrace, 118B Wodehouse Road, Colaba (2215-2513). **Open** 11am-7.30pm Mon-Sat. **Credit** AmEx, MC, V.

Accessories designer Rina Shah makes glam shoes that work. She also does boots with Indian embellishments.

Travellers' needs

Dry cleaning

Akash Dry Cleaners

Shop No 2, Ratan Manzil, 64 Wodehouse Road, Colaba (6516-1616). CST or Churchgate stations. **Open** 10am-8pm Mon-Sat. **No credit cards**.

American Express Dry Cleaners

Hill Road, Bandra (W) (2643-1743). Bandra station. **Open** 8.30am-1pm, 3.30-8pm daily. **No credit cards**.

Beauty Art

Stadium House, Veer Nariman Road , Churchgate (2282-1039). Churchgate station. **Open** 9am-2pm, 4-7pm Mon-Sat. **No credit cards**.

Opticians

Colaba Opticians

A/8 Fatima Manzil, Near Sassoon Dock, Colaba (2287-4244). CST or Churchgate stations. **Open** 9.30am-9pm Mon-Sat; 10am-7pm Sun. **Credit** AmEx, MC, V.

Lawrence & Mayo

Dr Dadabhai Naoroji Road, Fort (2207-6049). CST or Churchgate stations. **Open** 10am-7.30pm daily. **Credit** AmEx, MC, V.

Travel agents

Akbar Travels of India

Terminus View, 169 Dr Dadabhai Naoroji (DN) Road, Fort (2263-3434). CST station. **Taxi** Crawford Market. **Open** 10am-7pm Mon-Fri; 10am-6pm Sat. **Credit** AmEx, DC, MC, V.

Atlas Tours & Travels

53 Haji Mahal, Mohammed Ali Road (6636-1000). CST station. **Taxi** near Noor Hospital. **Open** 10am-8pm Mon-Sat. **Credit** AmEx, DC, MC, V.

Globe Forex & Travels

102 Modi Chambers, First Floor, French Bridge Corner, Opera House (4091-6666). Churney Road station. **Taxi** French Bridge. **Open** 9.30am-6.30pm Mon-Fri; 9.30am-4.30pm Sat. **Credit** AmEx, DC, MC, V.

Riya Travels & Tours

Atlanta Arcade, Ground Floor, Marol Church Road, Andheri (E) (2925-8611). Andheri station. **Taxi** near Leela Kempinski Hotel. **Open** 9.30am-7pm Mon-Sat. **Credit** AmEx, DC, MC, V.

Eat, Drink, Shop

ART. GRAND HYATT MUMBAI

The finest collection of art created by renowned as well as
upcoming talents from across the country.
Homage to the mythic and contemporary presence of Lord Shiva.
A reflection of the mythological and everyday life of the metropolis and
its rich cultural heritage. Experience excellence at Grand Hyatt Mumbai.

FEEL THE HYATT TOUCH®

For further information contact +91 22 6676 1234

GRAND
HYATT
MUMBAI
TM

Off Western Express Highway, Santacruz (East), Mumbai – 400 055, India
TELEPHONE +91 22 6676 1234 FACSIMILE +91 22 6676 1235 mumbai.grand.hyatt.com

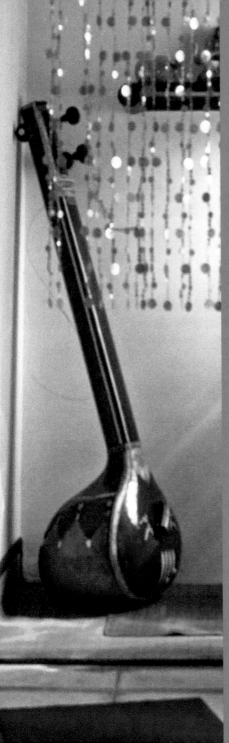

Arts &
Entertainment

Festivals & Events

Every day is a holy day.

Ganesh Chaturthi at Chowpatty Beach. *See p136.*

With practically every single religion on earth, except maybe Rastafarianism, represented in Mumbai's population, almost every day is a festival for someone, somewhere in the city. In the past, the vast number of religious festivals (all but three of the 17 holidays allowed to public servants are related to religion) have provided fodder for thunderous newspaper editorials blaming them for India's poor economic growth. Indians, it was claimed, were too busy celebrating their festivals to get any work done. The theory doesn't hold much water – most Indians work six-day weeks, so the time lost evens out – and got soundly kicked into irrelevance by 21st-century India's economic boom.

In Mumbai the biggest and most widely celebrated festivals are **Holi**, the festival of colour (and of *bhang*, a marijuana derivative) in March, the noisy and spectacular **Ganesh Chaturthi** around September and the firework frenzy of **Diwali** in October or November – all Hindu festivals, but marked in some form by nearly every community.

January-March

Mumbai Festival

Across the city (www.mumbaifestival.in). **Date** Jan.
Founded in 2004, the Mumbai Festival aims to bring all things Mumbai under one banner, with

For music festivals, *see p155* **Music**.

auto-rickshaw races, arm-wrestling challenges, fishing-trawler pulling contests, concerts, dance performances, handicrafts and, of course, local food.

Pongal

Across the city. **Date** Jan.
The four-day Pongal festival is a South Indian harvest festival traditionally celebrated in the home. Pongal means 'to boil over' in Tamil, representing abundance. On the second day, Surya Pongal, the sun-god Surya is worshipped for protection and nurturing crops through the previous year.

Makar Sankranti

Across the city. **Date** 15 Jan.
Makar Sankranti is a harvest festival celebrating the transition of the sun from Sagittarius to Capricorn, according to Hindu astrology. Across the city, children and adults go kite flying, using strings embedded with crushed glass to try and cut each other's lines in friendly dogfights. Kites are sold at shops across Mumbai, with some of the most intense aerial battles taking place at Chowpatty Beach.

Kala Ghoda Arts Festival

Kala Ghoda, Fort (www.kalaghodaassociation.com). CST or Churchgate stations. **Date** Feb.
Started in 1999 to promote the Kala Ghoda neighbourhood in Fort as an arts district, this ten-day festival is the city's premier showcase for painting, sculpture, film, music, dance and literary events, and another opportunity to eat lots of food. *Photo p137.*

Mahashivratri

Across the city. **Date** 23 Feb 2009.
When the dreaded *halahala* poison threatened to kill them all, gods and demons prayed to Lord Shiva

Arts & Entertainment

to save them. On the night now known as Mahashivratri, Shiva drank the poison and held it in his throat, turning his throat blue and earning two new names in the process – Vishakantha ('The One Who Held Poison in His Throat') and Neelakantha ('The One With a Blue Throat'). That night is now celebrated every year with offerings of *bhel* leaves to Lord Shiva, and fasting. But the highlight of the festival is a night-long vigil when devotees sing *bhajans* in homes and temples to honour Lord Shiva.

Mumbai International Film Festival

Various venues (www.filmsdivision.org/ www.miffindia.in). **Date** Feb 2010.
The Mumbai International Film Festival is a biennial competitive event that showcases films from across the world. It's also a rare platform for independent Indian films, with a programme that includes documentaries, shorts and animated films. Delegate passes are available for around Rs 100.

Holi

Across the city. **Date** 11-12 Mar 2009; 1-2 Mar 2010.
One of the city's most popular festivals, celebrating the death of the demoness Holika. On the morning of Holi, the festival of colours, the whole city becomes an interactive Jackson Pollock painting as Mumbaikars gleefully spray each other with brightly coloured water – called 'playing Holi' – and eat and drink dishes made with a kind of marijuana called *bhang* which is sold at temples on the day of the festival. Cars, tourists, anyone out on the street on Holi is fair game – so grab your colours and join the meleé.

April-June

Gudi Padwa

Across the city. **Date** Apr.
Also known as Ugadi, Gudi Padwa marks the beginning of *basant* or spring. It's also celebrated as the start of the New Year for Maharashtrians. *Gudis* – poles decorated with silk, marigolds, mango leaves and coconuts, with upturned metal pots sitting on the end – are hung out of windows and displayed in traditional households.

Ramnavami

Across the city. **Date** 3 Apr 2009; 24 Mar 2010.
Celebrating the wedding day of Rama and Sita, as well as Rama's birthday, Ramnavami sees devotees performing mock wedding ceremonies with small idols of the deities. In the evening, the brightly adorned statues are paraded through the streets.

Good Friday

Holy Name Cathedral, Colaba; St Michael's Church, Mahim; St Andrew's Church, Bandra & across the city. **Date** 10 Apr 2009; 2 Apr 2010.
Christian prayer services across the city mark the day of Jesus's crucifixion. Some churches stage ornate tableaux of the event, using a combination of human actors and life-sized clay figures.

Easter Sunday

Holy Name Cathedral, Colaba; St Michael's Church, Mahim; Mount Mary Church, Bandra & across the city. **Date** 12 Apr 2009; 4 Apr 2010.
Easter is the most important religious festival of the Christian liturgical year, celebrated in March or April to mark the resurrection of Jesus. Easter eggs, made of marzipan and chocolate, are sold in confectionery stores across Mumbai.

July-September

National Theatre Festival

Nehru Centre Auditorium, Annie Besant Road (2496-4676/nehrucentremumbai.com). **Date** Aug.
The Nehru Centre puts together a festival of drama from all over India every August. The plays are often disappointingly amateurish but every season has a gem or two.

Raksha Bandhan

Across the city. **Date** 16 Aug 2008; 5 Aug 2009; 24 Aug 2010.
Raksha Bandhan commemorates the bond between brothers and sisters. Across India, sisters tie decorative bands – called *rakhis* – on their brothers' wrists to remind them that sisters need protection; in return, brothers give their sisters cash or fancy presents. It isn't only siblings who celebrate the festival: girls can blunt the affections of ardent suitors by making them their symbolic '*rakhi*' brothers'.

Pateti

Across the city. **Date** 19 Aug.
Pateti is celebrated by Parsis on the eve of their New Year, with visits to fire temples or *agiaries*. After the *jashan* (prayers), sandalwood is offered to the holy fire. Parsi homes are decorated for the festival: white powder is used to fashion intricate designs of birds, flowers and fish (an art called *rangoli*) at the entrance to homes. Families exchange

Feasting during **Ramzan**. *See p136.*

Arts & Entertainment

gifts and sweets and tuck into special dishes like *patra ni machchi* (fish wrapped in banana leaves), *sali boti* (meat with potato chips) and a sweet, milky drink called *falooda*.

Janmashtami or Gokulashtami

Across the city. **Date** 23 Aug 2008; 14 Aug 2009; 2 Sept 2010.
The birthday of Lord Krishna, the eighth incarnation of Lord Vishnu, is celebrated with prayers, plays and fasting. Clay pots of yoghurt are strung between buildings high above the street, and bands of young men form spectacular human pyramids in an effort to reach and break the vessels. Onlookers try to hamper their efforts by pouring buckets of water on them from out of their windows. Success brings cheers from the crowd – and cash too.

Ramzan

Mohammed Ali Road, Bhendi Bazaar. CST station. **Date** 2 Sept 2008; 22 Aug 2009.
The Muslim month of fasting starts in August/ September. Mohammed Ali Road and Bhendi Bazaar turn into giant food courts and stay open all night as the feasting begins every evening. *Photo p135.*

Ganesh Chaturthi

Lalbaug, Girgaum Chowpatty, Dadar & across the city. **Date** 3 Sept 2008; 23 Aug 2009; 11 Sept 2010.
Ganesh Chaturthi marks the birthday of Lord Ganesha, the elephant-headed Hindu god of auspicious beginnings. During the ten-day festival, families install idols of the deity in their homes, while some neighbourhoods get together to erect tents (known as *pandals*) in which gigantic statues of Ganesha – some three storeys high – are

An idol being readied for **Durga Puja**.

enthroned. The idols are immersed in the sea or in lakes after either one and a half days, three, five, seven or ten days. While they are in residence, the idols are treated to music concerts and films late into the night – or at least as late as noise regulations permit. It's Mumbai's most popular festival, but is a relatively new addition to the festive calendar, devised only in 1901, when nationalist leader Bal Gangadhar Tilak decided to create the festival to mobilise public opinion against British colonial rule. *Photo p134.*

Bandra Fair

Mount Mary Church, Bandra. **Date** 14 Sept 2008; 13 Sept 2009; 12 Sept 2010.
The birthday of the Virgin Mary and the associated Church feast are celebrated with a noisy fair.

Navratri

Colaba, Andheri & across the city. **Date** 30 Sept-8 Oct 2008; 19-27 Sept 2009; 8-16 Oct 2010.
A popular festival with the city's Gujarati community, the 'nine nights' of Navratri are a countdown to Dussehra, the 'tenth day' on which Lord Rama killed the demon Ravana, as told in the *Ramayana*. Dance events, some attended by up to 10,000 people, are held on each night; couples holding batons in their hands dance the *dandiya raas* and the *garba*. They're a rare occasion on which teenagers of conservative households are allowed to mix with the opposite sex unsupervised by their parents. (City legend has it that some plastic surgeons offer to perform hymenoplasties after the festival, to 'revirginise' women before their weddings.)

October-December

Eid-ul-Fitr/Ramzan Eid

Mohammed Ali Road & across the city. **Date** 2 Oct 2008; 21 Sept 2009.
Eid-ul-Fitr, often referred to simply as Eid, is an Islamic holiday that marks the end of Ramzan (or Ramadan), the month of fasting. Muslim men attend special prayers, after which there's a swirl of visiting friends and eating festive meals.

Durga Puja

Tejpal Road, Gowalia Tank & across the city. *(2380-2679).* **Date** 5-9 Oct 2008; 24-28 Sept 2009; 13-17 Oct 2010.
Every year, the goddess Durga comes down to earth and stays for five days. The first time she did this she was busy killing the demon Mahisasura. Since then, her homecoming has been an excuse for Bengalis to make merry. Held on the last five days of Navratri, this festival brings out the epicurean nature of Bengali culture. Everyone wears shiny, new clothes, and singers and theatre groups from Kolkata visit Mumbai and perform at the different *pandals* (the venue for the *puja* – 'ritual prayer'). Some would argue religion is simply an excuse for Bengalis to tuck into the free, well-cooked vegetarian meals that are served to everyone at the *puja*.

Dussehra decorations in a local train.

A **Kala Ghoda Arts Festival** exhibit. *See p134.*

Dussehra

Across the city. **Date** 9 Oct 2008; 28 Sept 2009;
17 Oct 2010.
Dussehra, the day on which Lord Rama killed the
demon Ravana, symbolises the victory of good over
evil. The slaying of the demon is recreated in colourful pageants called *Ram Leelas*, which conclude with
the burning of large effigies of Ravana.

Diwali

Across the city. **Date** 28 Oct 2008; 17 Oct 2009;
5 Nov 2010.
Diwali (the 'festival of lights') celebrates Lord
Rama's return to the kingdom of Ayodhya after
the momentous assassination of demon Ravana,
described in the *Ramayana* epic. It's an Indian
Christmas, marked by fireworks, sweets and
merry-making. Diwali is also the day on which
Indian businessmen open new accounts books for
the year, and perform *puja* ceremonies at their
places of work to invoke the blessings of Lakshmi,
the goddess of wealth. The nights before Diwali are
spent gambling at cards, inviting luck to favour
you for the rest of the year.

Prithvi Theatre Festival

*Prithvi Theatre, Juhu Tara Road, Juhu (2614-9546/
www.prithvitheatre.org); National Centre for the
Performing Arts, Nariman Point (6622-3737/
www.ncpamumbai.org).* **Date** Nov.
Since 1983, the Prithvi Theatre Festival – held in
a cosy auditorium in Juhu, as well as in the National
Centre for the Performing Arts complex in South
Mumbai – has become the high point of the
Mumbai theatre season. It showcases the talents of
groups from around India, and often features international acts, with an emphasis on encouraging
originality in local drama groups.

Celebrate Bandra Festival

Across Bandra. **Date** Nov 2009; 2011.
In recent years, the once-sleepy northern suburb of
Bandra has become the city's hottest neighbourhood, with new nightclubs, bars, chic restaurants
and trendy boutiques popping up all the time.
Every two years, the 'Celebrate Bandra' festival
enlivens the area with events ranging from theatre
and music to sports and even a parade.

Guru Nanak Jayanti

Four Bungalows, Andheri & across the city.
Date 13 Nov 2008; 2 Nov 2009.
Celebrating the anniversary of the birth of Guru
Nanak Dev, the founder of the Sikh faith, Guru
Nanak Jayanti begins with early morning proces-
sions of devotees from *gurdwaras* (Sikh temples)
performing *shabads* (hymns). The celebrations also
include the three-day *akhand path*, during which the
Sikh holy book, the *Guru Granth Sahib*, is read from
beginning to end without a break.

Thespo

*Experimental Theatre, National Centre for the
Performing Arts, NCPA Marg, Nariman Point
(6622-3737).* **Date** Dec.
A platform for young actors to parade their talents,
Thespo only invites participants under the age of
25. Apart from full-length productions, Thespo
offers short performances and theatre workshops.

Muharram

Bhendi Bazaar, Mohammed Ali Road. **Date** 18 Dec
2009; 7 Dec 2010.
An important festival in the Shi'a Muslim calendar,
Muharram marks the anniversary of the Battle of
Karbala when Imam Hussain ibn Ali, grandson of
Muhammad, was martyred. The mourning reaches
its climax on the tenth day, known as Ashura, when
processions of devotees walk the city's Shi'a Muslim
areas flagellating themselves with razor-tipped
chains to experience the pain of Imam Hussain.

Christmas

*Holy Name Cathedral, Colaba; St Michael's Church,
Mahim; Mount Mary Church, Bandra & across the
city.* **Date** 24-25 Dec.
Christmas in Mumbai is much like Christmas in
the west – a midnight mass on Christmas Eve
(except it's actually over long before midnight
thanks to noise regulations), followed by an
exchange of presents and a Christmas Day
spent with the family. However, with temperatures
reaching up to 25ºC, a white Christmas is unlikely;
some make up for that by showering flecks of cotton over their carefully tended fir trees, while
street urchins and vendors roam Colaba Causeway
working up a sweat in red Santa hats.

Arts & Entertainment

Children

Don't despair, there is some magic among the mayhem.

At first glance, Mumbai looks like the world's worst city for kids. It's noisy, crowded, has few parks, terrible air pollution and the pavements – where they exist – are often too uneven to walk on. You'll rarely see parents with pushchairs in Mumbai; kids are carried, perched on the petrol tanks of motorbikes or found rattling around the backs of cars. There are very few clean public toilets and almost no facilities where babies can be changed, even in major stores, forcing hassled mums and dads to look for a vacant park bench (and good luck finding that park) to change a dirty nappy. Mumbai's maddening traffic congestion can be another downer for restless kids. Allow yourself ample time to get around, and make sure you're carrying plenty of drinks and snacks.

But take a second look and you'll see that Mumbai is not quite the worst city in the world for kids. It's probably only the fourth- or fifth-worst. With a little imagination and persistence you can find activities to keep children amused, like a ride through the lion and tiger enclosures at Sanjay Gandhi National Park (see p82) or a trip to Mani Bhavan; the spectacle of festivals like Diwali (see p137) and Ganesh Chaturthi (see p136) also make unforgettable experiences for young travellers. And it helps that the sun is often shining.

ANNUAL EVENTS FOR KIDS

January is crowded with activities for kids in the city-wide Mumbai Festival (see p134), closely followed by the Kala Ghoda Arts Festival (see p134). **February** sees a large flower, fruit and vegetable show hosted at the Veermata Jijabai Technical Institute grounds in Matunga by Friends of the Trees (2287-0860). World Book Day on **23 April**, Shakespeare's birthday, is marked by literary events for kids at the British Council Library at Nariman Point (2282-3560) and libraries and bookstores across the city. **June** brings in Environment Week, with events showcasing the region's flora and fauna organised by the Bombay Natural History Society (2282-1811) and the Worldwide Fund for Nature-India (2207-8105). On the first Sunday after **8 September**, the quiet lanes of Bandra come alive with a week-long fair around the Basilica of Mount Mary, celebrating the birthday of the Virgin Mother. Also around September is Ganesh Chaturthi (see p136), when devotees throng Chowpatty Beach to immerse large, multi-coloured idols of the

elephant-headed Ganesha in the Arabian Sea. In **October** or **November**, Diwali, the Hindu festival of lights (see p137), turns the city into a giant fireworks display.

The great outdoors

Chowpatty Beach
Marine Drive, Girgaum. Charni Road station.
Spin on the creaking, hand-cranked merry-go-round (when was the last time you saw one of those?) and miniature ferris wheels. Located at the northern end of Marine Drive, the beach is flanked by the Balodyan children's garden with play equipment.

Hanging Gardens
BG Kher Road, Malabar Hill (2363-3561). Grant Road station. **Open** 5am-9pm daily. **Admission** free.
Hanging Gardens has broad lawns, animal-shaped hedges and breathtaking city views. Across the street stands the Kamala Nehru Park with a slide coming out of a giant cement old woman's shoe, much like the nursery rhyme that inspired it.

Mahalaxmi Racecourse.

Juhu Beach

Juhu Tara Road, Juhu. Vile Parle station.
About 18 kilometres north of downtown, Juhu Beach is a veritable carnival at weekends, as families throng the beach and itinerant vendors sell colourful pinwheels, balloon monkeys and candy floss, and women apply henna tattoos. Swimming isn't advisable in these waters, though.

Mahalaxmi Racecourse

Amateur Riders' Club, Mahalaxmi Racecourse, Gate No.8, Keshavrao Khadye Marg, Mahalaxmi (6500-5204). Mahalaxmi station. **Open** 9.30am-5.30pm daily. **Classes** Rs 400 for 30mins. **No credit cards.**
Aimed at beginners of all ages, but especially popular with children, the Amateur Riders' Club's horse-riding course at Mahalaxmi lasts for ten days and is conducted by friendly trainers with many years of experience.

Maharashtra Nature Park

Sion-Bandra Link Road, Sion (W) (2407-7641). Sion station. **Open** 9am-3pm daily. **Admission** Rs 5.
A charming nature trail along Mahim Creek, following leafy paths and chasing dragonflies and frogs. This park is lush with fragrant medicinal plants, under a thick canopy of trees.

Mumbai Port Trust Garden

Women Graduates Union Road, Colaba. CST or Churchgate stations. **Open** 6-11am, 4.30-8.30pm daily. **Admission** Rs 2.
A beautiful 11-acre botanical park, with more than 450 flowering shrubs, spacious lawns, and woods with rose gardens and seashore flora. Kids get to play Tarzan on the hanging roots of banyan trees.

Veermata Jijabai Bhonsle Udyan (Byculla Zoo)

Dr Ambedkar Road, Byculla (E) (2374-2162). Byculla station. **Open** 9am-5pm Mon, Tue, Thur-Sun. **Admission** Rs 10; Rs 5 children.
Mumbai's lacklustre zoo, dating back to 1861, can be more depressing than educational, with animals confined in small, poorly maintained enclosures. But the surrounding gardens and paths are attractive and make a good spot for picnics. There's also a children's play area with slides and swings, and old statues from the British Raj era.

Indoor fun

Chhatrapati Shivaji Maharaj Vastu Sangrahalaya (Prince of Wales Museum)

Mahatma Gandhi Road, Kala Ghoda, Fort (2284-4484/4159). CST or Churchgate stations. **Open** 10.15am-6pm Tue-Sun. **Admission** Rs 300; Rs 5 under-12s; free under-5s. Audio tour in English, French or Japanese Rs 150.
The natural history section of this beautiful museum is a hit with kids and is filled with whales, rhino, deer and birds from across the region. The armoury and the collection of Indian miniature paintings are also interesting – shame about the lack of explanations though.

House of Horrors

Prime Mall, Irla, Vile Parle (W) (2621-3042). Vile Parle station. **Open** 11am-10.30pm daily. **Admission** Rs 200.
A ten-minute walk through a corridor of horror has mechanised dogs, severed heads and men in *Scream* masks waiting in ambush. The walk is meant for ten-year-olds and above; children below that are only allowed in with their parents or guardians.

Mani Bhavan

19 Laburnum Road, Gamdevi (2380-5864). Grant Road station. **Open** 9.30am-5.30pm daily. **Admission** free.
Mahatma Gandhi lived here from 1917 to 1934, planning and co-ordinating the peaceful civil disobedience movement that led to an empire's downfall. The museum here is a perfect introduction to Gandhi for kids, with cute clay doll figures depicting scenes from the great man's life.

Monetary Museum

Amar Building, Sir Pherozeshah Mehta Road, Fort (2266-0502/2261-4043). CST or Churchgate stations. **Open** 10.45am-5.15pm Mon-Sat. **Admission** Rs 10; children free.
Show them the money at the first-class Monetary Museum, with superb displays of ancient coins and crisp text explaining the 'Story of Money in India'.

Nehru Planetarium

Annie Besant Road, Worli (2492-0510). Mahalaxmi or Byculla stations. **Open** 11am-5pm Tue-Sun. **Admission** Rs 40; Rs 20 under-12s.
The planetarium conducts high-standard sky shows in English starting at 3pm. There's also a 'Discovery of India' exhibition exploring India's intellectual and cultural achievements at the Nehru Science Centre across the street.

Nehru Science Centre

Dr E Moses Road, Worli (2493-2667/4520). Mahalaxmi or Byculla stations. **Open** 10.30am-5.30pm daily. **Admission** Rs 20.
It's not a world-class science museum but it does have interactive exhibits for kids explaining everything from how pulleys work to how the eyes see. Call direct or check *Time Out Mumbai* for the centre's regular child-oriented workshops on astronomy, electronics, aero-modelling and rocketry.

Orama 4D Theatre

Atria Mall, First Floor, Annie Besant Road, Worli (2481-3380). **Open** noon-9.30pm daily. **Tickets** Rs 110.
Orama 4D Theatre shows short animated 3D films. The fourth dimension comes courtesy of leg ticklers, air blasts, foam and fog and wind. Two categories of seats are available: 'Fun' seats which are stationary but offer enhanced effects, and motion-based 'Krazy' seats that make you swirl and twirl.

Arts & Entertainment

Film

Multiplex mania has arrived but the single-screen gems are still flickering.

Over the last decade, the experience of going to the movies in Mumbai has been transformed immeasurably. Middle-class families now trek to the nearest multiplex, sometimes a 30-minute drive away, to watch the latest release in a hall that has excellent sound and superior projection. They often pay between Rs 200 and Rs 300 per ticket.

Until the late 1990s, Mumbai's hours in the flickering light were always spent in single-screen halls – spacious cinemas with an average capacity of 800 seats, with just one film showing three or four times through the day, where the audience would make its opinion known by whistling, singing along to the music or hurling things at the screen.

Until multiplexes arrived, almost every neighbourhood had at least one cinema hall – usually located close to the railway station – that screened new movies, recent releases or re-issued prints of older movies. English films were the preserve of a clutch of halls in the south of the city, including the still-surviving Regal and Sterling cinemas. The intimate association between single-screen cinema halls and a single film meant that a box-office hit could ensure a cinema's success. For instance, Ramesh Sippy's 1975 action epic *Sholay* ran for over five years at Minerva in central Mumbai. (When the movie was briefly re-released in 2004, it was at Minerva that *Sholay*'s posters first reappeared.) Sooraj Barjatya's melodrama *Hum Aapke Hain Kaun...!* helped yank the splendid Liberty cinema out of the red by ticking up just over 2,300 shows in 847 days.

The relationship between movie and cinema hall is more fragmented in the day of the multiplex. Their pricing, improved sound and seating, and location – many are inside shopping malls – make most multiplexes unaffordable to the city's underprivileged. The experience of going to the cinema – once India's great unifier – has now fractured, with the middle and upper classes visiting multiplexes while the city's poor keep the single-screen cinema alive.

Apart from the weekly dose of new releases, Mumbai gets added shots of cinema from a

Regal cinema.

handful of film clubs and cultural centres that bring international cinema of all hues to the city. Mumbai also hosts three international film festivals – the **Mumbai International Film Festival** (www.miffindia.in) of shorts and documentaries every second February; the **Mumbai Academy of Moving Images Festival** (www.iffmumbai.org), in March; and the Asian cinema-focused **Third Eye Festival** (2413-1918, www.affmumbai.com) in November.

BUYING TICKETS

Multiplexes allow advance bookings by credit card via phone or website, or you can buy direct from the box office. You should book ahead for first-night shows to be sure of getting a seat. Single-screen cinema halls do not take advance bookings except at the venue, and you will need to buy direct from the box office in cash. Hindi films generally do not carry English subtitles.

Single-screen cinemas

South Mumbai

Edward
Kalbadevi Road, Kalbadevi (2202-2109).
Marine Lines station. **Tickets** Rs 15-Rs 21.
No credit cards.

For more on Mumbai's cinema,
see pp36-39 **Bollywood**.

Its impressive frontage makes it look more public library than movie hall. Edward screens mostly 1970s and '80s re-runs. Patrons must park their bottoms on wooden seats under ceiling fans, but the theatre is much prettier than the posher 'plexes.

Eros
Khambatta Building, Churchgate (2282-2335). Churchgate station. **Tickets** Rs 60-Rs 100. **No credit cards.**
Built during Mumbai's fascination with art deco, Eros almost lives up to the romance of its name. With two wings topped by a domed baby-blue ceiling, access to its 1,000-seater hall is afforded by two grand marble staircases.

Regal
SP Mukherji Chowk, Colaba (2202-1017). CST or Churchgate stations. **Tickets** Rs 70-Rs 150. **No credit cards.**
India's first cinema hall equipped with air-conditioning and an underground car park opened in 1933 and is considered one of Mumbai's finest examples of art deco architecture. Though much of its thunder has now been stolen by the multiplexes, Regal remains the queen of South Mumbai's single-screens.

Suburbs

Chitra
Dr BR Ambedkar Road, opposite Fire Brigade, Dadar (E) (2418-2264). Dadar station.
Tickets Rs 40-Rs 75. **No credit cards.**
Chitra suffered the same woes that beset other single-screens in the late 1980s and early '90s – falling footfalls due to the video boom and, later, competition from multiplexes. It fought back by jazzing up its façade and pitching for new movie releases rather than 1980s re-runs.

G7
SV Road, Bandra (W) (2642-6963). Bandra station.
Tickets Rs 55-Rs 100. **No credit cards.**
Triplets Gaiety, Galaxy and Gemini morphed into a quasi-multiplex in the mid-1990s by converting the 40-seater preview theatres Gem and Glamour into fully-fledged auditoria. G7 later added siblings Grace, a new preview theatre, and Gossip, which screens non-mainstream films.

Maratha Mandir
Opposite Mumbai Central rail terminus (2307-0119). Mumbai Central station. **Tickets** Rs 45-Rs 65. **No credit cards.**

Metromorphosis

When the single-screen Metro cinema (*see p142*) shut in 2004 to be converted into a fancy new multiplex, there was a collective cry of protest from older Mumbaikars, who associated the stylish art deco theatre with gentler times. The cry was especially loud since several single-screens in the city have shut in recent years and been replaced by far uglier structures.

In its early days, Metro was less a cinema hall and more a place to be seen. Built in 1938, it was American studio Metro Goldwyn Mayer's effort to showcase its own musicals. The studio built art deco Metro theatres in several cities around the world, including New York, Toronto, Sydney and Chicago. In 1939 MGM built the Mumbai theatre on land it had leased for a period of 999 years. Worldwide, Metro theatres were distinctive in form and location, and Mumbai's was no exception: located at the meeting of six roads, the Metro in Mumbai was meant to be accessible to everyone. Every new release drew a faithful crowd who, says Nester D'Souza, the theatre's long-time manager, 'knew the ushers and doormen by name'.

The institution reopened as Metro Adlabs in August 2006 and thankfully not all has been lost in restoration. The façade stands untouched (save for a lick of paint and some repairs) and though the single king-size hall has been cut into six small screens, the rest of the layout remains unchanged; the plush interiors retain many of their original features, such as the magnificent Belgian chandeliers, iron and glass railings, and tall mirror panels.

Metro is listed as a heritage structure, which means that any plan to alter it requires the approval of the municipal council's heritage committee. When consulting the blueprints, the architects found one of the loveliest features of the building had been lost over the years: the original lobby had three ceiling-to-floor window panels on the right wall. However, World War II broke out soon after it was completed. Wartime restrictions meant all windows had to be painted black, and the over-enthusiastic owners went a step further and built concrete walls on either side of the building. When architects had the walls knocked down, they found the glass windows still intact, albeit rotten. Today, the tall sunlit windows are the high point of the lobby.

Metro's makeover raises hopes that theatres protected by heritage regulations will be preserved rather than erased in future.

Arts & Entertainment

If location is king, Maratha Mandir should be wearing the crown, with unbeatable positioning opposite Mumbai Central rail terminus. Maratha Mandir screens Hindi films and is home to the longest running flick, *Dilwale Dulhaniya le Jayenge*. Released in 1995, it is still playing as the matinée.

Multiplexes

South Mumbai

INOX
CR2 Mall, Nariman Point (6658-8888/www.inox movies.com). CST or Churchgate stations. **Tickets** Rs 89-Rs 200. **Credit** AmEx, MC, V.
Art deco for fat wallets. Designed to resemble the architectural style of its single-screen neighbours, INOX screens Hindi and English movies through the day, starting with morning shows at reduced rates. As far as seating and sound go, it's one of the best multiplexes around, though the snacks are so-so. **Other location** Second floor, Milan Mall, Milan Subway, Santa Cruz (W) (6659-5959).

Metro
Dhobi Talao, Marine Lines (3989-4040/ www.adlabscinemas.com). CST or Marine Lines stations. **Tickets** Rs 180-Rs 500. **Credit** MC, V.
A one-time single-screen behemoth, now lovingly converted to a multiplex (*See p141* **Metromorphosis**).

Sterling
Murzban Road, Fort (2207-5187). CST station. **Tickets** Rs 120. **No credit cards.**
One of South Mumbai's best-known single-screens has now become a multiplex. Yet location, rather than decor, remains Sterling's biggest advantage. Throw a piece of popcorn and you'll hit both CST and the delights of Colaba.

Suburbs

Cinemax
Infiniti Mall, Versova, Andheri (W) (2631-3355/ www.cinemax.co.in). Andheri station.
Tickets Rs 40-Rs 500. **Credit** MC, V.
Cinemax has been busy making sure that 'a theatre near you' is a Cinemax one, with multiplexes in Bandra (E), Sion, Kandivali, Goregaon, Thane and Mira Road. This is its swankiest property, with the option of recliner seats for Rs 500.
Other locations Andheri-Kurla Road, Andheri (E) (2631-3355); Kalanagar, Bandra (E) (2656-1501); Off Sion Circle, Sion (2404-1130); and throughout the city.

Fame Adlabs
New Link Road, Andheri (W) (6699-1212/www.fame cinemas.com). Andheri station. **Tickets** Rs 70-Rs 250. **Credit** MC, V.
As the exhibition wing of Shringar Films, which distributes and produces Hindi movies, Fame was the first of many multiplexes that now dot New Link Road, and is still a comfortable option.

Other locations Fame Nakshatra, Dadar (W) (6699-1212); Fame Malad, InOrbit Mall, Goregaon-Malad Link Road, Goregoan (W) (6649-0490).

Fun Republic
Shah Industrial Estate, Veera Desai Road, Andheri (W) (6675-5675/www.funcinemas.com). Andheri station. **Tickets** Rs 70-Rs 180. **Credit** AmEx, DC, MC, V.
Fame's rival in Andheri shares a strip with the offices of mega-producers Yashraj Films and record label T-Series. The multiplex often takes a break from Hindi and English movies to hold special screenings of international films.

PVR
Dynamix Mall, Juhu (2628-0101/www.pvrcinemas. com). Vile Parle station. **Tickets** Rs 175-Rs 250. **Credit** MC, V.
PVR set up the first multiplex in India in New Delhi in 1997. The group took its time to come to Mumbai, finally sinking roots in the Juhu neighbourhood in 2006.
Other locations Nirmal Lifestyle Mall, LBS Marg Mulund (W) (2565-7770).

Other film venues

Alliance Française
Alliance Française Auditorium, Theosophy Hall, New Marine Lines, Churchgate (2203-6187/ www.afindia.org). Churchgate station. **Taxi** next to Nirmala Niketan. **Tickets** free.
The French Consulate's cultural wing screens movies throughout the year.

British Council
British Council Auditorium, Mittal Court, C Wing, Nariman Point (2279-0126/www.british council.org.in). CST or Churchgate stations. **Taxi** Vidhan Bhavan. **Tickets** free.
The British government's cultural wing in Mumbai has a library of British television and film DVDs available for rent. It also holds film screenings.

Max Mueller Bhavan
Kala Ghoda, Colaba (2202-2085). CST or Churchgate stations. **Tickets** free.
Max Mueller Bhavan waves Germany's cultural flag in Mumbai with German-language screenings of films that are as edgy and experimental as a government-supported centre can get.

Vikalp
Bhupesh Gupta Bhavan, Leningrad Chowk, near Ravindra Natya Mandir, Sayani Marg, Prabhadevi (2437-4930/www.freedomfilmsindia.org). Dadar station. **Tickets** free.
The only space dedicated to Indian and international documentaries. Vikalp means 'alternative', and the organisation grew out of a protest movement by local documentary filmmakers against government censorship of the state-sponsored Mumbai International Film Festival in 2004. Check the website for dates and alternative venues.

Galleries

Looking for a brush with fame.

Every decade has its buzzword. The 1980s saw video rental stores popping up at every corner of Mumbai while the cyber café was the cash calf of the '90s. Now, with Indian art crossing the million-dollar mark on the auction circuit, art is the flavour of the times.

Mumbai's local art scene started with three private galleries that were established in the 1950s and a small, elite group of collectors. As of February 2008, the number of galleries has gone up to 82. Everything from apartments to sheds in the dockyard are being converted to galleries. Very few of these fold up because with growing affluence in the city, there are buyers for the most unlikely art. Whether it's the new auction-house favourite Subodh Gupta's sushi belt or veteran Jehangir Sabavala's figurative paintings, there's someone who wants it. There are old buyers who have been collecting Indian art from the days when paintings could be bought for a few hundred rupees, and there are the yuppies looking for some culture to flaunt in their handkerchief-sized flats. The old-timers may moan about how the world of art is turning into a business but the flood of new money has also meant that, for those of us who just want to wander around galleries, there's a bigger range of cool art to behold than ever before.

Each week brings news of a new price barrier crossed. When veteran Hindi film actress Leela Naidu bought her first SH Raza (the eminent India artist) in the 1960s, she paid a few thousand rupees. Today, a Raza of that vintage would fetch around Rs 3 million. For many of today's breed of nouveau riche art buyers, aesthetics are secondary to economics. Mumbai financial papers carry stories about the rise in Atul Dodiya's graph, the drop in the per-square-inch price of a Husain, and whether one should hold on to Akbar Padamsee or buy more. Each week brings a new breed of collector sniffing around, looking for an investment bargain that will also give its owner the aura of high culture. Art show openings are now social events filled with air kissing and shrieks of delight at seeing the same faces from the night before. No more will we have cheese sandwiches and orangeade; sponsored wine and canapés are de rigueur.

Where can you see all this art outside of a private gallery? Unfortunately, nowhere. Mumbai was home to some of the biggest names in the business, including Mehta, Husain, Padamsee and Ara. Some of them were part of the very influential Progressive Artists' Group, who were concerned with negotiating convergences and contrasts between traditional Indian art forms and Western styles, but the Indian government had no inclination to collect modern art when it was still affordable. Only the **National Gallery of Modern Art** (*see p146*) has a small collection – but even that is not on permanent display.

With the new boom, contemporary Indian art is now well out of the government's reach and out of sight, but it's possible to see some of the best new work at established private galleries. With prices rising faster than the water level around the Arctic, no one can be sure if or when the art boom will bust. But for now the euphoria of Mumbai's art scene mirrors that of a city riding a seemingly unstoppable high.

Check *Time Out Mumbai* magazine for details of the latest art shows.

Colaba

Art Musings

1 Admiralty Building, Colaba Cross Lane, next to Sassoon Dock, Colaba (2216-3339/www. artmusings.net). CST or Churchgate stations. **Taxi** opposite Dunne's School. **Open** 11am-7pm Mon-Sat. **No credit cards**.
Renovated in 2007, this gallery shows art that is decorative and sophisticated. In the past, it's had sell-out shows by established names like Akbar Padamsee, Anjolie Ela Menon and Jitish Kallat. It's

Autosaurus Tripous by **Jitish Kallat**.

Jehangir Art Gallery.

also serious about giving platforms to promising artists like Smriti Dixit and Maya Burman.

Bombay Art Gallery

First Floor, 02/19 Kamal Mansion, Arthur Bunder Road, Colaba (6507-0699/www.bombay artgallery.com). CST or Churchgate stations. **Taxi** Radio Club. **Open** 10.30am-6.30pm Mon-Sat. **No credit cards.**
Bombay Art Gallery shifted from Malabar Hill in search of a what proprietor Aditya Ruia describes as a place with a 'classic contemporary' feel. The gallery shows works by a wide range of artists, like Anita Dube, Shivani Aggarwal and DJ-photographer Talvin Singh.

Chatterjee & Lal

First Floor, Kamal Mansion, next to Radio Club, Arthur Bunder Road, Colaba (6521-5105/ www.chatterjeeandlal.com). CST or Churchgate stations. **Taxi** Radio Club. **Open** 11am-7pm Mon-Sat. **No credit cards.**
After promoting a host of young, cutting-edge artists for the past few years, Mortimer Chatterjee and Tara Lal took the plunge and opened up their own gallery in Colaba in 2007. From performance art to paintings, they're open to everything as long as it's 'high art'.

Collector's Paradise

17/19 Mahakavi Bhushan Road, Apollo Bunder, Colaba (2282-4765). CST or Churchgate stations. **Taxi** near Regal Cinema. **Open** 10.30am-6.30pm Mon-Sat. **No credit cards.**
This gallery doesn't hold regular exhibitions but it does have a fair collection of works that buyers (and oglers) are able to browse.

Galerie Mirchandani + Steinruecke

2 Sunny House, 16/18 Mereweather Road, Colaba (2202-3030/www.galeriems.com). CST or Churchgate stations. **Taxi** behind Taj Mahal Hotel. **Open** 10am-6.30pm Mon-Fri; 10am-4pm Sat. **No credit cards.**
Mother-and-daughter team Usha Mirchandani and Ranjana Steinruecke closed their Berlin gallery and came back to Mumbai to open a space to mount solos of major artists from around the world – they have hosted shows by high priestess of feminist art in America, Kiki Smith, and Saatchi Gallery's Jonathan Messe – as well as high-quality group shows.

Guild Art Gallery

First Floor, 2A Prince Chambers, Colaba (2218-0057/www.guildindia.com). CST or Churchgate stations. **Open** 10am-6.30pm Mon-Sat. **Credit** AmEx.
Gallery owner Shalini Sawhney displays works by contemporary Indian artists from the Progressive Artists' Group to works by the newer Bombay Boys; it also sells limited-edition prints.

Project 88

BMP Building, NA Sawant Marg, Colaba (2281-0066). CST or Churchgate stations. **Taxi** near Colaba Fire Station. **Open** 11am-6.30pm Mon-Sat. **No credit cards.**
It's one of the most striking art spaces in the city and owner Sree Goswami has cultivated a reputation for having exciting shows that don't seem particularly saleable but make for great viewing. It's also the only gallery in the city that also shows architectural projects. Among its more avant-garde exhibitions have been projects shown at Germany's Documenta in 2007 and the architectural biennale in Venice.

Sakshi Gallery

Tanna House, 11A Nathalal Parekh Marg, Colaba (6610-3424/www.sakshigallery.com). CST or Churchgate stations. **Taxi** opposite YMCA. **Open** 11am-7pm Mon-Sat. **No credit cards**.

In 2007, this gallery moved from mid-town and set itself up in the heart of the city's art district. Sakshi shows a range of established and upcoming artists, including traditional faves like Sudhir Patwardhan, known for his figurative paintings of Mumbai's underbelly, and new media artist Shilpa Gupta.

Kala Ghoda

Art Land

Third Floor, Esplanade Mansion, MG Road, Kala Ghoda (6635-0776/www.artlandindia.com). CST or Churchgate stations. **Taxi** Army & Navy Building. **Open** 10am-7pm Mon-Sat. **No credit cards**.

Owner Sunil Chauhan opened this 800-sq-ft space as a platform for emerging Indian artists. Now renovated and extended, Chauhan hosts large shows and has widened the gallery's brief to include exhibitions by established artists like Prafulla Dhanukar, Padmanabh Bendre, Nayanaa Kanodia and Asit Kumar Patnaik.

Artists' Centre

First Floor, Ador House, 6 K Dubash Marg, next to Rhythm House, off MG Road, Kala Ghoda (2284-5939). CST or Churchgate stations. **Taxi** Rhythm House. **Open** 11am-7pm Mon-Sat. **No credit cards**.

Housed on the first floor of a heritage building, this was the first gallery to open in Mumbai's art district in 1950. It used to be the meeting point for renowned artists like KH Ara, FN Souza, MF Husain, SH Raza and S Bakre – the core of the Progressive Artists' Group that took Indian art in a new direction. It now has regular shows by young artists who haven't yet been snapped up by richer galleries.

Bodhi Art

28 K Dubash Marg, Kala Ghoda (6610-0124/ www.bodhiart.in). CST or Churchgate stations. **Taxi** near Rhythm House. **Open** 11am-7pm Mon-Sat. **No credit cards**.

This three-storey gallery is a stunning space, with a repertoire running the gamut from cutting-edge to classic. Indian art's wunderkinds are all here, from Subodh Gupta to Anju Dodiya. **Other location** Ground Floor, 14 Elphinstone Estate, Malet Bunder Road, near Orange Gate, Wadi Bunder.

Gallery Beyond

First Floor, 130/132 Great Western Building, Shahid Bhagat Singh Road, Fort (2283-7345/ www.gallerybeyond.com). CST or Churchgate stations. **Open** 10.30am-6.30pm Mon-Sat. **Credit** AmEx, DC, MC, V.

Owner Vibhuraj Kapoor is committed to hosting debut solo shows by young, emerging hot properties like Prajakta Palav, Minal Damani, Anu Agarwal and Preetam Bhatty.

Jehangir Art Gallery

MG Road, Kala Ghoda, Fort (2204-8212). CST or Churchgate stations. **Taxi** Elphinstone College. **Open** 11am-7pm Mon-Sat.

This is the largest art gallery in Mumbai, with four exhibition halls, an art shop and a café. Opened in 1951, it's now the city's most popular contemporary

Follow your art

In Mumbai, the arts village is in Colaba and Kala Ghoda, nestled between the docks and the financial district. This is the neighbourhood where the best of the city's art galleries are located, and covering all of them makes for an enjoyable walk; just wear comfortable shoes.

Start with **Bodhi Art** (*see above*) in Kala Ghoda where you'll almost always see one or more celebrities. Almost opposite is the **Museum Gallery** (*see p146*), which is generally worth a visit. Go past **Jehangir Art Gallery** (*see above*) towards Colaba. Check to see if the **National Gallery of Modern Art** (*see p146*) has a new show and if not, head straight down to **Sakshi** (*see above*). If there's no show on, check out its permanent collection. Come out onto Colaba Causeway and go across to **Galerie Mirchandani + Steinruecke** (*see p144*), in Sunny House, which often shows interesting work. Walk

down towards the Radio Club and up to **Chatterjee & Lal** (*see p144*) where exhibits are always funky and intelligent. Get back on the causeway and turn left at Colaba Fire Station to reach **Project 88** (*see p144*), one of the coolest spaces (with some of the most bizarre shows) in the city. Come out and walk towards Sassoon Dock but keep an eye out for the sign for **Art Musings** (*see p143*) on your left. The gallery generally shows paintings and has a nice seating area in which to browse past catalogues and rest your feet.

For those who love cheap wine as much as they love art, gallery openings are held on Thursdays; you can tell there's an opening by the groups of scruffy-chic men outside, and the belligerent-looking women wearing lots of kohl. Even though these events are officially for invited audiences, Mumbai galleries love gatecrashers and no one checks for invites.

art space, with hundreds of visitors each day. But Jehangir rarely offers the best of Mumbai's contemporary art. It's run by a trust that rents out the space on a first-come-first-served basis, often without careful attention to quality.

Museum Gallery
K Dubash Marg, Kala Ghoda, Fort (2284-4484). CST or Churchgate stations. **Taxi** *Jehangir Art Gallery.* **Open** *11am-7pm Mon-Sat.* **No credit cards.**

Sharing a wall with the landmark Jehangir Art Gallery (*see p145*), this 1,000-sq-ft gallery is also a space-for-hire, but with more discriminate taste than its neighbour; it has hosted some of the city's best solo shows.

National Gallery of Modern Art
Cowasji Jehangir Hall, MG Road, Colaba (2288-1969/www.ngmaindia.gov.in). CST or Churchgate stations. **Taxi** *opposite Regal Cinema.* **Open** *11am-6pm Tue-Sun.* **No credit cards.**

One of the city's most interesting art spaces. From time to time it mounts retrospectives of major Indian artists as well as shows from abroad.

Nariman Point

Jehangir Nicholson Gallery of Modern Art
National Centre for the Performing Arts, Nariman Point (6622-3737). CST or Churchgate stations. **Open** *10am-6pm Mon-Sat.* **No credit cards.**

Housed within the National Centre for the Performing Arts building (*see p166*), this gallery is named for legendary collector Jehangir Nicholson, who donated a significant part of his collection to the NCPA. The gallery is regularly rented out by curators and gallery owners for various exhibitions.

Fort

Fourth Floor
Kitab Mahal, Fourth Floor, DN Road, Fort (2207-9119/www.kitabmahal.org). CST or Churchgate stations. **Taxi** *near New Excelsior Cinema.* **Open** *10.30am-7pm Mon-Sat.* **No credit cards.**

Situated opposite Chhatrapati Shivaji Terminus, Fourth Floor is an 8,000-sq-ft event space with an avant-garde emphasis. Located on the top floor of a heritage building, Kitab Mahal, it's a gorgeous space that occasionally plays host to very interesting shows.

Pundole Art Gallery
369 DN Road, Flora Fountain (2204-8473). CST or Churchgate stations. **Taxi** *next to American Dry Fruit.* **Open** *10.30am-6.30pm Mon-Sat.* **Credit** AmEx, MC, V.

This gallery became the main building block of the Progressive Artists' Group (PAG). Run by Dadiba and Khorshed Pundole, Pundole specialises in the works of the PAG and you'll also find unique prints

by these artists here. In recent times, they've been showing mid-range artists like Ebenezer Sunder Singh and Sharath Kulagatti.

Breach Candy

Studio Napean
Matru Ashish, 39 Nepean Sea Road (3264-9532). Grant Road station. **Taxi** *Matru Ashish.* **Open** *10.30am-8pm Mon-Sat.* **No credit cards.**

Interior designer and collector Kavita Singh may be better known as Bollywood star Anil Kapoor's sister-in-law but she's trying to change all that by breaking into the world of art as a gallerist. Run by her daughter Nandini, the gallery's exhibits are mundane but not bad for a casual wander.

Prabhadevi

Birla Academy of Art & Culture
Century Bhavan, Annie Besant Road, Worli (2432-0316). Dadar station. **Taxi** *Century Bhavan.* **Open** *10.30am-8pm Mon-Sat; 4-8pm Sun.* **No credit cards.**

This gallery reopened in 2005 with a fresh new look and an agenda to display works by debutant artists from across India. The quality level varies, but it's always interesting fare.

Worli

Gallery Art & Soul
1 Madhuli, Annie Besant Road, Shivsagar Estate, Worli (2496-5798). Mahalaxmi station. **Taxi** *Poonam Chambers.* **Open** *11am-7pm Mon-Sat; by appointment Sun.* **No credit cards.**

Tarana Khubchandani's gallery, on the ground floor of a Worli seafront high-rise, is a platform for young artists, as well as a venue for talks by artists, art historians and critics. The group shows at the gallery are generally well conceived and offer a range of experimental works.

Priyasri Art Gallery
4 Madhuli, Annie Besant Road, Shivsagar Estate, Worli (93235-82303). Mahalaxmi station. **Taxi** *Poonam Chambers.* **Open** *11am-7pm Mon-Sat.* **No credit cards.**

The glorious sea view from Priyasri is reason enough to visit the gallery, and the young artists from Baroda and Bengal that the gallery hosts are often pretty good too.

Tao Art Gallery
Sarjan Plaza, Annie Besant Road, Worli (2491-8585/www.taoartgallery.com). Mahalaxmi station. **Taxi** *Lotus.* **Open** *10.30am-6.30pm Mon-Sat.* **No credit cards.**

Established by collector and artist Kalpana Shah, this gallery is known for large group shows spread over its three exhibition rooms. It regularly shows the work of S H Raza, Sujata Bajaj and A Anwar.

Gay & Lesbian

Mumbai's gay scene is finally coming of age.

Mumbai's gay culture may be inching out of the closet, one painfully slow step at a time, but for every petition to decriminalise homosexuality is an incident like the February 2008 police raid of a gay party in a farmhouse just outside Mumbai, in which six men were booked for drinking without a permit. This doesn't help gay travellers to India, who are faced with confusing contradictions. They've read the warnings about how gay couples should be discreet but men keep looking at them in the street and no, not just in the way all foreigners get stared at. It's a bold, direct look straight in the eyes, which seems to suggest something. But what?

There's no easy answer. It could be an invitation to sex: as in all cultures where homosexuality is criminalised, gay men see foreigners as a relatively safe option, less likely to betray them to the local police. The gaze could also hold hope – some Indian gay guys have fairy-tale fantasies of a foreign who'll sweep them off their feet and take them far from the problems of being gay in India. The gaze could hold an acquisitive gleam. Male hookers in Mumbai hang around railway stations or the bylanes of tourist areas like Colaba and could be sizing you up as a potential customer. The gaze could also have a darker edge: blackmailers prowl the same areas looking for easy targets to set up for a scam. Or it may not mean anything dramatic at all. Perhaps he just wants to have coffee with you. Maybe he wants to sell you a carpet.

Scratch the surface and you'll find that the gay scene in Mumbai is not that closeted. There are gay and lesbian support groups (*see p233*) in Mumbai and regular parties. Websites list treks and film screenings for the gay and lesbian community, bookshops have gay- and lesbian-themed books from India and cinemas now show gay and lesbian films. A few years back the film *My Brother Nikhil* received critical acclaim as the first mainstream Bollywood production with a gay relationship at its core, and while many more such films haven't followed, gay characters are now quite common in bit-parts on-screen.

The media too now regularly reports on queer issues, and on the protracted battle to change the law in India. There's no gay pride parade in Mumbai yet but open demonstrations have taken place and with the knowledge of the police, who rarely seem interested. Spend time

An image by gay photographer **Sunil Gupta**, from his series 'Exiles'.

in Mumbai and you'll meet many gays and lesbians who are living life on their own terms.

At the same time, don't expect things you might take for granted elsewhere. There are no fixed gay clubs (except **Voodoo** on Saturday nights, *see below*) and no restaurants flying rainbow flags. But the reasons are more Mumbai than intolerance: rents are so high that niche venues of any kind are rare. There seems to be a tacit understanding between the city and its gay and lesbian community: you can do your own thing as long as you're discreet. If that sounds repressive, it's more than most Indian cities allow.

However, there's been a disturbing rise in cases of blackmailers targeting gay men in Mumbai. Some use the internet to lure victims so be careful with online hook-ups. Take the usual precautions: don't carry too much money, make sure a friend knows where you're going, lock up all valuables if you're bringing someone back to your hotel. A favourite scam is for the blackmailer to go back to your room with you and then pretend to be an undercover police officer threatening to arrest you for 'illegal sex'. Don't fall for this. Shout as loudly as you can, attract the attention of the hotel management, demand identity cards and say you'll go to the tourist police – they'll be gone long before that.

Mumbai's dyke community is very choosy and closed about letting in new members, and for good reason. Women in India have a lot less access to public spaces than gay men or men in general, with overbearing parents and siblings and Cinderella deadlines. However, once a new member visits the right circle of friends, she is happily inducted into the group.

One good way to find other women is to call the helpline **Lesbians and Bisexuals in Action** (98332-78171) or email them at stree.sangam@gmail.com; their aim is to reach out to the community. They usually make it a point to meet new members before they introduce them to the rest of the group, to ensure a protective layer for those who aren't out. Attending a **GayBombay** party is another way of meeting the few lesbians who do frequent larger spaces. **Symphony in Pink** (symphonyinpink@rediffmail.com) is an online discussion group for lesbians and bisexuals in Mumbai, and is pretty vibrant, though you may have to bear many approaches before you get to the good stuff. If you just want to pick someone up, parties and club nights are the best option.

What you get depends on what you're looking for. If you want a full-on gay scene, you should go to Bangkok instead. But if you want to tap into a young and lively scene, growing in size and confidence, but still small enough to be friendly, then take your chances with Mumbai.

Out and about

Voodoo (*see p158*) is the only club in Mumbai with a regular gay night, every Saturday. The place is small and rather grotty, the Rs 250 entry is somewhat excessive, the music variable and the loos best avoided. The crowd has a high percentage of hookers, male and female, and their clients. Yet Voodoo has real character, unlike the mirror-and-chrome places opening all over the place. It's also a curiously relaxed and easy-going place where anything goes – which can be a relief from the repressions of the moralists outside.

There are two organisations currently running regular parties for the LGBT community in Mumbai. **GayBombay** (www.gaybombay.org) is the better-established group that caters to the wider community with a taste for popular Indian music (read Bollywood). Its rates are lower and it gets slightly larger crowds at its parties, which are held at regular venues. **Salvation Star** (www.salvationstar.com) are the enthusiastic new kids on the block, catering to a more niche, trendy crowd with a taste for the latest in global music. It has a fixed venue, at a downtown club. Queer women are welcome at both venues, of course, but for occasional lesbian specific parties you need to check with the women's support groups.

Hotels in Mumbai usually don't bat an eyelid at two men or two women sharing a room. If you're a couple and don't want separate beds, ask for a single large one and they'll comply. But taking someone back to your room can be tricky. Most hotels don't object but a few might so be prepared.

Gay couples can sometimes run into problems getting into bars and clubs thanks to the 'couples only' policy that many places follow. Ironically, this is meant to deter boisterous straight men who might cause problems for women. It's usually easier to get in if you're a (white) foreigner, but if you have problems you might want to try convincing the bouncers you're gay (use your imagination) or you could persuade women friends to come along.

Mind, Body & Soul

Mumbai's calming side.

Iyengar Yogashraya. *See p152.*

Although India has a 5,000-year heritage of traditional holistic therapies, such as ayurveda, it is only in this decade that the demand for modern spas has seen a surge in cities like Mumbai. Over the past few years, wellness centres have popped up across the city, from barebones facilities like the Kerala Ayurvedic Health Spa, which offer age-old (and affordable) treatments to swanky five-star spas like Quan at the JW Marriott, which represents the last word in luxury.

If you're looking for one discipline that will have an enduring effect on your body and mind, forget fad diets and quick fixes and stick with yoga. Mumbai might lack the new-fangled versions now popular in the West, but you can find the real thing in yoga centres across the city, as well as little-known centres (Satyananda yoga, anyone?) if you're feeling adventurous. Be warned: most yoga centres are utilitarian and spartan, so leave the Louis Vuitton yoga tote at home and experience the science in its most unadorned form.

Like yoga, ayurveda is an ancient Indian science that believes in the philosophy of rejuvenation from the inside out. Rituals like the *shiro dhara* (a full-body massage in which a steady stream of warm medicinal oil is poured

on the forehead to awaken the 'third eye') are over 2,000 years old and continue to be popular across the social spectrum. Meanwhile, beauty treatments incorporate a range of organic spices, herbs, fruit, flowers and vegetables. Even the wealthiest brides indulge in the pre-wedding custom of smearing turmeric paste over their bodies, and posh South Mumbai housewives dab La Mer cream on their cheeks only after cleansing with all-natural rosewater.

A novelty not to be missed is the old Indian *champi* or *tel maalish*, a vigorous scalp massage with coconut, olive or herbal oil, which improves blood circulation, cures headaches and is often credited with giving Indian women their thick, healthy locks (*see p151* **Champions**). But as the city becomes more global, so do its offerings: you can now choose from Hawaiian, Javanese or Balinese massages by qualified masseuses in world-class spas. Spirituality is such an integral part of the Indian psyche that you won't have to look far to find offerings of interest. Newspapers are flooded with classifieds advertising everything from aromatherapy to reiki. Exercise some caution with these, but for the most part just go with the flow and don't worry too much: it isn't good for your soul (or your skin).

Arts & Entertainment

Ayurvedic healing

Ayushakti
Bhadran Nagar, Cross Road 2, opposite Milap theatre, off SV Road, Malad (W) (2806-5757). Malad station. **Open** 10.30am-8pm Mon-Sat. **Credit** V.

Dr Pankaj Naram is famous for diagnosing patients just by taking their pulse and then prescribing a customised combination of herbs, rigorous diets and much-needed detoxification. Legend has it Naram learned the art of pulse reading from a 115-year-old Tibetan monk. Today, the centre is spread over 15,000 feet in a leafy part of Malad and has a residential complex for long-term treatments (although you'll need to book at least two years in advance). Treatment sessions start at Rs 300.

Kerala Ayurvedic Health Spa
Neelkanth, Marine Drive (2288-3210/98204-35344). Marine Lines station. **Open** 8am-8pm daily. **Credit** MC, V.

For an authentic and affordable taste of South India's natural ayurvedic treatments, visit this chain, the best-known for good reason. Sample the famous *shiro dhara* – a full body massage carried out simultaneously by two practitioners who pour a vessel full of medicinal oil onto your forehead in a steady stream (supposedly to awaken the 'third eye'). It's an experience you'll want to sample at least once. Be warned though: you don't get to keep your undies on. The *ayushman bhava* rejuvenation therapy (Rs 1,685) is also popular. The clean but no-frills set-up feels cosy and authentic, thanks in large part to the sari-clad practitioners who studiously ignore the fact that you're naked. Treatments range from Rs 900 to Rs 3,000.
Other locations Louis Mansion, VS Road, Prabhadevi (2430-2336); Sun 'n' Sand Hotel, 39 Juhu Beach, Juhu (6602-4043).

Massage

See p151 **Spas** for addresses and timings.

Balinese
The massage that originates in the only Hindu state in the Indonesian archipelago involves acupressure, stretching, reflexology and a variety of kneading and rolling movements to balance the blood, oxygen and *qi* in the body. It's a medium-intensity massage to deal with specific stress.
Oberoi Spa *Available only with spa packages. Day spa at Rs 10,300 per person or Rs 14,700 per couple. Rs 3,850 for 60mins for residents. Weekend spa package Rs 16,500 per person or Rs 23,000 per couple.*

Hawaiian Lomilomi
'Lomi' is the Hawaiian word for the way in which a contented cat works its claws in and out. Lomilomi works your pressure points, but unlike acupressure or reflexology, the pressure is not held for very long; the masseuse uses her forearms and elbows in smooth, gliding movements to turn you into putty.
Oberoi Spa *see above.*
Rudra *Rs 3,372 for 60mins.*

Javanese Lulur
Lulur is Javanese for the rice and turmeric scrub used during a bride's prenuptial massage but spas also use the term loosely to describe the technique that involves thumb pressure and long palm strokes.
Rudra *Rs 4,383 for 60mins.*

Shiatsu
Shiatsu is an acupressure massage that follows the Japanese meridian system of energy flow in the body. *Shi* translates to fingers and *atsu* means pressure. So instead of being poked all over, pressure points in your body are merely tapped, rubbed, squeezed and pressed.
Rudra *Rs 2,360 for 60mins.*

Sea, sand and saline drips

Outsourcing has its benefits. Why shell out $1,000 on a root canal in the US when you can do it in Mumbai for $100 and use the rest of the money for a fab holiday in India?

Cheap laser eye corrections and hip replacements have now become compelling reasons to take a trip to Mumbai. In the West, long waiting lists for routine procedures and rising drug costs have helped push India as a health-care destination, where everything from heart surgery to dental care can be had at excellent facilities and performed by first-rate doctors.

Medical tourism is a growing industry that could be worth around $1 billion a year to the Indian economy. Organisations like the **Medical Tourism Council of Maharashtra** (2496-8000) arrange for packages that include travel, accommodation and medical expenses. On its website, the **Apollo Group of Hospitals** (www.apollohospitals.com) has a section devoted to international patients – explaining everything from blood screening standards to a virtual patient visit. In Mumbai, the private **Lilavati, Jaslok** and **Hinduja** hospitals (*see p233*) have state-of-the-art health-care facilities that have been serving foreigners for years. Medical tourism could save you a fortune, but it's a new industry and poorly regulated.

Thai

Thai massage practitioners don't believe in letting you lie back and blissing out. Expect to go 'ouch' as your pressure points are firmly pressed and your body stretched, folded and twisted into various yoga poses on a mat on the floor. This is somewhere between an alternative therapy and a less strenuous workout. If it makes you feel any better, you get to keep your clothes on.

Antara *Rs 2,529 for 90mins.*
Quan *Rs 3,000 for 60mins.*

Spas

Antara

The Club, 197, DN Nagar, Andheri (W) (6693-9999). Vile Parle. **Taxi** DN Nagar. **Open** 8am-8pm Mon-Fri; 8am-9pm Sat-Sun. **Credit** AmEx, MC, V.
Antara, which means 'looking within' in Sanskrit, offers a modestly priced getaway from the chaos of the city. The six-room spa is high on value and low on frills. While there, remember to try the spa's signature treatment: a body wrap followed by 'dry floatation' on a specially designed waterbed, which glows red, blue and purple according to the temperature of the water. It looks straight out of *2001: A Space Odyssey* and adds a bit of humour to the treatment, which is supposed to produce deeper muscle relaxation in twenty minutes than two hours of shut-eye would. *Photo p152.*

Aquamarine Day Spa

202 Patel House, Bomanji Petit Road, Kemp's Corner (2381-1118). Grant Road station.
Open 10am-7pm daily. **Credit** AmEx, MC, V
Aquamarine was started by European beauty giant Thalgo and offers a range of treatments including lymphatic drainage massages, facials, body wraps and hot-stone therapy.

Centre for Colon Therapy

92 Lady Ratan Tata Medical and Research Centre, Maharshi Karve Road, Cooperage (6585-4474/ www.thecoloncentre.com). CST or Churchgate stations. **Open** 10am-6pm daily. **Credit** AmEx, DC, MC, V.
Dedicated solely to colonic irrigation, or hydrotherapy, the Centre is small, friendly and private. It employs the latest US technology, which 'offers the most advanced methods in lower bowel evacuation'.

Kerala Ayurvedic Health Spa

See p150 **Ayurvedic healing**.

Lakme

Arsiwala Building, Wodehouse Road, Colaba (2218-1747/6631-5277). CST or Churchgate stations.
Taxi Wodehouse Road **Open** 10am-7pm daily.
Credit MC, V.
Lakme salons offer a range of beauty services, including waxing, threading and hot-oil scalp massages.
Other location Shop No. 1, Kailash, Waterfield Road, Bandra (2642-1410/2643-7220).

Champions

Google '*champissage*' and you'll find scores of reflexology clinics and spas in the UK that offer this hybrid variant of *champi*, the traditional Indian head massage, with some places even offering to make it oil-less so that you can enjoy it in the office. The humble *champi* has gone places. Traditionally, '*champi*' meant an oil massage for the scalp and hair, which is supposed to encourage hair growth, improve blood supply to the brain and relax the neck, shoulders and upper arms. The technique is said to have been handed down from generation to generation; largely self-taught masseurs offer it as an add-on service in barbershops, where they use a vibrating massage machine for enhanced pleasure.

For an authentic *champi* that's light on the pocket, visit one of the no-frills barbershops that dot the city or hang around at Chowpatty beach, where masseurs look for clients. You can expect a massage that will invigorate your head, neck, shoulders and, if you wish, the rest of your body as well. For a more genteel experience, go to one of the day spas listng below that offer the same service minus the knuckles cracking on your head.

Air-cool

IMC Marg, Churchgate (2287-3839). Opposite Churchgate station. **Head massage** Rs 50. **Open** 8am-8.30pm.
No credit cards.

Jiva Grande

Taj Wellington Mews, 33 Nathalal Parekh Marg, Colaba (6657-4401). **Champi** Rs 1,910. **Open** 9am-9pm daily. **Credit** AmEx, DC, MC, V.

Oberoi

Oberoi Hotel, Nariman Point (6632-5757).
Churchgate station. **Open** 8am-8.30pm.
Credit AmEx, DC, MC, V.
It's Asian exotica through and through at this spa
run by the Thai Banyan Tree chain. The Thai
masseuses with soft hands and softer voices are
experts at pampering you and they have fancy, natural ingredients. Steam, sauna, jacuzzi – this place
has the works. All you need to do is lose your inhi-
bitions when faced with the mirrored walls and let
their hands do the rest.

Parcos

*White Hall, Kemp's Corner (2364-3685). Grant
Road station.* **Open** 10.30am-7.30pm. *Studio*
10am-6pm. **Credit** AmEx, DC, MC, V.
This Clarins-run spa is small but neat, and offers
signature face and body treatments.

Quan

*JW Marriott, Juhu Tara Road, Juhu (6693-3610).
Santa Cruz or Vile Parle stations.* **Open** 9am-9pm
daily. **Credit** AmEx, DC, MC, V. Prior appointment
required for all treatments.
For five-star comfort and cutting-edge design, visit
Quan at the JW Marriott in suburban Juhu. Quan
earned itself the new spa of the year award in 2006
at the Asia Spa Baccarat Awards, which honour
innovation in the spa industry. And if you're travelling with your significant other, don't forget to lux-
uriate in the couples room.

Rudra

*Kwality House, Kemp's Corner, Hughes Road
(2387-2530/31). Grant Road station.* **Taxi** Kemp's
Corner. **Open** 8am-9.30pm daily. **Credit** AmEx,
DC, MC, V.
Rudra's interiors display attention to detail: the
mood lighting, ornate furniture and meditative
chants are all carefully chosen to provide 'souli-
tude'. All 13 rooms feature DVD players that play
the music of your choice, and high-end showers
which double up as saunas. But while the interiors
are fancy, the treatments emphasise traditional

'Dry floatation' at **Antara**.
See p151.

Tibetan and ayurvedic techniques. Give the
Himalayan herbs scrub a shot: the two-hour
treatment involves a massage with aromatic herbs
like turmeric, sandalwood and cinnamon and is
likely to lull you into deep sleep.

Yoga

Ishwardas Chunnilal Yogic Health Centre – Kaivalyadhama

*43 Marine Drive (2281-8417). Charni Road
station.* **Open** 6.30-9.30am, 3.30-6.30pm Mon-Sat.
No credit cards.
The Kaivalyadhama at Marine Drive is part of
a 60-year-old organisation set up by Swami
Kuvalayananda to promote yoga for health and
healing. Roughly 4,000 members visit this roomy
centre to study yogic practices every year. It costs
Rs 300 for a check-up and approximately Rs 500
for a monthly class.

Iyengar Yogashraya

*Elmac House, Senapati Bapat Marg, Lower
Parel (W) (2494-8416). Lower Parel station.*
Open 7am-4pm Mon, Sat; 7am-8pm Tue-Fri.
No credit cards.
Though the 90-year-old BKS Iyengar personally
conducts classes only in Pune, the Mumbai branch
of the Iyengar Institute, which opened in 2002, is a
good place for beginners. The warm and welcoming
you-can-do-it-too attitude will put even the most
insecure first-timer at ease with the idea of standing
on his or her head. That's not to say the *asanas* are
even remotely comfortable, but props designed by
the master – wooden gadgets, belts and ropes – help
tremendously. *Photo p149.*

Satyananda (Bihar) Yoga Centre

*Group classes at Walkeshwar Mon-Thur 7-8am,
10-11am, 7-8pm. Private classes also available on
request. Call Sarvath Palanpur on 98701-11094
for details.* **No credit cards.**
Practise yoga in the comfort of your hotel room
under the guidance of instructors from the
Satyananda Centre. Founded by Swami
Satyananda Saraswati, the school integrates techniques from various traditional branches of yoga,
including *Raja, Bhakti, Karma, Hatha, Kundalini*
and *Kriya*. It costs around Rs 1,000 per month for
two classes a week.

Yoga Institute

*Prabhat Colony, Shree Yogendra Marg, Santa
Cruz (E) (2611-0506). Santa Cruz station.*
Open 7am-7.30pm daily. **No credit cards.**
If you want a serious crash course in the funda-
mentals of yoga, try the Yoga Institute's seven-day
health camp (Rs 2,200 inclusive of four meals) which
includes an introduction to the philosophy of yoga
and its practical applications. The centre combines
traditional yogic values and techniques with
Western science to spread the word about wellbeing. Put down the self-help book and register.

Music

Everything from Indian classical to classic rock.

Mumbai is the home of Bollywood, and by extension, the home of Indian pop music, almost all of which is film songs. Bollywood music blares from every nightclub, autorickshaw, radio station and music channel; it would seem that the city listens to nothing else. Yet, there's a thriving scene of classic rock and death metal among college students, a burgeoning local hip hop culture (as evident at 50 Cent's gig in November 2007, where the audience knew every word of every song), a slow revival of interest in jazz and the occasional regional pop and rock act performing in the language of their home state. The number of gigs and the variety of acts has jumped over the last couple of years, thanks in no small part to new venues and a growing interest in new sounds.

However, it's Hindustani (North Indian) and Carnatic (South Indian) classical music that dominate Mumbai's live music scene, despite accounting for just ten per cent of record sales. That's because of the improvisational nature of the music, in which a single *raga* (a fixed set of notes, somewhat akin to a scale) can last anywhere from ten minutes to two hours and sound entirely different each time it's performed, making each concert a unique event. Most classical concerts are organised by *sabhas* or music circles, whose members pay an annual subscription fee to attend concerts arranged by the circle, which is usually associated with a particular venue. Non-members can attend by paying a nominal guest fee (*see p154* **Buying tickets**). There are also larger concerts during the winter, the traditional classical music season, when famous names like Ravi Shankar and Zakir Hussain make their annual visit to the city for a series of performances.

Mumbai had a vibrant jazz music scene from the 1930s to the '60s, when the erstwhile Churchgate Street (now Veer Nariman Road) was lined with venues, each with its own jazz band. Today, your best chance to catch some Bombay jazz is at **Not Just Jazz by the Bay** (*see p113*) – where the octogenarian Jazzy Joe and the Jazz Junkies play regularly – and bars such as **Blue Frog**, **Henry Tham** and **Soul Fry Casa** (*see p110* **Pubs & Bars**). Mumbai also has one of India's biggest college rock scenes. Classic rock and extreme metal are the dominant sounds and though most bands stick to covers, there are a handful of young acts putting out original (albeit derivative) music. Three of the biggest Mumbai bands are **Zero**,

Janmashtami Flute Concert. See p156.

Pentagram and **Pin Drop Violence**, who play occasionally at college festivals (visit www.gigpad.com for details) and at rock-friendly venues such as **Razzberry Rhinoceros**. There are also occasional larger festivals like **Independence Rock** (*see p155* **Music festivals**). You can find Indian rock CDs at the shop **BX Furtado** (*see p131*).

As for international acts, Mumbai is a retro-loving city and you're more likely to see a veteran rock band play here than the pop world's latest superstar. However, India's newfound status as one of the world's fastest growing economies has led a lot of big names to include the country in their world tours. Beyonce, 50 Cent and Shakira have performed in Mumbai in the recent past but the city tends to lose out to other urban centres such as Bangalore and Delhi on account of the high entertainment tax that's levied on ticket sales by the Maharashtra government.

There's also a small Western classical music scene, which plays at just one venue – the **National Centre for the Performing Arts** (NCPA; 2282-4567, 6654-8135/www.ncpamumbai.com) at Nariman Point. The **Symphony Orchestra of India**, formed in 2006 and currently under the direction of Kazakh violinist Marat Bisengaliev, performs seasonal concerts every February and September; *photo p154*.

Not Just Jazz by the Bay. *See p153*.

Symphony Orchestra of India. *See p153*.

One of the city's most interesting live music experiences takes place on the first, third, seventh, tenth and 11th days of the annual **Ganesh Chaturthi** festival (*see p136*) around September, when the city streets are taken over with lines of devotees dancing to the sound of *nashik bajas* – amateur bands who beat out frenetic rhythms of Maharashtrian folk music.

BUYING TICKETS

Check *Time Out Mumbai* magazine and city newspaper supplements to find out what concerts are on during your stay, or call music circles (*see listings below*) for information on upcoming classical performances. Guests are welcome to attend music circle concerts for a fee of Rs 50-Rs 100 payable at the venue on the night. Concerts of Hindi film classics usually take place around the birth or death anniversaries of famous singers, composers and lyricists. Again, check *Time Out* or the newspapers. Tickets cost between Rs 50 and Rs 300. Except for larger concerts or performances at the NCPA, concert organisers generally do not accept credit cards or take advance bookings.

Music circles

Most of today's household names in Indian classical music made their debut at concerts organised by *sabhas* or music circles, which emerged in the late 19th century to popularise classical music. Indian classical music still lacks funding and music circles remain vital in supporting the form. Most of the venues listed below are small with simple facilities, and often lack air-conditioning.

Dadar Matunga Cultural Centre

122A JK Sawant Road, near Ruparel College, Matunga (2430-4150). Matunga Road station.
One of the city's oldest music circles, it puts on at least one concert a month. It also hosts two annual events dedicated to the memory of musicologist Vishnu Narayan Bhatkhande: a music festival in January and a lecture in September.

Fine Arts Society, Chembur

Sivaswamy Auditorium, Fine Arts Society, Fine Arts Chowk, near Chembur Flyover, RC Marg, Chembur (2522-2988). Chembur station.
One of the city's main venues for Carnatic classical music performances.

Indian Music Group

St Xavier's College Hall, St Xavier's College, 5 Mahapalika Marg (2263-4548). CST or Churchgate stations.
Founded in 1974 by former students of St Xavier's College, the Indian Music Group organises four prestigious Hindustani concerts every year.

Kala Bharati

Karnataka Sangha, Dr Vishveshawarayya Samarak Mandir, CHM Marg, Matunga (W) (2437-7022). Matunga Road station.
Hosts a classical music or dance performance every Sunday morning in an air-conditioned auditorium. It also organises three major festivals every year in memory of three Hindustani classical stalwarts. Festivals honouring vocalist Krishnarao Shankar Pandit, tabla player Nizamuddin Khan and singer Sharadchandra Arolkar are held in August, September and December respectively.

Sri Shanmukhananda Fine Arts & Sangeet Sabha

Shanmukhananda Hall, Plot No. 292, behind Gandhi Market, Comrade Harbans Lal Marg, Sion (E) (2407-8888). Sion station.
Carnatic music dominates this Sabha's calendar and the monthly list of performers includes both established and new artists. The Shanmukhananda Hall, with seating for over 3,000, was once the premier venue for local rock gigs and has been rented out for performances by acts as varied as *ghazal* singer Jagjit Singh and British dinosaur rockers Jethro Tull.

Swar Sadhana Samiti

Mumbai Marathi Sahitya Sangh Mandir, Dr Bhalerao Marg, near St Mary's High School, Gaiwadi, Girgaum (2385-6303). Charni Road station.
Stages a monthly concert to showcase the work of upcoming Hindustani classical musicians.

Udayan

National Gallery of Modern Art, Cowasji Jehangir Hall, near Regal Cinema, MG Road, Colaba (2288-1969). CST or Churchgate stations.

Udayan organises classical music, dance and theatre performances on Saturdays at the National Gallery of Modern Art in Colaba. Send an email to udayan_cultural_organisation@hotmail.com.

Music festivals

The most important events in Mumbai's musical calendar. Call ahead for the exact dates as performances often correspond to festivals and events in the Hindu calendar that vary from year to year. See also page 134 **Festivals & Events** for cultural festivals featuring music performances.

January/February

Alla Rakha Khan Barsi Concert

Shanmukhananda Hall, Plot No. 292, behind Gandhi Market, Comrade Harbans Lal Marg, Sion (E) (2407-8888). Sion station.

Zakir Hussain and his brothers pay tribute to their father, the legendary tabla player, in a one-day festival at Shanmukhananda Hall.

Banganga Festival

Banganga Tank, Walkeshwar (2202-4482/ www.maharashtratourism.gov.in). Grant Road Station. **Taxi** Banganga.

A two-day festival featuring the top names in Hindustani classical music from across India on the banks of the Banganga tank. The temple-town-like location set between high-rises and the Arabian Sea makes the festival an exceptionally memorable experience.

Elephanta Festival

Elephanta Island (2202-4522/ www.maharashtratourism.gov.in).

The country's classical music and dance maestros perform against the backdrop of the historic caves of Elephanta Island at this festival hosted by the Maharashtra Tourism Development Corporation.

Hridayesh Arts Vile Parle Festival

Parle Tilak Vidyalaya Ground, Hanuman Road, Vile Parle (E). Vile Parle station.

This festival, formerly known as the Sureshbabu Mane-Hirabai Badodekar Smriti Sangeet Samaroh after two Kirana gharana vocalists, is one of the most prestigious Hindustani classical music events held in the Western suburbs. Organised by Hridayesh Arts (2614-8556).

Get your own guru

Want to be able to scat like Ella? Then Hindustani classical singing lessons might be just what you need. Over the past 11 years, jazz singers from the US and Europe have been visiting Mumbai to learn how to sing *alaaps* and *nom-tom*, studying improvisation techniques employed in Indian classical music. For a few hours every week, they play the role of devoted *shishyas* (students) to their guru, Dhanashree Pandit-Rai of the Jazz India Vocal Institute. Although they visit for lessons, they don't actually move into the home of the mother of two, as they would have done in the good old days.

The *guru-shishya parampara* (literally 'teacher-student tradition') is a 3,000-year-old education system in which students lived with their teachers in an ashram and were taught the Vedas – ancient texts that dealt with everything from mathematics to medicine. Although the *guru-shishya* tradition has been replaced with the scholastic system, one-to-one oral teaching remains the main way of passing on skills in Indian classical music.

The name of your guru is still considered a keen indicator of how good you are. All the stalwarts of 20th-century Indian classical music, including sitar maestro Ravi Shankar and sarod virtuoso Ali Akbar Khan, are

products of the *guru-shishya* parampara. If you'd like to learn the sitar, and are ready for the commitment, you could try and get your own guru. There are several gurus teaching both vocal and instrumental music in Mumbai. Fees range from Rs 200 to Rs 1,000 per lesson. Check music shops like Rhythm House and Bhargava's Musik (*see p131* **Shops & Services**) for directories of music teachers. There are also several city institutions teaching classical music; enrolments usually take place in June (*see p237*).

JanFest
St Xavier's College Hall, St Xavier's College,
5 Mahapalika Marg (2263-4548). CST or
Churchgate stations.
College kids outnumber the oldies at this concert
by students of St Xavier's College. Organised by
the Indian Music Group.

One Tree Music Festival
MMRDA Grounds, Bandra-Kurla Complex,
Bandra (E). Bandra station.
Two to three days of rock, blues and funk.
Organised by Fountainhead (2600-4640).

Smriti Sandhya
St Andrew's Auditorium, St Andrew's College,
St Dominic Road, Bandra (W) (2640-3041/
www.bimalroymemorial.org). Bandra station.
A concert of film music held in memory of one of
India's greatest directors, Bimal Roy. Organised by
the Bimal Roy Memorial Committee.

March/April

Alladiya Khan Festival
Balvikas Sangh Hall, Balvikas Sangh Marg,
near Gandhi Maidan, Chembur (2527-2388).
Chembur station.
This four-day concert pays tribute to the founder of
the Agra *gharana* of Hindustani classical music.

May/June

Aarohi
YB Chavan Centre, near Mantralaya, General
Jagannath Bhosle Marg (2285-2081). CST or
Churchgate stations.
Performances by the future stars of Hindustani
classical music. Organised by Pancham Nishad
(2412-4750).

Megh Malhar
Nehru Centre Auditorium, Annie Besant Road,
Worli (2496-4676/www.nehrucentremumbai.com).
Mahalaxmi station.
Maestros perform romantic monsoon ragas.

Rabigeetika
Mysore Association Hall, 393 Bhau Daji Road,
near Maheshwari Udayan, Matunga (E) (2402-
4647). Matunga station.
A concert of Rabindra Sangeet, the music written
and composed by Bengali writer Rabindranath
Tagore. Organised by Rabigeetika (2262-4709).

July/August

Independence Rock
Various venues (www.gigpad.com).
Two adrenaline-charged days of headbanging courtesy of the country's best-loved rock and metal acts,
this two-decade old festival is meant to coincide with
the Independence Day weekend in mid August but
is often postponed by a few weeks.

Janmashtami Flute Concert
Brindavan Gurukul, Haridwar Marg,
Versova Link Road, Andheri (W) (2646-3535/
www.brindavangurukul.org). Andheri station.
Legendary flautist Hariprasad Chaurasia and his
students perform a 24-hour concert (*photo p153*) at
his music school during the festival of Janmashtami
(*see p136* **Festivals & Events**).

Khazana
Various venues (www.pankajudhas.com).
An annual *ghazal* festival organised by singer
Pankaj Udhas.

September/October

Zia Mohiuddin Dagar Barsi Festival
YB Chavan Centre, near Mantralaya, General
Jagannath Bhosle Marg (2285-2081). CST or
Churchgate stations.
The city's only Hindustani classical festival dedicated to *dhrupad*, a style of singing that was the
dominant form until the 18th century, when *khayal*
– the style rendered by most singers today –
started gaining popularity.

November/December

A Festival of Festive Music
National Centre for the Performing Arts, Nariman
Point. CST or Churchgate stations.
Twelve choirs from around the country perform
Christmas music. Organised by the Stop Gaps
Cultural Academy (2421-2120).

Jazz Utsav
Land's End Amphitheatre. Bandstand, near Lands
Ends Hotel, Bandra (W). Bandra station.
The foremost exponents of Indian jazz perform
alongside musicians visiting from around the world,
most of whom tend to be from Europe. The venue is
one of Mumbai's prettiest: an amphitheatre inside
Bandra Fort at Land's End, against the backdrop of
the Arabian Sea. Organised by Capital Jazz. Email
Prakash Thadani (prakash@jazzutsav.com).

Ruhaniyat
Horniman Circle Gardens, Horniman Circle, Fort
(2363-3561). CST or Churchgate stations.
A Sufi music festival. Organised by Banyan Tree
Events (2826-0674).

Sangat
National Centre for the Performing Arts, Nariman
Point (www.ncpamumbai.com). CST or Churchgate
stations.
A chamber music festival organised by the Mehli
Mehta Music Foundation (2382-3644).

Spiritual Morning
Gateway of India, Apollo Bunder, Colaba. CST or
Churchgate stations.
Morning *ragas* at the Gateway of India. Organised
by Pancham Nishad (2412-4750).

Arts & Entertainment

Nightlife

Clubbing under a curfew.

Mumbaikars like to think of their city as the nightlife capital of India but clubland is actually in a bit of a funk. It's been a downward spiral ever since the state government's conservative Deputy Chief Minister decided in 2005 that 'dance bars', uniquely Mumbai establishments in which fully clothed women danced to Bollywood songs for the enjoyment of their male patrons, were dens of vice and must be shut to protect the virtues of bar girls.

Many of these bars were part-owned by police officers, who decided that if they couldn't continue running their bars, clubs for middle- and upper middle-class clients had no business staying open until 5am either. That year, the palm-greasing of the police by club owners, which had allowed them to stay open beyond the official 1.30am deadline, came to a halt.

This made life very tough for a lot of city clubs. Clubbers rarely step out before 11pm, meaning there simply isn't time to make enough money before the 1.30am deadline kicks in. The only beneficiaries of the new regime are the clubs within luxury hotels, which are allowed to operate until 3am. But the biggest fallout of the 1.30am law has been its effect on creativity. With restricted business hours, club owners are wary of experimenting with new music, and prefer meainstream sets that are indistinguishable from venue to venue. This may be popular with the majority of clubbers (*see p160* **The Bombay sound**), but it keeps the city from developing any niche scenes.

In 2006, things looked like they might improve, as independent DJs started club nights in venues across town but by early 2007, the last of them had withered away thanks to high costs and low turnout. To add to the city's woes, the once-thumping Insomnia at the Taj Mahal Hotel turned off the music for the last time in 2007, when the management decided that high-end retail stores would be more profitable than a club.

It's not all doom and gloom though. Mumbai has found an increasing interest in live music, and artists from the city and around the country now regularly play at venues like **Blue Frog**, **Hard Rock Café** and **Soul Fry Casa** (for all, *see pp110-116* **Pubs & Bars**), and the proliferating lounge bars often book DJs to perform house and electronica sets, ensuring that Mumbai may not be the best city in the country in which to go dancing, but it's still tops for good gigs and an energetic, buzzing vibe.

DOS & DON'TS

Mumbai nightclubs have notoriously complicated cover charges, depending which night of the week you go, whether you are a male-female couple, a single woman or a stag (a single male). Most cover charges range between Rs 600 and Rs 1,500 and include the cost of a few drinks. Clubs occasionally enforce no-stag policies on Friday and Saturday nights, but they're often more lax when it comes to (white)

Arts & Entertainment

Poison. *See p158.*

foreign men, thanks to the continuing popularity of the idea that foreigners spend more or that they add a touch of glamour – but don't count on this. Clubs are notorious for turning away black men; bouncers commonly assume that if you're black and in Mumbai you must be Nigerian and therefore involved in the drug trade. If you suspect that you're the victim of a racist entry policy, demand to see the manager and tell him you're going to call the local press – stories like that make club owners very uncomfortable.

The admission prices given in the listings are for male-female couples and stags, with the lower price applying for weekdays, and the higher price for Fridays and Saturdays. Single women can expect to pay about half that, or sometimes nothing at all.

Colaba

Polly Esther's
First Floor, Gordon House Hotel, Battery Street, Apollo Bunder, Colaba (2287-1122). CST or Churchgate stations. **Open** 9pm-3am Tue-Sun. **Admission** Rs 1,000-Rs 1,200.
A fun, roomy club that's part of the Gordon House Hotel, decked out with flower-power decor, posters of *Rocky* and a young Bollywood-starlet-of-yesteryear Zeenat Aman toking on a chillum. Most nights at Polly's are dedicated to retro at its purest – Prince, the Pet Shop Boys and the Bee Gees all do heavy duty rotation – but there's also plenty of present-day fare. Few places in this town offer as much plain, pure fun on a Saturday night. The enthusiasm and the gay abandon with which the crowd sings along is infectious. Best of all, it's free entry on weekdays.

Voodoo
Arthur Bunder Road, off Colaba Causeway, near Radio Club, Colaba. Taxi Radio Club. **Open** 8pm-1.30am daily. **Admission** Rs 250.
Voodoo is the most risqué little bar in Mumbai. It's got girls aplenty and they certainly do dance, but they also sit, talk and drink with the male clientele – a motley collection of minor-league businessmen, both local and visiting. In other words, you can look and you can touch. The lights are dim, the air is heavy and the atmosphere is sweaty, going on edgy. For entertainment value, nothing beats it (but don't visit the loos alone). It's also the only club in town with a gay night, on Saturday.

Fort

Red Light
Above Khyber restaurant, 145 Mahatma Gandhi Road, Kala Ghoda, Fort (2267-3227/6634-6248). CST or Churchgate stations. **Open** 7pm-1am daily. **Admission** Rs 1,200-Rs 1,800.

A destination for the prettiest students in South Mumbai, paying for their drinks with plentiful allowances from daddy. The music on weekends is a mish-mash of Hindi commercial grind (and you really have to like crowds), but the DJs serve up some old school Snoop, Dre and Pac on Wednesdays, and there's plenty of Brit-Bolly-bhangra beats on offer for the city's bling bling crew. However, be warned: a clear head is necessary for a visit to the loos, where the mirrored corridor causes such disorientation that desperate and dazed patrons have been known to relieve themselves on the floor.

Lower Parel

Play
High Street Phoenix, 462 Senapati Bapat Marg, Lower Parel (6661-4343). Lower Parel station. **Taxi** Phoenix Mills. **Open** 9pm-1.30am Wed-Sun. **Admission** Rs 1,500.
Until the last few months of 2007 it was called Ra but in an effort to revive flagging interest the management gave this club a minor makeover and a new name: Play Superclub Mumbai. While this is patently untrue – Play is not particularly large nor terribly cutting-edge – it's certainly an excellent club to listen to Bollywood and hip hop and to watch kids wear oversize dollar sign pendants without a fleck of irony. The new name and design changes are little more than a reboot of an old franchise; the dancefloor is still exactly where it used to be, the bar hasn't moved and even the cover charge is the same. Located in between town and the 'burbs, Play attracts a mixed crowd; and with an unabashedly mainstream bent to the setlist and a liberal attitude towards the way you dress, it's the sort of place that has no hang-ups, as long as you don't.

Bandra & Khar

H2O: The Liquid Lounge
Sheetal Bukhara, off Linking Road, Khar (W) (2649-5151/98203-49168 guestlist). Khar station. **Taxi** Khar Telephone Exchange. **Open** 6.30pm-1.30am daily. **Admission** Rs 500-Rs 1,000.
Four split levels, three open-air terraces each with its own bar, walls in seven hues of blue and circular water-filled windows with colourful plants dancing in the currents. H2O is like an underwater lair from a Bond film (minus the bikini babes). The music is upbeat lounge in the early evening, followed by a smattering of house, ending up with Bollywood beats – standard Mumbai fare to keep the boys and girls bouncing.

Poison
Basement, Krystal, 206 Waterfield Road, Bandra (W) (2642-3006). Bandra station. **Taxi** ICICI Bank, Bandra. **Open** 9.30pm-1.30am Tue-Sat. **Admission** Rs 1,000-Rs 1,500.
Poison is without question Mumbai's favourite place to party. Since it opened in July 2006, it has been consistently packed; not an easy task when you have

Enigma. *See p160.*

over 10,000sq ft of space in a notoriously fickle city. But Poison has it all neatly worked out: commercial tunes on the weekends, house on Wednesdays, hip hop on Thursdays and big name acts, including the likes of Christopher Lawrence, Paul Oakenfold, Brian Transeau, Paul Van Dyk and Mylo every couple of months. It's a favourite with the Bollywood crowd. *Photo p157.*

Photo p157.

Juhu

Enigma

JW Marriott Hotel, Juhu Tara Road, Juhu (6693-3000). Vile Parle station. **Open** 8.30pm-2.30am Tue-Sat. **Admission** Rs 1,000-Rs 2,500.

Enigma, the JW Marriott's superclub, has defied the competition by managing to keep pulling in the crowds almost continuously since 2003. Known as Bollywood's favourite nightclub, it tends to get filled up with paunchy movie producers, but you won't hear the girls complaining when they also get the chance to shake booty alongside regulars like movie stars Abhishek Bachchan and Fardeen Khan. The decor radiates an appropriate aura of kitsch-cool: a dramatic chandelier is suspended above a large circular bar in the centre of a space decked out with dark-hued drapes, plush sofas, flickering candles and ottomans. Show up before midnight if you don't want to encounter serpentine queues. *Photo p159.*

Rock Bottom

Hotel Ramee Guestline, AB Nair Road, Juhu (6693-5555). Vile Parle station. **Open** 9.30pm-2.45am Tue-Sun. **Admission** Rs 600-Rs 1,500.

When Rock Bottom opened for business in late 2003, the hype was huge, with no less than living Bollywood legend Amitabh Bachchan seen regularly striding through this sleek Juhu nightclub. It isn't quite so hip any more but it remains an attractive club, with a cavernous dancefloor, vast screens over the DJ booth, a stellar sound system and a late-night licence. The crowd is largely suburban kids who don't want to travel (especially since the drink and drive laws were stringently implemented in 2007). Expect standard commercial fare as far as music is concerned.

The Bombay sound

Mumbai has about half a dozen nightclubs that can call themselves clubs in the truest sense of the term. Even the ones that make up this short list tend to look like clones, all long, sleek bars and minimalist lounge decor. This is because most club owners travel to South-East Asia or Europe, comb nightspots and come back to tweak their space to give it an adequately 'international look'. Most clubgoers also judge a new venue by how closely it 'feels like abroad'. If there's one thing that distinguishes our clubs from those in the rest of the world, it's the music. No matter how exclusive or high-minded a space purports to be, when it comes to pulling in the crowds you can always count on this city's love for the Hindi film song.

'Nothing goes down better with the crowds than Bollywood and whiskey,' says Sunny Sara, co-owner of Colaba's **Red Light** (*see p158*). Bollywood's invasion of clubland is deeper and more thorough than it has ever been before. Suburban clubs such as **Enigma** (*see above*) in Juhu, an area many of the biggest film stars call home, were the first to start Bollywood nights in the late 1990s, and over the past five years even establishments such as Red Light and **Polly Esther's** (*see p158*) in South Mumbai have succumbed. After all, hit film tunes such as 'Kajra Re' from *Bunty Aur Babli* (2005) and 'Deewangi' from *Om Shanti Om* (2007) fill dancefloors in seconds.

It wasn't always like this. DJ Akhtar, who was the resident DJ at the now shuttered Insomnia – the legendary club at the Taj Mahal Hotel – for 14 years, remembers being forbidden from playing any kind of film music by the management at 1900s (an earlier incarnation of Insomnia) in the early 1990s. This, despite being inundated with requests. The music was in high demand at private parties, but clubs remained off-limits. Akhtar credits the acceptance of Bollywood music to UK-based British-Asian DJ Bally Sagoo's mid-'90s remix of RD Burman's 'Chura Liya' and the bhangra craze that followed. These days, Saturday night playlists are incomplete without remixes of old Bollywood tracks and current Hindi film chartbusters. Most soundtracks come with ready remixes – to a large extent a new song's success depends on the number of times it's spun in clubs.

Why do we insist on hearing the same music inside a nightclub when it's already around us? Not only is Hindi film music one of the most open genres in the world – one that has embraced everything from rock 'n' roll to hip hop and electronica – it is perhaps also the easiest type of music to dance to in the universe. Thanks to the relatively simple choreography – Bollywood actors aren't trained dancers – all you to have do is shake your shoulders and sway your hips to feel like Shah Rukh Khan or Priyanka Chopra.

Sport & Fitness

Where cricket is king.

Stroll down to the Azad Maidan on a weekend afternoon and watch as dozens of cricket matches take place simultaneously, with no sign of even a token football anywhere on the ground. Such is the dominance of cricket in Mumbai that it knocks every other sport off the calendar and away from the collective consciousness. Enthusiasm for it runs so high that one of the most popular tournaments in the city is the Kanga League, which is played during the rainy season (a practice that is said to have been started to familiarise Mumbai players with conditions in England).

No wonder, when cricket bats and balls are thrust into Mumbaikars' hands as soon as they're old enough to grip them, and when the city has produced so many Test cricketers for the national side, including the great Sachin Tendulkar. Many Mumbaikars have fond memories of days spent at **Brabourne Stadium** watching visiting teams play the Board President's XI and at **Wankhede Stadium**, watching the great Bombay cricket team crush opponent after opponent to win the inter-state Ranji Trophy 37 times since the trophy's inception in 1935.

Public parks and sports grounds are few, but do-it-yourself 'gully cricket' prevails in alleys, patches of ground and even busy streets everywhere in the city. **Oval** and **Azad Maidans** in South Mumbai, though home to cricket in the dry months, are colonised by football when the monsoon begins in June, and the maidans turn into muddy battlegrounds. Mumbai has a lively football league run by the Western India Football Association, in which sides with names like Maharashtra State Police battle Orkay Silk Mills at the **Cooperage** ground in South Mumbai and at other venues. Hockey, once a thriving city sport that produced numerous players for India's national side, now comes a distant third, popular in the schools and colleges of suburban Malad.

As they have done for over a century, private sports clubs and gymkhanas like the Bombay Gymkhana remain important, although snobbish, centres for amateur and recreational sports like squash, tennis, badminton, cricket, rugby and swimming. Club memberships are expensive and waiting lists long, and these aren't accessible to visitors. But modern gyms have mushroomed in recent years, some offering short-term or day memberships.

Major events in the city's sporting calendar include the **Ranji Trophy** from October to January, the Royal Western India Turf Club **Derby** at the Mahalaxmi Racecourse in February and the **Mumbai Marathon** (www.thegreatestrace.com; *photo p163*), started in 2004 and now an annual January event that attracts thousands of runners (and a surprising number of men in Gandhi costumes) for prize money of up to $30,000.

Spectator sports

Check the newspapers for details of sporting events during your stay, or call sports associations directly.

Cricket

Teeming maidans like the **Oval** (Maharshi Karve Road, Churchgate) and **Shivaji Park** (Veer Savarkar Road) have become part of cricketing folklore for being training grounds for future superstars. The 24-year-old Wankhede Stadium, the second largest in the country with a capacity of 45,000, is currently

Oval Maidan.

being renovated to prepare for the 2011 One-day World Cup final. The Mumbai Cricket Association's plans for the ground include improved drainage, more seats and air-conditioned stands. Until the renovation is completed, the much prettier **Brabourne Stadium** (Dinshaw Wachha Road, Churchgate, 6659-4100) in Churchgate will host international fixtures as well as domestic league matches.

Football

Mumbai has two major football venues, the larger of which is the **Cooperage** (Cooperage Road, Churchgate), a no-frills 12,000-capacity stadium near Colaba. There's also **St Xavier's Ground** (near Parel Flyover,

Parel). Both the grounds are plain and functional, with simple facilities. Call the **Western India Football Association** on 2202-4020 for match details.

Hockey

Mahindra Stadium

D Road, Churchgate (W). Churchgate station.
The Bombay Hockey Association's Mahindra Stadium is the only hockey stadium in Mumbai with an AstroTurf surface. Situated right next to Wankhede stadium, it hosts Mumbai Hockey League games and all the city's major tournaments, most famously the Bombay Gold Cup in April-May and the women's Tommy Emar Gold Cup in April. Call the **Bombay Hockey Association** on 2281-1271 for match details. Entry is free.

'Kabaddi, kabaddi, kabaddi…'

Mumbaikars' obsession with cricket has batted aside popular interest in most other sports, including traditional Indian ones like mallakhamb, kabaddi and kho kho. Fortunately there are a few pockets left where indigenous games are played – and the largest centre is ironically the spiritual home of Mumbai cricket: **Shivaji Park**, a giant public park in the heart of Dadar. Every weekday, roughly 800 children come here to learn traditional games, led by instructors from Shree Samartha Vyayam Mandir, an organisation dedicated to preserving India's erstwhile sporting culture.

   Kabaddi is a kind of tag game played by two teams who score by touching or capturing players of the opposing team. The attacking side sends a raider who enters the opponents' half of the court chanting 'kabaddi, kabaddi' repeatedly to prove he is not breathing in. His aim is to touch an opposing player (who is then out of the game) and return to his team's side of the court, all in one breath. Meanwhile, the defending team attempts to capture the raider and hold him until he's forced to take a breath, in which case he's also out of the game.

   Another popular traditional sport is **kho kho**, also a tag game in which members of one side squat on their haunches while their opponents run around them. One member gets up to chase and capture opposing team members; if he fails, he then passes the job of chasing to a teammate by touching the teammate's back while saying 'kho'.

   But the most dramatic local sport is **mallakhamb**, a traditional form of Indian

gymnastics involving intricate twists, turns, grips, coils and catches around a pole. 'In modern gyms you have different machines for each part of the body; mallakhamb allows you to work out every part with just one wooden pole,' says Uday Deshpande, head of the Shree Samartha Vyayam Mandir. Using yoga moves and dynamic acrobatics, this 200-year-old Maharashtrian sport is a combination of control, speed, strength, agility and grace. Climbing the greasy pole was never more fun.

Shree Samartha Vyayam Mandir

Shivaji Park Maidan, Dadar (W) (2445-7870). Dadar station. **Fees** Rs 30 per month, free trials available.

Mallakhamb.

Mumbai marathon. *See p161.*

Horse racing

Mahalaxmi Racecourse
Keshavrao Khadye Marg, Mahalaxmi (2307-1401). Mahalaxmi station. Admission Rs 25.
Mumbai has one of India's top horse racing venues at the Mahalaxmi Racecourse, also the headquarters of the **Royal Western India Turf Club**, equipped with the smart Gallops restaurant. The year's biggest races are the Indian Derby, the Poonawalla Breeders' Multimillion and the Indian 2000 Guineas, held every February. On these days, the racecourse becomes an Ascot-style photo-op for Bollywood stars and local celebs.

Active sports

Golf

Bombay Presidency Golf Club
Dr C Gidwani Road, Chembur (2520-5874). Ghatkopar or Chembur stations. **Open** 6am-7pm Tue-Sun. **Green fees** Rs 790 Tue-Fri; Rs 1,350 Sat, Sun and government holidays. **Credit** AmEx, MC, V.
Mumbai's premier golf club has an 18-hole, 6,189-yard course, a swimming pool, gymnasium, billiards room and a cards room. Comfortable rooms are also available for visitors at Rs 2,400 a night. The Presidency Club hosts several major amateur and pro tournaments.

Horse riding

Amateur Riders' Club
Mahalaxmi Racecourse, Gate No. 8, Keshavrao Khadye Marg, Mahalaxmi (6500-5204). Mahalaxmi station. **Open** 9.30am-5.30pm. **Classes** Rs 400 for 30mins. **No credit cards.**
Take a half-hour horse ride at the racecourse or take a riding course pitched at your level. Choose from two modules: a beginner's course or an advanced course. But don't expect to spend all your time charging around on Seabiscuit; the courses are in-depth and you're also expected to take theory classes to familiarise yourself with horse riding equipment as well as the anatomy and psychology of the animal.

Swimming

Bodyrhythm
Advent, 12A Gen J Bhosale Marg, Churchgate (2284-8011). Churchgate station. **Taxi** next to YB Chavan Auditorium. **Open** 7am-12.30pm, 3.30-9pm daily. **Fees** Rs 12,000 annual membership; Rs 300 one visit. **No credit cards.**
Look for the staircase at the right side of the Advent building for Bodyrhythm's 22-metre pool. Nothing fancy, but those who just want to hit the water will have no complaints.

Mahatma Gandhi Pool Camp
Mahatma Gandhi Public Pool, Veer Savarkar Marg, Shivaji Park (2445-2062). Dadar station. **Fees** Rs 2,300 annual membership; Rs 1,100 for three months. **No credit cards.**
Cheap, cheerful, and at 50m by 25m, the L-shaped MG pool is one of the city's biggest.

Tennis

Maharashtra State Lawn Tennis Association (MSLTA)
Maharshi Karve Road, Cooperage (2287-4806/ 4808/4809). Churchgate station. **Open** 10am-1pm for non-members. **Court charges** Rs 200 per hour; Rs 300 extra for partner. **No credit cards.**
Work on your backhand at the state-run MSLTA. You can hire a court and play against a partner supplied by the Association or bring your own willing opponent along.

Water sports

H20 Water Sports Complex
Chowpatty (2367-7584/2367-7546). Charni Road station. **Open** 10am-7pm daily. **No credit cards.**
The H20 Water Sports Complex on Chowpatty Beach offers waterskiing (Rs 1,600 for 15 mins), speedboating (Rs 175 per person), kayaking (Rs 150-Rs 200 for 30 mins), plus jetskiing, parasailing and even beach volleyball. They also conduct week-long classes in windsurfing, waterskiing and rowing.

Arts & Entertainment

Gyms & fitness centres

South Mumbai

Befit Zone
Amarchand Mansion, Madame Cama Road, near Regal Theatre, Colaba (2288-0055). CST or Churchgate stations. **Open** 6am-10.30pm Mon-Sat; 10am-8pm Sunday. **Membership** Rs 1,400-Rs 1,500 one week; Rs 400 one visit. **No credit cards.**
One of the city's biggest gyms, with cardio-vascular training, weight training and steam rooms.

Euphoria
DSK Towers, opposite Taj President, Cuffe Parade (2216-2525). CST or Churchgate stations. **Open** 6am-11pm Mon-Sat; 10am-6pm Sun. **Membership** Rs 3,829 one month; Rs 2,755 two weeks. **Credit** AmEx, DC, MC, V.
Euphoria specialises in resistance, or strength training. They also provide cardio-vascular training, and have a full-time nutritionist on hand.

Fariyas Health Club
25 Off Arthur Bunder Road, Colaba (2204-2911/ www.fariyas.com). CST or Churchgate stations. **Open** 7am-8pm daily. **Membership** Rs 15,000 six months; Rs 300 one visit. **Credit** AmEx, DC, MC, V.
Compact to the point of being claustrophobic, this hotel gym nevertheless does have some good equipment as well as a steam bath, sauna room and swimming pool.

Fitwell Fitness Centre
Colaba Police Compound, behind Buckley Court, Colaba (2288-2728). CST or Churchgate stations. **Open** 6am-10am, 4pm-9pm daily; 10am-4pm women only. **Membership** Rs 5,400 for six months; Rs 3,600 three months; Rs 200 one visit. **No credit cards.**
This smart 1,000sq ft gym is a fave with Colaba residents. It's open to both sexes in the morning and evenings, with women only between 10am and 4pm.

Gold's Gym
Garden View Chambers, opposite St Elizabeth Nursing Home, J Mehta Marg, Nepean Sea Road. (2367-9392/www.goldsgym.com). Grant Road station. **Open** 6am-10.30pm Mon-Sat; 9am-8pm Sun. **Membership** Rs 4,500 one month. **Credit** AmEx, MC, V.
Yes, the same Gold's Gym that's famous for giving Arnold Schwarzenegger his body. The Mumbai branch of the California-based chain offers trainers, equipment, chiropractic massages, rehabilitation therapy and a spinning studio. It also sells sports clothing, hydration and meal-replacement drinks, and a range of energy food and supplements. **Other location** Landmark, Pali Naka, Bandra (W) (6699-2291).

Inch by Inch
95 Parijat Building, Marine Drive (2282-8885). Churchgate station. **Open** 6am-10.30pm daily.

Membership Rs 4,494 one month; Rs 561 one day. **Credit** AmEx, MC, V.
Gaze at the Arabian Sea as you work the treadmill at this airy, modern gym.

Martial arts

Judo

Cawas Billimoria
BJPC School, Charni Road (98211-35870). Charni Road station. **Open** 7pm-9pm Tue-Thur. **Fees** Rs 300 one month. **No credit cards.**
Instructor and six-degree black belt Cawas Billimoria won a silver medal in judo at the 1992 Commonwealth Games and a bronze at the 1989 Asian Games.

Karate

Rajesh Thakkar
Fellowship School, Nana Chowk, Grant Road (98201-57738). Grant Road station. **Taxi** near August Kranti Maidan. **Open** 6.45-8.15am, 7-8.30pm Mon, Wed, Fri. **Fees** Rs 400 one month. Free trial available. **No credit cards.**
Indian legend has it that karate originated in the kalaripayattu martial arts tradition of Kerala and was then taken to Japan by Malayalee Buddhist monks. Rajesh Thakkar, who has worked as an instructor for the past 25 years, brought karate back to Mumbai with an emphasis on discipline, but has softened up in recent years: 'These days we allow short breaks for water and visits to the bathroom. Not like the old days; the new generation just can't take the pain.'

Tae kwon do

Vijay Kumar
Call Vijay Kumar (98192-08504), Maker Towers, Cuffe Parade. CST or Churchgate stations. **Open** Mon-Sat flexible timings. **Classes** Rs 1,000 one month. Free trial available. **No credit cards.**
A Korean martial art that emphasises attacking an opponent using the power of your legs. Vijay Kumar has been teaching for the last 15 years.

Tai chi

Rakesh Menon
Call 98194-59694. **Fees** Rs 500-Rs 900 per month; Free trial available. **No credit cards.**
Rakesh Menon teaches tai chi, the meditative Chinese martial art, at three different locations across the city, with a regimen that's aimed at the older generation. 'As people age, it becomes harder to attempt flying kicks or do repeated push-ups,' reasons Menon.
Venues National Centre for the Performing Arts, Nariman Point; St Andrew's School, Bandra (W); Saraswati Vidyalaya, Chembur.

Theatre & Dance

A moveable feast.

Theatre

English-language theatre in Mumbai has come a long way since the 1980s, when it was mostly the preserve of wealthy South Mumbai amateurs who produced classic British and American plays and musicals, sometimes with an Indian twist. Now a growing citywide movement, English theatre has a cadre of writers producing original drama, such as Cinematograph theatre company's *C for Clown,* which is partly in English, mostly in gibberish, and hugely popular. Yet Mumbai's theatre scene is dominated by productions in Hindi, Gujarati and Marathi. Gujarati theatre and Hindi drama to a certain extent consist largely of commercial drama – mostly coarse bedroom comedies and Indian-adapted versions of Neil Simon plays. But Mumbai's most popular, exciting and innovative theatre is without doubt Marathi, which has a strong modern history of experimental drama (*see p166* **Pushing the boundaries**). One of India's most caustic and cutting-edge playwrights is the Mumbai-based Marathi playwright Vijay Tendulkar, whose plays are regularly performed in Mumbai theatres.

In recent years, an increasing taste for innovation has led theatre groups to move out of the usual venues for one-off performances and short runs in unconventional spaces like bars, libraries and out on the street – no mean feat in a desperately crowded city. In 2005, the **Prithvi Theatre** in Juhu, one of Mumbai's most popular, had performers take to the streets at its annual festival; in March 2006, the 19th-century David Sassoon Library at Kala Ghoda hosted a production of Shakespeare's *Much Ado About Nothing.* In 2007, the art gallery Project 88 hosted a number of productions by avant-garde director Rehaan Engineer (including *The Secret Love Life of Ophelia*; *photo p167*). Frequent theatre festivals also offer a chance to catch independent drama from around the country and the occasional visiting international company.

BUYING TICKETS

Check *Time Out Mumbai* and city newspapers for details of productions showing during your stay. It's also worth taking a look at www.mumbaitheatreguide.com – although their listings are not exhaustive – and www.bookmyshow.com, at which you can buy tickets for shows at Juhu's Prithvi Theatre. There are no one-stop ticketing agencies and tickets must usually be bought direct and in person from the box office. With the exception of the **National Centre for the Performing Arts** in Nariman Point, Mumbai's theatres do not accept credit cards. Theatre box offices are usually closed on Sundays unless there is a performance scheduled on that day. Calling the theatre in advance to enquire whether tickets are available is always a good idea. Ticket

Cinematograph's *C for Clown.*

prices vary considerably depending on the production, but normally cost between Rs 30 and Rs 400 each. The average price for a ticket for an international production is Rs 1,000.

Venues

South Mumbai

Mumbai Marathi Sahitya Sangh
Dr Bhalerao Marg, Gaiwadi, near Charni Road station, Charni Road (2385-6303). Charni Road station. **Box office** 5-9pm Mon-Sat. **No credit cards.** Mumbai Marathi Sahitya Sangh is a theatre devoted to experimental Marathi work. The hall suffers from poor acoustics, compensated for by some ridiculously low ticket prices – a mere Rs 30 – and high standards of performance.

National Centre for the Performing Arts
NCPA Marg, near Oberoi Hotel, Nariman Point (6622-3737/www.ncpamumbai.com). CST or Churchgate stations. **Box office** 9am-7pm Mon-Sat. **Credit** MC, V.
The National Centre for the Performing Arts is Mumbai's one claim to a world-class performance space. A complex of theatres, galleries and outdoor spaces set at the very end of the narrow strip of Nariman Point and against the backdrop of the Arabian Sea, the NCPA includes the Jamshed Bhabha, Experimental, Tata, Little and Godrej Dance Academy theatres. The jewel in its crown is the Jamshed Bhabha, resembling a Victorian town house with its double marble staircases, but the smaller Experimental Theatre remains the most popular venue for plays. Despite the name, the Experimental is indiscriminate in its

Pushing the boundaries

In Marathi playwright Sachin Kundalkar's riff on power in relationships, *Fridge Madhe Thevalele Prem*, a quarrelsome couple decide to preserve the meagre remnants of their love in the fridge, then consume a daily ration and top it up once a week. But when the husband demands a second helping, the system breaks down with disastrous consequences. Offbeat, funny and shamelessly absurd, *Fridge Madhe Thevalele Prem* finds few equivalents in the plays of Mumbai's other theatre scenes, but is nothing out of the ordinary in effervescent Marathi stagecraft, which consistently outperforms other theatre productions in terms of both originality and productivity.

That's partly thanks to the Maharashtrian community's long and distinguished heritage in the performing arts, with traditional forms like *sangeetnatak*, a kind of musical, and *tamasha*, which typically features raunchy

dancing to risqué songs. Theatre-going remains a popular community recreation, with middle-class Maharashtrian families going to see plays in the way other communities go to the movies, storming theatres from Thane to Dadar every weekend. This has fostered an audience accustomed to theatrical conventions, and who are open to seeing them broken, giving rise to an energetic sub-culture of experimental Marathi theatre.

It's a sub-culture that's produced Vijay Tendulkar, regarded as the most controversial as well as greatest living Marathi playwright. Tendulkar is best known for *Sakharam Binder*, *Ghashiram Kotwal* and *Gidhade*, plays which altered the course of Marathi theatre in the 1970s with a furious critique of the Indian caste system and shocking on-stage depictions of violence and blasphemy – something Maharashtrian theatre audiences had never seen before.

Tendulkar was joined by other innovators like Satish Alekar, famous for his darkly witty *Mahanirvan* and the fantastical *Begum Barve*, and Mahesh Elkunchwar, whose gritty modern plays include the *Wada Trilogy* (*pictured*), *Party* and *Vasanakand*. Following in their footsteps, a new breed of young Marathi writers continue to push the boundaries with politically driven plots and experimental dramatic forms. But after Tendulkar, it's become harder to shock Maharashtrian audiences.

line-up – romantic comedies and avant-garde drama all find a home here. All the theatres serve delicious sandwiches in the intervals.

Nehru Centre Auditorium
Nehru Centre Auditorium, Annie Besant Road, Worli (2496-4676/www.nehrucentremumbai.com). Mahalaxmi station. **Box office** 10am-6pm Mon-Sat. **No credit cards.**
Apart of the Nehru Centre complex, the auditorium hosts plays and music concerts. The highlight of its theatre calendar is a month-long festival in August of works from around the country.

Ravindra Natya Mandir
PL Deshpande Maharashtra Kala Academy, Sayani Road, Prabhadevi (2431-2956). Elphinstone Road station. **Taxi** near Siddhivinayak Temple. **Box office** 11am-10pm Mon-Sat. **No credit cards.**
Ravindra Natya Mandir and its smaller sister in the same complex, the PL Deshpande Hall, host performances from all the city's language theatres, plus regular Bengali dance dramas and college theatre festivals.

Sophia Bhabha Hall
Sophia College Campus, off Bhulabhai Desai Road (2353-8550). Grant Road station. **Box office** 10am-6pm Mon-Sat. **No credit cards.**
This large, plush auditorium is part of the palatial Sophia College campus, which was home to the Maharaja of Indore and subsequently the Maharaja of Bhavnagar between 1923 and 1940. The theatre offers a decent line-up of both serious and light English drama.

Tejpal Hall
Tejpal Road, August Kranti Maidan, Gowalia Tank (2380-2679). Grant Road station. **Box office** 9am-noon, 4-7pm Wed-Sun. **No credit cards.**
Monopolised by Gujarati plays, Tejpal Hall is a spacious theatre that's tucked away in a quiet corner of Gowalia Tank. Dance dramas and plays in Bengali are performed at Tejpal during the Durga Puja festival (*see p136*).

Suburbs

New Mahim Municipal School
Miya Mohammed Chotani Marg, Teesari Galli, Mahim (W) (2444-5871). Mahim station. **Box office** 7pm onwards Mon-Sat. **No credit cards.**
Awishkar, one of Mumbai's most active Marathi experimental theatre groups, operates out of this state-run school, and regularly performs plays by the country's upcoming playwrights (*see p166* **Pushing the boundaries**).

Prithvi Theatre
Janki Kutir, Juhu Church Road, Juhu (2614-9546/ www.prithvitheatre.org). Vile Parle station. **Taxi** near Juhu Market. **Box office** 10am-1pm, 2-7pm daily. **No credit cards.**

Rehaan Engineer's *The Secret Love Life of Ophelia*. See p165.

Built in 1978 to promote Hindi theatre, the Prithvi managed to snatch audiences away from the older, classier National Centre for the Performing Arts, despite being far away uptown in Juhu. An intimate 200-seater, Prithvi is partial to Hindi drama but also hosts English, Marathi and Gujarati plays. It has a casual, cosy atmosphere with a leafy outside café that attracts the occasional Juhu celeb and is famous for its (non-alcoholic) Irish coffees. In November, Prithvi hosts its popular annual theatre festival (*see p137*).

Rangsharda
Hotel Rangsharda, Bandra Reclamation, near Lilavati Hospital, Bandra (W) (2643-0544). **Box office** 10am-6pm Mon-Sat. **No credit cards.**
Located in Hotel Rangsharda, the theatre hosts commercial plays in Hindi, Gujarati and English.

Shivaji Mandir
Shivaji Mandir, NC Kelkar Road, Dadar (W) (2438-9387). Dadar station. **Taxi** opposite Plaza Cinema. **Box office** 8.30-11am, 5-8pm daily. **No credit cards.**
A pit-stop for those with a taste for ribald humour and slapstick – the mainstays of commercial Marathi theatre – Shivaji Mandir is also a venue for travelling *lavani* troupes. A Maharashtrian folk performance form, *lavani* features peppy dancing to risqué songs.

St Andrew's Auditorium
St Dominic Road, Bandra (W) (2645-9667). Bandra station. **Box office** 10am-6pm daily. **No credit cards.**
Musicals and English comedies take centre stage at the cavernous St Andrew's Auditorium, which boasts an excellent sound system.

Dance

There are seven classical dance forms in India, but only three – *bharatanatyam, kathak* and *Odissi* – are regularly performed in the city. The rest, *Manipuri, mohiniattam, kuchipudi* and *kathakali,* are taught in some of Mumbai's established dance schools but rarely seen on stage. Traditionally, dances were performed in temples as an expression of devotion, later becoming courtly entertainment under Mughal rule in the 16th and 17th centuries. Most of the dances were performed by men; it was only in the 18th century that dancing became a socially acceptable pursuit for women, who today dominate the form.

Bharatanatyam was first performed in temples in the state of Tamil Nadu by *devdasis*, girls who devoted their lives to Lord Shiva. Its origins can be traced to the *Natya Shastra*, a 2,000-year-old discourse on dance and drama written by the sage Bharata. Even today, most Indian classical dances' vocabulary is based on Bharata's comprehensive work, which gives dancers guidelines to adhere to. *Bharatanatyam* is characterised by powerful movements and an erect torso and is performed to Carnatic music played at an upbeat tempo.

Sculptures of women dancers and musicians discovered in caves in Orissa suggest that **Odissi** was being performed as far back as 200 BC, but it gained acceptance as a classical dance form only in the 1950s, through the efforts of celebrated male performers such as Pankajcharan Das and Kelucharan Mahapatra. *Odissi* is a subtle dance of lyrical, curving movements of the wrists and torso.

Kathak comes from North India and is a storytelling dance form (*katha* means 'story'). *Kathak* originated with the *kathakars*, dancers and musicians who travelled from village to village performing tales from the *Mahabharata* and the *Ramayana*. There are three *gharanas* or schools of *kathak* in Lucknow, Jaipur and Varanasi. Each has a different style, but the form is generally characterised by vigorous, fast-paced footwork.

While classical dance continues to rule the stage, the occasional contemporary performance also finds space in Mumbai and institutes specialising in western styles such as salsa, modern dance, ballroom and Latin have gained prominence. Such is their popularity, dance nights have been started at popular bars like Zenzi (every Sunday) and Blue Frog (twice a month, call for details), which offers Latin dance and free entry. To break free from the dogmatic nature of the classical dances, freestyle forms – such as Bollywood, which owes its success to the industry's music directors and choreographers – are immensely popular; Bollywood instructors combine the best of classical, Western, folk and trademark *jhatkas* (pelvic thrusts) to create an eclectic style. To learn the popular Bollywood moves, contact the Shiamak Davar Institute of Performing Arts (2353-7930) or Rajiv Goswami's RG Company of Dance (93243-36721).

BUYING TICKETS

To find out what's on during your stay, check newspaper listings or look in *Time Out Mumbai.* Also worth a look is website www.narthaki.com, where Indian classical and contemporary dancers and groups post updates about their tours. Ticketed events are rare; most dance performances are arranged for free by cultural organisations or for a 'guest charge', typically Rs 50-Rs 100. Guest passes can be bought from the box office on the night of a show or up to three days before a performance. Tickets are also sold at the Rhythm House music store at Kala Ghoda (*see p131* **Shops & Services**). Credit card bookings are not available except at the Godrej Dance Academy at the National Centre for the Performing Arts.

Venues

Blue Frog

Todi & Co, Mathuradas Mills, Senapati Bapat Marg, Lower Parel (4033-2300/www.bluefrog.co.in). Lower Parel station. **Credit** MC, V.

Godrej Dance Academy Theatre

National Centre for the Performing Arts, NCPA Marg, Nariman Point (2283-3838/www.ncpa mumbai.com). CST or Churchgate stations. **Box office** 9am-7pm daily. **Credit** MC, V.

Mysore Association Hall

Near Maheshwari Udayan, 393 Bhau Daji Road, Matunga (E) (2402-4647). Matunga or King's Circle stations. **Box office** 10am-6pm daily. **No credit cards.**

Nehru Centre Auditorium

Annie Besant Road, near Shiv Sagar Estate, Worli (2496-4680/www.nehrucentremumbai.com). Mahalaxmi station. **Box office** 10am-6pm daily. **No credit cards.**

Sivaswamy Auditorium

The Fine Arts Society, Fine Arts Chowk, RC Marg, Chembur (2522-2988). Chembur station. **Taxi** near Chembur Flyover. **Box office** 10am-6pm daily. **No credit cards.**

Zenzi

183 Waterfield Road, Bandra (W) (6643-0670). Bandra station. Salsa Sundays 6.30pm. **Credit** MC, V.

Goa

Features

Maps

Corina Bar, Panjim. *See p206.*

Getting Started

Small is beautiful.

Goa is India's smallest state by a considerable margin, but its pocket-sized charms exert a powerful allure. You feel the difference immediately on arrival – the familiar subcontinental bustle and jostling give way to a measured languor and broad smiles, and the skies clear to a distant horizon. Just 1,429 square miles, with a population of 1.5 million, this is where the crowded cityscapes of urban India give way to coconut groves; traffic fumes fade under the perfume of cashew blossoms and ripening mango. The blare of traffic yields to birdcalls and the insistent whisper of sea on

The best Of Goa

For a journey back in time
Old Goa was once one of the world's great cities – bigger than London – and home to grandees, adventurers and slave-traders. Its surviving churches and convents are designated a World Heritage Site by UNESCO (*see p210*).

For India's only Latin quarter
Wander the narrow lanes of **Fontainhas**, a charming area full of beautifully maintained Indo-Portuguese houses, chapels and public shrines (*see p205; photo p173*).

For a glimpse of the grandees
Take a peek into the gorgeously detailed world of the South Goan aristocracy at the **Figueiredo Mansion** at Loutolim (*see p220*).

For the wilderness experience
Spend a night at one of the most beautiful eco-tourism resorts in the world. **Wildernest** occupies a stunning location in the Western Ghats, at the lip of the Mhadei Valley (*see p190*).

For the art of the ancients
Visit one of the greatest Mesolithic art sites in the world and one of the most accessible. Awe-inspiring rock carvings cover a riverside shelf of laterite rock at **Pansaimol**. You can walk right up to them to feel the ancient grooves under your fingers (*see p223*).

sand. No wonder this is India's most popular resort destination – not just for travellers from Europe, Israel and Russia, but increasingly for India's growing middle class, for whom Goa is famously summed up by the Konkani word *sussegad*, meaning 'laid-back' or 'relaxed'.

Goa's landscape is remarkably varied, ranging from the thickly forested Western Ghats mountain range on its interior border through lush river valleys to the beaches of its roughly 75-mile-long coast. It has a tropical climate, with average temperatures of 25 to 30 degrees Centigrade from November to April, and up to 40 degrees with high humidity in October and May. The Goan monsoon lasts from early June to late September, with the heaviest rains in July. Other than tourism, Goa's main industry is iron ore mining for export, which earns the state around $1 billion a year. Much of the trade is with China. Between highland mining areas lie relatively inaccessible forests; protected reserves that feature great biodiversity, including leopards, tigers, elephants, hundreds of bird species, crocodiles and wild boar. Another resident is the gaur, the largest wild cattle species in the world, and the state's official animal.

GOA TODAY
Goa's tourism development in the last 30 years has been anything but *sussegad*. The northern coastal strip from Aguada to Arambol has a vibrant, noisy, multinational resort culture, with restaurants lined along winding access roads and hundreds of beach shacks crowding the dunes. None of this existed when the first tourists started arriving in Goa in the 1970s, when backpackers and hippies trickled in on an overland route from Europe. They found idyllic, empty beaches fringed with thick coconut groves, and friendly locals familiar with Westerners. The so-called 'Goa Freaks' lived hedonistic lives on the cheap, giving the state an international reputation as a party paradise with unbeatable sunsets, memorable moonlight parties, and cheap drugs and alcohol (*see p187* **Hippie and you know it**).

In the mid 1980s, charter operators began to run regular flights to Dabolim from Europe despite vocal resistance from local activists who issued prescient warnings of dangerous environmental and social damage from mass tourism. The first charters patronised five-star hotels, which then made up most of the tourism

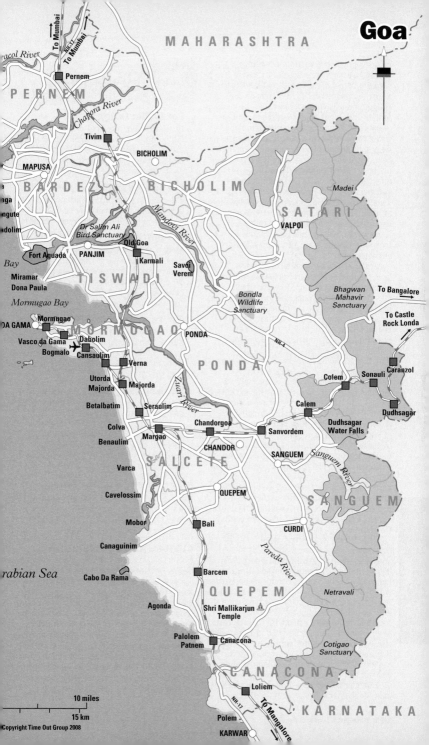

infrastructure, but small hotels and guesthouses immediately proliferated to occupy the rest of the beachfront landscape as entrepreneurs rushed to cash in on the emerging tourism boom. More than two million foreign and domestic tourists now visit Goa every year, a number set to rise as Indians travel more. In recent years, there's been a clear shift from budget accommodation to the boutique hotel, with some stunning and unique properties like **Pousada Tauma** (*see p190*) offering visitors exclusive and luxurious surroundings with price-tags to match. Thousands of foreigners, and an equal number of India's moneyed elite have bought property and permanently settled in Goa in the last seven years, seeking a high standard of living at prices that are a fraction of almost anywhere else.

A giant new international airport has been planned at Mopa in North Goa, sure to decisively tilt the balance towards greater mass tourism. Deep-pocketed foreign and Indian developers are racing to meet the projected demand. But the majority of Goans bemoan what is happening to their once peaceful land. An impressive show of force in 2007 halted a controversial Regional Plan that would have opened huge swathes of the hinterland to real estate and other development. Mainstream Goan society also remains resolutely opposed to drug use, rave parties and trance tourists, who are seen as an immoral influence on their relatively conservative society. Responding to a series of legal judgements, raves have been banned by the Goa state government since the 2005-06 tourist season, though some underground parties still take place in and around Arambol in the north and near Palolem in the south. It's hard to predict what will happen next to the rave sub-culture that spawned the globally popular Goa Trance groove. While it is unlikely to recover its past glories, parties are certain to continue on a smaller, more discreet scale.

There is also widespread anger about illegal construction, the abuse of strict coastal land laws, and the state government's decision to allow casinos to operate in the state's waters. Legislation forbids new permanent construction within 500 yards of the high-tide line and restricts it for another 500 yards. These laws have been blatantly flouted along the entire coastline of the state, often with the connivance of government officials (*see p185* **Enemy of the estate**). The state claims to have several hundred cases ready for 'appropriate action', a claim at which most Goans ruefully laugh. The number of illegal developments has clearly mounted far higher, and transgressors include many of the five-star hotels in the state.

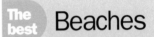

The best Beaches

For idyllic lazing
Once deserted, most of Palolem is now firmly on the beaten track, but its smaller adjunct **Patnem** is a good place to get a taste of the idyllic experience that put Goa on the global tourism map (*see p222*).

For following the hippie trail
The legendary paradise beach of the 1970s hippie scene, **Arambol** retains an edgy counter-cultural atmosphere (*see p200*).

For getting back to nature
Morjim and **Ashvem** are a half-hour drive from the tourist hub of North Goa, but a world away in atmosphere. A few protected Olive Ridley turtles come here every year to lay eggs, fending off most major construction in the process (*see p196*).

For an escape from the tourists
The last undeveloped beach in North Goa, **Keri** remains a long and almost empty stretch of sand, where you can sit blissfully alone in the shadow of casuarinas trees (*see p202*).

For watching locals at play
Miramar beach in Panjim isn't safe for swimming but it is impressively broad, and well-situated at the mouth of the Mandovi. Crowds of Indian tourists and Panjim residents head to the water to watch the sunset in a pleasant, convivial atmosphere (*see p208*).

However, with the real estate and tourism lobbies hand-in-glove with a thoroughly corrupt political class, a serious effort to deal with illegal developments seems unlikely.

CULTURE AND COMMUNITIES
Despite 250 years of the Portuguese Inquisition (*see p177* **Bloody inquisitive**), Hindus have always been the majority population in Goa, though you might not guess it from all those whitewashed churches. Hindus now make up around 65 per cent of the population, with the same caste divisions as the rest of India. In recent years, Goa has felt a surge in rightwing Hinduism, part of a nationwide phenomenon, but it remains relatively free of religious feuding. In early 2006, Goa experienced its first religious riot when a mob vandalised Muslim businesses in Sanvordem. Public reaction was nearly

Goa

Fontainhas. *See p170.*

unanimous in condemnation; Goa's communities tend to respect (and even worship at) each other's holy sites, even as they maintain a certain social distance from each other.

Christians in Goa have tenaciously hung on to caste affiliations, though these have been adapted into three broad categories – Brahmin, Chardo (or Kshatriya) and Sudra (*see p33* **Stuck in the caste**). Despite the strenuous efforts of the Portuguese, strict Christian conservatism never really took root in Goa. The majority of Goan Catholics continue to cherish the indigenous influences that have helped create a mystical, goddess-centred Christianity with deep roots in pre-colonial Goan culture and beliefs.

Islam has a long history in Goa but today Muslims have a small presence, grown through migration from nearby states and Kashmir. Konkani is the native language of Goa and remains ubiquitous despite centuries of colonial efforts to eradicate it. By law, all state-funded primary schools must teach in Konkani, and there are hundreds of Konkani books published each year. Readership is dwindling, however, as the language steadily loses relevance in the face of competition from giant national media markets for English and Hindi. Portuguese is surprisingly widespread, although Goans will usually clam up rather than speak it around outsiders.

Getting there

More information on getting there and around is given in individual Goa chapters.

From Mumbai

By air

Over 20 direct flights make the short hop from Mumbai to Goa each day. Jet Airways (www.jetairways.com) and Air India

(1800-180-1407/www.airindia.in) offer impressive service and inflight meals, but you might find better deals from Kingfisher Airlines (1800-1800-101/www.flykingfisher. com), or low costs airlines Deccan (3900-8888/ www.airdeccan.net); GoAir (1800-222-111/ www.goair.in), Indigo (1800-180-3838/ www.goindigo.in) and SpiceJet (1800-180-3333/ www.spicejet.com). For easy booking, metasearch websites like www.cleartrip.com and www.makemytrip.co.in crawl through various airline websites and present all available flights and on a single page. One-way flights range from Rs 2,000 to Rs 5,500. Book at least a week ahead in the peak winter season.

By bus

Dozens of bus services make the 12- to 14-hour trip from Mumbai to Goa each day, from decrepit decades-old coaches to comfortable modern Volvo behemoths with air-conditioning and reclining seats. Go for the latter. Paulo Travels (022-2645-2624 Mumbai, 0832-243-8531/8537 Panjim, www. paulotravels.com) is the biggest coach company, with daily services. Return fares range from Rs 700 to Rs 1,400.

By train

Trains chug into Goa five times each day from Mumbai. The 11-hour trip offers magnificent views of the Ghats and the lush riverine plains of the Konkan coastline if you travel in the daytime, or you can take a sleeper overnight and be there fresh in the morning. The major stops are Tivim for North Goa, Karmali for Panjim and Margao for South Goa. You can book online (www.konkanrailway.com/ www.irctc.co.in) but it can tend to be a little complicated. In peak season berths can be hard to come by, but there's a 'foreigners' quota' for one-way tickets (*see p230*). Return tickets for berths in air-conditioned carriages range from Rs 1,600 to Rs 3,500.

Goa

Goa's motorcycle taxis – '**pilots**'.

Getting Around

By autorickshaw

Unlike Mumbai, autorickshaws are neither plentiful nor hassle-free; you have to bargain hard for a price that's outlandish anywhere else in the country. But they're good for short trips and can usually be rented by the hour or day. A half-day rental costs around Rs 250.

By bus

Goa has a well-connected bus network, with stops in every major village. Buses aren't particularly clean or punctual, but they are cheap; a ride from Panjim to Candolim, for example, costs just Rs 10. Non-stop Kadamba shuttle buses run between major towns, charging Rs 7-Rs 20.

By motorcycle

Goa's motorcycle taxis are known as 'pilots', whose bikes are distinguished by their bright yellow front fenders, with the name of the 'home stand' painted on. Designated stands can be found near all main bus stops, and village and city markets. Around Rs 15 per mile.

By ferry

Goa's rickety, slow-moving, flat-bottomed ferries offer a scenic way to cross the state's many rivers. Pedestrians ride for free and two-wheelers are charged Rs 10, cars Rs 15. Ferries

on the Mandovi cross from Betim Jetty to Panjim, from Ribandar to Divar and Chorao, from Old Goa to Divar, and from Pomburpa to Chorao. They ply on the River Zuari from Agassaim to Cortalim and the River Tiracol from Keri to Tiracol.

Bicycle rental

Much of Goa's coast is flat and perfect for bikes. Bicycles can be rented for around Rs 25-50 per day; look for signs near village bus stands, or ask at the nearest petrol station. Be careful: drivers show little consideration for cyclists.

Motorcycle rental

Hundreds of people informally rent out motorbikes and scooters; you'll see them advertised everywhere in the coastal areas. Paulo Travels offers two-wheeler rentals available from their garage near the Mahalaxmi Temple in Panjim (0832-243-8531/8537; Scooter Rs 300/day, 100cc motorbike Rs 350/day, Enfield Bullet Rs 450/day.) Two-wheelers are well-suited for Goa's narrow roads and parking is rarely a problem. Check the vehicle carefully before renting because you will be asked to pay for any damage.

Taxis & car rentals

Goa's semi-regulated taxi industry can create headaches for tourists. Drivers routinely charge extortionate rates, especially to anyone emerging from an upmarket hotel or restaurant. If you intend to run around a bit, hire one for the day for around Rs 1,000. Most car rentals include a driver; drive-your-own deals offer only negligible savings. You must have an International Driving Permit and third-party insurance, available from the rental company. Check the car carefully. Reliable taxis and rentals are available from Joey's in Panjim (0832-222-8989, fully insured Hyundai Santro Rs 1,000/day) and Vailankanni in Candolim (0832-248-9047/9658, Hyundai Santro Rs 800/day, cheaper rates for long rentals). Beware, parking can be a nightmare in North Goa's tourist hotspots and in Panjim.

Tourist information

Directorate of Tourism Rua de Ourem
Patto, Panjm. 0832-222-6515. **Open** 9.30am-1.15pm, 2-5.45 pm.

Prices in Goa change depending on the time of year. They are at their highest in the winter season (Oct-Jan) and their lowest in the off-season (Apr-Sept). The prices in this guide are an indication of the average and may be different when you visit.

Goa

Goa History

Commerce, colonials and Christendom.

Goa's distinct character set it somewhat apart from the rest of the subcontinent, even many centuries before the Portuguese colonial episode. The territory had always been an entrepot for trade with the rich hinterlands of the Deccan, and a window on the outside world for Indian kingdoms. For centuries, the ports of Goa were the main points of entry for Arabian warhorses into the fiercely contested neighbouring kingdoms. This trade continued for centuries, with many Arab traders settling in Goa. The territory was exchanged between subcontinental empires and then slumbered for 500 years under the Kadamba dynasty that reigned from their capital on the Zuari River. But the relatively tolerant atmosphere changed in 1312, when Muslim armies from the Delhi Sultanate swept into power, destroying temples built by the Kadambas. Just 30 years later, the Delhi Sultanate was itself challenged by a breakaway group from the Deccan, the Bahamanis, who unleashed another orgy of destruction. Both were finally displaced by the Hindu Vijayanagaris, who oversaw an interlude of prosperity and relative calm.

Successive waves of conquerors were lured by Goa's superb ports and lucrative trade. By the late 15th century Goa had fallen under the control of the Sultanate of Bijapur, a splinter of the Bahamani Empire ruled by the Turkish-born Sultan Yusuf Adil Shah. Under his relatively enlightened rule, Goa developed once again into a rich trading post and crossroads between East and West, crowded by ships from Arabia and the Far East. In 1497, the Portuguese explorer Vasco da Gama made a historic turn round the horn of Africa and set off towards the Indian coast. The Portuguese had recently emerged independent from Moorish domination and were determined to wrest control of the near-priceless spice trade from the Arabs and win souls for Christendom. On his first trip, Da Gama landed to the south of Goa in Calicut. There he harvested no souls but gathered plenty of black pepper – a treasure that was to spur future European colonial adventures in the Indian Ocean.

Vasco da Gama never made it to Goa. But his successor, Afonso de Albuquerque, kept his eye on the territory on a trading voyage to Calicut, where he received word that Goan Hindus were unsatisfied with the rule of the Sultan of Bijapur. They were struggling under heavy taxes and would support a transfer of possession to these unknown foreigners should they manage to take control. Albuquerque duly seized what is now Old Goa on 1 March, 1510. The Bijapuris briefly regained possession but were ejected by the Portuguese in a bloody rout nine months later.

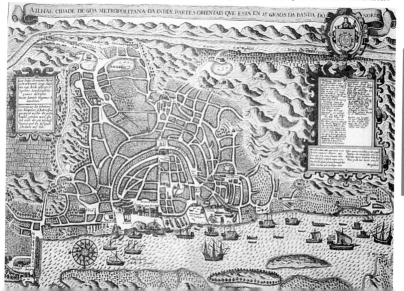

Phallical feast

The grandest baroque structure from Goa's colonial period isn't among the churches that make up Old Goa's UNESCO-designated World Heritage precinct. Instead, the genuinely magnificent Church of St Anne is some distance away in Talaulim, standing alone in a landscape of ruins that are covered by thick jungle, at the rim of a vast bowl of rice fields. This outsized building, described by the World Monument Fund as 'a living treasure', stands empty most of the year, with only the sun's rays to light up its lavishly detailed plaster interior. But on its feast day of 26 July, Santana de Talaulim, as the church is popularly known, draws thousands of Hindus and Christians to a fertility oriented 'cucumber feast', where offerings of cucumbers are reputed to yield unfailing results of male offspring.

It's not easy to get to Santana de Talaulim by public transport, despite its proximity to Panjim (5km) and to National Highway 17 (3km). Take NH 17 to the junction with Goa Velha, and then stick to the sole village road that runs north on a winding path through fields and backwaters, and winds up at the foot of the church's imposing laterite stairways.

The first colonial possession of the Portuguese was Tiswadi, a huge promontory containing two natural harbours between the Mandovi and Zuari rivers. In time, the Portuguese added the territories of Bardez and Salcete, lands that are still commonly known as the 'Old Conquests'. By the middle of the 16th century, the *Estado da India* had developed into one of the great international trading outposts, and a magnet for foreign adventurers. A new elite of Portuguese (and other European) administrators and soldiers were married off to the widows and daughters of the erstwhile ruling class. Franciscan, Jesuit, Dominican and Augustinian priests arrived in Goa and were each granted territories in which to begin converting native Goans to Catholicism. A unique European-Indian cultural exchange began that would completely remake Goa, and eventually the entire subcontinent. Chillies first entered India via Goa, as did cashews, corn, potatoes, papayas and countless other imports now taken for granted, including Asia's first modern printing press, medical college and lighthouse.

THE ERA OF 'GOLDEN GOA'

By the end of the 16th century, the Portuguese-controlled city that mushroomed on the bank of the Mandovi was one of the richest places in the world, a crowded metropolis bigger than London or Paris, and home to what are still the largest church and convent complexes in Asia. It was known as *Goa Dourada*, or 'Golden Goa', of as much importance to the Portuguese court as Lisbon itself, and raked in such vast profits that it came under constant threat from envious newcomers to the Indian Ocean trade. The Dutch levelled crippling blockades against the city twice in the early decades of the 17th century, and a series of plagues devastated the European population. Portuguese interest in the colony eventually waned, as the royal court became preoccupied with its new holdings in Brazil. The colony was occasionally threatened by the Marathas to the north, and was almost conquered by Shivaji's Maratha Confederacy before the Mughals distracted them away, and Goa remained in European hands.

From the 18th century, a native aristocracy steadily gained power and influence at the cost of a distracted ruling class in Lisbon. This cadre of converted upper-caste landlords and the offspring of Indo-Portuguese marriages embarked on a spate of estate building that left a permanent mark on Goa's landscape, a constellation of agrarian villages organised in a largely feudal manner, with a few landlords holding sway over large numbers of subject tenants. Unlike British India, there was never any colonial emphasis on secular education, infrastructure improvement or the exploitation of natural resources. Goans began to leave their homeland to pursue opportunity elsewhere, initially to the Portuguese territories in Africa and Asia.

During the Napoleonic wars, when British troops were stationed in Goa to deter French attacks, the aspirations of ambitious Goans shifted to the British Empire. Thousands of Goans left to work in British cantonments in India and in British East African colonies where they became administrators, clerks, cooks, musicians and *ayahs* or nannies.

LIBERATION

At the end of World War II, the writing was on the wall for the European imperial project. India became independent in a cataclysm of sectarian violence in 1947, and the Portuguese immediately came under heavy pressure to hand Goa over to the new Indian government. But though there were only a few dozen Portuguese officials left in the territory, the

fascist dictator Salazar declared that it would remain eternally Portuguese and embarked on a violent, occasionally lavish campaign to persuade Goans that their future lay with Portugal and not the Indian republic. The majority of Goans became increasingly impatient for change, and increasingly radicalised when Portuguese police responded to minor provocations with heavy-handed tactics, including firing on unarmed crowds and mercilessly beating peaceful protestors. In 1961, India's first prime minister, Jawaharlal Nehru, sent in the Indian army and took Goa virtually unopposed on 19 December, ending at last the European colonial era on Indian soil. Almost immediately afterwards, Goan voters rejected a proposal to merge with the state of Maharashtra, choosing to remain a territory administered by the central government. On 30 May, 1987, Goa finally became a full-fledged state of the Indian Union and Konkani became an official national language.

Bloody inquisitive

'If everywhere the Inquisition was an infamous court, the infamy, however base, however vile, however corrupt and determined by worldly interests, was never more so than in Goa.'
– Archbishop of Evora, Portugal

In 1542, Francis Xavier of Navarre, a Basque priest who co-founded the Jesuit order, arrived in Goa as an ambassador of the Pope. He was 35 and had most recently worked at the newly established Court of the Inquisition. Over the next few years he spent just six months in Goa, but it was enough time for him to form a deep distaste for the louche behaviour of its Portuguese residents and utter disgust at the newly converted Indian Catholics, whom he called 'half-baked, semi-pagan, Eurasian converts'. With characteristic impatience, he fired off numerous appeals to the Court of the Inquisition to export its cleansing offices to Goa. Eight years after his death, they did so.

The Portuguese Inquisition was imposed in Goa in 1560, and was formally renounced only in 1812, under pressure from the British. Officially, it was meant to seek out and eradicate religious heresy; in practice, it was a convenient tool for ethnic cleansing, suppressing dissent and eradicating threats to Portuguese rule. Confessions were extracted by the careful amputation of limbs

and slicing-off of eyelids, done in a manner to keep the victim alive as long as possible. Bizarre and arbitrary laws were imposed on Hindus, including the banning of betel nuts, Indian musical instruments, the sarong-like *dhoti*, Sanskrit names and even the ritual feeding of the poor. Every few years, those deemed heretics were burned at the stake in an *auto da fe*, heralded by the tolling of a grand bell. The terror of the Inquisition in Goa – considered by many historians to be the bloodiest Inquisition of all – prompted a mass exodus of Hindus and Christians alike.

Ironically, St Francis Xavier today remains a deeply venerated saint in Goa. Xavier died on an island in the mouth of the Canton River in 1552, where his body was buried in a wooden coffin packed with lime to ensure its speedy decomposition. Ten weeks after, a Portuguese ship went to recover the body and – so the story goes – found it miraculously preserved and unmarked. The body was buried and disinterred yet again in Malacca, with similar tales of its incorruptibility. The body eventually made its way back to the seat of Portuguese power in Goa, where it is kept in the Basilica of Bom Jesus in Old Goa (*see p212*). Every decade, the relic is displayed at an exposition which draws hundreds of thousands of pilgrims from across the world.

Goa

North Goa

So much more than hippies.

The original, iconic hippie trail of the early 1960s started off in Europe, and proceeded slowly overland through Turkey and Iran to Pakistan, and then on through Kathmandu and other parts of the Himalayas all the way down to a handful of remote beaches inset in the rocky coastline of North Goa. In the decades since the Goa Freaks first tumbled onto their sands, that handful is now multicultural and multinational, with thousands of permanent resident expatriates from around the world, and almost two million visitors a year. The beachfront stretches all the way from the **Aguada Plateau**, which drops to the Mandovi River, to the **Tiracol Fort** on the Maharashtra border – a drive you can make in about two hours. In between, there's charter tourism congestion in **Candolim**, the Indian middle class packing the sands of **Calangute**, party central for India's twentysomethings at **Baga**, and the sprawling luxury villas of India's rich and famous in **Sinquerim**. Further up the coast are the dream beaches of the '60s hippie trail, the first of which was **Anjuna**, where a remnant of septuagenarian Goa Freaks linger on in a wildly international mix that still retains its alternative vibe. There's also the more edgy **Chapora** and **Vagator**, where cafés are jammed with tokers openly puffing on smokestack-sized chillums under the watchful gaze of well-connected locals.

North of Vagator, the beaches begin to empty out and some are relatively deserted. **Morjim**, where protected Olive Ridley sea turtles still come to lay eggs on the beach, now hosts a thriving Russian sub-culture. **Ashvem**, with its rugged rock outcrops and windswept sands, is home to Goa's best beach restaurant, **La Plage** (*see p197*). Beyond **Mandrem**'s unique marriage of swift-running freshwater and ocean surf, all roads lead to the legendary **Arambol**, where latter-day versions of the first flower children spend months living in thatched huts under coconut palms. In peak season, your day on the beach here could easily be spent with 10,000 other travellers, with Hebrew as the lingua franca and waiters and hawkers the only Indians in sight. Apart from the beaches, North Goa is also home to some of the most ambitious restaurants in India, including Burmese, Turkish, Italian and French establishments – but there's always recourse to the inevitable steak and kidney pie and mushy peas so beloved of the Brits who still outnumber all other foreign visitors by a tidy margin.

North Goa's attractions aren't just confined to the coast, they extend to hill-hugging cashew plantations that blanket much of **Pernem** taluka (Goa's feni-producing heartland), the noisy riot of colours that is **Mapusa** market in the heart of Bardez district, and the hidden, curiously hybrid Hindu temples of **Ponda**.

Anjuna Beach. *See p191.*

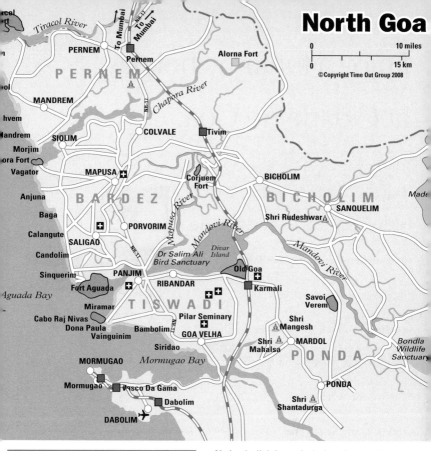

0   10 miles

0   15 km
©Copyright Time Out Group 2008

Sinquerim & Fort Aguada

Goa tourism began here, at the far end of
what was once a pristine four-mile stretch
of broad golden sand lined with rolling dunes
and backed by acres of coconut plantations.
Long before strict coastal development laws,
the hotel arm of the Indian business house Tata
built a sprawling five-star hotel complex amid
the crumbling ruins of an early 17th-century
Portuguese fortress. The **Fort Aguada Beach
Resort** threw open the floodgates to mass
tourism when it started operations in 1972.
By the late '90s the beach had become lined
elbow-to-elbow with beach shacks and a
warren of hotels, shopping centres, pubs,
restaurants and supermarkets. The plateau
atop the Sinquerim headland, near the modern,
squat **Aguada Lighthouse**, offers one of the
best ocean views in Goa, with the wide mouths
of the Mandovi and Zuari rivers on one side,
and that glorious beach on the other. Next door
sits its ancestor – the first lighthouse in Asia,
built by the Portuguese in 1864.

Under the lighthouse is the low-rise complex
of Goa's main prison, the **Fort Aguada Jail**,
once packed with anti-colonial activists in
the days of the Portuguese, now home to local
crooks plus a couple of dozen foreigners busted
under India's severe but selectively applied
anti-drug laws. The nearby **Church of St
Lawrence** (open for Sunday mass at 8am),
built in 1630, commands another spectacular
view of the Mandovi River, receding to the east.

Down the hill, past a curve overlooking the
quiet **Nerul River**, tourist development takes
over both sides of the road. The Fort Aguada
hotel complex covers almost 90 acres onto the
beachfront right up to its sister **Taj Holiday
Village**. The Taj is now building a massive
stone bulwark to protect the property from
the rapid, destructive beach erosion that has
followed the grounding of the River Princess,
a huge iron-ore cargo ship, during a storm in
2001. The rusting hulk is still stuck just off the
beach, as its powerful mining-company owner
fights through the courts to ensure he never
has to pay the huge cost of removing it. Off the

Goa

Enjoy a funtastic holiday at Cidade de Goa.

Imagine an intimate beachside resort at Goa that lets you get away from it all, where you are pampered with only the finest indulgences. Whatever your ideal - a secluded honeymoon, total rejuvenation, a feast of traditional cuisine, incredible water sports, or simply the lure of Goan hospitality; your dreams become reality at Cidade de Goa.

Make **everyday** a holiday
and **celebrate** just living!

Idyllic destination.

Hectic vacation.

Find a million things to do. At a tranquil beachside setting.

Where fun-filled activities help recharge your senses.

It's a perfect place to relax. Or plunge into non-stop activity.

road, just beyond the gardens of the Taj complex, is the palatial entranceway to **Kingfisher Villa**, the private pleasure palace of flamboyant brewery and airline tycoon Vijay Mallya (he makes Kingfisher beer). Around New Year, these gates are jammed with eager locals and frantic paparazzi clamouring to catch a glimpse of Mallya's celeb-heavy guest list.

Where to eat & drink

Sinquerim and Fort Aguada are the most exclusive, expensive parts of the North Goan tourism strip, so expect high prices for good quality throughout. The **Banyan Tree** (Taj Holiday Village, 0832-664-5858, main course Rs 350 noon-2.30pm, 7.30-10.30pm daily), one of Goa's best Thai restaurants, sits beside a magnificent specimen of its namesake in the Taj Holiday Village. North of Fort Aguada, there's **Santa Lucia** (Fort Aguada Road, 0832-561-5213, main course Rs 180, 6.30-10.30pm daily), a tiny, relaxed terrace restaurant serving zesty Italian and Swiss food.

Nightlife

Near the Taj Village is **Sweet Chilli Garden Restaurant and Lounge** (on the Lighthouse Road, 0832-247-9446, main course Rs 120, 11am-midnight daily), a popular open-air restaurant on several levels, with live music every night and lively jazz jams on Friday evenings. Down the road towards Candolim is **Butter** (98221-26262, main course Rs 150, noon-midnight), a stylish lounge and live music venue that hosts well-attended parties every weekend.

Entertainment

Although Sinquerim beach has been cut to a tiny sliver of its former breadth by the erosion caused by the marooned ore-carrier River Princess, it's still a good centre for watersports. Morgan D'Souza of **Thunder Waves** (on the beach near Fort Aguada, 98221-76986, 9am-sunset daily) offers dolphin trips (Rs 400 per head for a half-hour excursion), speedboat-driven parasailing from the beach (Rs 1,000-Rs 1,500 for 3-10mins), and jet-skiing (Rs 900 for 15mins). The Taj Aguada has one of the best spas in India, **Jiva** (0832-664-5858, 8am-8pm daily), which offers popular Balinese massages for Rs 3,000 per hour, and a signature Jivaniya package (including spice scrub, wrap and deep-tissue massage) for Rs 3,650.

Feni for your thoughts

The French have their wine, the Greeks have their ouzo, but Goans have feni – and they don't really need anything else, thank you very much. Every April and May, the heavy scent of fermenting cashew drifts across the countryside and traditional stills fire up to make the year's batch of this deeply loved drink – a drink as synonymous with Goa as beaches and fish-curry-rice. Feni (pronounced fey-nee) is a clear, powerful spirit that comes in two varieties: cashew

and coconut. Coconut feni (also known as palm feni) is made all year round, mostly in South Goa, but is considered by purists to be an inferior version of the 'original' cashew feni, which can only be made after the cashew fruit harvest in March. The fruits are crushed and the juice left to ferment, which is then heated in large copper or earthen pots over firewood and the distillate collected through

a coiled pipe. The first distillate is weak and makes a drink called urrak; it takes two or three distillations to make proper, strong feni, which is around 40 per cent alcohol.

Connoisseurs insist that good feni can be as smooth and nuanced as the finest single malt whiskies. It's by far the state's most popular drink, available at hole-in-the-wall taverns everywhere, which serve homemade varieties poured from jerry cans or unlabelled plastic bottles. **Hospadaria Venite** in Panjim (see p206) sells an excellent home-produced feni by the bottle for about Rs 150, but there are lots of big-name brands like Big Boss (Rs 150 for 750 ml) available from wine shops. Drink it neat, with a squeeze of lime, a pinch of salt, or with lemonade. It's also fabulous in fruit cocktails. Watch out though – it has a kick like a gaur.

Where to stay

The **Fort Aguada Beach Resort** (Fort
Aguada, 0832-664-5858, www.tajhotels.com,
Rs 7,000-Rs 11,000 double), the luxury tourism
pioneer, is showing its age but is still the
playground for India's A-list, especially during
New Year celebrations. But it's questionable
whether the experience lives up to the hype.
The **Taj Holiday Village** (0832-664-5858,
www.tajhotels.com, Rs 8,000-Rs 9,000 double)
offers attractive individual villas with private
balconies. Near the Taj is the **Marbella
Guesthouse** (Fort Aguada Beach Road,
near Jojo's Corner restaurant, 0832-247-9551,
Rs 1,200-Rs 2,500 double) with six eccentrically
decorated but well-appointed rooms in a pretty
house under a mango tree.

Getting there

Tivim is the nearest train stop to the north beaches;
the half-hour taxi ride from Tivim to Sinquerim
costs Rs 350. From Dabolim Airport, it's Rs 650 and
takes an hour. From Panjim, take the Mandovi
Bridge towards Mapusa and turn left off the NH-17
at O Cooqueiro junction. Turn left at St Alex Church
and Sinquerim is three miles down the road. Taxis
cost Rs 250 from Panjim.

Nerul (Coco Beach)

Before the beach road hits Candolim, a sharp
right turn onto a narrow, scenic road leads to
Nerul and Coco Beach on the Mandovi River,
with views of the Panjim waterfront. Nerul
feels slightly schizophrenic, alternating between
the ultra-luxurious villas of Indian and foreign
millionaires, and small village homes of local
fishermen and farmers. The beach is popular
with Goan families, wealthy Indians and older
Europeans. The water off Coco Beach is a little
murkier than that of Candolim or Calangute
but it is clean and safe to swim 100 yards out.

Where to eat & drink

Under the Nerul Bridge (off which Matt Damon
crashed a car in the action film *The Bourne
Supremacy*) is **Amigo's** (0832-240-1123, main
course Rs 120, 11am-10.30pm daily), a local-run
restaurant in a beautiful spot on the mangrove-
fringed riverbank, with strong ties to local
fisherfolk – hence the super-fresh mussels,
shrimp and estuarine crabs.

Candolim

Once a deserted expanse of banyan trees and
soaring palm trees, Candolim is now mass-
tourism's ground zero in Goa. It's a maze of

The Rebelos of **Café Chocolatti**.
See p185.

lanes and by-ways lined with hundreds of
guesthouses, shops and restaurants and
choked with traffic in peak season. Candolim
is the epicentre of the British invasion, both by
budget travellers and expatriates, and abounds
with fish-and-chip shops and pubs festooned
with Premier League memorabilia. Candolim
is as close as Goa gets to mass-tourism hotspots
like Cancun and the Costa del Sol, but it's still
reasonably relaxed and has some excellent
restaurants hidden among the neon-lit also-
rans. Unlike the beaches to the north, Candolim
is a one-stop vacation destination – everything
you need is within walking distance.

In the interior of the village, about a mile
from the main road, the impressive **Our Lady
of Hope Church** (open for Sunday mass
5.45pm) sits on an elevated location with
a good view of the carefully tended *bund*
(earthen dam) system that keeps the acres of
surrounding farmland protected from flooding
from the Nerul marshes. The sluices for these
bunds are called *kandoli* in Konkani – hence the
name Candolim. The village played a prominent
role in Goan history, and was the site of a major
campaign of revolt against Portuguese rule
in 1787 led by disaffected Catholic priests,
including the clergyman father of the
adventurer-hypnotist Abbe Faria (*see p208*
All the fun of the Faria). The revolt was put
down, but locals proudly refer to the episode as
just the second anti-colonial uprising in history
after the American Revolution of 1776. In the

TAJ
Holidays

Fine dining at its best

Taj Exotica | **Taj Holiday Village** | **Fort Aguada Beach Resort**
Goa   Goa   Goa

Enemy of the estate

India's economic boom has sent real estate prices rocketing in cities across the country, but even against that backdrop, Goa stands out for the sheer frenzy of its property market. Prices have more than doubled since 2003, with two-bedroom flats near Candolim now fetching around Rs three million, up a million in the last two years. Demand for property still far outstrips supply. Indians from across the country – now wealthy enough to afford holiday homes – are snapping up anything that doesn't move in India's premier resort destination. The market is also being fuelled by foreigners: over 25,000 Europeans, Israelis, Russians and North Americans have invested in Goan real estate since 2000.

Goan society has become increasingly anxious about shifting demographics and there's widespread anger against the corrupt local politicians who have conspired to get rich by selling land. In 2007, a broad-based people's movement hit the streets of Panjim and Margao, managing to force a stunning withdrawal of a dubiously formulated plan that wanted to open huge swathes of land

for commercial development. The non-party affiliated Goa Bachao Andolan, led by a charismatic young physician, Dr Oscar Rebello, continues to give voice to what seems to be a majority of Goans saying 'development yes, but not this mess'. In January 2008, the Chief Minister promised to pursue stricter laws that would limit land purchase by outsiders.

Should you catch the property bug, like countless others before you, get started by looking through the classifieds in Goa's three English-language newspapers – *O Heraldo*, the *Navhind Times* and the *Gomantak Times*. You'll have to get to grips with complex rules governing foreign ownership of property in India, which some buyers have got around by setting up dummy companies in Mauritius or Panama that become the official owners. Consult good lawyers at every step; land deals in Goa are notoriously unreliable and can collapse with investors losing all of their money. But if you do find that dream property, enjoy the seclusion while you can. You'll have lots of neighbours soon enough.

north of the village stands the **Casa dos Monteiros**, a beautifully preserved 17th-century private home. It can be approached from the road, but like the similarly impressive **Casa dos Costa-Frias** near Bosio Hospital, no visitors are allowed.

Where to eat & drink

Candolim has some of Goa's best restaurants, but the stand-out eatery here is **Bomra's** (Souza Vaddo, 98221-49633, 98221-34857, main course Rs 200, 7-10pm Mon-Sat, closed Apr-Sept), which serves innovative versions of Burmese and Kachin dishes, prepared by a London-trained Burmese chef. Opened in the 2006 season, Bomra's has received lots of attention and makes a credible claim to being the world's best Burmese restaurant. Another unusual eating option is **Cuckoo Zen Garden** (near Bob's Inn, Ximer 98221-26031, www.cuckoozen.com, main course Rs 150, 7-11pm, Mon-Sat, closed Apr-Sept), Goa's only authentic Chinese restaurant, run by an eccentric commune of Taiwanese (with names like Soup and Elephant) who live in the shadow of Cuckoo, a Taiwanese acupuncturist and self-styled Zen master. Down the road, near Tarcar ice factory, is **Lloyd's** (94224-38230, main

course Rs 120, 7pm-6am Mon-Sat), a basic space with dismal bathrooms that becomes extremely popular late at night for alcohol-soaked home-cooked dinners including Goan-style spare ribs. The beach road opposite the Tarcar ice factory leads to the Italian-run **La Fenice** (0832-228-1182, main course Rs 150, 11am-10pm daily). At the top of a long flight of stairs are some spacious, atmospheric terraces where you can dine on tasty and authentic Italian food – the best on offer in the state. Down on the beach, the pick of Candolim's endless line of shacks is **Calamari** (0832-309-0506, main course Rs 150, 8.30am-9.30pm daily, closed May-Sept), where the motto is 'Bathe and Binge'. It has very friendly staff, nice Goan-style seafood, and offers patrons an outdoor shower and free towels. Down the road, a branch of Colva's **Amici Gelato** (no telephone, 11am-11pm daily) serves outstanding Italian-style ice-creams. Right opposite is a fabulous breakfast and lunch choice, **Café Chocolatti** (Fort Aguada Road, 0832-247-9340, main course Rs 200), run by Ricardo and Nazneen Rebelo (*photo p183*). Chocolatti specialises in superb salads, sandwiches and baked goods (with delicious biscuits and chocolates for sale in the tiny attached store).

Goa

Nightlife

These days, nightlife in Candolim is relatively sleepy. However, an ambitious entry into the Goan market by Mumbai landmark **Shiro** (0832-645-1718, 11am-1am daily) occupies a prime stretch of beachside land, and draws a loyal crowd of well-heeled Mumbai visitors. Opposite St Anthony's Chapel is the **Bar** (no phone, noon-3am daily), a cosy bar with low cane seating, a couple of pool tables and a club-like feel. Try the masala feni.

Shopping

One of Goa's most popular shopping centres is the **Acron Arcade** (283 Fort Aguada Road, 0832-564-3671, 10am-10pm daily). Downstairs, half the building is devoted to home decor from **Yamini**, an Indian chain of stores selling beautiful hand-made fabrics and furnishings. It has a variety of men's and women's clothes with an emphasis on handloom and reasonably-priced designer labels from Pondicherry and Bangalore. Down the road from the Tarcar Ice Factory, after La Fenice and in a charming old converted house, is the **Literati Bookshop & Café** (98226-82566, 0832-227-7740), Goa's best bookstore/café and hangout for India's A-list writers when they're on vacation. Not far away, the Swiss-owned store **Sotohaus** (1266F Anna Vaddo, Candolim, 0832-248-9983, www.sotodecor.com) offers beautifully worked iron-and-paper lamps, tables and other furniture, many made using found objects like banana, elephant-ear, papaya leaves, driftwood and even shed snakeskins, all under thick layers of lacquer.

Where to stay

This is charter tourism country, so most hotels in Candolim are built to specifications dictated by travel companies – virtually everything is identical, clean and well-run but there are few non-full board options available. The pick of this bunch is the lovingly decorated **Aldeia Santa Rita** (near Kingfisher Villa, 0832-247-9868, Rs 4,000-Rs 7,500 double), close to the beach. Nearby is **Whispering Palms** (off Candolim Main Road, 0832-247-9140, www.whisperingpalms.com, Rs 6,000-Rs 8,000 double), which has an excellent swimming pool and well-appointed rooms. More basic than either of these, though equally packed with British charter tourists, is the **Summerville Beach Resort** (off Candolim Main Road, 0832-247-9075, www.summervillebeachresort.com, Rs 1,500-Rs 1,800 double), which has 20 well-maintained rooms, a pleasant rooftop restaurant and a small swimming pool.

Resources

Internet

Sify I-way *Bake N Byte, Laxmi Apartments, near Candolim Market (no phone).* **Open** 9am-10pm daily.

Getting there

Taxis from Tivim take around half an hour and cost Rs 350. From Dabolim Airport, it's Rs 600 and takes an hour; from Panjim, it's around Rs 200 for a 20-minute trip. When driving from Panjim, cross the Mandovi Bridge and go about two miles straight up the NH-17 highway towards Mapusa. Turn left at the O Coqueiro junction, and pass through Sangolda until you reach the Church of St Alex in Calangute. From there, turn left onto Candolim Road.

Calangute & Baga

Long before tourists washed up on Goan shores, **Calangute** was a seafront idyll for genteel Goan families from all over North Goa and Panjim. Through the hot summer months of April and May, they retired here to simple rented accommodation and borrowed villas to take early morning 'sea baths' and evening walks along a rudimentary boardwalk. All that is long gone: Calangute's broad sands are as

Literati Bookshop & Café.

Goa

Hippie and you know it

In 1969, Gilbert Levey left the Haight-Ashbury district of San Francisco and took the overland trail through Afghanistan and Pakistan, first to Bombay and then Goa. He'd been a roadie for Sons of Champlain, a pioneering acid rock band, but in Goa he adopted the saffron robes and matted hair of a Hindu *sadhu*, or wise man, and became Goa Gil, a pioneer of the early hippie scene at Anjuna Beach. Throughout the 1970s, Gil organised legendary parties at Anjuna – moonlight jams and non-stop music and drugs that lasted from Christmas Eve to New Year's Day for a tribe of fellow overland travellers who called themselves the Goa Freaks. Gil describes these epic parties as efforts to 'tell the story of humanity'.

In the '90s, Gil started to use snippets from industrial music, ethno-techno, acid house and psychedelic rock to create Goa Trance, dance music with a heavy spiritual accent. Today, Goa Trance (sometimes known to fans simply as 604, a numerical approximation of the word Goa) has morphed into a global multi-million dollar industry and is played at clubs as far away as New York and Israel. Gil remains at the centre of the scene, DJing full-moon parties around the world in what he calls attempts 'to redefine ancient tribal ritual for the 21st century' and 'to uplift the consciousness of the participants', although a cynic might say that good, old-fashioned ecstasy has as much to do with that as the music. For Gil, Goa Trance is a logical continuation of what hippies were doing back in the '60s and '70s. 'The Psychedelic Revolution never really stopped,' he said. 'It just had to go halfway round the world to the end of a dirt road on a deserted beach, and there it was allowed to evolve and mutate, without government or media pressures.'

But government pressure has finally caught up with the revolution in Goa. Because of their association with drugs, raves are viewed with suspicion by a government anxious to mend the state's reputation as a destination for low-rent travellers, hoping instead to attact high-end tourists. Raves have been banned entirely since the 2005-06 tourist season. Still, underground raves do happen surreptitiously, sometimes starting at 4am on remote beaches or in forests. Ask staff at local bars and the 'pilots' who operate motorcycle taxis to find out when and where the next party is happening.

Goa Gil in Anjuna in 1972.

Still here in the 21st century.

Goa

Candolim's **Calamari** shack. See p185.

golden as ever but have been swamped with Goa's most congested tourist scene, with thousands of Indian visitors rubbing elbows with Scandinavians and Brits, and a beach lined with paragliders, jetskis, speedboats and tightly packed sunbeds. The interior is just as crowded, with buses constantly disgorging Indian day-trippers from neighbouring states, and the usual collection of Kashmiri rug merchants, fast food outlets, and cheap souvenir shops.

It's hard to tell where Calangute ends and **Baga** begins. Baga is now one of the most famous party hotspots in India, with a range of bars that pack in twentysomethings from Mumbai, Bangalore and Delhi. Slightly quieter is Baga Creek, across a concrete bridge, where a long line of some of Goa's best eating options operate out of converted old houses just yards from the river bank.

A couple of reminders of the past do remain, notably the private home **Casa dos Proenças**, just north of the main Calangute market. It was built with several unusual features, including a gorgeous seashell-screen enclosed verandah and an ingenious natural cooling system. Away from the beach, on the road towards Saligao, stands the spectacular rococo **Church of St Alex**, an 18th-century construction with a bulging dome and Indianised bell towers. Regular returnees to Calangute like to begin their vacation with a shave and a haircut in the barber shop (the sign reads 'Barberia') in the mirrored octagon in the centre of the Calangute market crossroads – a 200-year-old colonial customs post.

Where to eat & drink

Baga Creek has numerous exciting and ambitious restaurants, of which **J&A's Little Italy** (Baga Creek, 98231-39488, main course Rs 350, 6pm-midnight daily, closed Apr-Sept), is easily the best, serving delicious Italian food with an emphasis on superb ingredients and flawless presentation. Close by is the hillside **La Terrase** (Baga Creek, 0832-395-0832,

www.laterrasse.in, main course Rs 250, 6.30-10.30pm daily, closed Apr-Sept) high up a couple of flights of steps with great views of the creek and authentic southern French food. On the same stretch is the brilliant daytime hangout **Lila Café** (0832-227-9843, main course Rs 150, 9am-6pm Wed-Mon, closed May-Sept) whose German owners keep a devoted crowd of regulars happy with fresh German bread, mushroom paté, water-buffalo ham and other Euro-style treats.

Heading towards the beach, there's old-timer **Britto's** (last corner on Baga Road, 0832-227-7331, main course Rs 175, 8.30am-10.30pm daily), a friendly Baga institution serving decent Goan dishes, and a fine selection of desserts and baked goods. A little further down the beach road towards Calangute is **Casa Portuguesa** (Beach Road, 0832-227-7024, www.casa-portuguesa-goa.com, main course Rs 250, 7-11pm, closed season May-Oct), a pleasant restaurant in a converted ancestral home specialising in authentic Portuguese food. Further along the beach road from Baga to Calangute, the next landmark is **Le Restaurant Français** (Milky Way restaurant, Baga Road, 98221-21712, main course Rs 200, 7.30-10.30pm Wed-Mon, closed May-Oct), an experimental French restaurant. The huge screens painted with Parisian scenes are a bit incongruous but the food is stunning and consistently innovative. Across the road is the lane that leads to **Tito's** (Tito's Lane, Baga, 0832-227-5028, 0832-227-6154, main course Rs 250, 7pm-midnight daily, closed May-Sept), the party hotspot that also serves decent pastas and steaks. Much better fare is available directly opposite at **Fiesta** (Tito's Lane, Baga, 0832-227-9894, 0832-228-1440, www.fiestagoa.com, main course Rs 300, 7-11pm Wed-Mon, closed Apr-Oct), a beautifully decorated open-air restaurant with a Caribbean feel and a German chef who makes superb wood-fired pizzas and outstanding desserts. Nearby is the pick of Baga's beach shacks, **Zanzibar** (no phone, main course Rs 175, 9am-11pm daily, closed May-Sept), which serves good Indian food with an emphasis on fresh fish and shrimp. Further down the road is an unusual little nook of a restaurant, **Simply South** (98231-28567, 6-11.30pm daily, main course Rs 200), which serves outstanding meals derived from the South Indian non-vegetarian cuisines of Tamil Nadu and Kerala.

Just before the Calangute roundabout is the old Goan favourite **Infantaria** (0832-227-7421, main course Rs 100, 8.30am-10pm daily) which has been dishing up old-fashioned chops and potato croquettes to generations of day-trippers. Heading south, **I-95** (0832-227-5213, main course Rs 250, 7pm-midnight daily) has quickly made a name for itself as one of the best fine-

Goa

dining destinations in Goa, with lavish ingredients and highly attentive service. The restaurant occupies the garden of an impressive art gallery, and the studio of Yolanda Kammermeier, one of the state's leading artists, and a former national soccer player. All the way back in Gaurawaddo, in the part of Calangute that merges into Candolim, **Waves** (0832-227-6017, main course Rs 200, 7-10pm daily, closed May-Sept) is another restaurant that fuses art and great food, in the pleasant Kerkar Art Complex. It specialises in Hindu Goan, or 'Gomantak' specialities.

Nightlife

Calangute and Baga are home to some of Goa's most hectic nightlife; both beaches are crammed with chilled-out shacks serving drinks until late, and the streets behind are lined with hole-in-the-wall bars. Baga's (and maybe Goa's) most famous club is **Tito's** (Tito's Lane, Baga, 0832-227-9895, www.titosgoa.com, 10pm-4am daily, Rs 500-Rs 600), a Baga institution that attracts hundreds of Kingfisher-fuelled boys and girls from Mumbai for Bollywood beats and dancing on three levels, with extra entertainment provided by professional dancers and the occasional magician. Just down the lane towards the beach is **Mambo's** (Tito's Lane, Baga, 0832-227-9895, 7pm-3.30am, cover charge Rs 200-Rs 300), a wooden beach pub run by the Tito's management but with a more relaxed vibe. They usually play a mix of hip hop and house, with some country music thrown in. **Kamasutra** (Saunta Vaddo, Baga, 98901-41879, noon-midnight) is a laid-back bar serving food and cocktails to a progressive lounge soundtrack, popular with both Indians

and Euro-kids. Open even during the depths of the monsoon, the bar at **Cavala** (Saunta Vaddo, Baga, 0832-227-6090, 9am-midnight daily), an old Baga hotel, offers a warm welcome to a friendly (and older) crowd of locals, expats and regular returnees, with live music and retro nights most Fridays and Saturdays.

Where to stay

Pousada Tauma (Porba Vaddo, Calangute, 0832-227-9061, www.pousada-tauma.com, Rs 12,000-Rs 20,000 double), is a lush complex of villas set around an inviting pool with an enchanting restaurant beneath a laterite colonnade and a top-notch ayurvedic spa. **Villa Goesa** (Cobra Vaddo, 0832-227-7535, www.vilagoesa.com, Rs 1,700-Rs 2,700 double) is particularly close to the beach and set in nicely maintained gardens. The nearby **Chalston Beach Resort** (Cobra Vaddo, 0832-227-6080, Rs 1,200-Rs 1,800 double) is a clean, reasonably priced option popular with Scandinavians. Its beach shack is one of the best on this stretch. On the road in the thick of Baga's action is **Cavala** (Baga Main Road, 0832-227-7587, www.cavala.com, Rs 600-Rs 1,700 double), not far from the beach and with attractive, great-value rooms.

Resources

Post office

Calangute Post Office *near St Alex Church (0832-227-6030).* **Open** 9am-5pm Mon-Fri.

Internet

Sify I-way *Shop No. 1, Sunshine Complex, Baga Road (no phone).* **Open** 9am-9pm daily.

Coco Beach. *See p183.*

Boutique beds

For years, visitors to Goa had to choose between beach huts and informal guesthouses with plenty of character but often little comfort, or sprawling five-stars where the reverse was true. But in recent years, Goa's hotel market has been energised by the rise of boutique hotels – small and stylish properties offering an exclusive experience much more suited to Goa's naturally laid-back vibe. Since 2000, the new boutique breed has become extremely popular, routinely charging more than the five-stars during the peak season around Christmas and New Year's Eve.

The grandfather of the trend is the **Nilaya Hermitage** (Arpora, 0832-227-6794, www.nilayahermitage.com, Rs 12,000-Rs 25,000 double), an ethereal fortress of domes on an Arpora hilltop, with an eagle's-eye view of the jungle landscape below. The atmosphere is otherworldly – *Arabian Nights* meets New Age – with twelve exceptional rooms themed according to the 'cosmic elements', with names like 'sun', 'earth' and 'fire'. Under its largest dome is a 'music room' decked out with white cotton mattresses and a superb sound system – a veritable temple of chill-out. Nilaya has attracted numerous famous guests, including designer Giorgio Armani, supermodel Kate Moss and Hollywood star Richard Gere.

Pousada Tauma (Porba Vaddo, 0832-227-9061, www.pousadatauma.com, Rs 12,000-Rs 26,500 double) is a secluded dell of lush greenery and beautiful cottages around an attractive pool. It also has one of Goa's most enchanting restaurants.

Getting away from it all is guaranteed at **Elsewhere** (Mandrem, 98200-37387, www.aseascape.com, Rs 6,100-Rs 24,000 per day, closed June-mid Oct), the ancestral home of Mumbai fashion photographer Denzil Sequeira and a stunning beach house-for-hire. It's set on an isolated strip of beach in Mandrem, with a verandah overlooking the surf, shuttered windows and servants on hand. Overlooking a creek to the rear, Sequeira has set up a few tents – the word doesn't really do them justice – each with hot and cold running water, a private jetty and a four-poster bed (Rs 2,300-Rs 5,700 per night).

Most unusual, and perhaps most stunning of all is Loulou Van Damme's creation, **Panchavatti** (Corjuem Island, 98225-80632, www.islaingoa.com, Rs 6,000-Rs 8,000 double, closed May-Sept), a magnificent hacienda on a headland above the coiled Mapusa River, blending design elements from Morocco, Latin America and the Caribbean. It's a retreat, Loulou says, 'for serenity, for you to redo your soul the right way'.

Far inland, around 90 minutes' drive from Panjim, is **Wildernest** (Swapnagandha, Chorla Ghat, off highway to Belgaum, 0831-520-7954, www.wildernest-goa.com, Rs 2,500-Rs 5,500 double), a unique complex of wood-and-glass cottages located 800 yards above sea level in the Western Ghats. Run by nature lovers, Wildernest offers secluded and highly comfortable cottages hidden away in the woods, with floor-to-ceiling glass walls that make you feel like you're camping out. Splash around the fabulous infinity pool, gaze out over the breathtaking Vazra Waterfall and the entire Mandovi River valley, and then strap on your boots for a leisurely hike in the woods.

Pousada Tauma.

Panchavatti.

Goa

Getting there

Taxis from Tivim cost Rs 300 for the half-hour trip. From Dabolim Airport, it's Rs 650 and takes around an hour and 15 minutes. From Candolim, turn right at St Anthony's Chapel for Calangute; for Baga, take another right at the main traffic circle just before Calangute beach.

Anjuna

Anjuna is where the first tie-dyed '60s refugees came in search of freedom, sunshine and cheap drugs. Some never left: you can still find Eight-fingered Eddie (now in his eighties) playing ball on the beach he 'discovered' 40 years ago, and the spirit of the Goa Freaks lives on in the hundreds of raised chillums that hail each sunset on the beachfront. But Anjuna is also home to writers and artists who simply like the vibe, and even has a strait-laced private school, the British-operated Little Yellow School House – by far the most expensive school in Goa, catering to expat children.

Long before the Goa Freaks skipped onto its beaches, Anjuna was a cosmopolitan trade outpost controlled by the Arabs (hence the name, derived from *hanjuman*, meaning 'trading post') in the 10th century. But most Muslim (and Hindu) traces were wiped out by the Portuguese zeal to Christianise the region as fast and as bloodily as possible. The sprawling **Church of St Michael the Archangel** (open for mass 7am Sun) dates back to that violent era.

Anjuna's famous **Flea Market** (South Anjuna, 8am-sunset every Wednesday) is a relic from the early hippie days in the 1960s and '70s when hashish was legal and sold just like today's vendors hawk cheap T-shirts and wooden knick-knacks. The market's original avatar was small-scale, sometimes relied on barter rather than cash, and was mostly used by foreigners looking to raise the money to stay on or get home. Now tens of thousands converge on the flea market every Wednesday from October to April in a convoy of scooters, motorbikes and trucks that throws up huge clouds of dust. The market sprawls over a plateau by the beach with hundreds of stalls selling everything from tie-dye bikinis to chillums and sitars to cushion covers.

In the late '90s and early 2000s Anjuna became famous all over again for its moonlight parties and raves – legendary open-air happenings that drew thousands of wildly dressed revellers. That scene is on hold while the Goa government wrings its hands over a coherent policy towards rave tourists. But it seems unlikely that the rave scene will ever return to Anjuna in quite the same way again.

Public crosses dot the Goan countryside.

Where to eat & drink

All roads lead to **Curlies** (South Anjuna Beach, 98221-68628, main course Rs 100, 6am-4am daily), a low-slung beach shack in South Anjuna, where a tightly knit staff of Anjuna villagers watches over a veritable United Nations of tokers. Sunset on the steps feels like an ancient ritual, with dozens of packed chillums making the rounds while children and dogs caper in the surf a few yards away. Up the beach is **Café Looda** (0832-562-9323, main course Rs 200, 8.30am-11.30pm daily, closed May-Oct), perched on the rocks overlooking the beach, at its best after the flea market slows down on Wednesdays. A bit further up the beach is the excellent **Shore Bar** (Anjuna Beach, no phone, 8am-11pm daily), a stylish beach shack for grown-ups, run by a chef who trained with the Roux brothers in England. Try the home-made seafood soup. Quite near all three, behind a small chapel, is the Anjuna landmark **Xavier's** (Praia de San Miguel, 0832-227-3402, main course Rs 150, 9am-11pm daily), once a small, basic shack and now a multi-cuisine establishment with three kitchens whipping up Indian, Chinese and Continental dishes. Another local landmark is **Basilico** (0832-227-3721, main course Rs 150, 11am-midnight daily), which serves excellent home-made pesto and wood-fired pizzas.

Goa

Occupying a prime corner nearby is one of Goa's best new restaurants, **Sublime** (99824-84051, 6.30-11pm) whose chef trained at the elite Culinary Institute of America. Closer to Anjuna village is **Bean Me Up** (Soranto Vaddo, 0832-227-3977, www.travelingoa.com/beanmeup, main course Rs 120, 9.30am-10.30pm daily), a world-class American-run vegetarian restaurant with super home-made tofu and salads. On the main Anjuna village road, the **Blue Tao Organic Restaurant and Café** (before Starco turn-off, 0832-309-0829, main course Rs 100, 9.30am-10.30pm daily) is a welcoming family restaurant selling home-made cakes and ice creams, herbal teas and fresh juices, and tasty, healthy breakfasts. At the far north end of Anjuna beach, near the Paradiso nightclub, is **Zoories** (no phone, main course Rs 150, 11am-11pm daily), with a stunning setting high on a cliff overlooking a rocky cove and a menu ranging from houmous and tahini to fajitas and enchiladas. A few minutes drive away from the beach is the outstanding **Yoga Magic** (Grand Chinvar Vaddo, next to Bobby Bar, 0832-562-3796, 93705-65717, www.yogamagic.net, main course Rs 400, 11.30am-1.30pm, 7-9pm daily, closed Apr), a popular eco-friendly getaway offering super 'Indian fusion' vegetarian meals to non-resident guests. Dinner bookings required.

Nightlife

Both **Curlies** and **Café Looda** (*see p191*) turn into lively beachside nightspots after sunset, with Curlies going heavy on the trance and ambient sounds for its stoner patrons. The

Shore Bar (Anjuna Beach, no phone), a few minutes' walk up the beach north of Café Looda, hosts regular trance nights from 6pm to 11pm. Goa's most stylish club is **Club Cubana** (82 Xim Waddo, Arpora Hill, 98235-39000, www.cubana.net, 9.30pm-5am daily, closed May-Oct, cover charge Rs 600-Rs 1,500), perched on an Arpora hilltop, a short drive from Anjuna. Cubana sprawls across a maze of levels and staircases, with terraces offering starry night views across Goa for its mixed crowd of European tourists and weekend-break visitors from Mumbai. Trance is firmly rejected here in favour of hip hop, house and R&B. Towels are provided for patrons who fancy jumping into the swimming pool, and the drinks are unlimited once you pay the cover charge (it can hit Rs 1,500 each for couples and single men around Christmas and New Year). Less fancy but even bigger is **Paradiso** (Anjuna, 93261-00013, 10pm-5am daily, cover charge Rs 300-Rs 600), a huge club built on a series of psychedelically-painted terraces overlooking the sea. Paradiso attracts some of India's best DJs and even the likes of Goa Gil (*see p187* **Hippie and you know it**). When it's packed, the energy level is hard to beat, pumped up by non-stop trance beats and the rhythm of the waves. **Underground Kingdom** (Grand Peddem, Anjuna, no phone, 10pm-6am daily, entry Rs 200) has got around the rave ban by burying itself in a large World War II-style concrete bunker in the middle of a forest, where DJs drop trance beats that echo insanely off the walls. Patrons can give their eardrums a break outside at relaxed open-air bars and canopies with soft cushions. The

Curlies.

Goa

famous **Ingo's Saturday Night Bazaar**
– a popular weekly night market at Arpora
– features an amazing array of foods and
artisanal crafts from around the world.
It seems back for good after more than a year
of legal limbo for the Swiss impresario, Ingo
Grill, who organises it each year. Make sure
to visit if it's on while you're in Goa. There's
nothing quite like this energetic, wildly
international mix of art, design, great food
and live music anywhere else in the world.
Highly recommended.

Where to stay

Anjuna is fast catching up with other beachfront
villages in the range and quality of its hotels
and guesthouses. The most atmospheric of
all is **Granpa's Inn** (Gaun Vaddo, 0832-227-
3270, Rs 850-1,750 double), the converted
ancestral home of the Faria family. It has a
great atmosphere, lovely gardens and terrace,
and a pool. A similar, though more downmarket
version is **Palacete Rodrigues** (Mazal
Vaddo, 0832-227-3358, Rs 800-Rs 1,100 double),
a converted 200-year-old house with the feel
of a family home. Back in the present century,
Laguna Anjuna (Soranto Vaddo, 0832-227-
4305, www.lagunaanjuna.com, Rs 2,500-Rs
7,500 double) is Anjuna's best hotel, a stylish
set of cottages set around an attractive pool,
although it is starting to look a little worse for
wear. In the far north of Anjuna is **Lotus Inn**
(Zor Vaddo, 0832-227-4015, www.lotusinn.com,
Rs 1,000-Rs 4,500 double), a family-friendly
modern hotel with a pool and a popular
restaurant serving a mix of German and Indian
food. Something different is offered by **Yoga
Magic** (Grand Chinvar Vaddo, near Bobby
Bar, 0832-562-3796, 93705-65717, www.yoga
magic.net), an environmentally friendly, tented
yoga camp (tents Rs 1,200 per person) which
also offers a luxurious room (Rs 5,000 per night)
in the main house.

Resources

Post office
Anjuna Post Office *near Football Grounds
(0832-227-3221).* **Open** 9am-5pm Mon-Fri.

Internet
Sify I-way *next to Tembi Café, Mazal Vaddo
(no phone).* **Open** 9am-9pm daily.

Getting there

The taxi from Tivim takes 25 minutes and costs
Rs 350. From Dabolim Airport, taxis take an
hour and 15 minutes and charge Rs 750. From
Panjim, take the NH-17 toward Mapusa and

Siolim Bridge takes you from Vagator
to Morjim. *See p196.*

turn left near the Green Park Hotel. Follow
the narrow road; Anjuna is signposted.

Vagator and Chapora

As Anjuna steadily turns more mainstream
and family-friendly, the hard core of trance
music pilgrims, dropouts and committed
stoners has shifted further north to the beaches
and headland in the shadow of the rugged
Chapora Fort. The Portuguese rebuilt this
bastion at the turn of the 18th century on the
ruins of a much older fort built by Bijapuri
Sultan Adil Shah (the name Chapora comes
from Shah-pura, or 'Place of the Shah'). In
the early 18th century, the son of the great
Mughal Emperor Aurangzeb holed up here
while scheming to topple his father in a pact
with the enemy Marathas. The fortress is
crumbling to bits and overrun with vegetation,
but the views are magnificent, with the Arabian
Sea on one side and the gorgeous harbour at
the mouth of the Chapora River on the other.
All this makes Chapora Fort one of the best
sunset spots in Goa, often attracting hundreds
of Indian tourists from neighbouring states.
    In recent years, the winding palm-lined lanes
of Chapora and the beaches of 'little' and 'big'
Vagator have become home to a hard-edged
sub-culture of Russians, Israelis, Italians
and other Europeans. Many visitors stay
for months, renting tiny no-frills rooms in
the same local houses each year, watched
over by Goan vigilantes well connected with the
local police. The atmosphere can be a little off-
putting, with hundreds of foreigners jammed
into pocket-sized tavernas and *chai* shops,
openly smoking chillums under the watchful
presence of slightly menacing fix-it men
and local minders. **Big Vagator** is a good

swimming spot, dramatically situated under the ramparts of the fort. It is a lovely beach that gets crowded in season (especially with Indian day-trippers). **Ozran** (aka **Little Vagator**), to the south, is where party folk congregate at beach shacks and the popular Nine Bar.

Where to eat & drink

There's a high turnover of restaurants in this area, but there are a few long-stayers like **Le Bluebird** (Ozran, 0832-227-3695, main course Rs 250, 9am-2pm, 7-11pm daily, closed May-Oct), a remarkably good French restaurant with an excellent (and pricey) wine list. There's also the trippy, somewhat down-at-heel **Baba Yaga** (House 408, Main Road, Chapora, 0832-227-3339, main course Rs 250, 11am-midnight daily) in the middle of Chapora village. A short flight of stairs leads to a rooftop den painted with Russian folk murals where an all-Russian clientele enjoys a huge selection of vodkas along with *pelmenyi* (dumplings) and Ukrainian-style borscht. There's also the local institution, **Primrose Café** (Coutinho Vaddo, 0832-227-3210, main course Rs 100, 9am-midnight daily) that fills up after 10pm. Another good option is **The Alcove** (no phone, main course Rs 200, 9am-9pm daily), a Goan restaurant on the cliff above Ozran.

Nightlife

Evenings kick off at **Nine Bar** (above Little Vagator Beach, no phone, 6-10pm daily) a mini version of Paradiso, with a cliff-top sea view and a packed house of the Indian and European party crowd warming up to some intense trance (what else?). That finishes early, and since the clampdown on raves, open moonlight party venues like Disco Valley and Spaghetti Valley have fallen silent; instead, many opt for the **Primrose Café** (Coutinho Vaddo, 0832-227-3210, 9am-4am daily, entry Rs 100-Rs 200), a grungy indoor trance club with a heavy stoner contingent. The **Hill Top** (Vagator, 98221-51690, closed Apr-Oct) is an isolated hotel with a sprawling garden filled with fluorescent-painted palm trees and is large enough for a few thousand revellers. They still manage the occasional rave; give them a ring to see if they're planning any. Chapora village is quiet late at night, but the friendly, Russian-dominated **Baba Yaga** (House 408, Main Road, Chapora, 0832-227-3339, 11am-1am daily) chills out until late on comfy cushions to an ambient soundtrack.

Where to stay

Chapora and Vagator have a few professionally run guesthouses, including the bright **Bethany Inn** (538/6 Vagator Road, near Chinatown Restaurant, 0832-227-3731, 0832-227-3163 www.bethanyinn.com, Rs 800-Rs 1,200 double), where each room has a private balcony and mini-bar. There are two other options run by the same management: **Julie Jolly** (near Ozran, 0832-227-3357, Rs 800-Rs 1,000 double), and the slightly more upscale **Jolly Jolly**

Beach shacks at **Morjim**.
See p196.

Roma (Vagator Beach Road, 0832-227-3001, Rs 1,000-Rs 1,500 double). To the right of the road leading to Disco Valley is **Leoney's Resort** (0832-227-3634, www.leoneyresort.com, Rs 1,500-Rs 2,600 double), with Indo-Portuguese villas and cottages set around a pool. Leoney's doesn't take advance bookings for high season. Inland, ten minutes drive away, is the atmospheric **Siolim House** (Wadi, 0832-227-2138, www.siolimhouse.com, Rs 3,000-Rs 5,000 double), a converted 200-year old Indo-Portuguese mansion with a beautiful courtyard, huge rooms and a swimming pool. Check their website for 'silent auctions' that can get you a cheaper deal on a room.

Getting there

Taxis from Tivim charge Rs 350 for a 30-minute trip to Chapora. From Dabolim Airport, it's around Rs 750 and takes an hour. To get there from Anjuna, turn left at the crossroads just outside the village.

Morjim & Ashvem

Across the long Siolim Bridge into Pernem district, the landscape shifts into deep countryside. This part of Goa was annexed by the Portuguese much later than the lands to the south, after the chieftain Deshprabhu family accepted a royal title, Viscondes de Pernem, and allowed their holdings to be assimilated into the *Estado da India*. There is a separate character to this part of the 'New Conquests', overwhelmingly Hindu rather than culturally mixed, and far less developed than Bardez district south of the river.

Until the bridge was built in 2002, mass tourism had never made it past the long queues for the ferries across the Chapora River. A few travellers made it to the strip of beach starting at **Morjim** and stretching north into **Ashvem**, but now that it's just a brisk 20-minute drive more development is on the way. The only thing holding back the hordes is the breeding habits of the migratory Olive Ridley Turtle. It's not a large nesting site (Orissa on India's east

Temples across the Ponda

Shri Mahalsa Temple.

For over a century after their arrival in Goa, the Portuguese conquistadors set out to destroy every single Hindu temple they could find, with one particularly zealous officer, Diogo Rodrigues, tearing down over 280 temples across 58 villages in 1567. By the turn of the 17th century, none were left standing.

However, many of the precious idols housed within them were spirited away by loyal devotees, who stole across the rivers towards Ponda, a redoubt that didn't come under Portuguese rule until the 18th century, by which time their religious fervour had waned. There, nestled in thickly forested valleys, new temples went up to house the idols, with the result that, today, Ponda is home to some of Goa's most important Hindu sites.

The most famous of all is the **Shri Mangesh Temple** (Priol, north-west of Ponda on NH-4, open 7am-6.30pm daily), a popular stop for domestic and foreign tourists alike. The resident *shivalingam* (a clay phallus representing Lord Shiva) was brought across the Zuari River from Curtorim and is housed in a temple of Mughal-type domes, baroque flourishes adapted from Goa's churches, and an impressive octagonal tower that can be seen for miles.

coast has far more) but this species is officially endangered and local officials have limited development in the area. In recent years, the influx of mainly Russian travellers has inhibited turtle hatchings to just twice a year, but the government plans to turn the beach into a nature sanctuary, putting paid to plans to develop the village and the beachfront. Even now, this stretch of very broad sands feels empty, with casuarinas and palm groves standing untouched, and traditional fishing boats lining the northern and southern ends of the beach.

Where to eat & drink

The Morjim/Ashvem culinary landscape is dominated by five very different eateries. **Glavfish** (Vithaldas Vaddo, 98812-87433, main course Rs 300, 8am-midnight daily) is an all-Russian hangout where patrons lounge on simple stone slabs and rough wooden benches. Just 100 metres away but radically different in atmosphere is the restaurant at **Montego Bay**

Beach Village (Vithaldas Vaddo, 98221-50847, main course Rs 150, 8am-10pm daily), a Goan family favourite serving excellent food, staffed by friendly and helpful locals. Nearby is **Mojito** (no phone, main course Rs 150, 8am-midnight daily), from the same crew that runs Palolem's iconic Café del Mar, a thatched-roof complex of huts which draws a nice mix of visitors and locals. Further down the road is the elegant, up-market **Ku** (93261-23570, main course Rs. 250, 8am-midnight) a little Balinese-style hotel/restaurant run by a European couple with kids. The pick of the bunch is in a stand of mature coconut palms down the beach in Ashvem. **La Plage** (98221-21712, main course Rs 250, 8.30am-10pm daily) is the best beachside restaurant in Goa, with an outstanding menu including superb carpaccio, zesty ceviche, and much more. Highly recommended.

Where to stay

This stretch of beach offers little outside the informal options of huts and ultra-basic rented

A few miles away is the **Shri Mahalsa Temple** (Mardol, north-west from Ponda off NH-4, 7am-6pm daily). At the end of a marble courtyard, there's a beautiful water tank fed by a freshwater spring, lined with coconut palms and traditional ghats used for ritual bathing (and for doing the locals' laundry).

South-west of Ponda, right on the edge of unbroken jungle, is Goa's largest and perhaps most important Hindu temple devoted to **Shri Shantadurga**, the Goddess of Peace (an avatar of Durga, Lord Shiva's consort), who remains one of Goa's most popular deities and is even venerated by Catholics. The temple was built by the Marathas in 1738, and is influenced by Goan church architecture.

But if you can only visit one temple in Goa, it should be **Tambdi Surla** (seven miles north of Molem in Sanguem Taluka, 30 minutes from Ponda along NH-4, take the left to Sancordem and follow signs, open 6am-4pm daily), a 12th-century survivor that escaped the Portuguese because of its remote, near-inaccessible location. Hewn from massive slabs of basalt that must have been carried across the mountains from the Deccan region beyond, it's a stunning and mysterious relic of the Kadamba era, the home-grown dynasty that ruled Goa until the 14th century.

Shri Shantadurga Temple.

rooms. The warmest welcome is found at **Montego Bay Beach Village** (Vithaldas Vaddo, 98221-50847) which centres around a charming two-bedroom beach house (Rs 2,500-Rs 6,000), but also offers well-appointed tents with attached bathrooms (Rs 2,000-Rs 5,500) and air-conditioned rooms (Rs 2,500-Rs 6,000) with breakfast included. The friendly owner, Alwyn Fernandes, is a mine of information on Morjim. Well up the beach towards Ashvem is **Papa Jolly's** (New Vaddo, 0832-224-4114, www.papajollysgoa.com, Rs 2,500-Rs 10,000 double), run by a resident Punjabi owner who lived for decades in Austria. Children are not welcome.

Resources

Internet
Sify I-way *C-Shell Café, Mendonsa Vaddo (no phone).* **Open** 9am-10pm daily.

Getting there

Taxis from Tivim Station charge Rs 500 for a 40-minute ride to Morjim and Ashvem. From Dabolim Airport, taxis cost Rs 850 and take around an hour-and-a-half. From Panjim, take the NH-17 past Mapusa and turn left at Vrindavan Hospital for Siolim. Cross Siolim Bridge and follow the signs for Morjim. Taxis from Panjim charge around Rs 650 and take about an hour.

Mandrem

Mandrem still offers the secluded beach experience that first brought travellers to Goa, with friendly locals, communal games of football on the beach in the evenings and total quiet by late evening. Many of the miles of broad sand sweeping north towards Arambol are bound by a narrow river running parallel to the ocean, and there's little development here, with a local economy that runs on fishing, toddy-tapping (*see p215* **Toddy and soul**) and a calm, low-key tourist industry. In the centre of the village is the **Ravalnatha Temple**, which contains some centuries-old paintings and carvings including an unusual depiction of Garuda, a divine eagle, here shown with a man's arms.

Where to eat & drink

There are few decent eateries in Mandrem but **Kimaya World Foods** (House 444, Junaswada, 0832-224-7604, 8am-8pm daily), in the centre of Mandrem village, has all the ingredients for a perfect picnic on the beach. Run by the engaging Tanishq Mahajan, Kimaya is a one-stop emporium for homemade products from an emerging local cottage industry in organic food. Grab bunches of peppery rocket, fresh multigrain bread, homemade tofu, pesto, brownies and peanut butter, and head for the beach.

Shalom, namaste

Take a walk on Vagator Beach during peak season, and you find yourself in a parallel Hebrew-speaking universe that could easily fit into the beachscapes of Tel Aviv and Haifa. More than 25,000 Israelis visit Goa during the winter months each year, and large stretches of the north Goan coastline have developed to cater almost exclusively to them.

This long-running cultural intermingling has historical antecedents. The Konkan coastline has ancient links to the Mediterranean Sea, and the commercial activity of Jewish traders in the area has been recorded for more than 2000 years. For example, the Chapel of Jesus of Nazareth at Siridao is no less than a crudely adapted synagogue.

For decades after the Portuguese takeover in 1510, Goa hosted thousands of European Jews (including many recent, forced converts to Christianity, aka *Marranos*) as they fled the Inquisition. Among these newcomers was the great Garcia da Orta, whose pioneering work on the medicines of India introduced a wholly new pharmacology to the West. Da Orta died before the Inquisition was imported into Goa in 1560, but his bones were burned at the stake nonetheless, as Goa quickly drained of its Jewish population; the terrors raged on for two and a half centuries.

In the 1990s, the Jewish presence under the coconut palms of this coast picked up again, as Israel and India renewed diplomatic relations. Tens of thousands of Israelis now head for Goa each year in what has become a national rite-of-passage after the mandatory stint of military service. Many stay on, as part of the countercultural world that survives in Goa. It's a new-age phenomenon with deep roots, these modern-day adventurers are completing an ancient circle that has always linked the Konkan Coast with the shoreline of the Levant.

Crossing the **River Mandovi** in the monsoon.

Where to stay

One of Goa's most beautiful beachfront properties is the secluded **Elsewhere** (*see p190* **Boutique beds**), the converted ancestral home of Mumbai photographer Denzil Sequeira, which also features luxury tents and three newly built guest-houses that mimic the original. Pleasant, but overrun with cats, is **Villa River Cat** (438/1 Junaswada, 0832-224-7928, www.villa rivercat.com, Rs 2,200-Rs 3,200 double), a highly individualistic riverside hotel run by fervent animal lover Rinoo Sehgal. It features 16 intensely decorated rooms, many with balconies and hammocks overlooking the shore, and a great little vantage point overlooking the beach.

Getting there

Taxis from Tivim take around 45 minutes and charge Rs 500. From Dabolim Airport, taxis cost Rs 850 and take just under two hours. From Siolim Bridge, go straight on the 'new road' and look for signs to Mandrem after five-six miles. Taxis from Panjim charge about Rs 600 and take around an hour.

Arambol

Arambol was once the Holy Grail of the later hippie years, the dream beach for travellers seeking the precise location of the middle of nowhere. Arambol is the largest coastal village in Pernem district, with a wide beach clustered with shacks that hosts several thousand visitors a day in high season from November to March. It's become part of the well-beaten track that so many once came here to avoid, with endless lines of travellers hiking up the coastal path to the 'lakeside' beach – an arc of soft sand between the sea and an increasingly polluted lake behind. The lake is bound by thick jungle where naked hippies still sleep under the stars like their 1960s ancestors.

Where to eat & drink

Relax Inn (Socoilo Vaddo, 98223-87618, main course Rs 120, 8am-11pm daily), run by five Goan brothers, is a friendly shack at the northern end of the beach, serving excellent Italian dishes made from recipes handed down by an expatriate chef who has now returned to Italy. Great for seafood is **Fellini's** (Arambol Beach, no phone, main course Rs 200, 11am-11pm daily) a popular Italian restaurant with outstanding homemade gnocchi and wood-fired pizzas. Decent Tibetan and other East Asian food is available at **Rice Bowl** (Socoilo Vaddo, 98507-27329, main course Rs 150, 8am-11pm daily), a Nepali-run restaurant which serves homemade noodles, dumplings and tempura. The new **Café Pacha** (93267-8123/22/21, 11am-midnight daily) has brought a bit of Baga nightlife to Arambol, and hosts ambitious parties every weekend in season.

Where to stay

Arambol's beach huts are basic compared to the sophisticated set-ups available at Palolem. The Naik family rents out over a hundred small huts with basic amenities (some have attached toilets, some do not) scattered across the cliffs on the northern end of the beach, with fabulous sea views. Call or ask at the Naik-run **Relax Inn** (Socoilo Vaddo, 98223-87618, huts Rs 500-Rs 750) for details. Modern, airy rooms are available at the Israeli-run **Lamuella Guesthouse** (Arambol Beach Road, 0832-561-4563, Rs 450-Rs 700 double), the smartest (and most expensive) guesthouse in Arambol.

Clams by the bucketload in **Siolim**.

Goa

Goan grub

*'Please Sir, Mr God of Death
Don't make it my turn today, not today,
There's fish curry for dinner.'*
- Bakibab Borkar, Goan poet

It tells you a lot about Goans that a common way of asking 'How are you?' in Konkani, the local language, is *'Nisteak kitem aslem?'* which translates as: 'What fish did you have today?' Food, particularly seafood, is a Goan obsession, and far removed from North Indian staples like butter chicken and biryani. But what Goans eat today would be almost unrecognisable to a 16th-century Goan. The cuisine was transformed by the arrival of Portuguese colonists, who brought with them a cornucopia of culinary treasures harvested from previous adventures: chillies, tomatoes, potatoes, pumpkins, fruit like guavas, pineapples and chikoos, and cashews; not to mention Iberian garlic sausages, and *garrafãos* of vinegar, wine and olive oil.

As Portuguese influence took hold so did their diet, edging out the traditional cuisine of Saraswat dishes from the Konkan region. The ubiquitous vindaloo (which tastes nothing like the British copy) is a corruption of *vinho e alhos*, a garlicky Portuguese wine-vinegar marinade. *Chouriço*, those chubby links of spiced pork, are a Goan version of the Iberian sausage. *Sorpatel* started off as *Sarabulho*, a Portuguese stew of pork meat and offal.

The Portuguese also introduced dishes and influences from their journeys to South East Asia, Africa and South America: like prawn *balchão* from Myanmar and chicken *cafreal* from Mozambique. Saraswat touches added to the mix as a new Goan cuisine evolved – turmeric, cumin, cinnamon and cloves found their way into Portuguese *assados* or roasts, coconut and semolina showed up in *bolos* (cakes), and the local taste for strong spices led to versions of Portuguese dishes with so much chilli and vinegar that they would have been intolerable to the colonisers' palates.

Today the staple dish remains fish-curry-rice, the exact ingredients of which vary widely from region to region, village to village, and even house to house. For most of the year, Goans tuck into prized estuarine shrimp and tiger prawns, mussels, langoustines, lobsters, pomfrets, kingfish and river perch – and shark in the hot-and-sour *ambotik* curry.

Links of spicy **Goa sausages**.

In the monsoon, deep-sea fishing is banned to allow stocks to replenish, and Goans take to eating the *muddasho* (ladyfish), a slender fish with a buttery taste. Other speciality Goan curries include the mild *caldine*, a children's favourite often made with eggs or vegetables, and the complex, vinegary *xacuti* usually made with chicken, goat meat or beef.

The original Saraswat cuisine did survive as what is now known as 'Gomantak' cooking. Goa's hidden cuisine generally consists of thick-grained, nutty, reddish parboiled rice taken with fish or shellfish that has been curried or fried. It's accompanied by mildly spiced seasonal vegetables, all flavoured with dark palm sugar (jaggery) and tamarind, with lashings of coconut in every form. Mud vessels and wood fires gave the food its characteristic smoky aroma, which is best captured in a steaming bowl of *canjee* (rice gruel) with a wicked piece of mango pickle.

Always leave room for dessert, an area where Goan cuisine truly excels. Along with *bebinca*, a layered cake made with dozens of egg yolks, comes *bolo sans rival*, a cake made with the left-over whites. Many sweet dishes are heavy on the coconut, including the *batika* cake and steamed coconut-jaggery festival favourite *pattoyos*, which come wrapped in a segment of banana leaf.

Goa

Shopping

Down the beach in Khalcha Vaddo is **Arambol Hammocks** (House 564, no phone, www.arambol.com), a cottage industry set-up selling excellent hand-made hammocks (from Rs 1,000) including extra-wide 'flying carpets'.

Resources

Post office

Arambol Post Office, *near Mount Carmel Church (0832-229-7665)*. **Open** 9am-5pm Mon-Fri.

Internet

Famafa Hotel, Khalcha Vaddo (0832-229-2516). **Open** 9am-11pm daily.

Getting there

Taxis from Tivim take an hour and charge Rs 600. From Dabolim Airport taxis cost Rs 850 and take just under two hours. On the 'new road' after Siolim Bridge, look for signs for the Arambol turn-off after 10 miles.

Tiracol

From Arambol, the coastal road climbs to the top of a rugged plateau, then descends through jungle back towards the shoreline and the pristine Tiracol river. Just before the tiny ferry point is **Keri**, a long sliver of shining sand untouched by development. You can spend hours here without seeing another soul, except at weekends when picnickers wander over from neighbouring Maharashtra. High on the headland **Tiracol Fort** stands sentinel over Goa's northern border. Now a heritage hotel, the fort courtyard contains a small, beautiful chapel that is still used by Tiracol villagers three times a week for mass. You can get there via the free ferry across the Tiracol (every half hour from 6.30am to 9.30pm). Built by the Marathas in the 18th century and then snatched by the Portuguese, Tiracol Fort became the base for a disastrous anti-colonial insurrection in 1825, which ended in a bloody rout for the rebels. A plaque in the fort commemorates a later act of anti-colonial resistance in the Gandhian tradition of *satyagraha*, or 'truth-led struggle', by unarmed Goan freedom fighters in 1954. They took the fort and raised an Indian flag, but were later captured after Portuguese troops opened fire, killing two.

Where to stay

In 2004, the **Fort Tiracol Heritage Hotel** (Tiracol, 0832-622-7631, Rs 4,500-Rs 7,000 double) was given a touch of glamour by new management – the owners of the Nilaya Hermitage, the pioneering boutique hotel in Arpora (*see p190* **Boutique beds**). It offers seven well-appointed rooms with a lovely self-contained air of privacy, including two suites, each with a turreted balcony and a superb cliff-top view of the Goan coast. It also has an impressive promenade lined with *charpoys* and tables for alfresco dining, and an excellent restaurant that welcomes day-trippers. It's a little isolated, but a speedboat is on hand to take you to the busier beaches to the south.

Mapusa

A half-hour drive inland from the beaches is Mapusa, the commercial, administrative and transport hub of North Goa. Mapusa is a dusty smudge of urban India amid rich, sprawling agricultural lands, and hosts a raucous market spilling across several acres close to the city's main road. Much of Mapusa can be safely avoided, although the Friday market is lively

Keri Beach.

Goa

Fort Tiracol.

and features an array of local produce trucked in from across the state. A little over seven miles east of the city is **Tivim**, the nearest stop on the Konkan Railway for North Goa's beaches. On the eastern edge of the city is the 'Milagres' ('Miracles') church, **Our Lady of Miracles** (open for mass at 7.30am daily), built on an ancient, sacred site where a Hindu temple once stood and now worshipped at by Goans of all religions.

Where to eat & drink

The Golden Oven (opposite Mapusa Market, 0832-226-4210, 8am-8.30pm Mon-Sat) is a highly popular and attractive bakery-café serving freshly-made baked goods – try the delicious beef patties (Rs 19) or the Goa sausage pizza (Rs 24).

Where to stay

The tourism strip's myriad options are a short drive away. But if you absolutely have to stay in Mapusa, the **GTDC Mapusa Residency** (opposite Kadamba bus stand, Mapusa, 0832-226-2794, Rs 550-Rs 750 double) offers just about adequate en suite rooms, and has a convenient tourist information kiosk in the lobby.

Shopping

Goa's most interesting bookshop lurks in an undistinguished building on the slope of Mapusa Hill. The **Other India Bookshop** (near Mapusa clinic, 0832-226-3306,

www.otherindiabookstore.com, 9am-5pm Mon-Fri, 9am-1pm Sat) has over 1,000 books on Goa and Goan history, organic farming, environmentalism, and what seems like every anti-globalisation text ever written.

Getting there

From Panjim, take the NH-17 straight to Mapusa. Taxis usually charge around Rs 200 and take 20 minutes. From Tivim by taxi, it takes around 20 minutes and costs Rs 300. From Dabolim Airport, it's Rs 650 for the one-hour trip.

Resources

Hospital
Vrindavan Hospital *off NH-17 Highway (0832-225-0022).* **Open** 24 hrs.

Internet
Sify I-way *Angod, near market, opposite the mosque.* **Open** 9am-9pm Mon-Sat.

Police
Mapusa Police Station *near Municipal Gardens, Mapusa.* **Emergency Number** 100.

Post office
Mapusa Post Office *next to Mapusa Police Station (0832-226-2881).* **Open** 9.30am-1pm, 2-5.30pm Mon-Sat.

Tourist information
Goa Tourism Development Corporation Information Office *Mapusa Residency Hotel lobby, opposite Kadamba Bus Stand, Mapusa (0832-226-2390).* **Open** 9.30am-5.30pm Mon-Fri.

Goa

Panjim & Old Goa

Raffish charms and crumbling relics.

The feast day procession leaves from the **Church of Our Lady of Immaculate Conception**.

Despite a real estate boom that has set prices soaring and apartment complexes sprouting on its outskirts, Panjim retains an old-fashioned character that feels quite different from any other state capital in India. The architecture is low-rise, Latinate, with plenty of green spaces, and the riverfront setting ensures a pleasant and breezy atmosphere that feels positively Caribbean. Panjim began to emerge around the late 18th century and by the 1820s had become the bustling administrative centre of the Portuguese *Estado da India*. Beautiful buildings from this period still crowd many of the old neighbourhoods and give the city its character. In recent years many of these architectural jewels have been restored and brightly repainted in characteristically Goan pastel shades.

The city is best explored on foot. Wander along the Mandovi riverfront, take a stroll under the overhanging street arcades of **18th June Road** (named for the day in 1946 when Indian socialist Ram Manohar Lohia called for the Portuguese to be chucked out) and amble through the old quarter of **Fontainhas** – a Latinate labyrinth of sun-kissed ochre and magenta buildings, pocket-sized balconies and tiny plazas, and trees laden with ripening papayas and guavas.

The original colonial capital, now known simply as **Old Goa**, is an area of empty avenues and ancient churches. It's a few kilometres away, linked to modern Panjim by a centuries-old causeway that stretches through backwaters and traditional salt pans, and passes through some of the state's earliest colonial architecture at **Ribandar**.

Panjim

City Centre

Panjim's commercial centre is dominated by the baroque **Church of Our Lady of Immaculate Conception** (*see p206*), near the municipal garden. An impressively large church sitting atop criss-crossing whitewashed stairways, it has become an instantly recognisable symbol of the city, and looms over the road leading to the **Altinho Hill**, with the **Garcia da Orta Garden** on one side. Along the Dada Vaidya Road that hugs the Altinho Hill is the **Mahalaxmi Temple**, the first new Hindu temple to be allowed in Portuguese territory after the Inquisition was finally abandoned in the early 19th century after pressure from the

Goa

British (*see p177* **Bloody inquisitive**). During the time of the holy terrors, the idol of the goddess Mahalaxmi now kept here was trucked around in the hinterlands in a bullock-cart by devotees anxious to save it from desecration. Just down the road is the attractive **Boca de Vaca Spring**, where fresh water flows year-round from a cow'shead spigot.

Panjim's old Latin quarter and heritage district is **Fontainhas**, where strict development laws now preserve hidden gems after senseless demolitions in the 1970s and '80s. A beautifully restored colonial mansion now houses the **Fundaçao Oriente** (Filipe Neri Road, 0832-223-0728), a European NGO founded on a pile of casino lucre from Macao, which works to maintain Goa's colonial-era cultural legacy. Nearby is the neatly maintained heritage inn complex run by the Sequeira-Sukhijia family, that includes **Panjim Pousada**, a restored traditional Hindu home; **Panjim Inn**, a quirky old Goan double-storey house; and the more upmarket **Panjim People's**, formerly a high school.

A short walk along the river leads to two iconic Panjim restaurants: **Horseshoe**, where Chef Vasco Silveira turns out superb Luso-Indian food, and the more modest **Avanti**, serving delicious home-style Goan food with an accent on pork and seafood.

Nearby is the landmark **San Sebastian Chapel**, which houses the large wooden crucifix that once towered over the bloody deliberations at the old Palace of the Inquisition in Old Goa. The collection of altars and paintings here is one of the best in Goa, gathered by refugees who fled the plagues that decimated Old Goa throughout the 17th century. The **Afonso Guesthouse** near here has a rooftop terrace where you can sip coffee and get a bird's-eye view of the neighbourhood. Literally in the middle of the crowded block, accessible only by narrow pathways, is the charming, family-style **Viva Panjim** restaurant.

On the other side of the concrete walkway that crosses the **Ourem River**, a short walk brings you to the ugly concrete high-rise locality called Patto and the **Goa State Archaeological Museum** (*see p206*). A leisurely amble through Fontainhas towards the Mandovi riverfront brings you to the delightful **31st January Road** (named for the date on which the Portuguese republican revolution erupted in 1910) which is lined on both sides with colonial-era buildings, many adorned with public shrines. In the evenings, these icons of Mary and ornate crosses are

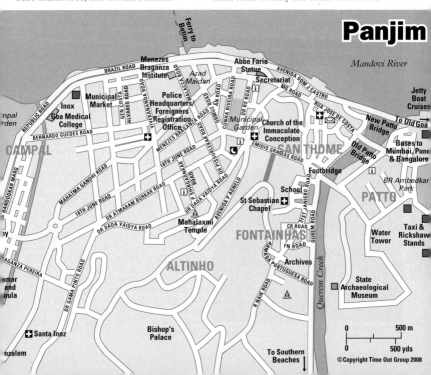

often visited by groups of hymn-singing supplicants, a village tradition that has survived the shift to the city. At the end of the street is the seashell-encrusted entrance to **Hospedaria Venite**, a popular backpacker hotel and restaurant, whose owner, Luis, is always happy to talk about the neighbourhood and Goa's history.

A couple of minutes' walk towards the waterfront, on one side of the Secretariat, is a low, crumbling double-storeyed building still owned by the Mhamai Kamat family, a Hindu clan that (well in the past) made its fortune trading opium, African slaves and socks (yes, socks) throughout the Portuguese colonies. Their 250-year-old ancestral home is now slowly falling apart and is subdivided like a rabbit warren, but you can still peer through open wooden doors to the colonnaded inner courtyard distinctive of palatial Hindu architecture. Right opposite is a statue of **Abbe Faria**, a charismatic 18th-century Goan abbot, political radical and hypnotist (*see p208* **All the fun of the Faria**).

Church of Our Lady of Immaculate Conception

Church Square, Emidio Gracia Road, near Municipal Garden.
A symbol of Portuguese ambition and power when it was built in 1541, with gilded and ornate interiors. The church was then expanded repeatedly, most

St Augustine Tower in Old Goa. *See p211.*

recently in 1871 to accommodate a huge bell that once hung at the Tower of St Augustine in Old Goa. The Church hosts one of the most popular Goan feasts in December, the Feast of Our Lady of the Immaculate Conception, when the nearby square is lit with thousands of candles. *Photo p204.*

Goa State Archaeological Museum

Near the State Bank of India building, Patto.
Open 9.30am-1.15pm, 2-5.30pm Mon-Fri.
Admission free.
A threadbare museum with a random collection of exhibits, but a few intriguing pieces as well, like the huge table used by the Grand Inquisitor in Old Goa, and an unusual antique lottery machine imported from Lisbon by the colonial administration for weekly state lottery draws.

Where to eat & drink

There's a smörgåsbord of eateries in Panjim offering excellent Goan cooking, with an emphasis on super-fresh seafood. In Fontainhas there's **Hotel Avanti** (Rua de Ourem, 0832-242-7179, Mon-Sat, main course Rs 100), one of Panjim's most typical and popular old-fashioned eateries, run by a hard-working couple who possess an expert home-style touch. Nearby is the great-value **Horseshoe** (Rua de Ourem, Fontainhas, 0832-243-1788, closed Sun, main course Rs 150-Rs 200) where Chef Vasco Silveira crafts outstanding Luso-Indian dishes with flavours from his years in Portugal and in the Angolan army. **Viva Panjim** (off 31st January Road, Fontainhas, 0832-242-2405, main course Rs 120) is a backpacker favourite with excellent Goan fare and a sweet courtyard for alfresco dining. The charming, 50-year-old **Hospedaria Venite** (31st January Road, 0832-242-5537, closed Sun, main course Rs 150) has old oak shipwreck timbers for a floor, tables-for-two on balconies and great food. Further down, set in the Old Bus Stand, the unglamorous **Corina Bar & Restaurant** (Near PWD, 0832-242-5740, main course Rs 100) serves outstanding Goan curries to a fervently loyal clientele. Near the town centre, the popular **Ritz Classic Family Restaurant** (18th June Road, 0832-564-4796, main course Rs 150) is always packed with Panjimites attracted by its super-fresh seafood at great prices. **Ernesto's** at **Clube Vasco da Gama** (Souza Towers, opposite the Municipal Garden, 98230-15921, closed Sun, main course Rs 100-Rs 150) is hard to beat for atmosphere as well as food; a relaxed social club with views of the Municipal Garden (*see p212* **Club Portugal**). For great pastries and snacks, visit the nearby **Mr Baker** (Jesuit House, opposite Municipal Garden, 0832-222-4622, closed Sun), a landmark Panjim bakery since 1922. Try the cashew

Goa

The heritage **Panjim People's** hotel.

drops, fantastically addictive little nut meringues invented by the owner, Delia Vaz.

Shopping

In Fontainhas, **Velha Goa** (4/191 Rua de Ourem, 0832-242-6628, www.costavin.com) sells *azulejos*, hand-painted tiles made in the Iberian tradition, and has a nearby studio where you can watch their artisans at work. Not far away, **Sosa's** (E245, Rua de Ourem, 0832-222-8063) offers clothes by top Indian designers, including funky retro designs by Goa's Savio Jon, all at reasonable prices. Make a quick trip to Lisbon by popping into **A Nau** (Jesuit House, near Municipal Garden, 0832-222-4567), a cheerful store filled with Portuguese food and drink imports. Over at Azad Maidan, **UK Traders** (0832-242-7172) sells super Goa-grown cashew nuts for around Rs 300 per kilo.

Where to stay

The **Directorate of Tourism** (Rua de Ourem, Patto, 0832-222-6515) has a list of private homes open to paying guests. The Fontainhas heritage district offers several attractive places to stay, including the family-run **Afonso Guesthouse** (San Sebastian Chapel Square, 0832-222-2359, Rs 600-Rs 700 double) with an attractive terrace. Nearby are the **Panjim Inn**, **Panjim People's** and **Panjim Pousada** (31st January Road, 0832-222-6523, www.panjiminn.com, Rs 2,000-Rs 5,500 double), three atmospheric heritage hotels with the same management, nestled together at a crossroads in the heart of the district. Near the centre of Panjim is **Manvin's Hotel** (Souza Towers, opposite Municipal Gardens, 0832-222-4412, Rs 1,000 double), an unremarkable hotel with basic rooms but pleasant river views. The modern **Nova Goa** (Borkar Road, 0832-222-6231, www.hotelnovagoa.com, Rs 2,500 double) offers a good location and excellent value in the centre of town.

Getting there

From Dabolim airport, pre-paid taxis for a ride into Panjim can be hired from a counter just outside the arrivals hall for around Rs 500. The nearest Konkan Railway stop to Panjim is Karmali (also called Carambolim) about 13 kilometres away. Taxis charge Rs 200-Rs 250, autorickshaws Rs 150-Rs 200 for a ride to Panjim.

The Waterfront

The Mandovi riverfront road that links the district of **Sao Tome** to the rest of Panjim, and then to **Campal** and **Miramar** is named after Dayanand Bandodkar, Goa's charismatic first chief minister after local government was established in 1963. A pleasant riverfront walkway runs along almost the entire length from the quayside where innumerable brightly lit tourist cruisers are berthed. Near here the waterfront is dominated by the **Idalcao Palace**, now known as the **Old Secretariat** (*see p208*), an imposing 400-year-old mansion. Further down D Bandodkar Marg is the **Mandovi Hotel**, once the city's premier hotel and still good value accommodation. Nearby is the somewhat down-at-heel **Central Library** (the oldest public library in Asia) and the **Menezes-Braganza Institute**, occupying one corner of a massive structure that also houses a dozen government offices and the Panjim police headquarters. Just outside is **Azad Maidan**, a cheerful open space teeming with schoolboys playing cricket through the afternoon. It holds a pavilion of Corinthian columns, salvaged from Old Goa, which shade a **memorial** to **Tristao Braganza Cunha**, an important Goan anti-colonial freedom fighter. Further up on DB Road is the vibrant **Municipal Market** (*see p210*), still holding on to its traditional patch in the face of efforts to shift vendors to a new building. Slightly further on, the recently renovated **Goa Medical College Heritage District** includes some of the cinema infrastructure that's used for the annual International Film Festival of India.

The pretty, aristocratic locality of **Campal** houses a set of the grandest houses in the city. They're all out of bounds for visitors, but an upper floor of one has been converted by Goan designer **Wendell Rodricks** (*see p210*) into an airy boutique selling elegant couture and all kinds of accessories from furniture to skin cream. Across the road stands a statue of **Francis Luis Gomes**, an eloquent orator who was the lone Goan representative in the Portuguese parliament, and argued passionately for pan-Indian nationalism

Goa

50 years before the freedom movement began in the rest of the country.

The statue overlooks the entrance to the **Campal Children's Park**, a beautifully situated public garden that spreads right up to the bank of the river under the shade of hundreds of casuarina trees. It's a great place to people-watch in the evenings, with Goan families from across the social spectrum happily wandering the curving pathways and hoisting ecstatic youngsters onto swings and slides. A similar riverfront garden is located a bit further down the road in the grounds of the **Kala Academy** (D Bandodkar Marg, Campal, 0832-242-0451, open 9am-9pm daily), where you can buy a cup of coffee for Rs 5, and relax on lawns and benches overlooking the river. The complex was designed by Charles Correa, the internationally-renowned Goan architect. It's a couple of kilometres on to **Miramar Beach**. The beach is broadest right off **Miramar Circle** where middle-class Panjimites gather every evening for sunsets, walks in the fresh breeze and streetside snacks. Unfortunately the water isn't clean enough for swimming, but the beach is long and pretty,

All the fun of the Faria

On the Panjim waterfront near the Secretariat building stands a 60-year-old bronze statue of **Jose Custodio Faria** looming with his arms outstretched over a hypnotised woman. It's an unusual piece of public art celebrating an unusual man. Faria was an abbot, military adventurer and pioneering 18th-century hypnotist, and one of the first Indians to become famous in the West.

Faria was born in Candolim in 1746. At that time, the priesthood was the only career with any prospects for ambitious Goans, and the young Faria followed his father into the Church. Sensing that the young man's prodigious intellect and charisma would be stifled in the colonies, Faria's father took him to Europe, where he was enrolled in Rome's elite Propaganda Fide college. Within a few years, his studies in theology had made him famous. He was invited by the Pope to deliver a Pentecost sermon at the Sistine Chapel, and soon after to preside over mass at the royal Portuguese Court at the Queluz Palace near Lisbon. Faria was struck with stage-fright at the sight of the queen and her dazzling courtiers, but a strange whispered phrase in Konkani from his father – '*Hi sogli bhaji, kathor re bhaji*' ('They're all vegetables, just cut the vegetables') – unfroze the young abbot. It was an early lesson in the power of suggestion that set Faria on the path to groundbreaking ideas about hypnotism.

Historical details are sketchy, but Faria and his father were later discovered plotting to expel the Portuguese from Goa and were forced to flee the Portuguese Court, turning up in 1787 in revolutionary France. There Faria plunged headlong into the turmoil, commanding a battalion in a campaign against the anti-Royalist National Convention, which was crushed by the young Napoleon Bonaparte, before he was locked up in the Bastille. During his time in jail, Faria supposedly invented the modern version of the game of draughts, further developed his scientific study of hypnotism and became so notorious that Alexandre Dumas even included a fictional version of him as the 'mad abbe' in *The Count of Monte Cristo*.

Faria emerged from prison at the start of the 19th century to engage in an acrimonious public debate with Anton Mesmer about the nature of hypnosis. The Frenchman had popularised the theory that hypnosis was the result of an exceptional 'animal magnetism' exuded by the hypnotist. Faria challenged this, declaring that the hypnotist merely implanted suggestions in the mind of the subject, and that hypnosis was a kind of pact in which the subject's own imagination was paramount. Faria's idea was later proved essentially correct, and is now known as 'post-hypnotic suggestion'. But although Faria provided a crucial insight that underpins modern psychoanalysis, it is his rival Mesmer who remains celebrated in the West with the word 'mesmerise'. Guess 'faria-ise' doesn't roll off the tongue quite as easily.

Monte Music Festival. *See p213.*

with sweeping views of the mouth of the Mandovi River and the Aguada headland.

A few miles further down the riverfront highway is Dona Paula, home to the huge **National Institute of Oceanography** at Dona Paula Circle (0832-245-0450, public science seminars every Thursday) a world-class research institute and the leading scientific authority on the biology of the Indian Ocean. Nearby is the tiny **British Cemetery** left over from a brief occupation during the Napoleonic Wars, and restored after a chance visit by Margaret Thatcher a couple of decades ago. Further up, the road leads to the **Cabo Raj Nivas** – the mansion of the state Governor. The complex includes a magnificently situated chapel on a promontory between the Zuari and Mandovi rivers. Visitors can only enter for Sunday services (from 8am) and Midnight Mass on Christmas Eve. The effort is worth it for the location, the beautiful chapel and a rousing choir considered the best in Goa.

Idalcao Palace/Old Secretariat
Panjim Waterfront.
A mansion built as a summer palace in the early 16th century by the Bijapuri ruler Yusuf Adil Shah. It stood virtually isolated on the island for centuries until Panjim began to grow around it under the rule of the Portuguese, who used it as the seat of the viceroys of the Portuguese East Indies for over a century. The grand arch over the main entrance used to carry the viceroy's ornate crest; it now displays India's national symbol, the Ashoka Chakra. Plans are underway to convert it into a museum.

Menezes-Braganza Institute
Malacca Road, opposite Azad Maidan. **Open** 9.30am-1pm, 2-5.45pm Mon-Fri. **Admission** free.

Before 1961, the Institute was named after Vasco da Gama and the entranceway still holds a mesmerising floor-to-ceiling mural of hand-painted tiles commemorating the colonisation of the Indies, adorned with stanzas from the epic *Os Lusiades* written by the Portuguese national poet, Luis Vaz de Camoens.

Where to eat & drink

At Azad Maidan, **Delhi Darbar** (0832-222-2544, main course Rs 150-300) is the best of Panjim's tandoori restaurants, with excellent service. Also on the Maidan is **Farm Products** (0832-222-5287), a cute three-seater snack shop run by octogenarian Goan freedom fighter Alvaro Pereira, who serves a clientele of old Panjim characters. Along the waterfront road, Miramar's **Mum's Kitchen** (98221-75559, Main course Rs 200) serves a fascinating menu of dishes from Goa's various culinary traditions, which it calls 'our move to save Goa's cuisine'.

Nightlife

For Indian tourists in Panjim the evening river cruises departing from the Santa Monica pier are a must-do. Boats leave all evening, starting from 5pm, and chug up to the mouth of the Mandovi with an enthusiastically performed song-and-dance routine to entertain passengers en route (Rs 100 per person). Night cruises depart from 8.30pm. Contact the **Goa Tourism Development Corporation** (0832-222-3396, www.goa-tourism.com) for further details. Panjim's only proper nightclub is **O-Zone** (Goa Marriott Resort, Miramar, 0832-246-3333, www.goamarriottresort.com, open from 7pm

Goa

daily, Rs 500 cover charge Sat), a bit on the small side but coolly lit and decked out in white. Open throughout the year, it's popular with Panjim's rich kids but usually comes into its own when there's nothing else to do – in the tourist off-season, from May to September. The newest nightspot in the area is **Ice Cube** (Miramar, 98221-02991, open from 7pm daily), which features live music almost every evening, including a range of international jazz acts. More and better live jazz becomes available a few times a year at an impromptu venue run out of a stately house in Campal by the genial Armando Gonsalves. Check www.heritage jazz.com for listings.

Shopping

Municipal Market

D Bandodkar Marg, Panjim waterfront.
Open dawn to dusk daily.
Lively and crowded, Goa's municipal market is packed with Goa-grown produce like Alphonso, Mankurade, Ilario and Monserrate mangoes and dozens of bananas, from delicate fingerlings to enormous green plantains. Early mornings here are the best time to visit, with fisherwomen in full voice and baskets spilling over with white river prawns, estuarine fish and baby sharks.

Wendell Rodricks Design Space

Campal, near Francis Luis Gomes garden (0832-2238-177, 0832-242-0604/www.wendellrodricks.com).
Open 10am-6.30pm Mon-Sat. **Credit** AmEx, MC, V.
Elegant couture by Goa's most celebrated designer and favourite of the Bollywood set.

Entertainment

A floating casino, the **MS Caravela** (0832-223-4077, Rs 1,300 per person, departs 9pm, no shorts/sandals) sails from the **Fisheries Building** opposite the Mandovi Hotel for a couple of hours of gambling on a short cruise up the river, with a buffet and drinks included in the price. For the die-hard gambler, there's the considerably less atmospheric **Chances**

The **Convent of Santa Monica**.

casino in Dona Paula (Vainguinim Valley Resort, Machado Cove, 0832-245-2201, 11am-4am daily). Alternatively, save your money and check out the latest Bollywood offerings at the **INOX Cinema** (behind Goa Medical College building, Campal, 0832-242-0999), a modern multiplex built for the first International Film Festival of India to be held in Goa, in 2004.

Where to stay

The **Mandovi Hotel** (D Bandodkar Marg, 0832-242-6270, www.hotelmandovigoa.com, Rs 3,000 double) on the riverfront road was once Panjim's most exclusive hotel. These days it's an art deco oldie in need of renovation, but still provides good service and value. It's been supplanted by the **Goa Marriott** (Mandovi waterfront, Miramar, 0832-246-3333, www.goamarriottresort.com, Rs 6,000 double), easily the most luxurious hotel in Panjim and a kind of clubhouse for Goa's moneyed elite, with an unbeatable location on the waterfront. Contending for the top spot is the excellent **Cidade de Goa** (Vainguinim Beach, 0832-245-4545, www.cidadedegoa.com, Rs 4,000 double), with its own private beach. A little cheaper is **Prainha** (Dona Paula 0832-245-3881, www.prainha.com, Rs 2,000-Rs 3,000 double), a cantilevered hotel with a secluded private beach and a lovely outdoor pool.

Old Goa

Old Goa was the original capital of the Portuguese colony, a European-style metropolis whose grand architecture reflected its tremendous power, wealth and prestige. Known as *Goa Dourada* or 'Golden Goa', it made a fortune in spices and slaves. In the Western part of the city lay a huge barracks, the first European-style hospital in Asia, a foundry and a vast arsenal. In the East was its sprawling marketplace and a waterfront slave market, which sent African slaves across Asia. Dominating the centre were churches, cathedrals, monasteries and convents built by the Franciscans, Dominicans, Augustinians and other religious orders. Plague outbreaks in the 17th century forced residents to flee. Today, only the soaring architecture remains.

On the crest of the city's tallest hill sits the **Chapel of Our Lady of the Mount**, one of the earliest Portuguese buildings in Goa, commissioned by Afonso de Albuquerque after he took control of the city in 1510. It's built on the site of a fierce battle between Bijapuri troops and the Portuguese. The chapel has been restored and hosts a classical music festival (*see p213*) every March. Come here

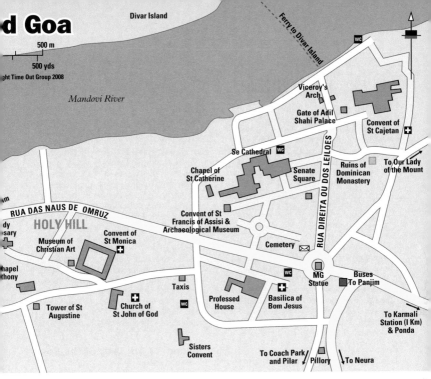

at sunrise to enjoy a magical view of slanting sunlight slowly illuminating the churches' whitewashed façades in the distance below. Perched on the slope of Holy Hill is the fortress-like **Convent of Santa Monica**, the largest convent in Asia. Access is restricted, but if you ask nicely, you might be allowed into the private chapel at the rear, which is covered with stunning 17th-century frescoes. One wing open to the public houses the **Museum of Christian Art** (0832-228-5299) – a beautiful if indifferently curated collection of intricate chalices and other ritual objects, along with a few important Christian paintings.

Opposite the Convent of Santa Monica a turret of laterite stone, now known as the **St Augustine Tower** (*photo p206*), is all that's left of a grand church complex of the Augustinian mission. There were once eight chapels, plus a convent and library, and the imposing tower housed a huge bell that now tolls at the Church of Our Lady of Immaculate Conception in Panjim. Over the centuries the entire complex collapsed, with the last sections crumbling in 1942. All except the tower, which now watches over a team of archaeologists.

Nearby is the **Royal Chapel of St Anthony**, another mid-16th century church (dedicated to the patron saint of Portugal) that fell into decrepitude until it was restored in 1960. The simple painted idol of St Anthony kept here was treated as a full captain in the Portuguese army and each year was taken for a ceremonial ride through Old Goa to collect his officer's wages from the colony's Treasurer.

Just behind is the beautifully detailed **Chapel of Our Lady of the Rosary**, one of the first buildings built by the Portuguese in Goa, on the site of a pitched battle that Afonso de Albuquerque considered the turning point in his campaign for a foothold in the subcontinent. Down the hill along Rua Das Naus de Omruz is the World Heritage Site precinct of the **Basilica of Bom Jesus**, Goa's most famous church and resting place of the body of St Francis Xavier. Each decade, his body is removed and put on public display at the impressive **Se Cathedral** (7am-6pm daily) across the central square from the Basilica of Bom Jesus (*see p177* **Bloody inquisitive**). This huge Dominican-built church remains the largest in Asia, despite one of its towers collapsing after being struck by lightning in the 18th century. Its typically Corinthian interior includes a barrel-vaulted ceiling and two long side aisles, and a masterpiece of a gilded altar.

Across the road towards the riverfront from the Se Cathedral sits another baroque architectural jewel, the **Convent and Church of St Cajetan**. Further on, at the riverfront,

Club Portugal

Colonial-era Panjim lingers on under the high ceilings and slow-spinning fans of the **Clube Vasco da Gama** (*see p206*) near the Municipal Garden. Established in 1909, Clube Vasco was a social club reserved for the Catholic landowners and government officers of the Portuguese-speaking elite until Liberation in 1961. After that, they faced resentment and suspicion from Indian nationalists, and many emigrated first to Portugal and Brazil, and later the UK, Canada and Australia.

Those who stayed behind self-consciously stepped into the shadows: they stopped speaking Portuguese in public, and bent over backwards to prove that they were as Indian as everyone else.

Over 40 years later, such families still reside in the houses they built in the city's sleepy Latinate neighbourhoods of Altinho, Campal, Fontainhas and Sao Tome. And

Clube Vasco remains at the centre of social life. Members still congregate there every day, to while away idle afternoons enjoying the steady breeze through the French windows, prop up the bar with glasses of *feni*, the local cashew liquor, and to listen to live music or sing karaoke in the evenings. Tourists are made more than welcome. The afternoons are particularly atmospheric: the clock ticks slowly, the roast tongue sandwiches on distinctive Goan bread go down well with *feni*, and the next thing you know, it's sunset.

In a newly self-confident India, Portuguese-speaking Panjimites feel a lot less reticent about expressing their hybrid identity. It'll only take a little prodding to hear nostalgic stories of life in Goa before the Indian 'invasion', when goods were imported tax-free from Europe, Panjim's roadways and marketplaces were clean, and law enforcement had an efficient, fascist bite.

---

new arrivals to the colonies first set eyes on the fabled *Goa Dourada* through the granite-faced **Arch of the Viceroys**.

Arch of the Viceroys
Near the riverfront, Old Goa.
This dilapidated stone gateway is the Portuguese equivalent of the Gateway of India built by the British in Mumbai – but this one came first, by 200 years. It was built by Vasco da Gama's great-grandson, Francisco da Gama, who became viceroy of Goa at the end of the 16th century and promptly erected this tribute to his ancestor. It was the main entrance to the city and the symbolic spot where Portuguese supreme commanders of the Indies handed responsibility to their successors.

Basilica of Bom Jesus
Rua das Naus de Ormuz, opposite Se Cathedral, Old Goa. **Open** 7am-6pm daily.
Goa's most well-known church and the one whose façade and layout shows no local influences – it has a clearly Italianate look. The last of the Medicis, Cosimo II, the Grand Duke of Tuscany, financed the opulent altar that now holds the body of St Francis Xavier. It was sculpted by the Florentine artist Giovanni Batista Foggini. He took ten years to carve the three tiers of marble and jasper with intricate scenes from Xavier's life. Inside, in a silver casket, lies the 'incorruptible' body, whose face can be seen through a glass window. The body has become an object of pilgrimage that draws hundreds of thousands to a solemn Exposition held once every decade, with the last one held in 2004.

Chapel of Our Lady of the Rosary
Near St Augustine Tower.
Built by Hindu and Muslim workmen inherited from the Bijapuri kingdom, the church developed a unique hybrid style of eastern flourishes and decorative detail combined with a Western layout. The chapel's style was later widely copied across the new territory, a crucible for the fusion architecture now called Luso-Indian.

Convent & Church of St Cajetan
Rua Direita, near the Arch of the Viceroys, Old Goa.
Built by a team of Italian friars dispatched to India by Pope Urban III, this is the last domed church in Goa, shaped like a Greek cross and supposedly modelled on St Peter's in Rome. At its centre lies a mystery, a large slab of stone that covers a well that supposedly belongs to a Hindu temple that once stood on this spot. The story of the temple is lost to history, as is the reason why the well was given such prominence in its Catholic replacement. The church altar is an exuberant work of art, with angels and cherubs rising to a spectacular gilded crown. In the crypt below, sealed caskets hold the remains of senior Portuguese officials who never made it home.

Where to eat & drink

Star Bar (Near Goa Institute of Management, Ribandar, no phone, main course Rs 100) has bad service, indifferent decor and a somewhat undistinguished location, but its mussels and fish are legendary; Goans will drive across the state for them.

Getting there

Old Goa is about six miles from Panjim on a scenic road alongside the Mandovi River. Taxis routinely charge an exorbitant Rs 300 one-way, autorickshaws Rs 200. Buses leave from the Kadamba bus stand (Patto, opposite Ambedkar Garden) every half-hour. One-way fare to Old Goa is Rs 20.

Festivals

Carnival
Panjim Waterfront. **Date** February.
Latin-flavoured bacchanalia with an afternoon parade of colourful floats along the waterfront. It's followed by a charming fancy-dress ball on the city streets behind.

Monte Music Festival
Chapel of Our Lady of the Mount, Old Goa.
Date March.
One of Goa's best annual events, a festival of Indian and Western classical music. Concerts take full advantage of the stunning setting: both inside the church and in a small amphitheatre nearby. Call Fundaçao Oriente on 0832-243-6108 for details. *Photo p209.*

Shigmo
Panjim Waterfront. **Date** March.
Shigmo is the spring festival celebrated as Holi in other parts of India. Goa's Hindu hinterland takes centre stage on the capital's streets with vibrant, noisy, colourful displays and floats.

International Film Festival of India
Kala Academy/INOX cinema, Campal, Panjim (www.iffigoa.org). **Date** November.
A pleasant Indian version of Cannes. The festival encompasses two weeks of non-stop movie viewing on Panjim's waterfront, and public viewings across the state. In the past, IFFI has been accompanied by open-air screenings on Miramar Beach, displays of public art and a parade of floats to add to the festive atmosphere.

Fontainhas Festival of the Arts
Fontainhas, Panjim. **Date** November.
A week-long event in which the heritage houses of India's only Latin Quarter turn into temporary galleries showcasing Goa's best artists.

Tiatr Festival
Kala Academy. **Date** November
Crowded, super-popular annual competition that functions as a kind of Olympics of Tiatr, the folksy, vaudevillian Konkani musical theatre that retains tremendous popularity in Goa. Call Kala Academy (0832-242-0451) for details.

Feast of Our Lady of the Immaculate Conception
Panjim Church Square. **Date** December 8.

The largest of Panjim's traditional street fairs. Stalls crowd the roads in front of the church selling everything from peanuts to plastic buckets to candles as big as your arm.

Resources

Hospital
Vintage Hospital & Medical Research Centre
Caculo Enclave, St Inez (0832-564-4401/ www.vintage3.com).

Internet
Reliance Infocomm *Campal, near Kala Academy (0832-243-8176).* **Open** 10am-8pm Mon-Sat.

Police
Police Headquarters *Opposite Azad Maidan, Panjim.* **Emergency number** 100.

Post office
Old Tobacco Exchange building, Sao Tome, Panjim. (0832-222-3704/3706). **Open** 9.30am-1pm, 2pm-5.30pm Mon-Sat.

Tourist information
Directorate of Tourism Rua de Ourem, Patto, Panjim. 0832-222-6515. **Open** 9.30am-1.15pm, 2pm-5.45 pm.

Feel the latin vibe, at Panjim's **Carnival**.

Goa

South Goa

The coast is clear.

Locals watch the bullfights in **Benaulim**. *See p219*.

The original charms of India's sunshine state are better showcased in South Goa. It's bigger, less developed, with far more imposing colonial architecture and by far the best beaches. Fifteen miles of shining, uninterrupted white sands stretch from **Cansaulim** to **Mobor** with the spectacular ruins of the **Cabo de Rama Fort** looming over a rugged stretch of coastline further down. In the interior, there are the astounding Mesolithic carvings at **Pansaimol**, resident tigers in the jungle of **Cotigao Wildlife Sanctuary**, and the lush agricultural bounty of the hinterland of **Quepem**.

Rich farmlands and a billion dollars in annual mining income have so far kept South Goa from racing to replicate North Goa's party strip, which means it has been relatively untouched by mass-market charter tourism. It's also the home turf of fading generations of Luso-Indian grandees – the aristocracy whose mansions still line the streets of **Margao**, where Portuguese is still widely spoken. These days, the south's idyllic character is coming under threat from a rash of proposed development. Construction companies and real estate entrepreneurs have snapped up stretches of land all the way down to the Karnataka border, and though it will probably take years

to become as hectic as the north, large-scale development looks inevitable. Until that happens, much of the south offers a glimpse of an older Goa, where farmers work the same fields and orchards that their families have tended for centuries. Spectacular rococo and baroque churches gleam whitewashed amid emerald paddy fields. Old colonial-era houses are still meticulously maintained, and locals retain the gracious culture and beautiful manners that still count in Goa.

Bogmalo

Right in the path of approaching jet-liners, the hidden cove-like beach of Bogmalo is becoming increasingly popular with visitors who want no-frills sun-and-sand holidays without the crowds of the north strip. Goans also come here to party when other beaches get too crowded, and there's a long line of bars trailing up Bogmalo Beach. It's relaxed and uncluttered, with a few family-run hotels and the somewhat dilapidated five-star **Bogmalo Beach Resort**. The beach road ends at **Joet's Bar and Restaurant**, a local institution that started out as a beach shack run by a fisherman serving his day's catch. Now it's a friendly bar and restaurant

Goa

run by his son, with a clean, good-value guesthouse at the back and the neat **Coconut Creek Hotel** a few hundred yards across the road. If you have just one day in Goa and can't stray far from the airport, Bogmalo would be your beach. *Photo p225.*

Where to eat & drink

Joet's Bar and Restaurant
Bogmalo Beach (0832-253-8036). **Open** 8am-midnight. **Main course** Rs 200. **Credit** MC, V.
Clean and bright, with a non-stop rock 'n' roll soundtrack, this is one of Goa's best beachfront hangouts and a favourite with locals, who will drive across the state to while away an evening here.

Entertainment

It's worth taking a 15-minute drive north from Bogmalo to Vasco's Baina Beach for **H2O** (Baina Beach, 0832-394-6052, closed after sunset), which offers a range of watersports including parasailing (Rs 900), kayaking (Rs 150 for 30mins), jet-skiing (Rs 250 for 5mins), glass-bottomed boat rides (Rs 150 for a 30min tour) and speedboat rides (Rs 450 for a six-seater for 5-10mins). The highlight is a Jules Verne-style underwater walk 12 feet down, in a giant fish-bowl helmet (Rs 1,500 for 20mins).

Where to stay

Coconut Creek
Bimut Ward, near St Cosme and Damian Church, Bogmalo (0832-253-8090). **Rates** Rs 3,950 double. **Credit** AmEx, MC, V.
Getting a room here can be tough in peak season because it's heavily booked up by repeat customers. The loyalty is well-deserved: Coconut Creek's staff go the extra mile with warm, friendly service (including keeping the bar open 'until the last guest leaves').

Getting there

A taxi from Dabolim Airport to Bogmalo takes about ten minutes and costs around Rs 200. From Margao Station, it's a 40-minute taxi ride for around Rs 400.

Cansaulim to Betalbatim

South of Bogmalo, the beach turns to rock for a few kilometres before descending onto a 15-mile stretch of white-sand beach from **Cansaulim** to **Betalbatim** and beyond through **Utorda** and **Majorda**. Much like North Goa, the entire beach is lined with palm-thatched restaurant-bar beach shacks, backed by thick coconut palms yielding to acres of well-tended paddy fields. The **Park Hyatt**, in Cansaulim is

arguably the state's most luxurious hotel but unfortunately it is loomed over by the colossal Zuari Agrochemical plant, a hideous industrial complex. **Zeebop by the Sea**, a restaurant in Utorda, is a pretty shack with tables on the sand and perfect sunset views.

Another couple of kilometres down the surf's edge and you're in Betalbatim, another popular hangout for Goans. One big reason is **Martin's Corner**, a kitschy and hugely popular Goan restaurant five minutes' walk from the waterline. If you feel like a change of scene, take a five- to seven-minute ride inland to **Casa Walfrido Antao** (next to the turning for Nanu Resorts), a whimsically ornate Indo-Portuguese home with windows made of oyster shells, unfortunately closed to visitors but worth admiring from the outside.

Where to eat & drink

Martin's Corner
Betalbatim (0832-288-0061). **Open** 11am-3pm, 6.30pm-midnight daily. **Main course** Rs 250. **Credit** MC, V.
A beloved South Goa institution, with a devoted Indian clientele that includes the Indian cricketer Sachin Tendulkar (his favourite dish is the king

Toddy and soul

They're not as common as they once were, but keep an eye on the tops of palm trees for toddy-tappers and if you spot one, ask him for a drink. Toddy is a fermented, mildly alcoholic drink made from the sap of the coconut palm. Using nothing but their hands and feet, and occasionally a strap of cloth for support, toddy-tappers shin up the trunk then cut small holes between the branches and attach clay gourds to collect the sap. The fresh sap, called *neera*, is sweet and colourless, and can be drunk straight away or left to ferment. Within eight hours, it turns into toddy, a white, sweet-sour drink with a strong smell and taste and an alcoholic strength of about five to six per cent. It has to be drunk that day, or it rapidly ferments into a palm vinegar that Goans use as a major ingredient in cooking. A lot of the palm sap collected in Goa is distilled into a palm *feni* (*see p182* **Feni for your thoughts**). There's no organised toddy manufacturing – toddy-tappers are itinerant workers – but ask at your hotel to see if they can arrange to get some for you. It's very cheap, around Rs 40 for a litre bottle.

Goa

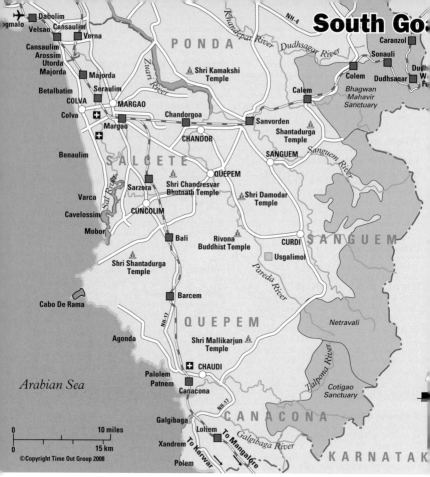

crab, as every waiter is sure to remind you). Dine under arches of red laterite and bamboo thatch under the gaze of caricatures of Goan folk. Serving mostly Goan seafood, Martin's cooking is not outstanding but it is decent – and there's virtually nothing else worthwhile around for miles.

Zeebop by the Sea

Opposite Kenilworth Beach Resort, Utorda Beach (0832-275-5333). **Open** Oct-Apr 10am-10pm daily. **Main course** Rs 200. **Credit** MC, V.

One of the best beach shacks in Goa, on an empty, atmospheric stretch of white-sand beach. It's by far the most popular beach restaurant for a cross-section of Goan families, who pile in on weekends and stay late into the night for the live music.

Where to stay

Despite the presence of a monstrous agrochemical plant nearby, the **Park Hyatt Goa Resort and Spa** in Cansaulim (Arossim

Beach, Cansaulim, 0832-272-1234, www.goa. park.hyatt.com, Rs 9,000 double) has won a clutch of awards for its magnificently landscaped grounds and offers every imaginable facility, including optional private gardens and the largest swimming pool in India. Further south in Utorda, the **Casa Ligorio** (near Kenilworth Beach Resort, Utorda, 0832-275-5405, www.casaligorio.com, Rs 2,500 double) isn't attractive to look at but offers decent value, with nine well-appointed rooms, each with its own balcony, set in pleasant gardens. In Majorda there's the **Kenilworth Beach Resort** (Majorda Beach, 0832-275-4180, www.kenilworthhotels.com, Rs 7000 double), a sprawling five-star just yards from the beach, with a huge swimming pool and a modern spa specialising in ayurvedic massages and treatments. Outstanding facilities make the difference at the **Majorda Beach Resort** (Majorda Beach, 0832-275-4871, www.majordabeachresort.com, Rs 7,500 double), which include separate gymnasiums for men and women, indoor and outdoor pools and squash and tennis courts. An ambitious new entry is **Vivenda dos Palhacos** (Costa Vaddo, Majorda, 0832-322-1119, Rs 5,000-Rs 7,000 double), a converted villa run by the Hayward siblings, British expatriates with a long family connection to India.

Entertainment

The **Go Kart Race Track** (Belloy-Nuvem, just off NH17, 98225-89313, open from 4pm Mon-Sat, all day Sun) is perhaps India's finest go-karting track – a quarter-mile of asphalt with fabulous views of the coastline and the Arabian Sea. Spin around at speeds of up to 40mph in four-stroke, six-horsepower karts. Ten laps cost Rs 120.

Getting there

Taxis from Dabolim Airport or Margao Station to Cansaulim, Utorda or Majorda both take around 20 minutes and cost Rs 300.

Colva

Like Calangute, its spiritual doppelganger in the north, poor old Colva gets a bad rap. Part of the reason is that, just like Calangute, it was once a favoured getaway for the landed elite during the summer months, and has now been taken over by tourists from neighbouring states, who paddle in the surf in their saris and generally behave like the first-time beachgoers they are. But Colva has an outstandingly broad expanse of sand and plenty of room for

everyone. Unlike Calangute and Baga, there are no deckchairs hogging the sand at high-tide mark, and relatively few vendors hawking rugs and massages. Also, it's still a working beach: dozens of fishing boats depart each day from here before dawn. On the downside the dunes have been levelled for no good reason, and the area near Colva bus stand is always strewn with unsightly garbage.

Where to eat & drink

Amici Gelato

Near Colva Police station, before turn-off to Benaulim (9822123173) **Open** 10am-midnight daily. **Ice-cream cone** Rs 100.

Kentuckee

Shop No 28, Colva Beach (0832-278-8107). **Open** 24 hours. **Main course** Rs 200. **Credit** MC, V. The best of an undistinguished scrum of beach-front restaurants and shacks. One of the original Colva institutions, Kentuckee has a decades-old reputation for good seafood.

Where to stay

A great location sets the excellent-value **Longuinho's** (Colva beachfront, 0832-278-8068, www.longuinhos.net, Rs 1,400-Rs 1,700 double) apart from the pack, on a prime spot of beach with lawns leading right up to the sand. The **Star Beach Resort** (near football ground, 0832-278-8166, www.starbeach resortgoa.com, Rs 1,000-Rs 1,400 double) is a newly-built hotel offering good value rooms, many with pleasant views of nearby rice fields, and the best pool in the area. **La Ben** (Colva Beach Road, 0832-278-8040, www.laben.net,

Palolem's **Café Del Mar**. *See p224.*

144 palm-flecked acres
180° ocean views
3 exotic properties

TAJ
Holidays

One incredible holiday

Taj Exotica, Goa

Fort Aguada Beach Resort, Goa

Taj Holiday Village, Goa

Rs 500-Rs 1,000 double) offers clean rooms in a modern building, with an open-air rooftop restaurant. **Soul Vacation** (Colva beachfront, 0832-278-8144, www.soulvacation.in, Rs 5,000-Rs 6,500 double) is a slightly cramped but ambitious 'concept hotel' located close to the beach, with an attached restaurant, **Shalom**, that's rapidly becoming a popular nightspot with young, moneyed visitors to South Goa.

Nightlife

The Boomerang (4th Ward, Colva Beach, 0832-278-8071, open until the last person leaves) has a circular bar right on the beach and attracts a crowd of locals and older Brits with regular live music and karaoke. **Gatsby's** (Colva Beach Road, 0832-278-9745, open 9pm-2am, entry Rs 250 including two drinks) is Colva's only 'nightclub'; a tiny, dark disco with mirrored walls playing house and hip hop for Euro-tourists.

Resources

Internet
Hello Mae *Colva Beach Road (0832-278-0108).* **Open** 7.30am-11pm daily.

Getting around

Taxis from Dabolim Airport take around 45 minutes to Colva and charge Rs 450. From Margao, it's a 15-minute ride for around Rs 150.

Benaulim

According to the *Skanda Purana*, an ancient Hindu text, Goa was created by Lord Parashurama, an avatar of Lord Vishnu. He stood atop the mountains of the Western Ghats and shot an arrow far into the sea, and commanded the waters to retreat to where it landed. That spot is 'Bannali', or 'where the arrow landed' – now named Benaulim. Just 15 years ago, this beach was deserted, used mainly by resident fishermen whose decorated wooden boats still line the sand. But tourism is steadily taking over as Benaulim's main trade as travellers branch out from the behemoth **Taj Exotica** resort to a range of new hotels. New holiday homes and apartment complexes aimed at retirees are mushrooming. Just beyond Benaulim village, the 'monte' (hill) is crested by the **Church of St John the Baptist** (open for mass at 8am daily). Built at the turn of the 16th century, it's one of the prettiest examples of classic neo-Roman church architecture in Goa. Benaulim, like other coastal villages in South Goa displays much enthusiasm for *dhirio*, old-fashioned bull-fighting, which is now strictly banned but continues nevertheless.

Where to eat & drink

As you'd imagine for a working fishing village, Benaulim's many shacks and restaurants all specialise in super-fresh seafood from the catch

The **House of Seven Gables** in Margao. *See p226.*

Goa

Grandee designs

Just like their fellow Iberians, the Spanish colonists in Latin America, the Portuguese administrators of Goa managed their territorial holdings on the lines of the ancient Roman system of *latifunda* – huge landed estates parcelled out to trusted supporters of the regime. Important native collaborators, staunch *mestiço* allies, and loyal compatriots who wished to settle permanently were granted vast estates that functioned as fiefdoms, with all authority ceded directly by fiat. The hybrid aristocrats, called grandees, served as an instant class of intermediary rulers, and as the Portuguese court's interest switched to its colonies in Brazil, they steadily gained in power and influence even beyond Goa to the rest of the Lusophone colonial holdings.

In South Goa, particularly in the rich agricultural lands of Salcete, this ambitious cadre of landowners celebrated their flourishing fortunes by constructing grand, luxurious mansions. The front rooms were designed for spectacular entertainment on the European model, with ballrooms and raised stages for orchestras, and imposing dining rooms for lavish banquets and receptions that were imagined to be exactly like those in faraway Europe.

After Goa's liberation in 1961, land reform took back these vast agricultural holdings and dismantled the feudal system that supported the grand estates. Many of the *palacios* survive in various states of disrepair, with absentee owners now in Portugal or Canada. Of the surviving grand mansions, the gorgeous **Figueiredo Mansion** (House No. 376, Loutolim, donations accepted), a 15-minute drive from Margao, is the most beautiful home open to visitors. Owned by a pair of septuagenarian sisters, Georgina Figueiredo and Maria de Lourdes de Albuquerque, the house retains much of its former grandeur, with magnificent collections of antique furniture and porcelain. One wing, the Heritage Inn (0832-277-7028, oldheritageinn@rediffmail.com, Rs 2,200-Rs 3,150 doubles), is open for paying guests. Or you can sample a taste of the grandee way of life with a full Indo-Portuguese meal (minimum six people, Rs 600 per head) in the formal dining room, complete with liveried service and century-old family crockery.

More imposing still is the spectacular **Menezes-Braganza House** in old Chandor (25 minutes drive from Margao, 0832-278-4201, admission Rs 100). Here gargantuan chandeliers dominate an opulent salon with marble walls and floors, filled with museum-quality antique furniture and Chinese porcelain. The east wing contains a famous private chapel, containing a sacred relic – a sliver of St Francis Xavier's fingernail, encrusted with gold and diamonds.

A great view into the ethos that produced these mansions is available at the 200-year-old **Palacio do Deao** (30 minutes' drive from Margao, opposite Holy Cross Church, Quepem, 98231-75639, www.palaciododeao.com), on the banks of the Kushavati River in Quepem. Built by a clergyman from Braga, Portugal, it lay in ruins until a young Goan couple, Celia and Ruben Vasco da Gama, agreed to take over its upkeep from Church authorities.

Celia and Ruben keep the house open to visitors, and the highlight of each visit is a traditional South Goan meal in an attractive covered courtyard behind the house (10am-6pm Mon-Sat, approx Rs 250 per head). A great place to learn more about these houses and the unique, distinctively hybrid Indo-Portuguese architecture is the excellent **Houses of Goa Museum** (Opposite Nisha's Play School, Torda, Salvador-do-Mundo, 0832-241-0711, Open 10am-7.30pm Tue-Sun, Tickets Rs 100), established by one of India's most prominent architects, Gerard da Cunha.

Palacio do Deao.

of the day. First among equals is **Johncy's Beach Shack** (Benaulim Beach, 0832-277-1390, main course Rs 220, open 7am-1am daily) which features excellent tandoori specialities. **Fiplee's Bar and Restaurant** (off Benaulim Beach Road, near Maria Hall, 0832-277-0123, main course Rs 150, open noon-3pm, 7pm-2am daily) is more of an entertainment magnet than a restaurant. Very popular with locals, it features an air-conditioned pub, a multi-cuisine menu, a cybercafé and 'leisure' zone with snooker tables and dart boards. **Joecon's Garden** (near Taj Exotica, 0832-277-0099, main course Rs 200, open 11am-midnight daily) is another favourite.

Where to stay

Camilson's Beach Resort (Sernabatim Beach Road, Colva, 0832-277-1582, Rs 1,000-Rs 2,500 double) has a great location just off the beach and offers clean double rooms with private terraces and a well-maintained garden. The super-cheap **Succorina Guesthouse** (1711 Vas Vaddo, Benaulim, 0832-277-0365, Rs 200 double) is about as low-budget as you can get, offering total peace and quiet, friendly service and small rooms with distant sea views. A few minutes' walk from the beachfront are the secluded, family-run **Palm Grove Cottages** (Tamdi Mati, 149 Vas Vaddo, Benaulim, 0832-277-0059, www.palmgrove goa.com, Rs 900-Rs 1,200 double) with spacious, airy rooms overlooking the greenery and a good restaurant. Set on over 50 acres of headland, with access to the prettiest part of the beach, is the sprawling **Taj Exotica** resort (Cal Vaddo, Benaulim 0832-277-1234, www.tajhotels.com, Rs 12,000-Rs 18,000 double), offering private villas and luxurious facilities.

Nightlife

Benaulim is quiet in the evenings but **Pedro's** (Benaulim Beach, near the Beach Road, 0832-277-0563) has live music every Tuesday and Saturday evening. Nearby, **Coco's Beach Shack** (Benaulim Beach, 20 yards north of Beach Road, 98224-88079) has live music every Friday and Monday evening. **Joecon's Garden** (near Taj Exotica, 0832-277-0099) has live music every night.

Shopping

A lovely old mansion has been turned into **Manthan** (near Benaulim church, 0832-277-1659, 9.30am-8pm daily), a many-roomed lifestyle boutique that sells everything from carpets to paintings.

Resources

Internet
New Horizon *1595, Beach Road (0832-277-1218/ 1219).* **Open** *9am-11pm daily.*

Getting there

From Dabolim Airport, taxi rides to Benaulim take 50 minutes and cost Rs 500. From Margao it's a 20-minute trip for Rs 200.

Varca, Cavelossim & Mobor

The beachfront runs straight down to **Mobor**, trailing through giant five-star complexes around **Varca** and the charter-tourist destination of **Cavelossim**. The beaches are beautiful but the fishing villages here have never been prosperous, and there's little to do outside the five-star hotels. Beyond Mobor, the beach tapers off at the junction with the Sal River estuary where another cluster of five-stars have sprouted up along with a mess of charmless fast-food outlets, imitation pubs and even an air-conditioned mini-mall.

Where to eat & drink

Outside the five-stars and beach shacks, **Fisherman's Wharf** (near Leela Hotel, Cavelossim, 93261-29810, main course Rs 200, open 11am-midnight daily) is a smart restaurant with tables overlooking the calm Sal River and a pretty wooden interior. Better still, take the free ferry boat across the river to Betul and the charming **Hotel River Sal** (near Cutbona jetty, Betul, 0832-309-6313, main course Rs 150, open 7am-midnight daily) which specialises in fresh seafood straight from the next-door trawler jetty. Instead of the ferry, simply wave from the beach next to the Leela hotel – they'll happily send a boat over for you.

Where to stay

Once part of the Marriott chain, the ostentatious **Ramada Caravela Goa Resort** (Varca Beach Road, Varca, 0832-274-5200, www.caravela beachresort.com, Rs 9,000-Rs 15,000 double) looms over its surroundings with an in-house casino and a nine-hole golf course. A favourite with charter tourists is **Dona Sylvia** (opposite shopping mall, Mobor Village, 0832-287-1321, www.donasylvia.com, Rs 7,000-Rs 13,000 double), with spacious cottages in large, manicured gardens. The **Holiday Inn Resort** (next to the Leela Hotel, Mobor, 0832-287-1303, www.holidayinngoa.com, Rs 6,500-Rs 9,500 double) is an undistinguished five-star but

Goa

The fish is always fresh in South Goa.

located very close to the beach. Arguably ahead of even the Park Hyatt for over-the-top luxury is **The Leela** (Mobor beach, 0832-287-1234, www.ghmhotels.com, Rs 9,000-Rs 20,000 double), a massive hotel complex built despite strong opposition from local environmental activists. It has seven restaurants, a spa, tennis courts and a 12-hole golf course.

Entertainment

Dolphin rides & deep-sea fishing
Boat rides to view the dolphins that frolic in Goan waters (the silvery Indo-Pacific humpbacked dolphin is the most common) are available through most hotels. Expect to pay around Rs 400 per person for an hour and a half on the water in the early morning, leaving around 7am. **Betty's Place** (near Leela Beach, Mobor, 0832 -287-1456, www.bettysgoa.com) offers dolphin boat rides departing at 8am and 10am (Rs 300 per person for around two hours) and deep sea fishing (Rs 500 per person for four hours).

Cycle tours

The British expat-run **Cycle Goa** (Shop 7, Mobor Beach Resort, Cavelossim, 0832-287-1369, 98223-80031, www.cyclegoa.com, 9am-1pm, 2-6pm) conducts a variety of rides, including pretty half-day village tours (Rs 750) and day-long rides pitched at different fitness levels, including a beautiful ride up to the Cabo

de Rama Fort (Rs 1,800). They also do a two-week cycling tour of Goa covering around 25 miles a day. They supply bikes, lunches and a back-up vehicle in case it all gets too much.

Getting there

Taxis from Dabolim Airport to Varca and Cavelossim take around an hour and 15 minutes and cost Rs 650. From Margao, it's a 30-minute ride, costing Rs 400, which takes you along the coast past Benaulim, then off a turn through Varca and Carmona.

Agonda

South of Mobor, a winding coastal road see-saws through valleys cut with rice terraces and coconut and areca nut palm groves. On the way, the road forks right to the forbidding Cabo de Rama fortress, which overlooks the sea from a dramatic headland. Leaving the cape, the road to Palolem cuts through cashew plantations and rice fields until another right turn leading to Agonda. This road is not officially marked, but look for signs advertising beach shacks. Agonda remains one of Goa's best beaches, a small stretch of tranquillity that has escaped major tourist development thanks to strong and organized local opposition. It's perfect for lazy beach days, and from October to April there are a few temporary shacks here offering food and drinks.

Cabo de Rama Fort
Off the Palolem Road.
The Cabo de Rama had already been a prized fortress for centuries when the Portuguese seized it in 1763. According to Hindu mythology, Lord Rama, the hero of the epic *Ramayana*, rested at this fort after being exiled from Ayodhya. A decrepit gateway leads to a copse of fruit trees alive with wide-eyed Hanuman langur monkeys. On one side are the remains of the battlements, still mounted with a rusting cannon, which afford spectacular views up and down the coastline. Walk past the monkeys and tangled vegetation, and you emerge on a small plateau that offers more superb views.

Palolem

The old coastal road is the most enchanting way to arrive in Palolem; turn a corner near the summit of the hill for an unmatched view of the beach's graceful arc far below. Palolem is the dream beach of picture-postcards – a beautiful bay lined with rippling golden sand and fringed by soaring coconut palms, with thick jungle rising from the southern end into the foothills of the Western Ghats. Once a distant point well off the beaten track, today Palolem has become the beach of choice for party-minded young backpackers and independent travellers. Palolem heaves with visitors from October to April, peaking at around 10,000 visitors during Christmas and New Year. Around 50 shacks line the bay like beads on a necklace, many of them run by expat foreigners – it's now easy to find wood-fired pizzas, homemade houmous, and artery-clogging English breakfasts. A leisurely 15-minute amble down the rocky coastline is Patnem, an escape from the crowds of Palolem.

Where to eat & drink

The restaurant scene in Palolem shifts wildly from season to season and even month to month, as itinerant entrepreneurs and chefs pick up and leave whenever they feel like it. One reliable institution is **Smuggler's Inn** (Palolem Beach Road, 98229-86093, main course Rs 250, 9am-10pm daily), a Brit-run eatery with friendly local staff offering decent Euro-fare including roasts, mountains of mashed potatoes and old-fashioned bangers. Another is **Magic View** (Colomb Cove, no phone, main course Rs 150, 10am-10pm daily) on a slope with a great view of the ocean, featuring excellent Italian home cooking including very tasty pizzas. **Home** (Patnem Beach, 0832-264-3916, main course Rs 140, 8.30am-5pm daily) is

an enthusiastically-run guesthouse and café offering real Lavazza coffee, bountiful fresh salads and very good homemade desserts. **Dropadi Beach Restaurant and Bar** (98226-85138, Palolem Beach Road, main course Rs 200, 8am-10pm, Aug-Apr) is a popular eatery for everything from lasagne to tandoori chicken, and is always the most crowded in the area.

Where to stay

The most interesting place to stay in Palolem is **Bhakti Kutir** (south end of Palolem Beach, take the fork right, near the mosque, and look for a sign, 0832-264-3469, www.bhaktikutir. com, Rs 1,200-Rs 2,200 double). Run by an idealistic Goan-German couple, the hotel has a strict environment-friendly philosophy, with non-AC cabanas entirely fashioned from local materials like rice straw, bamboo and mud. Most rooms have Indian-style squat toilets. Cleanse yourself with wheat-grass juice drinks and mud baths at their ayurvedic healing centre, and enjoy equally rejuvenating meals at the attached restaurant, which is one of the best health-food eateries in Goa. Of the beach huts, **Ciaran's Camp** (Palolem Beach, 0832-264-3477, www.ciarans.com, Rs 1,500-Rs 2,500 double) is the most established and attractive, with a smart lawn and well-designed cottages

Pansaimol

In 1993, a group of Goan villagers led a team from the Archaeological Survey of India to a football field-sized shelf of laterite near a bend in the Kushavati River at Pansaimol. Scraping away some of the silt that accumulates in the monsoon months, the villagers revealed ancient carvings of hulking bison and deer, some with shafts of spears sticking from their sides. The astonished archaeologists went on to uncover over 100 carvings spread over

600 square yards, many of them depictions of hunts. They most likely date back to the Upper Paleolithic or Mesolithic eras between 20,000 and 30,000 years ago. Alongside the animals are elegant line etchings of human figures, including an energetic 'dancing woman', and several strange triskelions – concentric rings which archaeologists speculate may have been used as rudimentary clocks. Large reproductions of the carvings are on display at the Goa State Archaeological Museum in Panjim (see p206).

The site is hidden in the rural interior of South Goa about an hour's drive from Margao (around Rs 1,000-Rs 1,200 in a taxi). Take the NH-17 south from Margao to the Tilamol crossroads, from where you head towards Rivona. From Rivona, head south through the tiny village of Colomb (also the last stop for toilets, food and drink) until you see a round red and green Archaeological Survey of India sign that points to the site along a winding dirt track.

Goa

Going wild

In April 2006, an adult 50-kilo male leopard wandered into the heart of residential Miramar in Panjim, causing panic until he was brought down by a tranquilliser dart. But what's most surprising is that it doesn't happen more often. Nature

preserves and sanctuaries cover a fifth of Goa's land; large stretches of which are unspoiled jungle filled with a wide variety of wildlife. In 2007, nature experts declared that Goa had registered the presence of resident tigers for the first time in decades, and border villages are frequently plagued by stray elephants that feast on sugarcane and other crops. Leopards are even more common; every year around half a dozen have to be rescued from wells or are trapped by rangers after eating dogs near human settlements.

Although the state's sanctuaries are open to visitors, most lack basic tourist facilities like trained guides, visitor centres or even bathrooms. Of all Goa's reserves, the

Cotigao Wildlife Sanctuary is perhaps the most accessible and rewarding, and is only 20 minutes from Palolem by road (along the NH-17 to Karwar, entry fees Rs 5 per person, plus Rs 100 car, Rs 50 motorbike, Rs 50 camera charge). Stretching across 33 sq miles of mixed deciduous forest, Cotigao is home to large numbers of gaur (the world's largest kind of cattle), langur and macaque monkeys, wild boar, porcupines, leopards, jackals and even a few sloth bears. Less wild, but a great option for families with kids, is **Bondla** (Ponda, Off NH-4, Rs 5, 9.30am-5.30pm, closed Thursdays), which is Goa's smallest sanctuary at just three sq miles, but contains a wildlife rescue centre that serves as the state's zoo. The animals are looked after well, and there are some excellent specimens to view – sleek leopards with glinting eyes, lots of hulking gaur, and even a magnificent King Cobra – the deadliest snake in the world.

with walk-in showers. The sea-facing cottages command higher prices, at Rs 2,000 to Rs 2,500 a night. A pleasant 12-minute stroll from the beach is **Oceanic** (Temba Vaddo, Palolem, 0832-264-3059, www.hotel-oceanic.com, Rs 1,500-Rs 2,000 double), run by a British expat couple to a good standard, with spacious and clean rooms equipped with mosquito nets. Unlike almost everywhere else in Palolem, it's child-friendly, with a good restaurant and the only swimming pool in the area. Slightly off the beaten track, a couple of minutes' walk from the beach across a bamboo footbridge is **Ordosounsar** (98224-88769, north end of Palolem Beach, Rs 400-Rs 800 cottages), a collection of 12 huts that feel nicely isolated from the rest of Palolem.

Nightlife

Rave parties do happen in and around Palolem – its remoteness makes it easier to evade late-night music bans. Details of when and where are circulated by word of mouth at the innumerable shacks along Palolem Beach. Otherwise, Palolem's nightlife is dedicated to shameless chilling out. Daytime beach parties sometimes happen outside **Café Del Mar**

(Palolem Beach, 98232-76520; *photo p217*), the most popular of Palolem's beach shacks and a sprawling, deeply relaxed wood-and-bamboo den serving hookah pipes, cocktails and snacks to a pounding soundtrack. Further down the beach is the **Cuba Beach Café** (Palolem Beach, 98221-83775), another popular lounge-vibe shack on a wooden platform on the sand, with sofas and chairs and a house guitar.

Resources

Internet
Bliss Travels *near main gate, Palolem Beach. (0832-264-3912).* **Open** 9am-11pm daily. **Rates** Rs 50 per hour.

Getting there

The nearest major train stop for Palolem is Margao. From Margao station you can then take a taxi to Palolem for about Rs 800. The trip takes about an hour. From Dabolim Airport taxis charge Rs 1,000 for the one hour and 45 minute-journey. From Panjim, the cab is around Rs 1,200 and takes an hour-and-a-half.

Goa

Bogmalo Beach. *See p214*.

Margao

Margao is a small city with a big opinion of itself. In the early 20th century, it was a town of opulent mansions that styled itself as a centre for scholars and the arts, and its grandee families prided themselves on their sophistication and refinement. After the 1961 liberation of Goa by Indian troops, many left for Portugal and Brazil and their huge estates were redistributed to tenant farmers. Residents still like to talk of Margao as Goa's second city after Panjim, but today much of Margao's character has been written over by modern concrete sprawl, its narrow streets are choked with traffic and for most people it is only the dusty little town they have to pass through to get to or from the railway station (maybe stopping for a drink on the way).

A walk around the **Largo de Igreja**, the old church square surrounding the impressive **Church of the Holy Spirit** (closed after 11.30am daily) in the centre of town yields a glimmer of Margao's former glory, lined as it is with ornate colonial-era buildings. The baroque church has definitely seen better days, but the façade is still impressive. Down from the church square, the road skirts some old grandee palacios, not open to visitors but worth a look from outside, particularly the so-called **House of Seven Gables** (*photo p219*), a mansion which lost four of its famous pitched roofs after generations of neglect. There's not much else to see in Margao other than the pretty **Chapel of Our Lady of Mercy** on the Monte Hill.

Where to eat & drink

The Margao branch of **Café Tato** (behind Collectorate, 0832-273-6014, main course Rs 30, Open 7am-10pm Mon-Sat,) serves fabulous vegetarian *thalis* and *puri bhaji*. **Banjara** (De Souza Chambers, behind Grace Church, 0832-271-4837, main course Rs 175, 11am-3pm, 6-11pm daily) is the best North Indian restaurant in the south, serving particularly good tandoori breads. A short drive away in neighbouring Raia is **Fernando's Nostalgia** (0832-277-7098, main course Rs 150, 11am-midnight daily), a labour of love of the late Fernando da Costa, who passionately pursued the preservation of old-style, painstakingly-prepared Goan food. The result is the best restaurant in South Goa. Near the old commercial centre, the 60-year-old **Longuinho's** (0832-273-9908, 8.15am-10.30pm daily, main course Rs 200) serves a selection of old-fashioned Goan dishes (try the beef roulade).

Where to stay

Nanutel

Rua Padre Miranda, opposite Clube Harmonia, Margao (0832-270-0900/www.nanuindia.com). **Rates** Rs 1,200 double. **Credit** MC, V.
Nanutel is an option only if you absolutely have to stay in Margao. A standard, uninspiring hotel but one that's located conveniently close to Margao Station and the Apollo Victor Hospital.

Entertainment

Crocodile spotting

Crocodile Station (61 Thana, Cortalim, 98221-27936, 0832-255-0334, Rs 750 per person) runs lazy rides up the ancient Cumbarajua Canal to view the two dozen or so crocodiles lazing around on the mud flats and canal banks. They promise your money back if you don't see a croc – and haven't needed to pay a penny back yet.

Getting there

Margao Station on the Konkan Railway line running from Mumbai to Kerala is the main station for South Goa. Buses run regularly to the station from Panjim (Rs 30, one hour) and Calangute (Rs 50, one hour 30mins). Or you can take a taxi from Panjim to Margao (around Rs 800, 50 minutes) or from Calangute (around Rs 1,000, one hour). Taxis from Dabolim Airport charge around Rs 450 for a 40-minute trip.

Resources

Hospital

Apollo Victor Hospital *near Carmelite Monastery, Aquem, Margao (0832-272-8888).* **Open** 24 hrs.

Internet

Cyberocks *Shop 5, Reliance Residency, Colmarod, Navelim (0832-270-2407).* **Open** 9am-9pm daily.
Phoenix *Apna Bazaar, behind Collector's Office (0832-271-2430).* **Open** 8.45am-9pm Mon-Sat.

Police

Police Station, near Municipal Gardens, Margao. **Emergency number** 100.

Post Office

Margao General Post Office *Municipal Gardens, Margao (0832-271-5791).* **Open** 9.30am-1pm, 2-5.30pm Mon-Sat.

Tourist Information

Goa Tourism Development Corporation Information Office *Margao Residency lobby, behind Municipality building, opposite Municipal Gardens (0832-271-5528).* **Open** 9.30am-5.30pm Mon-Fri.

Directory

Getting Around

By air

Chhatrapati Shivaji International Airport

www.csia.in
International Terminal (2A & 2C)
2681-3000

Mumbai's international airport, recently sold to a private consortium and currently being upgraded, is located off the Western Express Highway about 13 miles north of Mumbai Central and 18 miles from Colaba by road. For transiting to the domestic terminal, there is a free bus that runs between the international and the domestic terminals every 15 minutes.

Domestic Terminal (1A & 1B)
2626-4000/01

The domestic terminal at Santa Cruz is about three miles south of the international terminal. The state-run Air India (formerly Indian Airlines) and Kingfisher Airlines fly out of terminal 1A (under renovation) while Jet Airways and the low-budget carriers operate out of swanky terminal 1B. The domestic airport is well connected to destinations across India. The Brihanmumbai Electric Supply & Transport (BEST) runs the BRTS-2 bus from the domestic terminal to Churchgate through the day. A single fare is Rs 13.

Taxis from the airports

Most five-star hotels offer pick-ups from the airport. If yours doesn't, you can take a pre-paid taxi from a counter at the exit of the arrivals lounge in terminal 2A (you can walk there from 2C), which saves you the trouble of haggling later. The standard charge for a ride into Colaba from the international terminal is Rs 350. Regular taxis and blue air-conditioned taxis called 'cool cabs' are also available from the taxi stand outside. Ignore the shouts from touts and take a place in the queue. A trip from the airport to Colaba in a metered taxi costs around Rs 250-Rs 300 (Rs 400-Rs 450 in a cool cab). Drivers routinely overcharge, demand inflated 'luggage charges' and offer sob stories about having to spend three days in line waiting for a fare. Ask for the tariff card to check the correct fare (*see p229* **Taxis**).

Airlines

Terminals are shown in brackets.

International

Air France-KLM (2C)
2495-4348/www.airfrance.com/in
Air India (2C)
2279-6666/www.airindia.com
Alitalia (2A)
6663-0800/0810/www.alitalia.com
British Airways (2A)
98925-77470/
www.britishairways.com/india
Cathay Pacific (2A)
6657-2222/www.cathaypacific.com
Delta Air Lines (2A)
2283-9712/www.delta.com
El Al Israel Airlines (2C)
2215-4701/www.elal.co.il
Emirates (2C)
4097-4097/www.emirates.com/in
Lufthansa (2A)
6630-1940/www.lufthansa-india.com
Qantas (2A)
2200-7440/www.qantas.com.au
Singapore Airlines (2C)
2202-8316/www.singaporeair.com
South African Airways (2C)
2282-3450/www.flysaa.com
Virgin Atlantic (2A)
6752-3701/02/
www.virgin-atlantic.com

Domestic

Air India (1A)
1-800-180-1407/
www.indianairlines.in
Deccan (1B)
98925-77008/www.airdeccan.net
Go Air (1B)
1800-222-111/www.goair.in
Indigo (1B)
1800-180-3838/www.goindigo.in
Jet Airways (1B)
3989-3333/www.jetairways.com
Kingfisher (1A)
6649-9393/www.flykingfisher.com
Spicejet (1B)
98718-03333/www.spicejet.com

By road

There are three points at which to enter Mumbai by road. The Western Express Highway runs in from the north-west through Borivali to the airports and the western suburbs. If you're coming in on the highway from Pune, you'll come off the bridge from Navi Mumbai into Chembur and then on to the city's central suburbs. For cars, a toll of Rs 25 is levied to take the bridge. The Eastern Express Highway enters from the north through Thane. Two tolls of Rs 10 and Rs 20 are levied on this road if you're in a car.

By train

Mumbai is well connected to most parts of India through the country's extensive railway network. The Western Railway's (2600-2977/www. wr.indianrail.gov.in) termini in the city are Mumbai Central, Dadar, Bandra and Vasai. The Central Railway's (2262-1450/ www.centralrailway online.com) are Chhatrapati Shivaji Terminus, Dadar and Kurla's Lokmanya Tilak Terminus.

Maps

General maps of the city and road maps are available at the Maharashtra Tourism Development Corporation office in Nariman Point (*see p237* **Tourist information**). Other city maps are available at bookstores and at stalls at major railway stations. The most detailed map is published by Eicher, priced Rs 250. For maps, *see pp248-255*.

Mumbai's tourist and business districts are located at its southern tip in Colaba, Fort and Nariman Point. Taxis and buses are a good way to get around this part of the city, although much of Colaba and Fort can be covered on foot. To travel north into the suburbs, especially if you're headed past Dadar, the local train service is far quicker than battling Mumbai's notoriously slow and noisy traffic in a cab. A train from Churchgate to Bandra takes 30 minutes; the same journey from Churchgate by car in rush hour will take at least an hour and a half.

Buses

Mumbai's public bus system is run by the Brihanmumbai Electric Supply & Transport, whose red double- and single-decker buses are marked with big 'BEST' signs on the side. They're efficient across city districts. BEST runs 3,500 buses on 350 routes, carrying 4.5 million passengers every day. A short trip costs Rs 4.

Local trains

Mumbai's suburban train network has three lines – Western, Central and Harbour. The Western line starts from Churchgate and ends at Dahanu Road, which is outside the city limits of Greater Mumbai. The Central and Harbour lines start at Chhatrapati Shivaji Terminus. The Central line has two branches, which extend to Khopoli on the mainland in the south-east and Kasara to the north-east. The Harbour line also has two branches. One runs to Panvel in the north-east, going via Navi Mumbai and Belapur while the other runs to Andheri in the north, running along the Western line from Mahim onwards. Mumbai's trains are reliable, efficient and frequent – you'll rarely wait more than ten minutes for a train. The service carries six million commuters a day and the general compartments are densely packed in rush hours (9-11am,

6-9pm) and can be a highly uncomfortable, sweaty experience. First-class compartments have padded seats and are less crowded because fewer people can afford the fares. There are separate coaches for women, marked 'Ladies 24 hours' which are usually less crowded and highly recommended for women travellers. These coaches are located at the north end of the train and in the middle, next to the general first class compartment. For a map of the suburban railway network, see p256.

Tickets

Travel in the general compartment is cheap, at just Rs 6 from Churchgate to Bandra, for example, jumping to Rs 52 for first-class travel. Tickets are sold only at railway station counters. Return tickets are valid for return travel up to the following day. You can save a lot of time by buying a booklet of travel coupons instead of tickets for individual journeys. Just punch coupons to the value of your ticket in a red machine near the ticket counter before you travel. These machines are often broken, in which case you must apply a rubber stamp, available at the coupon booklet window, on your coupon. Fares for different destinations are displayed on a chart at each station. The railways also offer one-day (Rs 170 first/ Rs 30 second), three-day (Rs 330 first/Rs 90 second) and five-day (Rs 390 first/ Rs 100 second) passes for unlimited travel on all lines. If you're staying for a while, you could buy a monthly or three-month pass for travel in either class, which allows unlimited travel between the stations you choose for great savings. A single route pass allows travel only on either the Central, Western or Harbour line, or you can buy

a 'two-route' or a 'three-route' pass which allows for universal travel.

Autorickshaws

Autorickshaws (often locally called 'ricks' or 'autos') are three-wheeled taxis that operate in the suburbs north from Bandra in the west and Sion in central Mumbai. They are not allowed to ply in South Mumbai. Many rickshaws are mobile art installations, with colourful upholstery, movie-star images adorning the cabins and blaring Hindi film music. The fare is calculated on the basis of the imperial system of measurement, the metric system and waiting time: the minimum is Rs 9 for one mile. Each additional 200metres adds one rupee to the fare. To figure out your total fare at your destination, multiply the number on the meter by ten, and subtract one. So if the meter shows 01.00, the fare is Rs 9; if it reads 03.40, the fare is Rs 33. Between midnight and 5am, there's a 25 per cent night charge.

Taxis

Mumbai's distinctive black-and-yellow Padmini taxis are elderly, but built like tanks. In the 1990s, they were converted from petrol engines to compressed natural gas as an environmental measure. They charge Rs 13 for the first mile and Rs 1.50 for every additional 200mts. As with rickshaws, there's a 25 per cent night charge for travel between midnight and 5am. Although many cabbies are honest, some will hike their prices dramatically for foreign tourists. Ask for the tariff card ('card dikhao') to check. Private operators also run taxi services, referred to as 'call cabs', but these cannot be hailed on the street. Call cabs offer new, air-conditioned vehicles, printed receipts and uniformed drivers, and must be booked at least a few hours in advance.

Gold Cabs *3244-3333*
Meru Cabs *4422-4422*

Long-distance

Coaches

An array of new luxury coach companies have made long-distance bus travel comfortable, though Indian buses still lack toilet facilities. Be forewarned that 'video coaches' will blare Bollywood films almost non-stop until you get to your destination.

Gohil Travels *64/66 Gohil Sadan, SJ Marg, Lower Parel (W) (2496-1211/1113/gohiltravels.com). Lower Parel station.* **Credit** AmEx, MC, V.
Neeta Travels *19 Saraswati Niwas, Rokadia Lane, SVP Road, Borivali (W) (2890-2666/ 2888-3335). Borivali station.* No credit cards.
Raj National Express *Shop No.5, Nimesh Kunj SV Road, opposite Gokul Hotel Borivali (W) (2890-7922).* No credit cards.
Sachin Travels *First Floor, Nirmal Sagar, near Sena Bhavan, next to Aswad Hotel, LJ Road, Shivaji Park, Dadar (2432-3235). Dadar station.* No credit cards.
Swarmeet Travels *41 Ganga Niwas, Ranade Road, Dadar (W) (98697-05166). Dadar station.* No credit cards.
Travel Today *104 Sapna, SK Bole Road, Agar Bazaar, Dadar (W) (2430-3686/2437-0801). Dadar station.* No credit cards.

Trains

Trains are a slow but comfortable way to travel long distances. Seats or berths on popular routes like Mumbai-Goa are often booked weeks in advance in peak season (November-March). For foreign travellers there is a 'foreign tourist quota' of seats that can be bought on the day before or on the day of travel from the Chhatrapati Shivaji Terminus first-floor booking hall (counter 52). It's open from 8am to 8pm Mon-Sat and 11am to 2pm Sun. A passport is required as proof of foreign nationality. US dollars, British pounds and euros are accepted, but if you pay in rupees you may be asked to show a foreign exchange receipt or an ATM slip. Tickets can also be reserved and bought online from www.indianrail.gov.in or irctc.co.in, which offer e-ticketing on certain routes. If you're doing a lot of travelling, you can buy an Indrail pass (from counter 52), which offers unlimited rail travel across India for up to 90 days.

Driving

Indians drive on the left (usually) but driving in Mumbai can be a nerve-racking experience; traffic is heavy and many roads are badly maintained. With few decent pavements, and encroachments on the ones that do exist, pedestrians are forced to walk on the road, and often wander in front of traffic without looking, apparently in the expectation that any approaching motorist will be equipped with good brakes. Motorists make ample use of the horn to inform everybody of their presence, jostling aggressively for position with routine disregard for lanes, traffic signals or other vehicles to the sides or behind. Do not expect other motorists to check what's behind them before pulling out. To drive you will need a valid driving licence and international driving permit, both issued in your home country. Carry them with you whenever you drive. Drink-driving is an offence: drivers found with over 0.03% alcohol in their blood can be prosecuted. Unlike most rules, this is one the traffic police have started taking seriously after a spate of incidents where drunk drivers mowed down pedestrians or homeless people sleeping on the streets. Since June 2007, over 3000 motorists have been fined or imprisoned for drink-driving. It is also an offence to drive without wearing a seatbelt or while using a mobile phone. Traffic is intense during rush hours, usually 9.30am to noon and 5.30pm to 9.30pm.

Car hire

Mumbai doesn't have any agencies that rent out self-drive cars; only chauffer-driven vehicles are available. A typical rental fee is about Rs 1,200 for eight hours or 80km (50 miles), inclusive of driver, fuel and insurance, with surcharges for every additional hour/km. Make sure to check carefully for terms and conditions, and any regional limits on where you can take the vehicle.

Car Care *42 Kedia Apartments, 29F Dongersi Road, Malabar Hill (98210-12685/2367-7724). Grant Road station.* **Open** 24 hrs daily. No credit cards.
Hertz *Mahakali caves road, next to BMC school, Andheri (E) (6570-1692/93).* **Open** 24 hrs daily. **Credit** AmEx, DC, MC, V.
Royal Cars *7/27 Grant Building, Arthur Bunder Road, Colaba (2283-2928/1844). CST or Churchgate stations.* **Open** 24 hrs daily. No credit cards.
Satnam Travels *E3, Green Park, Off New Link Road, Oshiwara, Andheri (W) (98210-32606/6575-8505). Andheri station.* **Open** 24 hrs daily. No credit cards.

Walking

Getting around parts of Mumbai on foot can be difficult – many roads do not have pavements and where they exist they are often broken or obstructed by hawkers. But walking is a really good way to enjoy some of the heritage parts of the city such as Colaba and Fort, where pavements are generally in better condition. Bandra is also best seen on foot though the suburb's pavements aren't always even or well-paved. *Fort Walks* by Sharada Dwivedi and Rahul Mehrotra contains a list of picturesque walks through the Fort district (*see p240* **Books**).

Resources A-Z

Addresses

Addresses usually begin with the flat number of the building or the housing compound, followed by the name of the house or building, followed by the street number and finally the street name and neighbourhood, with an E or W in brackets indicating whether the address is on the eastern or western side of the local railway line. For example, 31 Pluto Building, 54 Turner Road, Bandra (W). Addresses also often contain a reference to a local landmark such as 'opposite Mahalaxmi Racecourse', and a Mumbai postal code, locally called a 'pin number', which is a six-digit number beginning with 4.

Age restrictions

The legal age for drinking varies according to the drink: You have to be 21 to drink beer or wine, and 25 for spirits. In practice, proof of age is rarely asked for. The age of sexual consent is 16; the driving age is 18. It's illegal for shopkeepers to sell cigarettes to anyone under 18, but this too is rarely enforced.

Attitudes & etiquette

Mumbaikars are usually very warm and hospitable towards foreign visitors. Shaking hands is the common greeting, but Indians also touch their palms together in front of the chest and say the Hindi greeting 'Namaste', or 'Namaskaar' in Marathi. This can be a more appropriate way to greet the elders and women from traditional families.

Mainstream society does not look fondly on the idea of a man greeting a woman who is not his wife with a kiss, even on the cheeks, although many upper-class Mumbaikars will have no problem with it – stick to shaking hands and *Namastes* if in doubt. Be aware that some Indian men labour under the idea that Western women are more open to casual sex than their Indian counterparts. This is unlikely to cause serious problems; rapes and sexual assaults against foreign tourists are rare in Mumbai. Still, women travellers should be careful of sending out the wrong signals.

Mumbai is a fairly liberal city and you will see women dressed in a variety of styles. Dress for the occasion: if you're going to a nightclub or a posh restaurant then a tight skirt or a skimpy top is fine; but if you're going for a bus ride or a walk on the beach then dress more conservatively if you don't want to be the focus of a thousand stares. When visiting religious sites, both men and women should cover their arms and legs, and remove their shoes before entering. Don't forget to cover your head before entering a Sikh *gurdwara* or a mosque.

Punctuality is not considered a great virtue in India and you can often expect to be kept waiting, even in business contexts. That's partly because Indians are very flexible with their schedules, which can be an advantage if you need to see someone at short notice. If you're being kept waiting, whether it's for a bus or an official, there is usually little to be gained from showing your anger about the delay – it will only cause resentment and embarrassment. Anticipate from the outset that tasks are likely to take longer than you would expect and just go with the flow.

Although Mumbaikars are in general a friendly lot, this is a big, crowded city and they don't have time to waste on niceties. You may be surprised at the cursory, sometimes rude way in which Mumbaikars deal with servants, wait staff and other people working in service jobs – 'pleases' and 'thank yous' are often not bothered with. On trains, buses and in traffic, Mumbaikars are cut-throat in jostling for an inch of space. Queuing does happen at railway stations, bus stops and banks, but is not universal – just as on the road, the biggest and fastest gets to the front first.

Couriers & shippers

Prices vary considerably, but the price of sending a 5kg package from India to the UK or North America is around Rs 6,000 inclusive of service tax and fuel charges, subject to customs.

Blue Dart

Ground Floor, Khaitan Bhavan, Jamshedji Tata Road, opposite Satyam Collection, Churchgate (2282-2495/www.bluedart.com). Churchgate station. **Open** 10am-8pm Mon-Sat. **Credit** MC, V.

DHL

Worldwide Express, 145A Embassy Centre, Jamnalal Bajaj Road, Nariman Point (2283-7179/7189/ www.dhl.co.in). Churchgate/CST station. **Open** 11am-8pm Mon-Sat. **Credit** AmEx, DC, MC, V.

FedEx

Jeena House, Plot No. 170, Om Nagar, Opposite Pipeline Road, Andheri (E) (6715-3535/www. fedex.com/in). Andheri station. **Open** 9am-7pm Mon-Sat. **No credit cards.** Call 2571-4444 to arrange for the parcel to be picked up.

Customs

Personal items can be brought in duty-free as long as they will be consumed or taken out of the country upon return. Up

Malaria

Malaria is a potentially fatal disease that is spread by the bites of infected mosquitoes. Malaria-carrying mosquitoes breed in Mumbai and Goa around areas with stagnant water, particularly at construction sites. Around 14,000 people a year are infected with malaria in Mumbai, with the riskiest season being the monsoon, from June to September. The typical incubation period is one week to one month, but travellers can fall sick up to one year after being infected, often long after returning home from India.

Symptoms include fever, body aches, chills, sweating, exhaustion, headaches, nausea and vomiting. Typically, malaria attacks last between six to ten hours and repeat after a period of abatement. The onset of malaria can be difficult to spot because the initial symptoms are flu-like and the disease must be diagnosed by a blood test. Consult a doctor immediately if you develop malaria-like symptoms. Severe cases can lead to seizures, comas, fluid in the lungs, hallucinations, kidney failure, respiratory problems and death.

Your chance of becoming infected on a short holiday to Mumbai or Goa are low, but both the UK foreign office and the US state department advise travellers to protect themselves against infection with anti-malarial drugs. Recommended drugs for India include chloroquine (sold under brand names like Nivaquine and Avloclor), taken once a week. There are some chloroquine-resistant strains of malaria present in India, so you should supplement that with a daily dose of proguanil. Start taking your medicine one week before travel and for four weeks after you return. The more expensive Malarone, a new-generation anti-malarial drug, combines atovaquone and proguanil, and is taken daily with food or milk. Start taking it two days before travel and for a week after you return. Bring enough medicine to last the duration of your trip; drugs like proguanil and Malarone will not be easily available.

Some anti-malarial drugs are associated with mild side effects, including stomach pains, mouth ulcers, nausea, itchiness, vomiting, sleep disturbances and headaches. Try switching to a different type if you suffer heavy side effects. Some drugs are not recommended for pregnant women, those with medical problems like epilepsy or those taking other drugs – consult your doctor.

Also protect yourself by using an insect repellent like Odomos. Use insecticide sprays in your room, sleep under a mosquito net, keep windows closed at night and cover your arms and legs. Pyrethroid coils to burn are readily available in India under the brand name Tortoise, as are repellents that can be plugged into electrical sockets (Good Knight Activ+ is particularly effective). Mosquitoes can bite through thin clothing, but you can spray a permethrine insecticide on your clothes, which offers protection for up to two weeks.

to 200 cigarettes or 50 cigars or 250 grams of tobacco and up to two litres of spirits or wine are permitted. For a complete list of duty-free rules see www.cbec.gov.in/travellers.htm.

Disabled

Bad pavements, heavy crowds and intense traffic all make Mumbai a challenge for travellers with disabilities. There is no legislation making it mandatory for shops, restaurants, hotels or office buildings to offer wheelchair access, and most do not. Nor do any of the city's public transport systems offer disabled access.

Drugs

Cannabis and other recreational drugs are illegal in India, and penalties for possession are severe, with prison terms of up to ten years. But that hasn't hampered a widespread drug culture across Mumbai's social classes. Hashish, locally known as *charas*, is more common and popular than grass (*ganja*) and finds its way into the city from Himachal Pradesh and Kashmir. In Colaba, tourists are likely to be approached by dealers peddling hash and heroin, and occasionally cocaine.

Electricity

The Indian domestic electric supply is 230-250V; 50 Hz UK appliances work with just a basic adaptor, but US 110V appliances will need a transformer as well. The plug sockets are round.

Embassies & consulates

Australia 36 Maker Chambers VI, 220 Nariman Point (6669-2000). CST or Churchgate stations. **Open** 9am-5pm Mon-Fri.

Canada *Sixth Floor, Fort House, 221 DN Road, Fort (6749-4444). CST or Churchgate stations.* **Open** 9am-5.30 pm Mon-Thur; 9am-3pm Fri. **Israel** *16th Floor, Earnest House, NCPA Marg, Nariman Point (2282-2822). CST or Churchgate stations.* **Open** 9am-5pm Mon-Thur; 9am-3pm Fri. **Italy** *First Floor, Kanchenjunga, 72 Pedder Road (2380-4071/ http://consmumbai.esteri.it). Grant Road station.* **Open** 10am-1pm Mon-Fri. **South Africa** *Gandhi Mansion, 20 Altamount Road, Cumbala Hill (2351-3725/3726). Grant Road station.* **Open** 8.30am-5pm Mon-Fri. **United Kingdom** *Second Floor, Maker Chambers IV, 222 Jamnalal Bajaj Road, Nariman Point (6650-2222/ www.ukindia.com). CST or Churchgate stations.* **Open** 8am-4pm Mon-Thur; 8am-1pm Fri. **USA** *Lincoln House, 78 Bhulabhai Desai Road, Breach Candy (2363-3611/http://mumbai.usconsulate.gov). Grant Road station.* **Open** 8.30am-5pm Mon-Fri.

Emergencies

To report an emergency, dial 100. For more information, consult www.mumbaipolice.com.

Ambulance *102 (Rs 200) and 1298 (Rs 600-Rs 1,500)*
Children distress line *1098*
Fire Brigade *101*
Mumbai Police *100*
Senior citizen helpline *1090*
Women's helpline *103*

Gay & lesbian

Under Section 377 of the Indian Penal Code, "carnal intercourse against the order of nature" is a crime in India. But the city has a vibrant gay and lesbian community, and activists continue to campaign strongly for a change in the law. Some of these groups meet regularly to discuss issues related to sexuality and gender (*see p147* **Gay & Lesbian**).

Gaybombay *www.gaybombay.org* Gaybombay's aim is to create safe spaces for the gay community in Mumbai. It does this through its website, the gaybombay@yahoogroups.com mailing list, regular meetings on the first, third and fifth Sundays of each month, parties, film screenings, treks and more.
Humsafar Centre *Girish Kumar (administrator), Post Box No 6913,*

Santa Cruz (W) (2667-3800/2665-0547/www.humsafar.org) **Open** noon to 8.30pm Mon-Sat. Humsafar is India's oldest organisation set up for creating support systems for sexual minorities. Its particular focus is communication and support on HIV/AIDS for gay men. It has open events on the second and fourth Sundays of each month.
Lesbians And Bisexuals In Action (LABIA) *98332-78171/ stree.sangam@gmail.com* LABIA is the a city group focusing on the issues of queer and trans-identified women. It has regular meetings and film screenings, brings out a magazine called *Scripts*, conducts actions on current issues relating to queer and trans-identified women, and networks with other activist groups.
Salvation Star *www.salvationstar.com* A group that runs a monthly party event at a bar in South Mumbai, with a focus on trendy, global music.
Samabhavna Society *1800-222-199* Samabhavna is involved with issues of human rights and advocacy for the LGBT community. They have an advocacy cell and a toll-free helpline (in English, Hindi and Marathi).
Symphony In Pink (SIP) *www.symphonyinpink.com* Symphony In Pink is an online discussion group for women only, to discuss issues relevant to lesbian and bisexual women in Mumbai.

Health

Accident & emergency

In case of accidents, call 102 or 1298. Use the name of the hospital if hailing a taxi.

Bombay Hospital *Bombay Hospital Road, New Marine Lines, near Metro Adlabs cinema (2206-7676/www.bombayhospital.com). Marine Lines station.*
Cumballa Hill Hospital & Heart Institute *93/95 August Kranti Marg, Cumballa Hill (2380-3336). Grant Road station.*
Jaslok Hospital *Pedder Road, (2352-3333). Mahalaxmi station.*
JJ Hospital *Ibrahim Rehamatullah Road, Byculla (2373-5555). Byculla station.*
Lilavati Hospital & Research Centre *A791 Bandra Reclamation, Bandra (W) (2642-1111/2655-2222). Bandra station.*
PD Hinduja National Hospital & Medical Research Centre *Veer*

Savarkar Marg, Mahim (2445-2222/2444-9199). Mahim station.

Pharmacies

Open 24-hour

Bombay Hospital Pharmacy *Bombay Hospital, New Marine Lines (2206-7676 ext 356/252). Marine Lines station.*
Dava Bazaar *32 Kakad Arcade, near Bombay Hospital, New Marine Lines (6665-9079/6655-9557). Marine Lines station.*
Hospital Chemist *Prarthna Samaj, Harkishondas Hospital, near Opera House, Charni Road. (2386-9219/2389-5553). Charni Road station.*

Other pharmacies

Bombay Chemists *Kakad Arcade, near Bombay Hospital, New Marine Lines (2200-1173). Marine Lines station.* **Open** 8.30am-11pm daily.
Colaba Chemist *27 Arthur Bunder Road, Glamour Building, Colaba (2284-8029/2283-2848). Churchgate/ CST stations.* **Open** 8am-11pm daily.
Real Chemists *Kakad Arcade, near Bombay Hospital, New Marine Lines (2200-4211). Marine Lines station.* **Open** 8am-10pm daily.
Red Cross Chemist *41/43 Kakad Arcade, near Bombay Hospital, New Marine Lines (6631-5766/2203-2410). Marine Lines station.* **Open** 8am-11pm daily.
RN Kapadia & Company *199B Gopal Bhavan, near Parsi Dairy, Shamaldas Gandhi Marg (2201-9659/2205-4824). Marine Lines station.* **Open** 9am-8.30pm Mon-Sat.
Royal Chemist *Liberty Cinema Building, New Marine Lines (2200-4051/4052). Marine Lines station.* **Open** 8.30am-8.30pm Mon-Sat.

Insurance

India has no reciprocal healthcare agreements with other countries and you should take a medical insurance policy before you travel.

Vaccinations

The most common vaccinations recommended for travel to India are against hepatitis A, typhoid and diptheria. You should also consider taking anti-malarial pills (*see p232* **Malaria**) during your stay. If you're planning a long visit or trips to far-flung rural areas

Directory

you may require additional vaccinations such as rabies, tuberculosis, hepatitis B, yellow fever and Japanese encephalitis. Check with your doctor at least three months before you travel.

Water

Visitors should avoid drinking water straight from the tap. Always drink bottled water or water that has been filtered or boiled or both. The most popular brands of bottled water are Bisleri and Himalayan. Evian is available at high-end restaurants and hotels. Always check the seal – bottles are sometimes refilled with tap water by unscrupulous vendors. Avoid salads unless they've been washed with boiled water and decline ice that hasn't been made with filtered water. Cylindrical ice with a hole running through it is factory-made and generally safe.

Internet

There are cybercafes across the city, many in the Fort area in South Mumbai. Fees vary, but are usually in the range of Rs 20 to Rs 30 for one hour of surfing at good connection speeds. Many hotels are hooked up, but usually at higher rates than those offered by cafés. Local service provider MTNL (mumbai.mtnl.net.in/instant) offers instant dial-up services from any landline using the user's phone number as the username and 'MTNL' as the password. Internet surfing charges (8p-32p per minute at 128 kpbs) are added straight to the user's telephone bill.

Asiatic cyber cafe

New India Assurance Building, next to Asiatic department store, Veer Nariman Road, Churchgate (no phone). Churchgate station. **Open** 10am-8.30pm Mon-Sat.

Cyber Craze

IMC Building compund, near Stadium restaurant, Veer Nariman Road, Churchgate (2284-8776). Churchgate station. **Open** 9.30am-7pm Mon-Sat; 10am-noon Sun.

Satyam Infoline

Prem Court Compound, Next to Samrat, Jamshedji Tata Road, Churchgate (98921-71047). Churchgate station. **Open** 9am-8.30pm Mon-Sat.

Language

Mumbai is the capital of the state of Maharashtra, the dominant language of which is Marathi. Although Marathi is commonly spoken in Mumbai, the lingua franca across the city's mix of communities is a form of Hindi known as Bambaiyya Hindi, which comprises elements of Gujarati, Marathi, Hindi and English, and is a bastardised version of the pure Hindi spoken in north India. English is commonly spoken, sometimes mixed with Hindi and other languages in an argot known as 'Hinglish'. Most public signs and notices across the city, and travel announcements at train stations and airports, are given in English and Hindi. Although Mumbaikars always appreciate efforts by foreign visitors to speak in Hindi and other Indian languages, English is common enough to allow you to get by without them.

Legal help

For legal assistance, contact your consulate or embassy (*see p232*) in the first instance.

Media

Newspapers

Mumbai has a rambunctious daily press in several languages, and is home to India's oldest newspaper, the Gujarati-language *Bombay*

Samachar, founded in 1822. Foreign visitors reading the English-language press are often struck by how flippantly the front pages of the city's broadsheets juxtapose political reportage with celebrity gossip; articles about Liz Hurley's shopping lists and Paris Hilton's latest exploits are common features in even the so-called quality press. The dumbing-down started about a decade ago, when the venerable *Times of India*, founded in 1838, decided to practise what it called 'aspirational journalism' and 'sunshine stories', focusing on beauty contests and society parties, allowing stories about poverty and infrastructure onto its pages only grudgingly. With a circulation of 700,000-plus, the *Times* is by far Mumbai's largest and most influential English-language newspaper.

Until recently, the feisty *Indian Express*, which prides itself on its investigative stories, especially about official corruption, was the *Times*'s only real competition. The *Asian Age*, notable for its wide international coverage (reproduced mainly from the *New York Times*), is weak on local affairs. But 2005 saw the birth of two new newspapers. While the multi-coloured *DNA*, which stands for *Daily News & Analysis* has seemed content to ape the *Times*'s infotainment model, the local edition of the Delhi-based *Hindustan Times* has won fans for putting serious issues back on the agenda. In the last year, it has run a 20-part series on the state of Mumbai's infrastructure, a series on slum rehabilitation scams and consistently reports on issues that really affect citizens.

For many Mumbaikars, the long train journey home after work affords the opportunity to browse through one of the two afternoon tabloids (a broadsheet would be impossible to read in a cramped compartment): the nearly-defunct *Afternoon Despatch and Courier* is mainly read by an older audience who have fond memories of its late founder-editor Behram Contractor, a man who fancied himself as an Indian Art Buchwald and went by the pen name Busybee. *Mid-Day*, meanwhile, is a zesty mixture of shocking crimes, political scandal and showbiz tattle. *Mumbai Mirror* is a tabloid that comes free with the *Times* in the morning, but also has an afternoon edition.

Radio

It's expensive to start up a radio station and more so to keep it running, and private radio stations in India aren't allowed to broadcast news. As a result, Mumbai's young breed of FM stations have been unable to appeal to niche audiences. Most stations seek the widest audience by playing the same songs as their competitors. The FM stations in Mumbai are Radio City 91.1, Big 92.7, Red 93.5, RadioOne 94.3, Radio Mirchi 98.3, All India Radio Gold 100.7, Fever 104, the women-centric Meow 104.8 and All India Radio Rainbow 107.1. All play Hindi film numbers and some English pop.

Television

TV sets started appearing in India only in 1959, and it wasn't until the 9th Asian Games in Delhi in 1982 that colour TV was introduced. But it was only in 1992 that private channels were allowed. Until then, Indian viewers had to make do with the state-run Doordarshan channel, which had a strong focus on education and socio-economic development. New channels MTV, Star Plus, CNN, BBC

and the Hong Kong-based Star TV, gave Indians new options.

Zee TV, the first privately owned Indian channel, brought a bevy of regional channels. A few years later, Discovery and the National Geographic Channel came in. Star also expanded its bouquet, introducing Star World, Star Sports, ESPN and Star Gold, among others. Regional channels flourished along with a multitude of Hindi channels and a few English channels. By the end of the '90s, HBO and Cartoon Network had made their appearance, as had Nickelodeon. MTV, which had become an entirely Hindi music channel, introduced popular international music channel VH1 in 2005.

A boom in news broadcasting in 2003 has left the market crammed with nearly 20 news channels. Of these NDTV (with NDTV India in Hindi and NDTV 24x7 and NDTV Profit in English) employs the most recognisable and experienced faces in Indian broadcast journalism. CNN-IBN formed as a breakaway from NDTV in 2005 and Times Now, a collaboration between the Times Group (which owns the *Times of India*) and Reuters, has novice reporters and sometimes tacky graphics. Other channels such as Headlines Today rely heavily on sensational pieces of gossip, crime and trivia-based news. Regional news channels all follow the trail of Aaj Tak (India Today Group), the first 24-hour Hindi news channel, which spawned a million clones.

In 2007, digital set top boxes were made compulsory in South Mumbai, ending the era of the cablewallah and ushering in crystal clear television reception thanks to direct-to-home providers like Tata Sky (whose remote looks exactly the same as every

other Sky box in the world) and Zee's Dish TV, which gave viewers the choice of subscribing to any or all of the 250-300 channels available on Indian television – everything from Fashion TV to God TV.

Money

India's currency is the rupee (short form Rs, although one rupee is written Re 1), which comprises 100 paise (p). Coins come in 50p, Re 1, Rs 2 and Rs 5 denominations. Paper money comes in denominations of Rs 5, 10, 20, 50, 100, 500 and 1,000. At the time of writing the tourist exchange rate was approximately Rs 80 for £1, Rs 40 for $1 and Rs 60 for €1. Avoid money-changers offering black market rates – it's illegal and they are frequently scamsters looking to short-change their victims.

ATMs

Most banks have 24-hour ATMs, often marked by an 'ATM' sign. They can also be found in shopping malls and some train stations. They dispense rupees only. Some are only for customers of certain banks, so look for the symbol of your card company. Links with international networks like Visa and MasterCard's Cirrus are common. You may be charged a small fee. Many ATMs are guarded by watchmen, but exercise basic caution and discretion if withdrawing large sums.

Banks

The banks below have branches throughout the city (except Barclays).

Barclays
501/503 Ceejay House, Shivsagar Estate, Annie Besant Road, Worli. Lower Parel Station (6719-6575/www.barclays.in). **Taxi** Planetarium **Open** 9.30am-5.30pm Mon-Fri; 9.30am-1.30pm Sat.

Directory

Citibank

Bombay Mutual Building, DN Road, Fort (2269-5757/www.citibank.co.in). CST or Churchgate stations. **Open** 10.30am-2pm Mon-Fri.

HDFC

Ramon House, HT Parekh Marg, off Maharshi Karve Road, 169 Backbay Reclamation, Churchgate station. **Taxi** Aakashwani. **Open** 9.30am-5.15pm Mon-Fri. *(6631-6000/2282-0282).*

HSBC

52/60 MG Road, Flora Fountain, Fort (4042-2424/6680-0001/ www.hsbc.co.in). CST or Churchgate stations. **Open** 9.30am-5pm Mon-Sat.

Standard Chartered

23-25 MG Road, opposite VSNL, Fort (2204-4444). CST or Churchgate stations. **Open** 9am-6pm Mon-Fri; 9am-4pm Sat.

Foreign exchange

ABN Amro Bank

Sakhar Bhavan, near Oberoi Shopping Centre, Nariman Point (2281-8008/www.abnamro.com). Churchgate station. **Open** 10am-7pm Mon-Fri; 10am-3pm Sat.

Thomas Cook

Thomas Cook Building, 324 DN Road, Fort (2204-8556). CST or Churchgate stations. **Open** 9.30am-6pm Mon-Sat. **Other locations** Terminal 2A, Chhatrapati Shivaji International Airport, Andheri (E) (2682-9217). *Andheri station.* **Open** 24 hrs daily.

Credit cards

MasterCard (MC) and Visa (V) are accepted at many shops, restaurants and hotels. Some will also accept American Express (AmEx) cards, while a rare few accept Diners Club (DC) cards. To report a lost or stolen credit card call these 24-hour helplines:

American Express 98926-00800
Diners Club 2834-4653
MasterCard 000-800-100-1087
Visa 000-117-866-765-9644

Natural hazards

Mumbai's famously moderate weather has turned a little nasty in recent years. The days between April and June are increasingly scorching and the monsoon between June and September causes floods every year, while the 2007-'08 winter was the coldest in 50 years. Bring plenty of sunscreen, dress in a T-shirt and loose pants to avoid sweat retention. Drink lots of water, but don't take it straight from the tap. Boil it first or buy bottled water. Mosquitoes are a problem in Mumbai due to the humid weather. Arm yourself with a repellent (like Odomos) and keep windows shut after sunset. For weather averages *see p239*.

Opening hours

General stores open by 10am and close around 8pm. Days vary; many businesses remain open on Sundays. Many liquor stores are shut on Thursdays. Banks generally open at 9.30am and stay open till 5pm on weekdays. On Saturdays, banks close around 2pm and are closed on Sundays.

Postal services

Post is delivered once a day from Monday to Friday. The city's main post office, the General Post Office near Chhatrapati Shivaji Terminus in Fort, is open from 10am till 5pm from Monday to Saturday. Stamps can be bought from post offices and some general stores. Most post offices also rent out post office boxes for a minimum of six months (Rs 250). See www.indiapost.gov.in for other services. *See also p231* **Couriers & Shippers**.

General Post Office *St George Road, behind Chhatrapati Shivaji Terminus, Fort (2262-0956). CST station.* **Open** 10am-5pm Mon-Sat.
Colaba Post Office *SBS Marg, Colaba (2215-3833). CST or Churchgate stations.* **Open** 10am-6pm Mon-Sat.

Safety & security

Mumbai is a remarkably safe city. Muggings, robberies and other serious crimes against tourists are rare, although pickpockets do operate in crowded areas. Still, it's always a good idea to take basic precautions, especially at night. Keep an eye on your luggage when travelling. In an emergency, dial 100.

For up-to-date info on the latest news on safety and security, health issues, local laws and customs, contact your home country's department of foreign affairs. For the UK, see www.fco.gov.uk/travel. For the US, http://travel.state.gov. *See also p233* **Emergencies**.

Smoking

Mumbai is generally tolerant of smoking, and non-smoking areas in public places are rare, although smoking is not permitted on railway station platforms or trains. It's frowned upon to smoke in or near temples and other places of religious importance. Under Indian law, selling cigarettes to persons under the age of 18 years is illegal.

Study

India follows a 15-year education format – four years of primary school, six years of secondary school, followed by two years of higher secondary education. This often precedes a three-year Bachelor's degree. Indian Master's degrees usually take two years. Student visas are granted for the duration of the academic course of study up to five years on the basis of letters of admission from the educational institution.

University of Mumbai

Founded in 1857, the Mumbai University offers a massive number of Master's and diploma courses, but it lags behind in teaching quality.

Fort Campus *Mayo Road, next to Mumbai High Court (2265-2825). CST or Churchgate stations.*

Vidyanagari Campus *Kalina, Santa Cruz (E) (2652-6091/2652-6226). Santa Cruz station.*

Studying music

There are several institutions in Mumbai teaching Hindustani and Carnatic classical music.

Bharatiya Vidya Bhavan's Sangeet Vidyapeeth *KM Munshi Marg, near Wilson College, Girgaum, Chowpatty (2369-8085). Charni Road station.*
Fine Arts School of Music & Dance *Fine Arts Society, Fine Arts Chowk, near Chembur Flyover, RC Marg, Chembur (2522-2988/ www.faschembur.com). Chembur station.*
Jazz India Vocal Institute *nmjazz@vsnl.com.*
Professor Deodhar's School of Indian Music *Mody Chambers, Pt Paluskar Chowk (2382-1940/ www.deodharmusicschool.com). Churney Road station.*
Sangeet Mahabharati *A6, 10th Road, Juhu Scheme, Vile Parle (W) (2620-7283). Vile Parle station.*
University of Mumbai Department of Music *Vidyapeeth Vidyarthi Bhavan, B Road, Churchgate (2204-8665). Churchgate station.*

Telephones

Dialling & codes

The country code for India is 91 and the area code for Mumbai is 022. To call India from abroad, dial the country code and drop the zero of the area code, followed by an eight-digit number, for example 91-22-2123-4567. To call a mobile phone, use only the country code, for example 91-22-98200-98200. You do not need to dial 022 from within the city except when dialling from a mobile phone. Mumbai landline numbers have eight digits. In 2002, MTNL, Mumbai's public sector telecom provider added an extra '2' to the start of all landline numbers, but some people, websites and other sources of information still quote the old seven-digit

numbers. Just add the '2' and the number should work. The area code for Goa is 0832, but if you're calling from a Mumbai landline, dial 95832. Private fixed phone service providers like Tata Indicom and Reliance Infocomm have eight-digit phone numbers beginning with 6 and 3. To find phone numbers, try these 24-hour directory enquiry services:

Just Dial 2888-8888, 2222-2222.
MTNL directory enquiry 197.
Times Infoline 6700-5555.

Calling long distance

Kiosks across the city marked 'STD' (Subscriber Trunk Dialling) and 'ISD' (International Subscriber Dialling) offer facilities to make calls around India and internationally. Rates depend on where you are calling and at what time.

Public phones

There are numerous pay phones around the city and every second shop is likely to have one. Look for yellow 'PCO' (Public Call Office) signboards or small boxy red phones at street stalls and outside shops. Local calls cost Re 1 for 90 seconds.

Mobile phones

Contact your local mobile phone provider for details on roaming facilities in India. Mobile phones are widespread in India. Several providers offer SIM cards with pre-paid/top-up billing. To buy one, you'll need two passport-size photographs and a photocopy of your passport. If you use your phone outside Mumbai city limits, you will be charged roaming rates.

Airtel
*Shop No 4, Yusuf Building, Veer Nariman Road, next to Akbarally's, Fort (98920-98920). Churchgate/ CST stations. **Open** 10am-8pm daily.*

BPL
*Ground Floor, Rajmahal, near Ambassador Hotel, Veer Nariman Road, Churchgate (98210-99800). Churchgate station. **Open** 9am-8pm Mon-Sat.*

Vodafone
*Shop No. 3, Indian Merchant Chambers Building, 76 Veer Nariman Road, Churchgate (98200-98200). Churchgate station. **Open** 10am-7pm Mon-Sat.*

Time

Indian Standard Time is GMT +5 hours and 30 minutes. India does not use Daylight Saving Time.

Tipping

In restaurants, a 5 to 10 per cent tip is appreciated, but not expected. Mumbaikars never tip in taxis and rickshaws.

Toilets

There are two styles of toilets in use in Mumbai – the Western-style toilet and the Indian 'squat' toilet. Squat toilets usually have ribbed areas to place your feet; stand on them and sit with your back to the hole. Although squat toilets take a bit of getting used to, it's worth the effort as the lack of a seat makes them more hygienic to use. Traditionally, toilet paper is not used; Indians usually clean themselves with a mug of water using the left hand. Public toilets in Mumbai are rare and where they exist are poorly maintained and unhygienic. However, most major stores and malls keep their toilets clean.

Tourist information

Maharashtra Tourism Development Corporation
Madame Cama Road, opposite LIC Building, Nariman Point (2202-4627/2202-7762/

Directory

www.maharashtratourism.gov.in).
Churchgate station. **Open** 10am-
5.30pm Mon-Fri; 10am-3pm Sat.

Visas & immigration

All foreign visitors to India
require a visa except for
citizens of Nepal, Bhutan
and the Maldives. There is
no provision for granting
visas upon arrival in India
and you should apply to the
Indian embassy or high
commission in your home
country. Visitors planning
to stay over 180 days must
register with the Foreigners'
Regional Registration Office
within 14 days of arrival.

Depending upon the purpose
of your stay in India, you should
apply for one of the following
visa categories: **Tourist** six
months, multiple entry. Tourist
visas are easy to get (proof of
residence is often enough) but
they cannot be extended or
converted into other visa
types; **Business** valid for
one year or more, multiple
entry. Applications should be
accompanied by a letter from
a sponsoring organisation
indicating the nature of
business, probable duration of
stay, places and organisations
to be visited; **Employment**
valid for one to two years,
multiple entry. Applicants
are required to submit a copy
of a contract of employment;
Student valid for the duration
of the academic course of study
or for a period of five years,
whichever is less. Proof of
admission from an Indian
educational institute is required.
Student visas cannot be
converted; **Transit** issued to
transit passengers for a
maximum of 15 days, single/
double entry; **Missionary**
valid for a non-fixed duration
at the discretion of the
Government of India, single
entry; **Journalist** issued to
professional journalists and

photographers, usually for
three months, single entry;
Conference issued to
attendees of conferences/
seminars/meetings held in
India. Applicants are required
to submit a letter of invitation
from the conference organiser.

Temporary Landing Permits

Temporary Landing Permits
can be granted to foreigners
without visas coming to India
in an emergency such as the
death or hospitalisation of a
relative. A cash payment of
US$40 (Rs 1,600) is required.
Permits can also be granted
to transiting foreigners with
confirmed onward journey
tickets departing within 72
hours, but the immigration
officer will retain the
passenger's passport for the
period. This facility is not
available to citizens of Sri
Lanka, Bangladesh, Pakistan,
Iran, Afghanistan, Somalia,
Nigeria and Ethiopia.

Foreigners' registration

Registration is compulsory
for all foreigners intending to
stay in India for more than 180
days. It should be done within
14 days of arrival.

Foreigners' Regional Registration Office
*Third Floor, Special Branch Building,
Badruddin Tayabji Lane, behind St
Xavier's College, Fort (2262-1169).
CST or Marine Lines stations.*

Weights & measures

India uses the metric system.
Indians also commonly use
the terms lakh for 100,000
and crore for 10,000,000.
For example, 'Rs 1 million'
is usually written as 'Rs 10
lakh', and 'Rs 1 billion' is
written as 'Rs 100 crore'.

What to take

Mumbai has a tropical climate,
so pack light summer clothes,
but also take a thin sweater or
thick shirt for cool January and
February evenings. Clothes
and shoes are widely available
at cheap prices but with a
limited range in larger shoe
sizes for men. The sun is
bright and burning, so bring a
hat, sunglasses and sunscreen.
Open shoes or sandals are a
good option, but closed shoes
are a must if you're coming
in the monsoon, between
June and September, as is an
umbrella (easy to purchase in
Mumbai). Foreign tourists are
notorious among Mumbaikars
for looking unkempt and
dirty; Indians always make
an effort to look neat and you
should pack at least one smart
ensemble for going out or
for visiting an Indian home.

Many medicines are
available in Mumbai over the
counter without a prescription,
so only bring specialised
personal medication.
Essentials include luggage
locks (bicycle locks are good
for securing luggage on long
train journeys), a money belt,
insect repellent, photocopies
of important documents like
passports, spare batteries and
an electrical adaptor. You
might also consider bringing
candles, a penknife (put it
in your check-in luggage),
a phrasebook, toiletries,
sanitary towels and tampons,
and an anti-bacterial hand gel.

When to go

Climate

The 'winter', from December
to February, is generally
considered the most pleasant
time to visit Mumbai, when
average daytime temperatures
dip to around 24°C (75°F) with
low humidity. It can get very
hot and humid in April and

May, when temperatures peak at 35°C (95°F). In June, the monsoon begins, bringing torrential rain and intermittent flooding across the city right through until September, with the heaviest rains in spurts in July and August. In October, the temperature and humidity rises again after the monsoon, cooling off by early December.

Public holidays

Republic Day 26 Jan.
Mahashivratri 23 Feb 2009; 12 Feb 2010.
Id-e-Milad 9 Mar 2009; Feb 26 2010.
Holi 11-12 Mar 2009; 1-2 Mar 2010.
Mahavir Jayanti 7 Apr 2009; 28 Apr 2010.
Good Friday 10 Apr 2009; 2 April 2010.
Ambedkar Jayanti 14 Apr.
Maharashtra Day 1 May.
Buddha Purnima 8 May 2009; 27 May 2010.
Independence Day 15 Aug.
Parsi New Year 19 Aug.
Ganesh Chaturthi 3 Sept 2008; 23 August 2009; 11 Sept 2010.
Mahatma Gandhi Jayanti 2 Oct.
Id ul Fitr or Ramzan Eid 2 Oct 2008; 21 Sept 2009.
Dussera 9 Oct 2008; 28 Sept 2009; 17 Oct 2010.
Diwali 28 Oct 2008; 17 Oct 2009; 5 Nov 2010.
Bhaubeej 30 Oct 2008.
Guru Nanak Jayanti 13 Nov 2008; 2 Nov 2009.
Bakri Id 9 Dec 2008.
Muharram 18 Dec 2009; 7 Dec 2010.
Christmas 25 Dec.

Weather averages

Mumbai

	Max (°C)	Min (°C)	Rainfall (mm)
January	30.6	20.1	0.0
February	30.7	21.7	4.2
March	32.4	23.8	0.0
April	33.3	25.9	0.0
May	34.2	27.9	0.7
June	32.7	26.6	803.3
July	30.5	26.1	524.8
August	29.9	25.3	687.4
September	30.4	25.2	420.5
October	33.3	24.5	0.0
November	33.2	23.1	2.4
December	32.0	21.2	0.0

Panjim

	Max (°C)	Min (°C)	Rainfall (mm)
January	33.4	20.2	0.0
February	32.7	20.6	0.0
March	32.6	23.5	0.0
April	33.8	26.3	0.0
May	34.1	26.2	93.8
June	30.4	24.8	1077.3
July	29.5	24.5	688.6
August	29.1	24.1	887.0
September	29.5	24.0	763.2
October	31.6	24.1	81.9
November	33.4	21.2	75.6
December	33.4	20.9	0.7

Women

Mumbai's women are not shrinking violets. Many are independent, assertive and are strongly represented in senior roles in industry and other walks of life. Women generally earn the same salaries as their male colleagues, but the glass ceiling persists at high levels of government and the corporate hierarchy. Even so, the streets and public spaces of Mumbai are more male-dominated than would be expected in a free and equal society. The level of independence that Mumbai's women enjoy varies for different classes and ethnic groups and the conservatism is driven by family mores rather than governmental disapproval.

Despite all the ever-present lurid Bollywood movie posters of skimpily-clad women, conservative dress for women is the norm – short skirts and tight tops are generally the preserve of the upper classes, although jeans and T-shirts are the city's college student uniform. 'Eve-teasing' is how Mumbaikars refer to cat-calls, sexual harassment and worse by men, which occur with distressing frequency, although rapes and other sexual crimes are not as common in Mumbai as in other Indian cities.

Foreign women are likely to be the objects of curiosity for some, and occasionally of lascivious attention; it's best to avoid revealing shorts and skirts or getting too friendly with strange men, who may get the wrong idea (*see p231* **Attitudes & etiquette**).

Working in Mumbai

Foreigners are not allowed to work in India without an appropriate visa. Employment visas are issued only in the applicant's home country (*see p237* **Visas & immigration**).

Directory

Further Reference

Books

Fiction

Chandra, Vikram *Sacred Games*
An enjoyable, if telephone directory-sized, cops-and-robbers thriller.
De Souza, Eunice *Dangerlok*
A finely etched portrait of an ageing English Lit professor struggling with life in a distant Mumbai suburb.
Desai, Anita *Baumgartner's Bombay* A German Jew, who has long made a new life in Mumbai, runs into a wild hippie from his homeland.
Jones, Nalini *What You Call Winter* A series of short stories set in the Roman Catholic enclave of Bandra.
Mistry, Cyrus *Radiance of Ashes* A young Parsi market researcher makes his way through the city's underbelly.
Mistry, Rohinton *Tales from Ferozeshah Baug, Such a Long Journey, A Fine Balance* and *Family Matters* explore the anxieties and joys of the city's diminishing Parsi community.
Nagarkar, Kiran *Ravan and Eddie* Mumbai's much-vaunted cosmopolitanism is stretched and tested in this brilliant novel, set in a tenement.
Roberts, Gregory David *Shantaram* An Australian convict finds redemption in this simplistic New Agey narrative, purportedly based on real life.
Rushdie, Salman *Midnight's Children, The Moor's Last Sigh* and *The Ground Beneath Her Feet* career through Mumbai (with tangents shooting through time and space) as India's best-known writer pays tribute to the city of his birth.
Shroff, Murzban *Breathless in Bombay* A collection of short stories about the problems that have become the natural order of city life.
Tyrewala, Altaf *No God in Sight* A cinematically constructed journey through the heart of the Muslim community of central Mumbai.

Poetry

Chaudhuri, Amit *St Cyril Road and Other Poems* Reflections on Bandra's Roman Catholic community, and other meanderings.
Ezekiel, Nissim *Collected Poems 1952-1988* Ezekiel's poems in Indian English display a verbal litheness that could only have been inspired by multi-lingual Mumbai.
Kolatkar, Arun *Kala Ghoda Poems* One of India's most famous English-language poets looks out across the city's most famous square.

Subramaniam, Arundhathi *Where I Live* It's a 'city of L'Oreal sunsets…of septic magenta hairclips…of hope and bulimia', says the poet.

Non-fiction

Chopra, Anupama *King of Bollywood: Shah Rukh Khan and the Seductive World of Indian Cinema* A primer to Bollywood, told through the story of its biggest star.
Dalmia, Yashodhara *The Making of Modern Indian Art* A lavishly illustrated, incisive look at the painters of the Progressive Artists Group, who invented a new idiom in the early years of Independence.
D'Monte, Darryl *Ripping the Fabric: The Decline of Mumbai and its Mills* An analysis of how the shuttering of Mumbai's textile mills has undermined the city's social and economic health.
Dwivedi, Sharada and **Mehrotra, Rahul** *Fort Walks* is an indispensable guide to the buildings of the Fort district and *Bangaga: Sacred Tank on Malabar Hill* is an illustrated history of the temple complex in Walkeshwar.
Dwyer, Rachel *Yash Chopra* surveys the success of this legendary Bollywood director, and is an insightful guide into the Indian film industry. *100 Bollywood Films* tells you which movies you can't miss.
Garga, BD *So Many Cinemas* A superbly researched history of Indian cinema, supported by film stills from the earliest movies.
Guha, Ramachandra *A Corner of a Foreign Field: The Indian History of a British Sport* Set largely in Mumbai, the home of sub-continental cricket, this book is a social history of India, told through its favourite sport.
Gupt, Somnath *The Parsi Theatre: Its Origins and Development* A study of a 19th-century theatre form that established the conventions still followed in Bollywood films.
Hansen, Thomas Blom *Wages of Violence: Naming and Identity in Postcolonial Bombay* How the nativist Shiv Sena party unleashed fundamentalist forces that polarised India's most cosmopolitan city.
Hoskote, Ranjit *The Complicit Observer* A showcase of the work of Sudhir Patwardhan, who paints Mumbaikars travelling on the train, on the street and sitting in Irani cafés and who delights in finding the extraordinary in the mundane.
Kabir, Nasreen Munni *Guru Dutt: A Life in Cinema* A biography of the brilliant director and actor who re-imagined formulaic Hindi cinema in

the 1950s.
Kapoor, Shashi and **Gehlot, Deepa** *Prithvivallas* The story of how India's most famous film family built the auditorium that is now at the centre of Mumbai's theatre scene.
Khote, Durga *I, Durga Khote* The journey of an upper-class woman through the disreputable world of Indian cinema. Khote debuted in 1931 and acted in over 200 films.
London, Christopher *Bombay Gothic* A pictorial history of Mumbai's fascination with a style that had its origins thousands of miles away.
Manto, Sadat Hasan *Mumbai: Stars from Another Sky* A catty collection of pieces from the time one of the greatest Urdu writers worked as a film journalist.
Mehta, Suketu *Maximum City* A painstakingly researched book about the numerous worlds that make up Mumbai.
Michell, George *Elephanta* A guide to the sixth-century rock-carved caves on the island just off Mumbai.
Moraes, Dom *A Variety of Absences* The shimmering memoirs of the famous poet and journalist.
Neuwirth, Robert *Shadow Cities* An American writer takes up residence in shanty towns on four continents, Mumbai among them.
Patel, Sujata and **Thorner, Alice** *Bombay: Metaphor for Modern India* and *Bombay: Mosaic of Modern Culture* are collections of academic articles that examine the city's past – and make prescriptions for its future.
Pinto, Jerry and **Fernandes, Naresh** (editors) *Bombay Meri Jaan* An anthology of writing and poetry about India's most vibrant city.
Ramani, Navin *Bombay Art Deco Architecture: A Visual Journey (1930-1953)* A fascinating survey of some of our city's finest art deco buildings, the picture-led book is also an excellent introduction to the ideas of the art deco style.
Seabrook, Jeremy *Life and Labour in a Bombay Slum* The author finds optimism amidst the squalour of Mumbai's shanty colonies.
Sharma, Kalpana *Rediscovering Dharavi: Stories from Asia's Largest Slum* A study of life in the district that has come to symbolise the urban policy which ensures that half of Mumbai's population has no hope of moving out of slums.
Zaidi, S Hussain *Black Friday: The True Story of the Bombay Bomb Blasts* A journalist's pacy reconstruction of the conspiracy that resulted in the explosions that killed 257 Mumbaikars on 12 March, 1993.

History

Dwivedi, Shardha and **Mehrotra, Rahul** *Bombay: The Cities Within* An immensely readable tale of how seven malarial islands grew into a major metropolis, with lots of pictorial evidence.

Edwardes, SM *Gazetteer of Bombay City and Island* The ultimate administrators' handbook to the city, completed in 1909, has sections on the city's history, trade patterns, headgear, and even lists distinctive hawkers' cries.

Farooqui, Amar *Opium City: The Making of Early Victorian Bombay* Opium, as much as cotton, boosted Mumbai's fortunes, says the author.

Marg Publications *Bombay to Mumbai: Changing Perspectives* An eclectic selection of articles, including pieces on early photography in Mumbai, 19th-century homes and the city's art deco architecture.

Menon, Meena and **Adarkar, Neera** *One Hundred Years, One Hundred Voices. The Millworkers of Girangaon: An Oral History.* A compelling history of how tumultuous changes in Mumbai's mill district shaped events across India.

Tindall, Gillian *City of Gold: The Biography of Bombay* A delightful stroll through the city's British history, told with a novelist's eye for detail.

Film

See also p36 **Bollywood**.

Aar Paar (1954) 1950s tragedy king Guru Dutt directs as well as stars as a working-class taxi driver who loses his job, starts working at a garage, has a run-in with gangsters and is the object of two women's affections.

Boot Polish (1954) Prakash Arora tells the story of Ratan Kumar and his sister, who survive on the streets of Mumbai by scrabbling for food and a few paise at railway stations.

Taxi Driver (1954) Chetan Anand's rambling tale of the relationship between taxi driver Dev Anand and runaway singer Kalpana Kartik is a grand excuse to shoot Mumbai's urban vistas.

Mr and Mrs '55 (1955) Made by Guru Dutt in the decade when the post-independence bubbly still hadn't gone flat, this is a satire on the feudal upper classes.

Shree 420 (1955) Raj Kapoor's guile-less tramp trips into Mumbai singing. The poor welcome him with open arms but he loses his way and starts working for a businessman whose plan wants to raze the slum where his com-rades and lady love Nargis live.

CID (1956) *CID*'s magic lies in its taut storytelling, business-like characters and snappy editing. Plus, this Bollywoodian film noir story has the unofficial Mumbai anthem: '*Yeh Hai Bombay Meri Jaan*'.

Aakhri Khat (1966) Chetan Anand's precursor to 1994's *Baby's Day Out* follows the adorable little Bunty as he stumbles about the city looking for his mother. Brilliantly shot, mostly in Mahim, with a jazzy soundtrack.

Chhoti Si Baat (1975) Basu Chatterji paints Mumbai as a truly romantic city, full of possibilities and a love of life. Amol Palekar's Arun meets Prabha every day at the bus stop. He's madly in love but has no confidence until he takes courtship lessons from a retired colonel.

Deewaar (1975) Directed by Yash Chopra and carried by Amitabh Bachchan, this has been interpreted by film theorists in different ways but it also happens to be a city film and a comment on how money-driven Mumbai drives a wedge between two brothers.

Ardh Satya (1983) Govind Nihalini's gritty cop story takes on a debate over violence, authority and control, with a hard-edged story unfolding through the eyes of a Mumbai police inspector, played by Om Puri.

Jaane Bhi Do Yaaro (1983) In this cult slapstick satire, directed by Kundan Shah, two bumbling photographers stumble onto a scam being hatched by corrupt builders and municipal officials, and embark on a series of madcap adventures to unearth the truth.

Saaransh (1984) Possibly Mahesh Bhatt's best film, and one of the few Hindi films to subtly explore the Shiv Sena's reign of terror in the city.

Nayakan (1987) Mani Ratnam's Tamil classic, also dubbed into Hindi, combines a respectful fan tip to Francis Ford Coppola's *Godfather* with a story based loosely on Vardharaj Mudaliar, the infamous smuggler who operated in Dharavi in the 1960s.

Salaam Bombay! (1988) Many Mumbaikars hate this movie, and dismiss it as urban exotica, but Mira Nair's debut is a moving portrait of the city's underbelly, seen through its street children, whores and pimps.

Tezaab (1988) N Chandra's movie is a great visual dictionary for the city: it has street lingo, gangster brawls, tough love and hip-shaking songs. Anil Kapoor plays Munna, an aspiring naval officer whose journey to gangsterhood is told in flashback.

Parinda (1989) A successful assimilation of the Hollywood film noir genre, *Parinda* remains Vidhu Vinod Chopra's most evocative film and one of the most well-crafted gang-ster films in recent times.

Salim Langde Pe Mat Ro (1989) Saeed Mirza tackles issues faced by Mumbai's marginalised Muslims in this beautifully shot movie, set in the teeming alleys of central Mumbai.

Sadak (1991) Eunuchs, taxi drivers, prostitutes, pimps, thugs. *Sadak* is the apogee of Mahesh Bhatt's series of films featuring street characters. Sanjay Dutt gives his all, and is brilliant, in a sort of neurotic tribute to Martin Scorsese's *Taxi Driver*.

Bombay (1995) One of the few films to look squarely at the 1992-'93 Mumbai religious riots, Mani Ratnam's love story has been dissected and dissed for its portrayal of events and characters – for example, the violence in the film is always initiated by a Muslim.

Rangeela (1995) Light at heart and on the feet, *Rangeela* is Ram Gopal Varma's ode to the magic of the movies.

Satya (1998) Through the character of Satya, a man with no background who emerges from the stone corridors of Chhatrapati Shivaji Terminus into the arms of the underworld, Ram Gopal Varma trawls through shoot-outs, betrayals and revenge. Bloody good fun, and a modern classic.

Dil Chahta Hai (2001) *Dil Chahta Hai* mostly plays out in spacious homes replete with leather sofas, electronic gadgetry, colour-coordinated walls, chic furniture and the kind of luxury you'd find in Nepean Sea Road or Juhu. Then the plot moves to Goa and Sydney but the heart is local; the portrait of the well-heeled universe is non-judgemental and accurate.

Munnabhai MBBS (2003) *Munnabhai MBBS*, a comedy about a street thug who teaches doctors a thing or two about treatment, isn't the first film to put Mumbai's street lingo into a film script. But it is the first to use the language almost as a living, breathing character.

Bluffmaster! (2005) A conman (Abhishek Bachchan) vows to go straight when his girlfriend (Priyanka Chopra) leaves him. When he's diagnosed with terminal illness, he decides to carry out one last heist.

Taxi No 9211 (2006) A rich brat (John Abraham) and a working-class taxi driver (Nana Patekar) collide in this imitation of *Changing Lanes*.

Black Friday (2007) A fast-paced yet detailed adaptation of S Hussain Zaidi's book about the 12 March 1993 bombings across Mumbai.

Guru (2007) A hagiography based on the life of Dhirubhai Ambani, a businessman who came to Mumbai with nothing and founded one of India's biggest corporations.

Metro (2007) The lives of several characters intersect in this ensemble about life in a modern Indian metropolis.

Traffic Signal (2007) A montage of how the poor live at one of the city's largest traffic signals.

Note page numbers in **bold** indicate
section(s) giving key information on
a topic, *italics* indicate photographs.

Advertisers' Index

Place of interest and/or entertainment . . .	
College/Hospital/University	
Railway station/Bus depot	
Ruins area	
Parks	
River	
Beach	
Main road	
Pedestrian road	
Airport	✈
Church	✚
Temple	🛕
Synagogues	✡
Hospital	✚
Post office	✉
Mosque	☪
Tourist information	ℹ
Area name . . . . FORT	
Hotels	➊
Restaurants & cafés	➊
Pubs & bars	➊

Maps

Mumbai

GORAI BEACH • GORAI NAGAR • DOKALI

SANJAY

Borivali • KANHERI CAVES • LOKMANYA NAGAR • NALPADA • HANEGA

MNADA • Kandivali • AKURLI • GANDHI • Tulsi Lake • WAGLE INDUSTRIAL ESTATE • THANE • Kal

SAI KRUPA NAGAR • MALGAI • NATIONAL • PODWAL NAGAR • Thane

RAM NAGAR • Malad • PATHANWADI • Mulund • MHADA COLONY • Air

DONGARPADA • Goregaon • PARK • Film City

RANGAI BEACH • OSHIWARA • LAXMI NAGAR • Vihar Lake • Bhandup • FRIENDS COLONY • Rabale

MADH BEACH • VERSOVA BEACH • Jogeshwari • AZAD NAGAR • Mahakali Caves • SEEPZ • Powai Lake • Kanjurmarg • NOCIL COLONY

Andheri • SAKI NAKA • Vikhroli • Ghansoli

JUHU BEACH • Vile Parle • Chhatrapati Shivaji International Airport • Kop Khair

Arabian Sea • JUHU • Domestic Airport • Ghatkopar • NAV

Santa Cruz • VAKOLA • Vidyavihar • MUMB

ALFHLD • Khar Road • Kurla • Tilak Nagar • SHIVAJI NAGAR • Vashi • Sa

BANDRA • Chembur • HERDI COLO

Bandra • Sion • Chunabhatti • Govandi • CIL COL

p249 • Mahim Fort • Mahim • Sion Fort • DEONAR • Mankhurd

Bandra Fort • Matunga Road • GTB Nagar • WADAVALI • UPPER TROMBAY

Worli Fort • Shivaji Park • King's Circle • ANTOP HILL • PANCHAVATI COLONY

PRABHADEVI • Matunga • MAHUL

Dadar • Wadala Road • TROMBAY

Elphinstone Road • Parel

Lower Parel • Currey Road • Sewri

Chinchpokli • Cotton Green

Mahalaxmi • Reay Road

Mumbai Central Terminus • Byculla • Dockyard Road • Butcher Island • NHAVA

CUMBALA HILL • p254-5 • Grant Road • Sandhurst Road • Elephanta Island

Charni Road • Masjid Bunder

Chowpatty Beach • Cross Island

Marine Lines • Chhatrapati Shivaji Terminus

FORT • p252-3

Back Bay • Churchgate

NARIMAN POINT • Gateway of India

CUFFE PARADE • Harbour • URAN

COLABA • p250-1

248 Time Out Mumbai & Goa

© Copyright Time Out Group 2008

0 — 3 miles
0 — 4 km

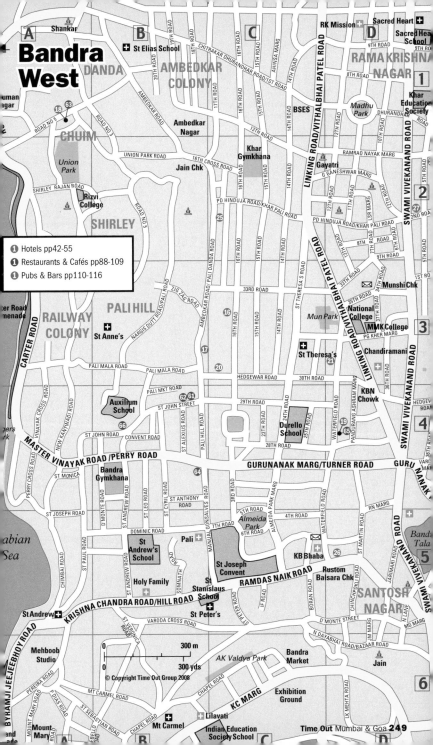

Bandra West

A Shankar

DANDA

St Elias School

AMBEDKAR COLONY

CHITRAKAR DHURANDHAR ROAD/1ST ROAD

C

RK Mission

Sacred Heart

Sacred Heart School

D

RAMA KRISHNA NAGAR

18 63

CHUIM

Ambedkar Nagar

Khar Gymkhana

BSES

Madhu Park

Khar Education Society

Union Park Road

Jain Chk

16TH CROSS ROAD

Gayatri

Union Park

SHIRLEY RAJAN ROAD

Rizvi College

SHIRLEY

PD HINDUJA ROAD/KHAR PALI ROAD

G GANESHWAR MARG

RAMRAO NAYAK MARG

PD HINDUJA ROAD/KHAR PALI ROAD

LSR MARG

25

2

Munshi Chk

33RD ROAD

National College

Mun Park

MMK College

3

PG KHER MARG

Hotels pp42-55
Restaurants & Cafés pp88-109
Pubs & Bars pp110-116

PALI HILL

RAILWAY COLONY

St Anne's

16

Chandiramani

St Theresa's

17

21

KBN Chowk

PALI MALA ROAD

PALI MALA ROAD

20

HEDGEWAR ROAD

30TH ROAD

4

PALI MKT ROAD

Auxilium School

29TH ROAD

Durello School

19

65

ST JOHN STREET

62 61

66

ST JOHN ROAD

CONVENT ROAD

28TH ROAD

MASTER VINAYAK ROAD /PERRY ROAD

GURUNANAK MARG/TURNER ROAD

GURU NANAK

ST MONICA

Bandra Gymkhana

64

ST LEO ROAD

ST ANTHONY ROAD

RN MARG

5TH ROAD

Almeida Park

4TH ROAD

ST MARTIN ROAD

D' MONTE ROAD

DOMINIC ROAD

Pali

6TH ROAD

KB Bhaba

26

Bandra Tala

ST JOSEPH ROAD

St Andrew's School

Holy Family

St Stanislaus School

RAMDAS NAIK ROAD

Rustom Balsara Chk

SANTOSA NAGAR

St Andrew

KRISHNA CHANDRA ROAD/HILL ROAD

St Peter's

VARODA CROSS ROAD

D' MONTE STREET

N DAYABHAI ROAD/BAZAAR ROAD

Mehboob Studio

300 m

AK Valdya Park

Bandra Market

Jain

300 yds

© Copyright Time Out Group 2008

KC MARG

Exhibition Ground

Mount Mary

Mt Carmel

Lilavati

Indian Education Society School

1 To Afghan Church

D NANABHAI MOOS MARG

Telegraph Quarters

1 PRAKASH PETHE MARG/CUFFEPARADE ROAD

Bus Depot

Dhobi Ghat

DALIT NAGAR

S.V.XAVIER'S MARG

2 St Francis Xavier's Church

Baptist

Colaba Woods

3 IDBI Tower

Maker Towers

J Maker I

J Maker II

J Maker III

GD SOMANI ROAD

World Trade Centre

CUFFE PARADE

4

E Mumbai Port Trust Garden

COLABA CAUSEWAY/SHAHID BHAGAT SINGH MARG

NATHALAL PARIKH ROAD

PRAKASH PETHE MARG

TAJA ROAD

K SAGANGADHAR ROAD

Gita Nagar

PHULE NAGAR

Back Bay

F Sessoon Dock

COLABA

WODEHOUSE ROAD

Naval Public School

4TH PASTA LANE

3RD PASTA LANE

2ND PASTA LANE

1ST PASTA LANE

S BHARUCHA MARG

BADHWAR PARK

KOLINAGAR

N SAVANT ROAD

RR STREET

SAIBKAR MARG

LALA NIGAM ROAD

STRAND ROAD

D VYAS MARG

NAZMI STREET

ARTHUR BUNDER ROAD

GARDEN ROAD

OLIVER ROAD

B BEHRAM ROAD

G Colaba Market

4TH PASTA LANE

MINOO DESAI ROAD

E VYAS MARG

Radio Club

PJ RAMCHANDANI/STRAND ROAD

1 Hotels pp42-55

1 Restaurants & Cafés pp88-109

1 Pubs & Bars pp110-116

H *Harbour*

0
0

© Copyright Time Out Group 2008

300 m
300 yds

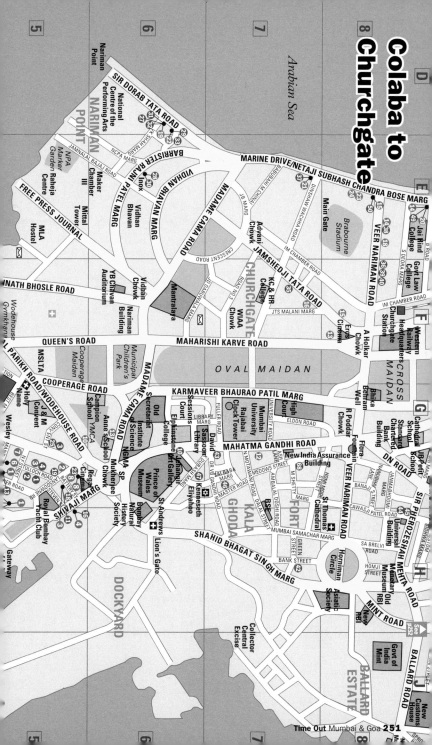

Arabian Sea

Nariman Point

SIR DORAB TATA ROAD

NARIMAN POINT

National Centre of the Performing Arts

NCPA Marg

SWATI MARG

JAMNALAL BAJAJ ROAD

NPA Marker Garden Raheja Centre

Maker Chamber III

BARRISTER RAJNI

VIDHAN BHAVAN MARG

FREE PRESS JOURNAL

Mittal Towers

Inox

MLA Hostel

Vidhan Bhavan

MADAME CAMA ROAD

MARINE DRIVE/NETAJI ChANDRA BOSE MARG

DINSHAW WACHHA ROAD

Main Gate

Brabourne Stadium

VEER NARIMAN ROAD

S DEORA MARG

B ROAD

Jai Hind College

Govt Law College

Western Railway Headquarters

Advani Chowk

JB MARG

IM CHAMBER ROAD

JAMSHEDJI TATA ROAD

CRESCENT ROAD

ROAD NO 3 DANMAR MARG

CHURCHGATE

KC & HR College

WIAA Chowk

Churchgate Station

NATH BHOSLE ROAD

YB Chavan Auditorium

Vidhan Chowk

Nariman Building

Mantralaya

IM CHAMBER ROAD

A Holkar Chowk

CROSS MAIDAN

JTS MALANI MARG

Eros Cinema

Wodehouse Gymkhana

QUEEN'S ROAD

MAHARISHI KARVE ROAD

OVAL MAIDAN

Bhika Behram Well

Cathedral School

UB Petit School

DN ROAD

SIR PHEROZESHAH MEHTA ROAD

L PARIKH ROAD/WODEHOUSE ROAD

MSLTA

Cooperage Maidan

COOPERAGE ROAD

Municipal Children's Park

MADAME CAMA ROAD

Campion School YMCA

KARMAVEER BHAURAO PATIL MARG

Old Secretariat Institute of Science

Sessions Court

Rajabai Clock Tower

Mumbai University

FULLER ROAD

High Court

R Poddar Chowk

Flora Fountain

Standard Chartered Bank Building

VEER NARIMAN ROAD

NAGINDAS MASTER MARG

Holy Name

J & M Convent

Anne School

NGMA Chowk

Elphinstone College

David Sassoon Library

LIBRARY MARG

UNIVERSITY ROAD

ELDON ROAD

MAHATMA GANDHI ROAD

New India Assurance Building

St Thomas Cathedral

Universal Building

Old Custom House RBI

Mandvi

Wesley

N TULLOCH ROAD

Regal Cinema

SHIVAJI MARG

Mukherjee Chowk

SP Mukherjee Chowk

Prince of Wales Museum

Bombay Natural History Society

Jehangir Art Gallery

Kennesseth Eliyahoo

Kenneseth

MUMBAI SAMACHAR MARG

HOMI MODY STREET

M SHETTY MARG

BSE

KALA GHODA

FORT

Royal Bombay Yacht Club

Gateway

St Andrews Cathedral

Lion's Gate

SHAHID BHAGAT SINGH MARG

BANK STREET

Horniman Circle

GREEN STREET

SA BRELVI ROAD

HOMJI STREET

SP PHEROZESHAH MEHTA ROAD

DOCKYARD

Asiatic Society

Collector Central Excise

MINT ROAD

New RBI

Govt of India Mint

BALLARD ROAD

BALLARD ESTATE

New Customs House

See p252

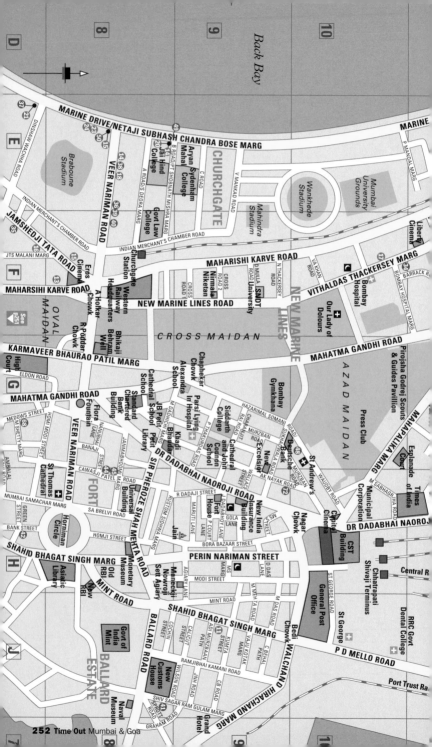

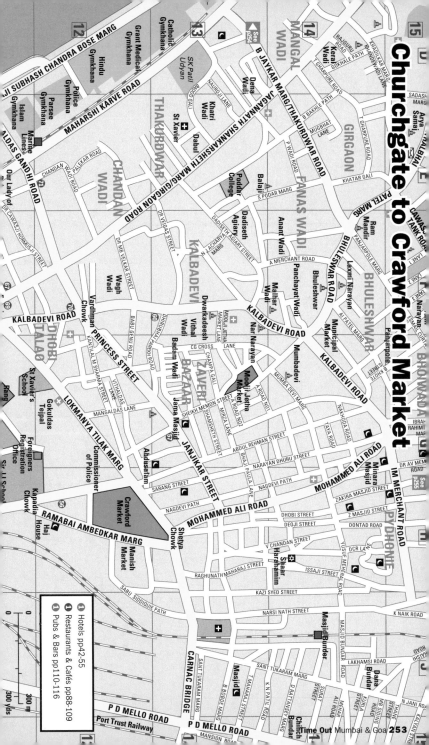

Churchgate to Crawford Market

CHHATRAPATI SHIVAJI SUBHASH CHANDRA BOSE MARG

MAHARSHI KARVE ROAD

Catholic Gymkhana
Grant Medical Gymkhana
Hindu Gymkhana
Police Gymkhana
Parsee Gymkhana
Islam Gymkhana

Marine Lines

Our Lady of
DR CAWASJI HORMASJI MARG
DALDAS GANDHI ROAD

THAKURDWAR
CHANDAN WADI
PALEKAR ROAD
CHANDAN WADI ROAD

SK Patil Udyan
St Xavier

THAKURDWAR ROAD
KALBADEVI
PRINCESS STREET
Vardhman Chowk

St Xavier's School
Rang
Gokuldas Tejpal
Foreigners Registration Office
Sir JJ School
LOKMANYA TILAK MARG
Commissioner of Police
Kapadia Chowk

Haji House
RAMABAI AMBEDKAR MARG
Crawford Market
Manish Market

B JAYKAR MARG
THAKURDWAR ROAD

See p254

MANGAL WADI
JAGANNATH SHANKARSHETH MARG
Dana Wadi
Khatri Wadi
NAUROJI LANE
P WADI ROAD
Dabul
BADO GALI
Balaji
S PODAR MARG
Pendar College
DR VEIGAS STREET
DADISETH AGIARY STREET
J ACHARYA MARG
DR ME VELKAR STREET
Wagh Wadi
Dwarkadeesh
Vithal Wadi
MARKET LANE
MODAJI JETHA LANE
BABU GENU ROAD
DHIRUBHAI PAREKH ROAD
KANTILAL M SHARMA STREET
ZAVERI BAZAAR
CHAMPA GALI
VITHALDAS LANE
MANGALDAS LANE
Badam Wadi
Moolji Jetha Market
Jama Masjid
SHEIKH MEMON STREET
SHAMSHETH STREET
MIRZA LANE
Abdulstan
JANJIKAR STREET
SARANG STREET
NAGDEVI PATH
Shetya Chowk
MOHAMMED ALI ROAD

GIRGAON
T GHARPURE ROAD
RAJGURU ROAD
Kerai Wadi
GOKHALE PATH
GHARPURE ROAD
THAKUDKAR MARG
KHANDERAO LANE
MUGBHAT LANE
T BAKHLE PATH
P WADI ROAD

FANAS WADI
Anant Wadi
A MERCHANT ROAD
Panchayat Wadi
Malhar Wadi
Nar Narayan
KALBADEVI ROAD
Mumbadevi
MUMBA DEVI MARG
C6 CROSS LANE
A ROAD NO.1
R ROAD NO.2
Jana Masjid
ABDUL REHMAN STREET
NARAYAN DHURU STREET
BHAT PAULA LANE
NAGDEVI PATH
MOHAMMED ALI ROAD
DHOBI STREET
DEOJI STREET
V CHANDAN STREET
Shaar Harahanim
RAGHUNATH MAHARAJ STREET
KAZI SYED STREET
NARSI NATH STREET

MANGAL WADI

Ram Mandir
PANJARPOLE LANE
Dadiseth Agiary
Bhuleshwar
BHULESWAR ROAD
Laxmi Narayan
AJ PATEL MARG
Municipal Market
Panjarpole
B KHOLE LANE
NAKHODA ROAD
Minara Masjid
TAIA ROAD
ZAKIRA MASJID STREET
Z MASJID STREET
DONTAD ROAD
YUSUF MEHRALI ROAD
ISSAJI STREET
MASJID BUNDAR ROAD

KHATAR GALI

KALBADEVI ROAD
BHULESHWAR
BHOIWADA

DR AV MEMON ROAD
IM MERCHANT ROAD
IBRAHIM RAHIMTOOLA MARG

See p255

PYDHONIE

Masjid Bunder

LAKHAMSI ROAD

CARNAC BRIDGE

SANT TUKARAM MARG
Masjid
K N PATIL ROAD
T MAHARAJ STREET
K BUBDE MARG
SURAT STREET
D RATTANSEY MARG

Masjid
SANT TUKARAM MARG
KAZI SYED STREET

Dana Bundar
Chinch Bundar
N JANI ROAD
KALYAN STREET
MB SIDING ROAD
KIJURA STREET
THANE STREET
MEHAR ALI ROAD
K NAIK ROAD

P D MELLO ROAD
Port Trust Railway
SABU SIDDIQUE PATH
P D MELLO ROAD
MANSION ROAD

1 Hotels pp42-55
2 Restaurants & Cafés pp88-109
3 Pubs & Bars pp110-116

0   300 m
0   300 yds

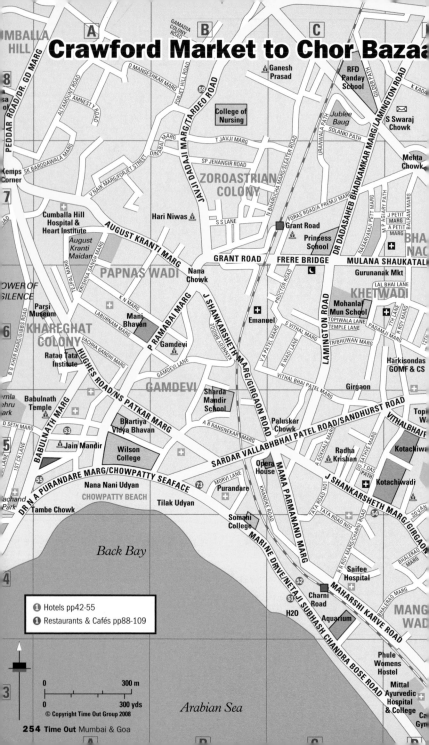

Crawford Market to Chor Bazaar

254 Time Out Mumbai & Goa

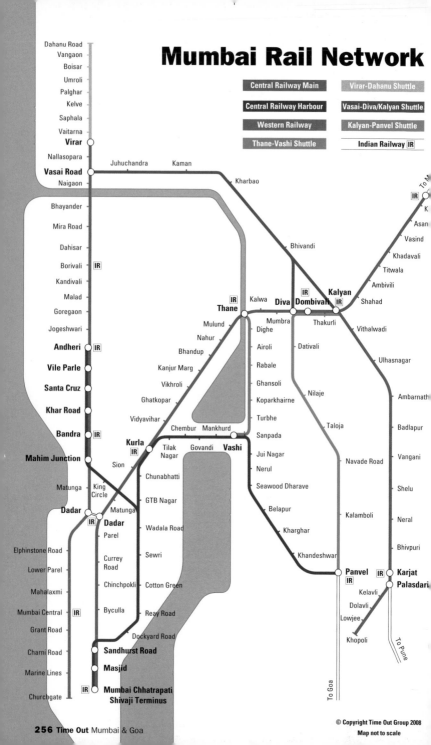

Mumbai Rail Network

Central Railway Main
Central Railway Harbour
Western Railway
Thane-Vashi Shuttle

Virar-Dahanu Shuttle
Vasai-Diva/Kalyan Shuttle
Kalyan-Panvel Shuttle
Indian Railway IR

Dahanu Road
Vangaon
Boisar
Umroli
Palghar
Kelve
Saphala
Vaitarna
Virar
Nallasopara
Vasai Road
Naigaon
Bhayander
Mira Road
Dahisar
Borivali **IR**
Kandivali
Malad
Goregaon
Jogeshwari
Andheri IR
Vile Parle
Santa Cruz
Khar Road
Bandra IR
Mahim Junction
Matunga
Dadar
Elphinstone Road
Lower Parel
Mahalaxmi
Mumbai Central **IR**
Grant Road
Charni Road
Marine Lines
Churchgate

Juhuchandra   Kaman
Kharbao
Bhivandi
Kalwa **IR** **Diva** **Dombivali IR** **Kalyan**
Thane IR
Mulund
Nahur
Bhandup
Kanjur Marg
Vikhroli
Ghatkopar
Vidyavihar
Chembur   Mankhurd
Kurla IR
Tilak Nagar   Govandi   **Vashi**
Sion
King Circle
Matunga
Dadar
Parel
Currey Road
Chinchpokli
Byculla
Chunabhatti
GTB Nagar
Wadala Road
Sewri
Cotton Green
Reay Road
Dockyard Road
Sandhurst Road
Masjid
Mumbai Chhatrapati Shivaji Terminus

Mumbra
Dighe
Airoli
Rabale
Ghansoli
Koparkhairne
Turbhe
Sanpada
Jui Nagar
Nerul
Seawood Dharave
Belapur
Kharghar
Khandeshwar
Panvel IR

Thakurli
Vithalwadi
Ulhasnagar
Dativali
Nilaje
Taloja
Navade Road
Kalamboli

To M
IR
K
Asan
Vasind
Khadavali
Titwala
Ambivili
Shahad
Ambarnath
Badlapur
Vangani
Shelu
Neral
Bhivpuri
Karjat IR
Palasdari
Kelavli
Dolavli
Lowjee
Khopoli

To Goa   To Pune